Church History

D1601091

PETER LANG
New York • Washington, D.C./Baltimore • Bern
Frankfurt • Berlin • Brussels • Vienna • Oxford

Dyron B. Daughrity

Church History

FIVE APPROACHES
to a GLOBAL DISCIPLINE

PETER LANG
New York • Washington, D.C./Baltimore • Bern
Frankfurt • Berlin • Brussels • Vienna • Oxford

Library of Congress Cataloging-in-Publication Data
Daughrity, Dyron B.
Church history: five approaches to a global discipline /
Dyron B. Daughrity.
p. cm.
Includes bibliographical references and index.
1. Church history. I. Title.
BR145.3.D38   270—dc23   2012026828
ISBN 978-1-4331-1695-7 (paperback)
ISBN 978-1-4539-0918-8 (e-book)

Bibliographic information published by **Die Deutsche Nationalbibliothek**.
Die Deutsche Nationalbibliothek lists this publication in the "Deutsche
Nationalbibliografie"; detailed bibliographic data is available
on the Internet at http://dnb.d-nb.de/.

Front cover: Lake Tana Monastery, Ethiopia.
Back cover: Monastic compound at Geghard, Armenia.
Both photos courtesy of Dyron Daughrity.

The paper in this book meets the guidelines for permanence and durability
of the Committee on Production Guidelines for Book Longevity
of the Council of Library Resources.

© 2012 Peter Lang Publishing, Inc., New York
29 Broadway, 18th floor, New York, NY 10006
www.peterlang.com

Printed in the United States of America

With profound gratitude, I dedicate this book to my church history professors:

Leonard Allen
Everett Ferguson
Douglas Foster
Stacy Patty
Douglas Shantz

CONTENTS

LIST OF TABLES AND ILLUSTRATIONS

Maps

Statistical Information

PREFACE

The field of Church History is changing rapidly, due mainly to the shift in Christian demographics from the northern hemisphere to the southern: Asia, Africa, and Latin America. Textbooks introducing students to the new context are scarce. The old books and the old paradigms persist in colleges and universities today, but changes are coming. This book is part of that corrective in the field.

This book is a primer for those wishing to explore Church History. It unpacks the history of Christianity, but it also explains how Church History is created and organized. In my teaching I have noticed a great need for this approach. Most of the current texts throw students into the deep end, assuming they already know something about the topic. This book however gets students started without overwhelming them. I want students to enjoy their first encounter with Church History, and I believe this book accomplishes that.

This book is different from traditional Church History textbooks in several ways:

- It has a global emphasis, rather than an exclusively Euro-American one;
- It explains the discipline of Church History in addition to the content;
- It is readable, lively, and inviting to new students;
- It makes the history of Christianity manageable rather than stressing myriad dates and obscure names.

Conceptually, this book is revolutionary. I tell the story of Christianity in five different ways. I have never seen this technique before. While introducing students to Church History methods, I immerse them in the content. There is a dual emphasis on content and method.

The book has five chapters, each offering a different angle for studying Church History. Each chapter advances student understanding in two ways:

1. It introduces students to a particular approach (method) to Church History, and

2. It provides a global perspective of the content of Church History by telling the story in five very different ways.

The book's chapter titles are carefully chosen biblical quotations, designed to frame a unique perspective on Christianity's fascinatingly complex history.

1) *At Many Times and in Various Ways*
   A Chronological Approach to Church History
   This chapter provides a Church History overview in seven epochs. It explains how and why church historians have to make decisions on what constitutes a new era in Christianity. I include dates that pique interest and raise eyebrows. In the spirit of Mark Noll's *Turning Points: Decisive Moments in the History of Christianity* this chapter selects some of the most notable events in Church History, using them as an illustration of larger trends in the 2000-year history of the faith.

2) *In My Father's House Are Many Rooms*
   A Denominational Approach to Church History
   This chapter explains how Christian history is generally broken into denominational categories for the sake of telling a coherent story. The chapter organizes the history of Christianity into three categories: Orthodox, Roman Catholic, and Protestant, devoting equal space to each of the three categories. As a comparison, very few textbooks give equal space to Orthodox Christianity. Many of the observations in this chapter come from personal experience in field research. The narrative does not advocate one denomination over another; it is sympathetic to the richness found in all three forms of Christianity.

3) *And the Lord Added to Their Number Daily*
   A Sociological Approach to Church History
   This chapter emphasizes sociology as a way to understand Church History. Sociological approaches explain how Christianity grew based on conversion rates, fertility rates, and demography. Using statistics, this chapter illustrates how Christianity grew to become the largest faith on earth. It presents key social trends that have affected the growth or demise of Christianity in various cultural blocks. Rodney Stark's writings—a hybrid between sociology and history—are a good reference point for how this chapter functions. I draw deeply from the statistical data generated by the respected World Christian Database.

4) *Go and Make Disciples of all Nations*
    A Geographical Approach to Church History
    This chapter divides the world's cultures into eight blocks: the Middle
    East, Eastern Europe, Western Europe, Asia, Africa, Latin America,
    North America, and Oceania. A brief history of Christianity in each of
    these areas provides a condensed snapshot of how the faith developed
    globally. I have anchored the narrative with useful examples from stra-
    tegic countries. For instance, Nigeria is an important touchstone for
    understanding African Christianity. Brazil is helpful for understanding
    Latin American Christianity due to the meteoric rise of Pentecostal
    Christianity there. This chapter contains detailed maps that help the
    reader along.

5) *Who Do People Say I Am?*
    A Biographical Approach to Church History
    This chapter consists of lively biographies from twenty centuries of
    Church History—with an emphasis on the global nature of Christiani-
    ty. From the age of the tortured martyrs to the Holy Roman Empire,
    from the crusades to the adventurous Nestorian missionaries, from the
    frightful years of medieval plague to the rise of Christianity in Africa
    and Asia, this chapter tells the story of Christians long neglected.
    Alongside Constantine, we take a good look at the significance of his
    mother, Helena. Instead of limiting our focus to Martin Luther, we
    look at the role his wife, Katharina, played in the Reformation. In-
    stead of limiting our scope to what is often considered mainstream, we
    take a more expansive view, for example the "heretical" life of Kongo-
    lese Beatriz Kimpa Vita, burned at the stake as a witch.

The story of Christianity is never complete. It only expands. This book allows
fresh players into the story. By broadening our perspective to include women,
the working class, heretics, and priests outside mainstream "orthodoxy," we
become open to new ways of understanding. And these new perspectives
enhance our comprehension of the endlessly surprising story of Christianity's
past.

I owe a debt of gratitude to many people. First off, I want to thank my
Church History professors at Lubbock Christian University, Abilene Christian
University, and the University of Calgary. I have dedicated the book to these
inspiring scholars. My colleagues at Pepperdine in the Religion Division are a
wonderful support; it is a privilege to work with them. I am grateful indeed to
Pepperdine's institutional support of research. Tim Willis, Rick Marrs, and
Lee Kats have been unfailingly supportive of my work. I offer many thanks to

Stan Litke for his excellence in editing, and his constant desire to improve the manuscript.

My hearty thanks go to Corey Williams and Nicholas Cumming for reading through my manuscript in the late stages of the book, and offering helpful feedback; it is a privilege to teach such quality graduate students. The book's compilation of statistics was largely the work of Corey Williams. He and I meticulously partitioned the world into eight blocks in order to make sense of often overwhelming data. He handled it with his typical grace and ease that will help to make him such a fine professor and colleague one day.

I am indebted to my family for encouraging me to develop as a scholar and as a Christian. Mom, Dad, Varen, Sunde, Clare, Ross, and Mande Mae—thank you for your stabilizing love. Sunde, words simply do not suffice.

Now unto him that is able to do exceeding abundantly above all that we ask or think, according to the power that worketh in us. Unto him be glory in the church by Christ Jesus throughout all ages, world without end. Amen. (Eph. 3:20–21)

Dyron B. Daughrity
Buenos Aires, Argentina
23 April 2012

CHAPTER ONE

AT MANY TIMES AND IN VARIOUS WAYS
A Chronological Approach to Church History

"In the past, at many times and in various ways, God spoke to our ancestors through the prophets, but in these last days he has spoken to us by his son." Hebrews 1:1–2

Introduction

It was a Christian bishop in North Africa who mused upon the concept of time with such profundity that his ruminations are required reading in virtually any liberal arts program in the Western world: Saint Augustine. Although Augustine died in the year 430, his insights into time are as rich today as ever. For example, in the *Confessions*, book eleven, "Time and Eternity," he writes:[1]

> What is time? Who can explain this easily and briefly? Who can comprehend this even in thought so as to articulate the answer in words? Yet what do we speak of, in our familiar everyday conversation, more than of time? We surely know what we mean when we speak of it. We also know what is meant when we hear someone else talking about it. What then is time? Provided that no one asks me, I know. If I want to explain it to an inquirer, I do not know.[2]

Augustine's assessment is profound. On the surface, time seems to be something we all understand. However, when asked to explain the concept, we stammer.

In his marvelously insightful book *The Gifts of the Jews*, Thomas Cahill argues that our concept of time comes directly from Judaism. Prior to Judaism, time was understood cyclically, as it is in Hinduism and other non-Western faiths. He writes:

For the ancients, the future was always to be a replay of the past, as the past was simply an earthly replay of the drama of the heavens: "History repeats itself"—that is, false history, the history that is not history but myth. For the Jew—the moral is not that history repeats itself but that it is always something new: a process unfolding through time, whose direction and end we cannot know.[3]

In other words, only God knows where time is headed. However, we can assume that it is indeed headed *somewhere* rather than *nowhere*. Time has meaning. We each have a place in it. Every human being is to be found by God somewhere in time. Perhaps most importantly, each human being can actually shape time, if ever so slightly. This is the unique understanding of time that was bequeathed to humanity by the Jews.

Christians have inherited this very Jewish understanding of "chronos," the Greek word for time. Perhaps no other Jew has shaped our understanding of chronology more than Jesus of Nazareth. By his birth much of the world organizes its sense of time: BC (Before Christ) and AD (Anno Domini, or, the year of the Lord).

We begin this book by looking at church history through the concept of chronology—a very Judeo-Christian thing to do. We will arrange key events in the life of this faith into a sequence, a timeline. The chronological approach to history helps us to make sense of what happened. By spreading out some of the most important events in church history, as onto a table, we begin to notice patterns, disruptions, idiosyncrasies, and transitions.

The Chronological Approach

The book of Hebrews says God spoke to us in various ways through our ancestors, through the prophets, and through Jesus Christ. Could it be the case that God continues to speak through these people, *in various ways?* If indeed God speaks through people, then the story of Christianity must be considered, in some sense, a divine story. If we accept this story as God-infused, then history becomes more than *just* history. History becomes—holy. Church history becomes, distinctively, the realm of the sacred. Pivotal moments in Christian history become much more than simple dates. Rather than merely a number, 1807 becomes the year Christians in England led the charge to abolish the slave trade in the British Empire. Captives were freed. Many of God's people from the continent of Africa could sigh and not fear. This was good news. It was much more than a number. The chronological approach to church history emphasizes dates, but the dates are remembered because of their power; because of their worthiness to be remembered.

This chapter tells the history of Christianity in the most traditional way—in a chronological story. The history of Christianity has been recounted, indeed, "many times and in various ways." Type "History of Christianity" into the Amazon.com search bar and you get inundated with 57,080 books from which to choose. Predictably, these books march the reader through the 2,000-year history of this massive faith, beginning with Christ and progressing, year by year, to the present. It can be an arduous journey. Moreover, if it is not recounted well, the journey can get awfully boring.

The chronological history of Christianity, traditionally, unfolds like this. First, there was the New Testament church. These people either knew Jesus, or they knew people who knew Jesus. Second, there was the era of the church fathers. These men figured out concepts such as the Trinity and decided who should be labeled a heretic. Third came that dense and backward era known as "the Dark Ages." Fourth was the Renaissance, and the Renaissance bled into the fifth era: the Enlightenment. It was during the Enlightenment we shook off our shackles of ignorance and entered into—sixth—the "Modern" period. Finally, at some point in the twentieth century we wandered into the seventh era—and nobody really knows how to explain it. Scholars say we are no longer in the modern era, but they feel it is too early to give this new epoch a firm label. They simply call it "Postmodern." What changed? Are we not really modern people anymore? How did that happen?

Church historians have to make decisions on what constitutes a new era in Christianity. While every historian is different, there has been remarkable continuity in figuring how to organize the general history of Christianity. One of my professors in graduate school, the eminent Everett Ferguson, required us to read one of the old classic texts in the field: A History of the Christian Church by Williston Walker, published first in 1918.[4] Walker began his narrative by looking at the early church up to the time of Constantine; no church historian can avoid that decision. Constantine represents a watershed where, essentially, Christianity became wedded to the state. Walker then organized Christian history into the categories that remain intact to the present day: the Middle Ages, the Late Middle Ages, the Reformation, and Modern Christianity. In 1918 the "postmodern" had yet to emerge. I loved the class, but I trudged through the book—all 756 pages. I had it easy, however. Some of my friends in other universities were reading Kenneth Scott Latourette's two-volume (fine print) A History of Christianity, first published in 1953.[5] It was a herculean accomplishment by one of the great church historians of all time. It was nearly as herculean to read it. I suppose most people who were assigned Latourette's history did not actually make it to page 1552. What is perhaps more interesting is that this is not Latourette's most important work. By far his most durable publication is the 7-volume, 3,600 page A History of the Expansion of Christianity.[6] Imagine having that on your syllabus!

In a traditional field like church history, the more things change, the more they stay the same. As I write this, the bestselling church history book on the market is Diarmaid MacCulloch's *Christianity: The First Three Thousand Years*, published in 2010.[7] One would think church history books would slenderize due to our society's rapidly declining attention span and need for quick information bites. However, MacCulloch's 3.6 pound, 1,200-page tome fits right into the classical approach. The more words the merrier. Some things you simply cannot exclude.

The present book is a departure from the traditional way of exploring the history of Christianity. I tell the history of Christianity in five very different ways. Not only am I introducing readers to historical content, but I am also explaining how church history is created, how it is put together, how it is organized, and how it can be understood. My goal is that readers will not only understand the history of Christianity, but will also be equipped to "do" church history. That is the innovation of this book.

In this particular chapter, however, we are going to take the traditional approach to "doing" church history. We will trek through 2,000 years of history, hopefully not for 1,200 pages. Readers will encounter a few twists. For example, I have chosen some unusual dates for anchoring the narrative. In the spirit of Mark Noll's *Turning Points: Decisive Moments in the History of Christianity*, I try to highlight strategic episodes when Christianity changed, failed, morphed, or expanded.[8] While Noll anchored his narrative around 13 "turning points," in this chapter I have organized church history into seven "epochs." I have never seen it done quite this way, so in some ways we will break new ground. By introducing new perspectives on the chronological history of Christian faith, we question old paradigms. The epoch of explaining Christianity in exclusively Western terms must end. At the very heart of this book is the conviction that when we look at Christianity through a global lens rather than an exclusively Western one, we realize the history of Christianity has always been so much more than a Western story.

Brief Overview

Christianity is truly a world religion. Today, it is the largest religion in six of the world's eight cultural blocks: North America, Latin America and the Caribbean, Western Europe, Eastern Europe, Africa, and Oceania. Only in Asia and the Middle East is it not the largest religion. For centuries, however, it was the major religion of the Middle East. It had a prominent place in Central Asia as well, especially in the centuries immediately prior to Islam. Christianity has never had a strong presence in South and East Asia, although South Korea is around 40% Christian while the Philippines are around 90% Christian. China, India, and Vietnam have significant Christian minorities, but in all three places, Christians amount to less than 10% of the population.

The point is this: Christianity is the one faith that can properly be understood as a global religion. Much of the world is either Christianized or was at one time Christianized. Islam, even though it claims over 20% of the world's population, is the primary religion in only one of the world's eight cultural blocks: the Middle East.

In this chapter we divide the history of Christianity into seven epochs. Every historian has to decide when one age ends and another begins. These categories are by no means official. They are simply my attempt to divide Christianity's history into meaningful periods. It is important to emphasize that historical epochs bleed into each other. History does not follow easy temporal meters. Categories spill. They are by nature arbitrary, imposed from without. However, in spite of many flaws, creating categories and delineating major eras can be quite helpful. They make the chaotic seem comprehensible.

What follows is my attempt to organize Christianity's global history into seven epochs. Here is a quick preview.

1. Apostolic Age: AD 33–60: the death of Christ to the middle of Emperor Nero's reign;
2. Post-Apostolic, Illegal Age: AD 60–313: Nero's persecution to Constantine's legalization of Christianity;
3. Constantine and Byzantine Age: 313–732: Constantine to Charles Martel's victory over Islamic forces in France;
4. Pivotal Age: 732–1204: Martel's victory to the first sacking of Constantinople;
5. Fractured Age: 1204–1517: Decline of Byzantine Empire to Luther's Protest;
6. Global Expansion Age: 1517–1906: Luther to the Azusa Street Revival;
7. Recession and Indigenization Age: 1906–Present: Azusa to the Present.

Christianity's Global History in Seven Epochs

The Apostolic Age: AD 33–60

How did Christianity grow from being a small, Middle Eastern Jewish sect to becoming the largest, most diverse religion in human history? The answer to that question must be intertwined with the lives of the apostles. A small cluster of twelve working-class men launched human history's largest institution. They must have been remarkable people. The *apostolic age* was their moment in the sun. These days we often hear teachers and motivational speakers tell us to get out there and "change the world." The apostles did. Why? Because of a Jewish rabbi named Jesus, from Nazareth.

Christianity began with the life and teachings of Jesus, a Jew. His ministry is recorded in the four canonical gospels of Matthew, Mark, Luke, and John.[9] These texts tell of Jesus' actions and personality: he could miraculously heal the sick, command the attention of crowds, show compassion and rage, but—most significantly—become resurrected from the dead. Indeed, Jesus' followers believed his significance was found in his resurrection. Did this actually happen? Historians are not sure. Modern science seems to indicate the possibility highly improbable. Rarely do people get resuscitated in today's world, although it is possible with machines and methods such as cardiopulmonary resuscitation (CPR). Generally, however, resurrection seems impossible without a miracle.

The gospels tell a gruesome story of a man sentenced to death on trumped-up charges of blasphemy. He was tortured according to Roman methods, demeaned, humiliated along the way, and ultimately put to death by crucifixion. Three days after his execution, his followers claimed to have entered his tomb and found it empty. Others claimed to have seen him walking around after his crucifixion. Still others believed him to have appeared to them, and one crowd witnessed him ascending into heaven. Jesus' followers believed he had been resurrected from the dead. Indeed, many of them were executed for believing this.

The resurrection, though, is by no means the end of the story. The disciples claimed he continues to exist in the lives of those who trust in him as their Lord and as the savior of humankind. Had early Christians capitulated to persecution, then Christianity would have been consigned to the history books as another Jewish sect or as one of the ubiquitous "mystery religions" of the Greco-Roman world. However, for one reason or another—modern historical methods fail to sufficiently explain—Christianity continued to grow in spite of (at times) fierce resistance from the cultures around them.

Perhaps the most significant event in the history of this religion was when an anti-Christian Jewish zealot named Saul claimed Jesus dramatically appeared to him on a road leading to Damascus. After something like scales fell from his eyes, he was baptized by water, his name was changed to Paul, and he became one of Jesus Christ's most devoted disciples in history. Due to his prolific New Testament writings, he is often called the second founder of Christianity.

Paul was stubborn, tireless, self-motivated, and thick-skinned. He was remarkably suited for the life of a missionary. He traveled around the Mediterranean world converting people to Christianity and was probably martyred in Rome after his extensive missionary career. The New Testament records Paul as traveling over much of the vast Roman Empire: modern-day Israel, Syria, Turkey, all around the Aegean Sea near Greece including the island of Crete, and finally Italy—including the island of Sicily. Paul was not alone in his indefatigable missionary ambitions. There were other early Christian mission-aries, but Paul's work was recorded and preserved in the Christian New Testament, bringing with it a higher level of historical respectability.

Christianity, in its early years, was a Jewish sect. Paul, though, believed the message of Christ was intended for everybody, regardless of their ethnicity or background. Even today, oral traditions circulate all over the Middle East, Africa, and Asia, explaining how Jesus' original apostles scattered across the known world. For example, the apostle Thomas supposedly went to India and established seven churches there, and the Christians in India will show you those churches. Andrew may have gone to Greece, and possibly as far as Kiev in the Ukraine. Today Andrew is revered for establishing a church in the city of Byzantium, later known as Constantinople—the capital of the Eastern Roman Empire. Bartholomew may have preached around the Black Sea (Turkey) and in Armenia. James the brother of John may have gone to Spain, which is conceivable considering Paul in particular thought it important to evangelize that distant shore. Barnabas and Mark—while not technically among the original apostles—are recorded in the book of Acts as having evangelized Cyprus. Mark may have founded a church at Alexandria; tradition states that he did and eventually served as the first pope of that important city. Many Africans salute Mark as the founder of Christianity on their continent. Considering Africa is the new center of gravity for world Christianity, his legacy will surely increase in coming years. Saint John seems to be the only apostle who lived to an old age; in church tradition he is believed to have been exiled late in life to the small Greek island of Patmos, just off the shores of Turkey. Patmos is still revered by many; the island's ancient Christian land-marks—such as the holy cave where John supposedly wrote the Apocalypse (Book of Revelation)—continue to be frequented by Christian pilgrims. Today Patmos hosts a seminary and is home to several Greek Orthodox monasteries.

The Post-Apostolic, Illegal Age: AD 60–313

Christianity began in modern-day Israel, and its influence radiated from there, most notably into what are now Egypt, Syria, Turkey, and Greece. Early on, Christianity was thought of as being a Jewish sect; all of the apostles were Jewish, and many of the early Christians believed that Jesus was the long-awaited Messiah. It is a misconception to think of "Christians vs. Jews" as some sort of clash of identity in the early church. Rather Christians under-stood themselves as part of the Jewish story, culminating in the Messiah, who, they believed, was Jesus of Nazareth.[10] In fact, it would be better to characterize the early church as being comprised of Jews who accepted Christ, and Gentiles who connected themselves to this ancient Jewish faith. These Jewish followers of Christ began to teach that God was not concerned with ethnicity. All were welcome to join the movement, as long as they connected themselves to Jewish texts and the larger Jewish narrative. Most importantly, they believed the Jewish God—Yahweh—had recently sent his son in the form of a human being to save all humankind, Jews and non-Jews, from their sins.

Christianity did not attract much hostility from the Roman government in the earliest years, simply because Christians were not easily distinguished from Jews. Jews were able to practice their religion, but with certain restraints. Since Israel, the Jewish nation, had historically been a powerful empire, the Romans were skittish about their strongly Jewish ethnic identity, their monotheistic ideas, and their insular cultural enclaves all over the Mediterranean region. The Jews were a strange, but in some ways admirable, people in the minds of Romans. They tended to be educated and literate, they were highly moral, and their faith was admirably ancient—with texts to back up their historical pedigree. However, the Jews were also something of a threat to the Romans. Jews would sporadically rise up and attempt to overthrow the Roman administrators in their little centers of influence, particularly around Jerusalem, the old Jewish capital city where the Temple proudly stood. Occasionally, Jews were perceived as being treasonous. They generally refused to participate in the pompous displays of Roman pride such as venerating Roman emperors and cheering for Roman soldiers as they paraded through towns and organized political gatherings intended to unite the people under Roman identity. At one point in time, Jews had that strong sense of victory and national pride. In some ways they lived in the past. Their glory years had long passed. David and Solomon lived about 1,000 years before the time of Jesus.

In time, Christianity became a thorn in the side of the Roman Empire. The government did not quite understand whether they were Jews, a Greek religion, or something else. In the decade of the AD 60s we begin to see Emperor Nero (ruled AD 54–68) take horrific steps to purge his cities of Christian influence. Whether the martyrological record is judged to be hagiographic or somewhat accurate, it is certain that Nero authorized the persecution of Christians. There exists evidence of Christians being noticed in the year 112 by the Roman Emperor Trajan; one of his informants, an official named Pliny, described the religion as a "wretched superstition" but could not provide any evidence of illicit activity. His descriptions of the Christians are rather mundane. He described them as singing anthems to Christ and eating food together. He wrote of their honesty in their dealings as well as their commitment to righteous living.[11]

However, Christians soon began to irritate the Roman political establishment and many of them paid with their lives. The first three centuries of Christianity are inspirational for Christians; however, they are also bittersweet because so many Christians were violently struck down. Christians often knew this going in; thus conversion to the faith was a solemn, sacred affair. Occasionally defections occurred, causing serious controversies. It was understandably difficult for Christians to worship with a "lapsed" Christian—one who abandoned the faith under pressure. Once the storm of persecution had subsided, these people often returned to faith.

Imagine a widow, whose husband had been crucified, sitting in church next to a couple who had abandoned the faith during a crisis, only to return later expecting the same rights and benefits of membership. It would have been difficult indeed to sort this all out. Tertullian (c. 160–220), a famous Christian theologian from the Berber people in North Africa, claimed that persecution was not always a bad thing, for, in his view, within the blood of martyrs lies the seed of the church.[12] It makes sense that a North African Berber would make a statement like this because the Christians of this region were brutally suppressed. There developed a crisis in the North African churches over whether to accept these "lapsed" Christians. It became so severe it split the church into several different groups in that region.

Among the most famous North African martyrdoms were two women, Perpetua and Felicitas, who were executed in Carthage in 203. Perpetua was a young woman with an infant child, and Felicitas was her eight-months pregnant slave. Both were found guilty in court and were killed by beasts in the arena in front of crowds of witnesses. The Romans underestimated the significance of these types of killings, and quite often the persecutions backfired. Christians were well known for their charity, their assistance to the poor, and their high standards in ethics and morals. In time the public execution of Christians began to be seen as an unjust act. This began to turn the tide of public opinion in favor of Christianity—something that reached fruition in the early 300s.

The Christian church did not quite know how to handle those defectors who tried to come back into the fold. This split became especially severe in the 300s in the Carthage area (modern Tunisia) and led to two distinct denominations: the mainline churches and the Donatists. The Donatists were led by a bishop named Donatus. They believed that traitors (which they called "traditores")—those who snitched on Christians or aided and abetted the persecution by turning them over to the authorities—should not be allowed into the church. They believed that traitors must deal with the consequences of their actions. The church must consist of only the faithful. They even declared that Christians who had been baptized by traitors should not be treated as true Christians, since by betraying Christ one's ordination was completely invalidated. In the end, the Donatists lost the larger debate. Perhaps the greatest theologian of Western Christianity, Saint Augustine, argued that the traitors were to be forgiven and allowed back into the churches.

Did these events water down Christianity in that region? Probably so, because the mainline group (led by Augustine) and the Donatists never fully repaired the fracture. When Muslim invaders came to town and captured Carthage in 698, Christianity fell quickly. It is somewhat predictable that many of the Donatists would admire the "moral rigor" of the Muslims, and converted to that religion rapidly.[13]

Could Christianity have withstood Islam in North Africa had it not divided? It certainly would have had a better chance. What we do know is that Augustine's less demanding approach to Christian membership backfired. Christians were relatively easy pickings for Islamic teachers who proselytized the people of North Africa. It is ironic that Saint Augustine, the greatest theologian in Western Christianity, may have instituted a policy that led to the demise of his faith in his homeland in just a few hundred years after his death. Obviously, Augustine believed in forgiveness. However, there may come a time when continued forgiveness weakens one's resolve to stand and fight.

Christianity was illegal in the Roman Empire prior to 313. However, even the mighty Roman Empire had borders, and there were several places outside the Roman Empire that saw Christianity grow in stature during the later part of the period under discussion. We will briefly highlight three of these places: Edessa, Armenia, and Axum.

Edessa was the principal city of Osrhoene, "the world's first Christian kingdom."[14] Osrhoene was a Syriac-speaking kingdom in what is today southeastern Turkey and Syria. The capital city simply became known as "Edessa the Blessed" due to its being a center of Christian theological training as well as "the birthplace of Syriac Christian writing."[15] Osrhoene citizens declared Christianity their official religion around the year 200. Today Edessa is known as the city of Sanliurfa; it is entirely Islamic. Tourists regularly visit the city because in Islamic tradition it is the birthplace of the patriarch Abraham.

Second, we should mention Armenia, which bears the distinction of being the oldest Christian nation that still exists. Armenia's famous king Tiridates III (ruled 287 to 330) converted to Christianity from Zoroastrianism in the year 301 after being miraculously healed from his insanity by Gregory the Illuminator. Gregory was a powerful Christian figure in that era; he and his family are known to have evangelized ("illuminated") the regions we know today as Armenia, Turkey, and Iran.

Our third example comes from Northeast Africa in what is today Ethiopia, another ancient Christian civilization. We know from the book of Acts, chapter 8, that "Philip the Evangelist" taught an Ethiopian eunuch who was a treasurer for Queen Candace.[16] This eunuch took the gospel back with him, paving the way for what became the Christian kingdom of Axum (or Aksum). While the precise dates are not certain, we do know that at some point in the fourth century the monarch of Axum, King Ezana (ruled from the 320s to 356) adopted Christianity for his empire. Ethiopians were known to have a strong

Jewish sensibility about them, which they claimed went back to Solomon having a love affair with the Queen of Sheba.[17] Ethiopians believe this queen returned to Sheba, pregnant with Solomon's son. Today, Ethiopia is over 60% Christian with strongly Jewish undertones.

Constantine and Byzantine Age: 313–732

The year 313 marks one of the more significant dates in Christian history. In that year, Constantine, one of the two Roman emperors at the time, co-authored the "Edict of Milan," allowing for religious freedom in the empire.[18] This was a tremendous reversal of fortune because only a few years earlier there had been a brutal persecution under Emperor Diocletian (ruled AD 284 to 305). Constantine favored Christianity because he believed the Christian God helped him rise to the position of Roman Emperor. In the year 324 Constantine became the sole ruler of the Empire and moved his capital from Rome to Byzantium—an ancient Greek city in modern-day Turkey. Constantine renamed the city Constantinople, after himself. Many people began to refer to the city as "New Rome" because it became the financial and administrative center of the empire. Today that city is called Istanbul.

Constantine probably did not become Christian until later in his reign, as he was for much of his life a follower of Mithraism, an ancient Aryan religion related to Zoroastrianism. Constantine eventually began to take up Christianity, however, possibly because of his mother. Constantine was very close to his mother, Helena, a devout Christian. She spearheaded many efforts to raise Christianity's appeal through benevolence work, building churches, searching for Christian relics, and discovering important Christian sites. It is quite possible that Helena's support of Christianity led to what would eventually become a wholesale embrace of the faith in the Roman Empire, and, eventually, the suppression of any non-Christian faiths; this is precisely what happened under Emperor Theodosius (ruled 378 to 395).

It is a very ironic story. In less than a hundred years, Christianity went from being ruthlessly purged to actively suppressing rival religions. In Darwinian fashion, Christianity's evolutionary chances for survival went from almost nothing to absolute within a century. Imagine being a non-Christian during those days: At the beginning of your life Christianity is an illegal, despised sect. At the end of your life, you are required to become a Christian in order to remain in good standing with the government!

One challenge to understanding Christianity during this age is defining exactly what we mean by the Roman Empire. This is a very difficult topic. In broad terms, the Roman Empire existed in some form from 44 BC to AD 1453. While many people understand the "Fall of the Roman Empire" to have occurred in 476, it actually continued in the Byzantine Empire, or, the Eastern

Roman Empire, until 1453. The Roman Empire split into two: Eastern and Western. Our period under discussion, 313–732, saw Christianity thrive in both sides of the Empire. When the Germanic peoples, the so-called "Barbarians," sacked the Western Empire, they became Christians. In the Byzantine Empire of the East, however, Christianity was thriving until the years of Muslim advance, which began in 632. After that, Christianity's fortunes reversed drastically.

We must not give the impression that Christianity was uniform during this period, because it certainly was not. The mainstream form of Christianity was known as the "Orthodox" or "Catholic" form. This is the form of Christianity that prevailed, at least numerically. It is important to mention, however, that Christianity east of the eastern border of the Roman Empire looked quite different. Many textbooks on the history of Christianity reflect a Western bias and scarcely mention that Christianity was vibrant and healthy outside of "the West" for a very long time. Some even associate Christianity with "the West" as if they were coterminous. The Christians who existed east of the Roman Empire were not usually considered "Orthodox" or "Catholic"; rather, they became known as Syrians, Nestorians, and Churches of the East. These groups of Christians still exist today, but they are small due to Islamic persecutions as well as by their being labeled heretics by Western Christians.

Christians in the Middle East, North Africa, southwest Europe, and Central Asia were decimated in the 600s and 700s. Islam spread very quickly and ruled over Christian populations in these areas, sometimes brutally, sometimes peacefully. It is a very mixed history during those years. Some people were not quite sure what to make of Islam. Was it a different religion? It shared so much with Judaism and Christianity. Muslims had a deep respect for Jesus and Mary. In fact they claimed to be a continuation and fulfillment of "the religions of the Book." Islam claimed to be, essentially, Part Three in the history of monotheism. Christians had always viewed themselves as being Part Two—a fulfillment of the religion of Judaism. The difference, however, was that Muslims conceived of their religion as a *final chapter* in the evolution of the faith from Judaism to Christianity to Islam. They claimed that their esteemed prophet, Muhammad, was the last messenger to relay God's teachings to humankind.

In the year 732, Islamic expansion suffered a surprising defeat when "the Hammer" struck with resounding force, causing Islam to lose its momentum in Western Europe. "The Hammer" was Charles Martel, leader of the Franks—a Germanic tribe that conquered most of Western Europe and ruled from the 300s to the 900s. Martel has become famous for being the grandfather of Charlemagne, known today as the father of Europe. However, there would be a very different Europe had Martel not defeated Islamic forces at the Battle of Tours (also known as the Battle of Poitiers) on October 10, 732. For the rest of his life (he died in 741), Martel devoted himself to pushing back Islam and checking its advance while expanding his own territory. Martel represents a pivot in Christian history. By pushing Islamic forces out of his land, over the Pyrenees Mountains—that natural border between France and Spain—he effectively removed the threat of an Islamic Europe. Islam continued to rule in Hispania—the Iberian Peninsula—for over 700 years. However, the grand ideal of conquering Europe in the name of Islam faltered because of Martel's battle prowess.

In the Eastern Roman Empire, Byzantium, it was a different story. Western Europe held safe distance from the Islamic world; the Byzantine Empire had no such luxury. Islamic forces chipped away at the Byzantine Empire, slowly but surely, during these years and beyond. Eventually, Islam won this titanic clash of civilizations. The city of Constantinople finally fell to Ottoman Muslims, but that did not occur until centuries later, in 1453.

East of the Roman Empire, in Persia, Christianity experienced ups and downs due to conflicts between Persia and Byzantium. Persian Christians lived amidst an officially Zoroastrian culture and were at times persecuted severely. Several cities in the Persian Empire achieved great status as being Christian centers of learning and piety. Mar Mattai, near Mosul in northern Iraq, became a center for theological training in the 300s and is today the home of the famous Mar Mattai Syriac Orthodox monastery. The cities of Merv and Samarkand were important Nestorian centers in the far reaches of the Persian Empire during the fifth and sixth centuries. These cities are virtually forgotten to Western Christians as Merv is located in Turkmenistan and Samarkand is in Uzbekistan. Other important cities that were home to Nestorian Christians during this period were Seleucia-Ctesiphon, the capital of the Persian Empire; Jundishapur (in Iran), possibly the first Christian university; and Nisibis (in Turkey), a famous training center for Syriac Christians that for centuries preserved the writings of Aristotle.

The Western side of the Roman Empire during the years 313 to 732 is a bittersweet story. The once invincible city of Rome became invaded, plundered, and eventually ruled by Germanic peoples to the north, often described as barbarians. "Barbarian" is a term of derision, used mainly to dismiss the civility of those who invaded—and eventually defeated—Roman troops in the Western part of the empire. In the year 410 the Visigoths overtook the city of Rome, led by their King Alaric I. The Gothic warriors proved too much, hammering away at the Italian Peninsula until eventually, in 476, the last Roman Emperor—Romulus Augustus—was deposed and no successor was appointed.

An important point here, however, is that while the political edifice in the West was in decline, this period was a defining one for what we know today as the Roman Catholic Church. Some scholars argue that when the Western

Roman Empire fell into disarray, the importance of the office of the papacy—the Bishop of Rome—increased significantly. Many great events occurred in the Roman Church during these years, for example:

1. Augustine (354-430), the preeminent theologian in the history of Latin Christianity, deeply impacted Western theology with his writings *The City of God* and *Confessions*, two of the most important works in Western civilization.

2. Jerome (c. 347-420), another important church Father, translated the Bible into Latin in the late 300s. His work was finished in the year 405, effectively setting the stage for a Latin Church that would in time distinguish itself from the Greek Church on linguistic grounds. The Greek/Latin diversion initiated by this groundbreaking translation of the Bible essentially led Western Christendom in a different direction than Eastern Christianities. Ultimately, the cultural divide, spawned largely by Jerome's work, would culminate in mutual excommunications. In the year 1054, the patriarchs of Constantinople and Rome declared each other to be non-Christians. We will cover this episode more carefully in the next chapter.

3. Rampant missionary work characterized the Western Roman Empire Christians during the period 313 to 732. We can briefly point to three: Patrick, Columba, and Boniface. Patrick (387-461; known in the West as "Saint Patrick") was a former slave who had great success evangelizing Ireland. Columba (521-597) was an Irishman who set up a base at Iona, Scotland, and successfully established Christianity there. The island of Iona is held dear to Scottish Christians. Boniface (672-754) has come to be known as the "apostle of the Germans" as he traveled across that land, rooting out paganism and planting Christianity in many towns and villages. Much of his effectiveness was due to his being protected by Charles Martel, "the Hammer," who ruled the region with an iron fist.

Pivotal Age: 732-1204

Christianity grew and flourished during the *pivotal age*, both in the East and the West. Even so, there were exceptions. For example, it began its long decline in the Middle East and North Africa during these years. However, in some places, Christianity reached high water marks during this period. In the East, around the year 800, we have a marvelous example of one of Christianity's golden eras in the ambitious career of Patriarch Timothy (died 823). Timothy was head of the Nestorian Church of the East and oversaw a prestigious Christian infrastructure that was far larger and more developed than the

Roman Church at the time. Based in the city of Seleucia, in modern Iraq, he presided over 85 bishoprics in the vast spread of land from Syria in the West to China and India in the East. He oversaw bishops in Iran, Armenia, Turkmenistan, Yemen, Tibet, India, and all the way to the city of Xian, in eastern China. His jurisdiction was huge in comparison with either the Western Roman or the Eastern Byzantine regions. More than anything, Timothy was missions-minded. He sent monks all over Asia to spread the gospel and establish Christian infrastructure through building churches and monasteries, and by commissioning gifted leaders. He was a highly literate man we know from his many letters; over 200 of them have been preserved. Timothy's work was strong in obscure nations Westerners know little about today such as Uzbekistan, Kazakhstan, and Tajikistan. Interestingly, Timothy's missionaries often intersected with Buddhist missionaries, and their interactions are documented as having been very cordial, often leaving lasting influences on both parties. For example, some believe Shintoism, the religion of Japan, may have been affected by Nestorian Christianity at some point in the past. This would make sense given the vast opportunities for cross-pollination among travelers in the cities and towns of the Silk Road.

Indeed, Nestorian Christians were so scattered over Asia that at times they became enmeshed into other religions in surprising ways. For example, in southeastern China in the fourteenth century, there was at least one example of a Nestorian Christian community and a Manichean group that lived and practiced their faiths under one bishop who supervised both. The Manichean movement arose in the third century and was a major threat to Christianity in some parts of the world. Their prophet, Mani, claimed to be "the seal of the prophets"—a title Muhammad would later adopt—and created a dualistic religion based on the eternal good and the eternal evil sharing equal power. The Turk-speaking Uyghur people of Central Asia were comfortable with Buddhists, Manicheans, and Nestorian Christians living together during the second Uyghur Empire spanning the period 850–1209.[19]

The case of the Nestorians raises important questions: When does Christianity end and culture begin? There is no definite answer because one person's syncretism may be another's orthodoxy. In other words, where is the theological arbiter who can decide whether a certain form of Christianity is correct or whether it has compromised itself and overly assimilated to another culture?

Christianity spread across this vast expanse on what we know as "The Silk Road"—a network of trade routes that connected the Mediterranean world with Asia. The Silk Roads were paths forged chiefly for commerce; however, they were very effective for missionary travels. From Syria to China, the Silk Road wound through the Persian world, Central Asia, East Asia, and back through India, Arabia, and Egypt.

North African Christianity as a whole was on the decline during this era (732–1204) due to Islamic expansion. The Christian communities of Sudan, Egypt, and Ethiopia dwindled because of Islamic Sharia law. Sharia does not normally allow Christians to evangelize, effectively limiting Christian growth to procreation. In addition, non-Muslims have to pay much higher taxes than Muslims, often leading to quick economic improvement simply by converting to Islam. Sudan, known historically as Nubia, was an important Christian kingdom from the sixth century to the fifteenth. Ethiopia has remained Christian-majority to the present day, an oddity for the northern half of Africa. Christianity remained strong in the luxuriously wealthy city of Alexandria, but in the surrounding region of Egypt, conversions to Islam became commonplace. Today, only about 10% of Egypt is Christian, but these ancient Christians, known as the Coptic Christians, are the heirs of a very ancient form of the faith.

The years 732 to 1204 are known as the *pivotal age* for another reason: during this era, Christianity became closely identified with Western Europe. This is not to say that Christianity was dying in the Byzantine area of influence. However, this period witnessed events that proved disastrous for the Eastern side of the empire. In fact, even at the beginning of this epoch, Islamic invasions had taken a heavy toll on Byzantine Christians and "By the 800s the East Roman Empire was reduced to the territories of Asia Minor and Greece on either side of the Bosporus, the southern end of Italy, and a scattering of islands in the Mediterranean Sea."[20] Constantinople was really the only major city left in this once proud Empire, and it was becoming increasingly vulnerable due to tenacious, relentless Islamic expansion at Byzantium's expense.

The year 988 marks another major pivot during this period. In that year, Vladimir of Kiev—who had just a few years earlier gained control of the Russian Empire from his brother—decided he needed a religion to consolidate his empire. The traditional story is that he investigated Judaism, Islam, Roman Catholicism, and Orthodoxy. He sent trusted envoys far and wide to determine which religion was most suitable for his people. After being disappointed by the other options, the delegates were dumbfounded when they entered the Hagia Sophia Orthodox Church at Constantinople, perhaps the most magnificent church building in Christian history. They simply did not have the words to explain how beautiful their experience was with all of the icons, incense, shimmering gold, cavernous naves, and sophisticated Greek liturgies. All they could tell the monarch was, "We knew not whether we were in heaven or on earth." Shortly thereafter, Vladimir expressed an interest in officially connecting his empire to the Byzantine Empire, which he did through marriage and baptism. He married the Byzantine Emperor's sister—a woman named Anna—and led a mass conversion of his people to Christianity. Many of Vladimir's people followed him as he solemnly descended into the Dnieper River to become baptized as a believer in Christ Jesus as Lord. It was one of the most rapid conversions of a people in Christian history. Monasteries and churches were built with astonishing speed and with splendid quality, as visitors to Russia today will quickly notice.

However, Islamic forces continued to hammer the Byzantine lands through the years, and increasingly the former Byzantine Empire was looking Islamic. Up in the Ukraine and in Russia, however, there was a blossoming of what began to become—and today remains—the heartland of Orthodoxy. The center of gravity of Eastern Christianity was moving north, out of the Middle East and into Russia.

Perhaps the single most important development between the years 732 and 1204 was the Christianization of Western Europe. We have already discussed some of the mission work in the British Isles and Germany; however, something of massive import changed the course of Western Europe in the year 800. Earlier, we discussed Charles Martel, the Frankish king who stopped Islam's advance into Western Europe in the year 732. That is not the end of the story. Martel went on to become an advocate of the Christian faith. Most importantly, Martel's grandson, a man we know as Charlemagne (ruled 768 to 814), officially accepted the title of Emperor of the Holy Roman Empire. Charlemagne mercilessly ruled the territory that included Italy, France, Germany, Austria, Hungary, and most of the Balkans. This man was a master warrior and immediately put to death any opposition be it military or civilian. He was also a ruthless enforcer of Christianity, giving his subjects the choice of Christian baptism or execution.[21] The Iberian Peninsula, containing Spain and Portugal, remained Islamic; no matter how much Charlemagne tried, he never could conquer it.

Charlemagne is known as the first emperor of the Holy Roman Empire. In the fateful year 800, he was crowned by the pope of Rome. The coronation was celebrated at the time, but it led to endless debates over who had more power, the papacy or the emperor. The story of Charlemagne's coronation is fascinating. It appears that he was in Rome to adjudicate over a political dispute involving Pope Leo II and the citizens. Charlemagne ruled in favor of the pope and condemned the accusers for treason. A short time later, on Christmas Day in the year 800, Charlemagne was praying in St. Peter's Basilica. While he was kneeling, the pope put a crown on his head and declared him to be the Roman Emperor. Why was this ceremonial act so significant? It was because the emperor of the Roman Empire was based in Constantinople, in the East. This location had been the seat of the Roman Empire since the year 330 when Constantine moved the capital from Rome. Thus, this occasion marks a symbolic break—a stark pivot—between the Latin West and the Greek East. The once united Roman Empire was now separated into halves—on an official basis. No longer did the Constantinopolitan emperor have jurisdiction in the West.

Why did the pope crown Charlemagne? Some historians believe the pope was trying to gain authority over the political sphere by essentially making the point that he was in charge—that he was able to select the emperor, but this idea is only a theory. We simply do not know what motivated this unprecedented move, nor do we know whether Charlemagne appreciated it or resented it. In any case, it did not really matter at the time because he was the undisputed ruler of the West, and the East was in decline. Charlemagne was king of "Christendom." In fact, it was right around this time that Europeans began to use that word to describe their culture—Christendom—the kingdom of Christ.

This was the heyday for Western Christianity: magnificent cathedrals were built higher and larger with each passing year, commanding the admiration of all who walked in the shadows of these towering masterpieces. Monasteries were full and wealthy, perhaps best exemplified in the French monastery of Cluny in the tenth century. Monks and missionaries pioneered all over the forests and countryside of this region, making Christianity the undisputed, official religion of Western Europe.

The Scandinavian nations were Christianized during this time. For example, Iceland became Christian in the year 1000 when their leader Thorgeir of Ljosvatn went into a Shamanistic trance for a full 24 hours, only to emerge from his cloak with the revelation that his land was to become subject to Christ. This was also a period of tremendous population increase in Western Europe, indicating ample food, abundant work, fruitful land, and widespread prosperity. Indeed this epoch in Western Europe was *pivotal*—the center of gravity of Christianity had moved out of Asia, the Middle East, and the Byzantine Empire, and more toward Western Europe.

The final episode that needs discussion here is the Christian crusades—a campaign to claim back land that had once been Christian but was now in Islamic hands. The holy city of Jerusalem was of course the great prize. Much has been written of this violent time, although it is difficult to isolate this as anything particularly bloody when comparing it to other events in history such as the expansion of Islam, the Mongol invasions, or the twentieth century's World Wars. While the crusades seemed to grind on from the year 1095 through the 1200s, historians usually point to four of them that truly merit the definition of an actual crusade. In 1095, the crusades began. That crusade ended with great success: the Latin Christians defeated Islamic defenders of the holy city and reclaimed it for Christianity. The victory was short-lived, however; Islam again recaptured Jerusalem in the year 1187 under the legendary Islamic war hero Saladin.

The fourth crusade, lasting from 1202 to 1204, was disastrous. It lives in the memories of Orthodox Christians and to this day is a stumbling block to relations between Eastern and Western Christians. It was initially an attempt to take back Jerusalem from Islamic power, but it went awry—terribly awry. The Latin crusaders began at Venice and sailed across the Adriatic Sea to the city of Zadar—a Christian city in the region of what we know today as Croatia. The crusaders pummeled the city and took all of the loot they could extract. Next, they sailed around the coast of Greece, up the Aegean Sea until they arrived at Constantinople—where they plundered the city, exiled the leaders, stripped anything of value, forced all priests to practice the Latin liturgy (as opposed to ancient Greek), and ruled the city until the year 1261, when the Byzantines finally rose up and drove the Latin Christians out.

Constantinople never recovered; it was weakened beyond repair. That event, punctuated by scores of murders and mass rapes in the aftermath of victory, has never quite disappeared from the consciousness of Eastern Orthodox Christians. In condemnation of his crusaders, the pope at the time, Innocent III, expressed horror at what had happened, "These defenders of Christ, who ought to have turned their swords only against the infidels, have bathed in Christian blood."[22] He came short of demanding that they withdraw, however. The exhilaration of capturing Christendom's most cherished city was too intoxicating. That horrific episode of Christian history set the agenda for a long and stubborn coldness between the East and the West, which has barely begun to thaw. Rather than what might have been: a united Christian civilization which functioned in two liturgical languages (Greek and Latin), we are left with two cultures that know little about each other, and probably trust each other even less.

Fractured Age: 1204–1517

The Byzantine Empire's days were numbered after the infamous sack of the city—by fellow Christians no less. The fall of Constantinople put into place a measure of hostility between the East and West that in many ways continues today. In this section we refer to that lamentable situation as a profound *fracture* in the Christian world.

Many books describe the big break between East and West as occurring in the year 1054—when the bishops of Rome and Constantinople excommunicated each other. However, the real straw that broke the camel's back was the sack of Constantinople in 1204. The city of Constantinople finally fell in the year 1453 when Ottoman invaders easily took the city. Ottoman troops outnumbered Byzantine fighters 200,000 to 8,000. Since that year, the city of Constantinople has been an Islamic city. Truth to be told, Constantinople remained Byzantine and Christian far longer than it should have, given its tiny force of defense. There was virtually nothing that could have been done to keep the glorious city of Constantinople in Christian hands. It had become a Christian dot in an Islamic world. Not even the famous walls of the city that had protected it for so long could have stopped the inevitable; it was only a matter of time before the entire region was subject to the powerful Ottoman Empire and the resurgent Islamic Caliphate.

I have named this period the *Fractured Age*. The two key fractures that occurred during this time need to be discussed here, justifying this somewhat dismal outlook on this period of Christian history: first, the fall of Christianity in the East; and, second, the Avignon Papacy and the resultant cries for Reform in the West. There were other developments in the Christian world that were not as bleak during this period. For example, the invention of the printing press and the resultant rise of literacy, the growth of the Ethiopian Church, and the beginnings of the Catholic transcontinental missionary movements. Indeed, the Catholic missions of the 1500s were truly exceptional, leading to what we can call, for the first time in history, a global religion. However, the two stories that dominated this period were the decline of Eastern Christendom and the Avignon crisis.

We should begin this section on the fall of Eastern Christianity by discussing the Nestorian Christians. Few in the Western world properly understand the Nestorian Church. Westerners tend to neglect Nestorian history, their great missionary work, and their rapid decline during the thirteenth and fourteenth centuries. The Nestorian Christians were anathematized in the year 431 at the Council of Ephesus—one of the great "seven ecumenical councils" of the Orthodox/Catholic Church. However, the Nestorians were a very successful branch of Christianity for centuries. They were especially strong in Central Asia and all along the Silk Roads. Think of their influence as a triangle from modern-day Iraq to Mongolia to India and back up to Iraq. Some people are surprised when they hear that Nestorians are still around. They have been heavily persecuted through the years and one wonders how in the world they have managed to survive so many catastrophes, but the fact remains that they are still among us, although drastically depleted. Their future, however, is precarious. Estimates are that there are only about 400,000 Nestorians alive today, though in their historical homeland of Iraq they have been decimated in recent years. Indeed, their patriarch, Mar Dinkha, now resides in Chicago in the USA simply because he is an endangered man in his own tumultuous country.

The thirteenth and fourteenth centuries were labeled "The Great Tribulation" by historian of religion Philip Jenkins. He writes:

> We can properly see the fourteenth century as marking the decisive collapse of Christianity in the Middle East, across Asia, and in much of Africa.[23]

Jenkins describes a harrowing tale. That century was disastrous for Christians in those regions, and Christianity scarcely exists in some of those parts today. For the Nestorians, however, the situation was more dire. This story is vague in the minds of most church historians. Some textbooks of Christianity ignore it altogether. Let me outline just a few of the incidents that led to the near-demise of Christianity in those parts, essentially pushing Christianity West and making it almost exclusively a Western religion at that time in history.

The thirteenth-and fourteenth-century atrocities against Christianity were perpetuated mainly by Muslim regimes that had historically been somewhat tolerant to the Christians living under their rule. For example, Egypt, which had officially become Islamic in the 600s, had a sizeable Christian population—until the fourteenth century that is. In that century there was an outbreak of persecution that saw the forced conversions of many, the confiscation of church properties and monasteries, and the erection of mosques on important Christian sites. The persecution grew so severe that mass conversion to Islam became the norm.

There was another force in the mix that proved equally devastating for Christians and Muslims alike—the Mongols. The Mongols were probably the greatest land fighters history has ever witnessed. This tribal people from the East managed to strike fear in the hearts of anyone and everyone in their path: Chinese, Christians, Muslims, various Central Asian peoples. Mongol invasions were particularly dreadful because their campaigns were unusually cruel. It was not uncommon for Mongols to slaughter entire towns, every man, woman, and child. Any survivors could become booty for the victorious warriors—a pleasure considered part of the spoils of war. Genghis Khan and his posterity were an ever present danger for nearly everyone on the Eurasian continent. They invaded as far West as Hungary and as far East as Japan. The Mongol Empire lasted from 1206 to 1368 and was the largest contiguous empire in world history, twice the size of either the Roman Empire or the Islamic Caliphate at their heights.

Religion in the Mongol Empire is a very complicated topic. The Mongols themselves were mainly Shamanistic—belonging to their own local, tribal religions. Sometimes the Mongol Khans indiscriminately executed entire cities regardless of religion; other times they seemed to prefer particular religions. In times of peace, Mongol leaders showed tremendous toleration for religious beliefs, whether Buddhist, Christian, or Islamic. A few of the Khans esteemed Christianity and occasionally members of the ruling families even embraced Christianity. This is not surprising, for Nestorian Christianity was the largest religious presence in central Asia at the time.[24] However, matters changed toward the end of the Mongol Empire. Around the year 1300, various Khans that governed this vast area began to adopt Islam as their religion—with disastrous consequences for Christians in the empire. This is why Central

Asian nations are today Islamic: Uzbekistan, Afghanistan, Tajikistan, Turkmenistan, Kyrgyzstan, and Pakistan. In other words, before the Mongol period,
Christianity was a majority; by the end of the Mongol period in 1368, Christianity's future in the region was in serious peril.

This period also witnessed various persecutions against Syrian Christians
in Armenia, Iraq, Syria, and southeastern Turkey. In Turkey, the Christians of
Ephesus were systematically put to the sword in 1304 or else sold as slaves. In
the city of Amida, known today as the Turkish city of Diyarbakir, there was a
massacre of Christians in the year 1317. If they escaped with their lives, they
were publicly humiliated; twelve thousand of them were carted off into slavery.
By the year 1500, free Christians made up less than 10% of what is today
Turkey; the rest were enslaved.[25]

Christianity in Iran and Iraq, previously lighthouses for Christian learning, nearly vanished due to Christians fleeing for the hills, leaving behind
wonderful resources that would be swiftly converted into mosques or Islamic
houses of learning. Armenian Christianity was ravaged during this period. Of a
particular siege that took place in 1387 by Islamic Tatars, one Armenian
historian records:

> Some, both men and women, they led away into captivity, and some they laid low
> with the slaying sword, their bodies trampled underfoot, priests and laymen alike
> falling dead and remaining unburied—Some were scorched with fire, and others
> through famine were exposed to the visitations of wild beasts, some tortured with
> cruel tortures, and others subjected to the distresses of terror.[26]

Somehow, Armenia has remained Christian. History proves, however, that
they were unique among their Christian peers during the persecutions of the
thirteenth and fourteenth centuries; most of their contemporaries died as
martyrs or else converted to Islam. Perhaps rather than using the word *fracture*,
the word more fitting for Eastern Christianity's decline during the years 1204–
1517 would be *amputation*.

The theme of *fracture* played out vividly in the Western European church
in a curious episode that is known to historians as the Avignon Papacy and to
the Roman Catholic world as the Babylonian Captivity of the Church. The
Avignon Papacy was a crisis in Western Christendom that gets little emphasis
in church history texts. Rather than merely a schism in the Roman Catholic
Church, the Avignon crisis led to a series of reform movements that would
culminate in the career of Martin Luther, better known as the world's first
Protestant.

In the 1300s, the Roman Church in the West began to enjoy the benefits
of a prosperous society. Cities like Venice and Genoa generated immense
capital, and much of that capital spread throughout the Roman Catholic
sphere of influence. Increased prosperity in this case meant increased spending

on benevolence—fattening church coffers. However, somewhere along the way, the church began to adopt a capitalist mentality not all that different from the business models they were witnessing in the Italian city states, a region some scholars believe is the seedbed of modern capitalism. Sociologist Rodney Stark writes, "Christianity created Western Civilization," and by that he means freedom and capitalism.[27] As the church gained wealth, it increased its building projects and this-worldly ambitions.

One of the best ways to finance the immense church infrastructure was through saving souls. Catholic theologians came up with the idea that indulgences could be purchased in order to increase one's likelihood of going to heaven, or of literally buying a loved one out of purgatory. This chapter of Roman Catholic history is not a pretty one as spending on structures—such as St. Peter's Basilica—required the church to think more in terms of finances than faith.

One of the most powerful popes in the history of the Roman Church ruled during this time: Pope Innocent III (pope from 1198 to 1216). Innocent believed himself to be the "Vicar of Christ," a term he introduced as meaning when he spoke, Christ was speaking. Innocent believed he was capable of ratifying church doctrine himself—which happened several times during his reign, such as in the case of transubstantiation. He also believed himself to be above any earthly position. This high view of the papacy persisted throughout the thirteenth and fourteenth centuries to the point that Clement V (pope 1305 to 1314) believed he could simply pluck up the office of the papacy and move it to France, which is indeed what happened in the year 1309. Between 1309 and 1377 the Roman pope was based in the French city of Avignon. Technically, this location was acceptable since Avignon was within Roman jurisdiction. However, it would ultimately prove to be a disastrous move. It seemed to show the people just how arrogant the clergy had become—if they wanted to move the church from Rome to France, then so be it.

The move to Avignon left a bitter taste in the mouths of many—particularly considering how lavish and luxurious the Avignon compound was. It did not sit well with most, particularly when factoring in the Black Death, a plague which terrorized Europe in the 1340s and 1350s, leaving anywhere between one-quarter and one-half of Europe's population dead. A richly ornamented, secure, and arrogant papacy was out of step with a culture of death that enveloped Western Europe. Nevertheless, in times of turmoil and uncertainty, people tend to turn to faith, and Western Europeans turned to their Holy Catholic Church—and the church grew wealthy and ever more powerful. Visitors to Avignon today will notice the pomp and splendor of the towering papal palaces from far away.

In the year 1377 disaster struck the Roman Catholic Church when the pope decided to move his seat of power back to Rome. This decision set into motion an intractable situation where one French pope was elected and one Italian pope was elected. In 1409 a new pope was elected and the two existing popes were deposed; however, neither of them resigned. Thus, Christendom was left with three popes, all ruling at once! It became a circus. This bizarre sequence of events ended in 1417, but for forty years—known as the "Great Western Schism"—there was a plurality of popes. Predictably, the office of the papacy was severely discredited. The papacy's legitimacy and authority were being questioned across Europe.

The Roman Catholic Church has never been exclusively identified with the clergy, the buildings, or the bureaucracy; rather, the church is the people. Then, between the years 1204 and 1517, people began to see their church in dire need of reform. Plainly evinced by the Avignon crisis, cracks existed in the institution of the church. By the year 1400, the church was no longer perceived to be an impenetrable institution. It was clear to many Catholics that their church needed saving. For people like John Wycliffe, Jan Hus, and Martin Luther, the church had to be reformed.

Martin Luther (1483-1546), a theology professor at Wittenberg, Germany, often represents a major turning point in history. His 95 theses that he nailed to the castle church door in Wittenberg on October 31, 1517, were originally intended to purge the church of what he viewed a sinister ploy on behalf of the church to raise funds for Rome—funds the German people did not have. Luther became particularly angry at circuit riding indulgence-salesmen like John Tetzel who came up with offensive jingles like "When the coin in the coffer rings, the soul from purgatory springs." The church had become so decadent by this stage that people were led to believe that if they gave enough money, they could save the souls of their deceased loved ones. Luther had previously taken a trip to Rome and had come to the conclusion that all of the glitz, pomp, money, and power were a sham. The church needed a complete overhaul.

First and foremost, Luther wanted to get the Bible into the hands of the people, so they could be informed on what the church should look like. This goal was impossible, however, because most people were illiterate, and if they were literate, they only read in their local dialect. The language of the Bible however, for the Latin West, was fixed. One had to go to theological college to learn Latin; it was a language for the intelligentsia. Thus, Luther realized he needed to translate the Bible into German, which he did with the help of several of his friends, completing the project in 1534. Luther believed the most fundamental task he could undertake to successfully argue that his interpretations of Christianity were correct was to show the people just exactly what the Bible said. Furthermore, in Luther's view, the sale of indulgences was not biblical. It was not only foreign to the scriptures, it was sinful. Luther felt

Rome was robbing poor people in the small, working-class towns of Germany in order to finance extravagant building campaigns and political objectives.

Luther had a tool on his side that helped him immensely. The printing press with moveable type had been invented the previous century around the year 1440. Ironically, it had been used previously for manufacturing thousands of these indulgences—these certificates which were essentially offerings of forgiveness, supposedly ratified by the "Vicar of Christ"—the pope. The printing press was Luther's best friend. Within days his theses were distributed all over Germany, and within two months most of Europe was fully aware of the crisis. The printing press exponentially increased the rapidity of knowledge distribution. It is ironic that a machine could be used for such diametrically opposed means. Nevertheless, Luther's Bible had the effect of increasing literacy rates quickly:

> From a secular viewpoint, surely the most far-reaching effect of Luther's activity was the radical increase in literacy from the early 1520s on through the rest of the century.[28]

Why did Luther's Bible have this effect? The reason literacy rates quickly improved was because Luther believed that only through the Bible could a person understand God's intent. Luther was essentially undermining papal authority. He believed everyone should read the Bible and try to figure out what was in that text before listening to someone else's interpretation. One Oxford scholar, Alister McGrath, described Luther's emphasis on "sola Scriptura" ("scripture alone") as "Christianity's Dangerous Idea."[29] Dangerous indeed. When information is distributed widely and people begin to develop interpretations that conflict, there are clashes. Luther's movement essentially split Europe into Protestant and Catholic. These were not merely ivory tower academic debates, either; they were bloody battles that left hundreds of thousands of people dead over a period of two centuries—even as far as the twentieth century in a few cases.

Luther was certainly not alone. There were others who preceded him. In many ways, Luther was repeating ideas that had been circulating in Europe for 150 years. The most obvious precursor to Luther was the Oxford scholar John Wycliffe (1320s-1384). Wycliffe argued the principle of sola Scriptura well before Luther. He also wanted to downplay the institution of the church and put the Bible at the center of Christian faith and life. This goal makes sense given the fact that he was almost an exact contemporary of the Avignon debacle going on within the papacy. No wonder he became disillusioned with Rome. Wycliffe wanted all people to read the Bible in their own language; thus, he translated it into English, completing his task the very year of his death in 1384—exactly 150 years before Luther's translation into German.

Wycliffe also preceded Luther in his opposition to indulgences and his belief that clerical celibacy was unscriptural. Luther later adopted both of these teachings as his own. Wycliffe was highly opposed to the church's involvement in secular and political affairs. In many ways, Wycliffe was an advocate of the separation of church and state—a viewpoint Luther did not share. Luther believed the church should be involved with the state, but more importantly, he wanted the church to purge its corruption. Thus, while Luther had hope in the church's ability to help govern, Wycliffe did not.

Wycliffe's ideas had a profound effect on Jan Hus (1372–1415), a theologian and professor in Prague, modern-day Czech Republic. England had connections with this area since the king of England at that time, Richard II, married a princess of that region—Anne of Bohemia. Anne was the daughter of the Holy Roman Emperor. In other words, Wycliffe's ideas travelled amongst the nobility as well as amongst the educated elite, and were obviously catching on. Jan Hus developed a large following, but he was burned at the stake for heresy in the year 1415. Hus's followers, however, founded many churches that were based on Wycliffe's ideas of reform. In fact, there were Protestant churches in the Moravian region of the modern-day Czech Republic nearly a century before Luther's famous protest. The Protestant churches of the Czech Republic are the oldest in Protestantism today; they are known as the Moravian Brethren. Hus's ideas were controversial; several local battles were fought between Hussite Protestants and the Roman Catholics. The whole reason these "Hussite Wars" (1419–1434) even began was because the nobility in Bohemia were outraged at the execution of their beloved professor and theologian, Jan Hus. Had it not been for Wycliffe and Hus, there would have been no Luther.

It was a *fractured* age. The fractures were deep, and there were no quick fixes; indeed, they are still hampering Christianity around the world. However, these fractures were always accompanied by those who wanted to heal them or introduce reform. The Avignon Papacy resulted in various cries for reform, notably the reform movements that remained *within* the Catholic fold: the monastic orders. A whole slew of monastic movements of renewal occurred during this time, arguing that the church needed to purify. Most of these orders are still in existence today. The monks and nuns involved in these reform movements continue to emphasize the core tenets of Christianity such as helping the weak, feeding the hungry, nursing the sick, spreading the gospel, teaching the poor, and always pressing the conscience of Christian elites. Some of the more prominent Roman Catholic orders that sprang up during this time were the following:

- Franciscans (est. 1209–founded by St. Francis in order to help the poor and sick; the nuns are known as the Order of St. Clare);

- Carmelites (est. 1214-a contemplative order);
- Dominicans (est. 1215-known for preaching and combating heresy);
- Augustinians (est. 1256 Martin Luther was a member).

Two great success stories between 1204 and 1517 need to be highlighted: the growth of the Ethiopian Church and the beginnings of the transcontinental Catholic missionary movements. The Ethiopian church is proudly ancient. Esteemed historian Martin Marty has written, "No branch of Christianity of any size matched the Ethiopian Church as a keeper of ties to the lore and ways of Hebrews, including the practice of universal circumcision of male babies."[30] Ethiopians have many Jewish customs that survive in their churches today. Perhaps most striking is their ancient practice of observing the Sabbath on its intended day—Saturday. Most Christians jettisoned this practice in the first century. Today, with few exceptions, Christians around the world normally gather on Sunday—the day Jesus resurrected.

The Ethiopians seemingly should have capitulated to Islam, as did many of the North African Christians, during "the Great Tribulation." In fact, the opposite occurred: "The thirteenth century was a time of significant Christian growth throughout the southern region of Ethiopia."[31] Historians of African Christianity call this period the "Solomonic Revival." During this period, the Solomonic tradition—which had formerly been a narrative for the upper classes—began to become adopted by the masses in the Ethiopian countryside. In addition, the monastic movements intensified in Ethiopia during this time, particularly in their emphasis on the Virgin Mary. Ethiopia was a strongly Christian nation "surrounded on three sides by Muslim-dominated states," a testament to their tenacious perseverance as an ancient Christian body.[32]

Finally, we should say a word about the Catholic transcontinental missionary era—an epochal event that transformed Christianity. Before the year 1500, the Roman Catholic Church was a western European religious movement. By the end of the sixteenth century, the Roman Catholic Church had been decimated in northern Europe due to Protestantism, but it was more than making up for this loss in its decision to expand globally. Most Westerners know the story of the Italian navigator Christopher Columbus sailing to the Americas in 1492. Less well known is the fact that on his second journey in 1493 he brought clergy with him, and the Roman Catholic missions to the Americas began. Thousands of missions were established from the island of Hispaniola (Haiti/Dominican Republic) to California to the southern tip of Patagonia. The Reformation had not occurred yet, and thus they were all Roman Catholic. It is a huge land mass for one faith to successfully evangelize.

The entire region bears the stamp of Spanish and Portuguese: "Latin" America. These are Catholic lands. Latin America boasts the largest Catholic population in the world. Brazil and Mexico each have more Catholics than any other country in the world.[33] With over 100 million Catholics in North America and 500 million Catholics in Latin America, we can surely say that Rome's decision to evangelize the "New World" paid unimaginably high dividends.

Roman Catholic expansion did not end there, however. Portuguese missionaries planted churches in the Congo beginning in 1491 when a Kongolese king was baptized. Even today the people of the Democratic Republic of the Congo are about half Roman Catholic. India, too, witnessed Roman Catholic Christianity's expansion in this period. In the year 1498 Vasco da Gama arrived to India's western shores, perplexed to realize that Christians were already there with traditions dating back hundreds of years. While Roman Catholic missions went global in the late 1400s, they really matured in the 1500s, especially with the founding of the Jesuits in the year 1540.

Global Expansion Age: 1517–1906

Christianity's *global expansion* will be discussed at length in later chapters; however, it may be helpful to highlight a few larger developments during this period. It is crucial to recognize that from 1517 to 1906 Christianity was by and large a Western faith. There were isolated pockets of non-Western Christians, but the Christians in Asia, North Africa, and the Middle East were decimated during the period between 1204 and 1517. The widespread persecution of Christians had the effect of shaping Christian geography—pushing its center of gravity unmistakably west. Here is some data that helps us realize just how "Western" the Christian faith was during these years:[34]

- *500*. In AD 500, 62% of the world's Christians were located outside the West, and 38% were located within the West.
- *800*. Charlemagne was the turning point. Around the year 800 Christianity was more or less 50/50, meaning about half of the world's Christians were in the West and about half were in the non-Western world.
- *1204*. This is the year Constantinople was sacked by Western crusaders. By 1204, Christianity in the East had declined to around 35%. While Christianity was by that year a Western-majority religion, the numbers in the East were still respectable: around one out of three Christians was non-Western.
- *1517*. The change was obvious by the time of Luther's protest in 1517. In that year, the numbers had shifted to 7/93: only 7% of the world's Christians were non-Westerners. This shift illustrates the devastating impacts during the thirteenth and fourteenth centuries due to excessive rounds of Christian persecution and mass defections from Christianity to Islam, usually under coercive circumstances.

- *1906.* Christianity was still a predominantly Western religion in this year; the numbers have been estimated around 25/75 at that time. Only one out of four Christians worldwide was a non-Westerner in that year. However, a demographic change was on the horizon. Christianity was making a comeback in the non-Western world.

In the twentieth century, the demographics of Christianity changed dramatically. Around the year 1980, Christianity became—again—a 50/50 religion distributed evenly between the Western world and the non-Western world. The year 1980 marks a major turning point in the history of Christianity. This shift will be discussed shortly.

Christianity began reaching its pinnacle at the very end of the period under discussion. Two key years illustrate:

- *500.* In the year 500, Christianity was about 22% of the world's population. This number changed very little for 1300 years. However, during the nineteenth century, Christianity made a huge surge in market share.
- *1906.* By the year 1906, Christianity had the allegiance of almost exactly one-third of the human race, around 34%. Christianity's market share has not altered much since.

Therefore, what is relevant to this section is the "global expansion" of Christianity during this period, particularly in the 1800s. While Christianity grew exponentially in its first few centuries, it stagnated for a full 1300 years between the years 500 and 1800. During those years Christianity fluctuated between 20% and 25% of the world's population. There was a major change that took place, however, between the years 1800–1900. During those years Christianity's market share spiked from around 23% to around 33%, where it remains today.

Obviously, the big story of this particular section is how Christianity managed to go from 20% of humanity to a full one-third of humanity during a mere 100 years. Indeed, there are other events that we must highlight in order to understand the complexity of this capacious period. We begin with the great Catholic-Protestant hostilities that enveloped Western Christendom. We will then say a word about the great missionary endeavors during this period, first the Catholic Jesuits and then the Protestants. Finally, we will look at the Azusa Street Revival of 1906, an event that epitomized the changing nature of Christianity in the twentieth century.

After Luther's protest, the Roman Catholic Church erupted into a long and disastrous series of wars that left millions dead over several centuries. Furthermore, the wars were not only between Catholics and Protestants; it was almost just as common for Protestant groups to battle one another. Luther authorized the suppression of thousands of peasants in a series of uprisings that took place in the 1520s; many of the uprisings were led by Protestants who believed they had Luther on their side, but they were wrong. Luther opposed them as anarchists. He had no problem with the government bearing the sword in order to keep the peace, which is precisely the view he took of the situation. Thousands were killed.

The most common scenario, however, was to see major blocks of territory having to decide between Protestant and Catholic. The Protestant-Catholic wars have continued into the present day, most notably in Ireland where the Protestant north and the Catholic south are just now emerging from several centuries of hostility and suspicion. The most devastating of the Protestant-Catholic wars occurred during the years between 1618 and 1648. This period is known as the Thirty Years' War. Europe was essentially ripped into two: a Protestant north and a Catholic south. Northern Germany, the Scandinavian countries, England and Scotland, and various parts of Switzerland and Holland became Protestant shortly after Luther's protest. Spain, Portugal, France, Italy, Austria, and southern Germany remained Catholic. All of the borders in between were battle grounds, particularly in Germany which saw massive loss of life. Some parts of Germany saw their populations cut in half.

The Thirty Years' War ended with the Treaty of Westphalia in 1648, a monumental treaty with long-term consequences. It was a success in some ways: at least it stopped the bleeding. At the end of it, northern Europe was Protestant, southern Europe was Catholic, and the border regions were mixed. The Treaty of Westphalia is seen by historians today as critical for the future of Western civilization, primarily in two ways: First, it represents the beginning of what we have in Europe today—nation states that have their own sovereignty. Before this, most of Western Europe was united under a Holy Roman Emperor who ruled somewhat conjointly with the pope, although the credibility of the papacy had been waning since the Avignon crisis. The second notable development is that the Treaty set into irreversible motion the concept of religious freedom in Europe, signaling the beginning of the long decline of papal power. The decision of the Treaty was *cuius regio, eius religio* which translates "whose realm, his religion." In other words, now that there were different nation-states, the pope did not have jurisdiction anywhere other than in his Papal States—only a few sections of Italy. The pope no longer had the political clout he enjoyed all throughout the Medieval Ages. Many historians believe this to be the beginning of the secularization of Western Europe, a phenomenon that continues to reverberate in Western Europe today.

The years 1517 to 1906 also represent the greatest years of Christian expansion since the first centuries of the church. Why? There are two answers: First, the Catholic missions in the 1500s; and, second, the Protestant missions in the 1800s. The Catholic missions have already been noted, but we would be remiss if we did not point out the astounding accomplishments of the Society of Jesus, also known as the Jesuits. The Jesuits were formed by a man named Ignatius Loyola in the year 1540. They enjoyed the benefits of a burgeoning colonial culture during their rise. Spain and Portugal were rapidly expanding their colonial territory in the 1500s, and the Jesuits rode the wave. Latin America was evangelized by the Jesuits and other Catholic orders such as the Dominicans and the Franciscans. However, the Jesuits were by far the most successful. They established missions all over the "New World" as well as in places all over Asia such as Japan, China, India, and the Philippines. The most famous Jesuit, and perhaps the most successful missionary of all time, is Saint Francis Xavier (1506-1552). Xavier is reported to have baptized 700,000 people himself![35] The Jesuits may have benefitted from the governments of Spain and Portugal, but many political leaders hated them. Famously depicted in 1986 in the Academy Award winning film *The Mission*, the Jesuits frequently opposed the government, particularly on human rights issues. They were resented for opposing slavery and working to keep natives under their jurisdiction rather than allowing them to fall under the yoke of slavery. They became such a nuisance to the political and ecclesial hierarchy that they were forced to disband in 1773. In 1814 they were reinstated and are today the largest and most powerful order in the Roman Catholic Church, acclaimed for their high quality educational institutions.

Worldwide Protestant missions were rather late on the scene, emerging prominently in the 1700s. In the 1800s, however, the Protestant missions became vast and successful due largely, as in the case of the Catholic missionaries, to safety of passage provided by colonial governments, in particular the great British Empire—the largest empire the world has ever known.

Britain became Protestant in the 1500s. Its missionaries were given great privileges in the British territories of North America, much of Africa, the Middle East, India, Oceania, and many islands in the Caribbean. The British also controlled some important Asian ports on the coast of China and all over the Indonesian archipelago such as in Malaysia and Singapore. Probably the most fortuitous event to date in the history of British Protestant missions was the decision to evangelize sub-Saharan Africa, a region that became strongly Christian in the twentieth century. Whether a person believes mission work to be right or wrong, the demographic changes in religion introduced by Christian missionaries are impressive indeed. Today, the majority of the world's Christians live in the global South.

We conclude this section with a few words about the Azusa Street Revival of 1906. That year marks the beginnings of what is known as the global Pentecostal movement. It began in Los Angeles, California, with an African-American man named William Seymour (1870-1922), a partially blind son of slave parents. The events of 1906 first appeared like an insignificant blip on the Christian radar. Seymour had learned about speaking in tongues and other gifts of the Holy Spirit when he was a student at a Bible school in Houston, Texas. He was invited to pastor a church in Los Angeles and taught his congregation about the charismatic nature of the Holy Spirit. The word "charisma" comes from a Greek word meaning "grace" or "favors" bestowed on someone. Seymour believed the spiritual gifts were directly from God.

The now legendary story goes something like this: Many of Seymour's congregants began to speak in tongues, as did he. It attracted all kinds of interest in Los Angeles, particularly among the Christians, and turned into a major revival that lasted years. Even the *Los Angeles Times* made the events front page news. People began coming from all over the world to attend the Azusa Street Revival. Participants reportedly received divine blessings from God: tongue-speaking, healings, prophecy, life-altering miracles, and more. Many committed their lives to Christ during that unique revival. Newcomers to the revival were struck by the conspicuously multiracial makeup of the church services; one journalist remarked that the color line was washed away in the blood of the lamb. Many "Azusa pilgrims" as they were called became convinced that God was doing something completely new.

The revival did not receive the full stamp of orthodoxy from most mainline Christian churches in America. In fact, many Americans considered these new "charismatic" Christians to be fraudulent: sects, cults, heretics. However, over the course of the twentieth century, charismatic/Pentecostal Christians became mainline. Today, the largest church in America is Lakewood Church, pastored by Joel Osteen, a Pentecostal believer. Some claim Pentecostal Christianity to be the fastest growing religious movement in the world today. The movement has spread rapidly into sub-Saharan Africa, Latin America, and all over Asia, propelling a seismic shift in the nature and demographics of Christianity worldwide. Estimates vary, but some believe there may be 500 million charismatic/Pentecostals in the world today, claiming around 20% of the world's Christians.

In retrospect, the Pentecostal movement was part of a larger context. The period between 1517 and 1906 saw the emergence of modern science. Many distinguished scientists such as Sir Francis Bacon, Isaac Newton, Copernicus, and Galileo were decidedly Christian. By the late 1800s, however, some argued that a person had to choose science or religion. Charles Darwin's *Origin of Species*, published in 1859, had something to do with that, although Darwin was by no means an outspoken critic of religion the likes of Richard Dawkins—the cantankerous atheist professor at Oxford. Darwin, like many around him, was simply fascinated by the discoveries of science. Many Christians were happy to embrace science, yet confidently remain Christian.

There was a distinctly American reaction to science that emerged in the 1800s and early 1900s: Christian fundamentalism. Fundamentalism represents a posture of defiance against interpretations of the Bible that might allow room for myth and allegory. Fundamentalists believe the Bible should be interpreted literally. This movement exists today, although somewhat outside the United States mainstream. Its impacts on other movements such as Evangelicalism and Pentecostalism, however, are unmistakable.

It must be stated that Fundamentalism and Pentecostalism are two very different movements, but united in their questioning of modern conceptions of reason. Fundamentalists have generally committed themselves to literal interpretations of the Bible; Pentecostals were concerned with the gifts of the spirit. Fundamentalists thought the Pentecostals to be "cults" in the early part of the twentieth century. The two groups began to absorb aspects of each other in time, however. The reason we are talking about them in the same context is that in the late 1800s and early 1900s they both represented a resounding "no" to the rationalists who believed reason superior to faith and the demise of religion imminent. During the 1700s there were some thinkers, like the French philosopher Voltaire, who seemed to be intoxicated with reason, worshiping scientific advance almost like a god. We must reiterate that most people were not so extreme; most scientists had no problem being both religious and scientific at the same time. There was a vocal minority, however, concentrated in the southern United States, which believed a person had to make the difficult decision of choosing one or the other.

Recession and Indigenization Age: 1906–Present

During the twentieth century there were numerous shifts in the nature of Christianity. The magnitude of these shifts cannot be overstated. Christianity's course of development completely changed during this epoch—and is continuing to change. The face of Christianity today is very different from the mainly European face evident in the early 1900s. The scholarly literature outlining these changes is vast, but the most conspicuous changes are the following: first, secularization in Western Europe; second, the rise and fall of atheism; third, global religious martyrdom; and fourth, independence movements in religion as well as in politics.

Many historians through the ages have referred to the Germanic invasions of Rome in the fifth century as being carried out by "barbarians." Obviously this designation suggests a pejorative term used to discredit the merit of a people who in all actuality must have been quite advanced and sophisticated—at least enough to conquer the once impenetrable, dazzling heart of the Roman Empire. Whether we consider the Gothic peoples to be barbarians or not, one thing is obvious: the twentieth century was more barbaric than the fifth. In fact, much of the blame is to be placed on the once-Christian part of the world: Europe—that twentieth-century graveyard of dead men and women who gave their lives and killed others for a whole variety of causes ranging from Marxist revolution to democracy, from liberation to colonialism. In the twentieth century, Europe and much of the world erupted into all-out war on two occasions. The casualties of war combined with bent ideologies reaches well into the hundreds of millions of lives, especially when figuring in genocides and famines that are often linked to despotic rule.

Christianity may be hailed as a peaceful religion, but the reality is that this claim cannot be maintained if we look at it globally and historically. Christian people-groups have been just as eager to participate in violence of all kinds—including genocide—as virtually anyone else. Alas, the primal instincts that seem to propel humans to eradicate their competitors run deep. Early in the twentieth century, Christian Russia became engaged in a series of conflicts both within and without: a failed war with Japan from 1904 to 1905 and a series of revolutions culminating in Vladimir Lenin's rise to power in the Bolshevik Revolution of 1917. The Christian countries of Rwanda and the Democratic Republic of the Congo were home to two of the twentieth century's last atrocities, capping off a terribly violent century.

Most Western Europeans seem to have reached the conclusion that no religion is good religion. One of the most important developments of twentieth-century Christianity is that Europe has become secular. Christian foreigners who visit Europe today are often shocked at how apathetic Europeans are toward religion. The traditional churches are virtually empty. This Christian heartland for so many centuries has, seemingly, left the building. There is now a substantial scholarly literature devoted to figuring out how and why this happened. Even Britain—the nation that spawned intensely religious America, the nation that supported thousands of missionaries throughout the 1800s, and the nation that birthed the King James Bible and the Puritans—has nearly fallen off the map in terms of active participation in the Christian faith. Most religious Brits today are immigrants.

The secularization of Britain is puzzling to Americans who have so much in common with the British. Recently I had a student in class articulate this with her question, "But what about C.S. Lewis? He was a practicing Christian, wasn't he?" Yes he was, but he died in 1963. Even during his lifetime, however, he was viewed by his colleagues at Oxford as something of an oddball due to his fascination with Christian apologetics. His belief in traditional Christian teaching such as miracles, angels, and demons was considered antiquated, even bizarre by many of those around him. In other words, C.S. Lewis may have been British, but he was decidedly atypical for Brits at the time, particularly in academia. Britain has continued on the path to secularization in the decades since. Thus while C.S. Lewis is something of a Protestant pope in America, in the U.K. he is more like a relic of the past.

Perhaps the most secular place of all is Scandinavia. Historically speaking, this northern European block is an enigma. Scandinavia was at one time a proud bastion of Christianity. However, religiosity has changed drastically in the region. Swedes are fond of reciting the mantra, "We don't believe in God in Sweden, we believe in people." In 2009 there was an ad campaign in Sweden that stated "Gud Finns Nog Inte," or, "God probably does not exist." In 1924, the people of Norway changed the name of their capital from Christiania back to the Old Norse name of Oslo. Denmark is almost thoroughly secularized; the U.S. Department of State clarifies: "Attendance figures —have fallen to record low levels —especially among young persons."[36] What is perhaps most striking is that while Scandinavians have secularized, they seem to be among the happiest people on earth. These countries consistently rank among the best in which to live.

Scandinavia is not alone in its faith recession; virtually all nations in Western Europe have secularized. While they consider Christianity to be their inherited religion, there seems to be little impulse to practice the faith. Most Europeans may attend only for Christmas, Easter, or a baptism. It is a bizarre story that we will investigate later in the book, but suffice it to say here that Western Europe is now unique among the world's cultural blocks: While most cultures in the world seem to be undergoing a religious resurgence—for example global Pentecostalism, the fall of religious restrictions in former Marxist heartlands, and a reinvigorated Islam—Western Europeans seem to be leaving the church behind. Perhaps the name change in Norway is indicative of the whole region.

The symbolic date of Western Europe's embrace of secularization began in 1648—the Treaty of Westphalia—when an exhausted population declared "enough." The Protestant-Catholic wars of religion had the cultural effect of discrediting Christianity, and this sentiment grew over the course of 350 years. In other regions of the world, secularization seems to have been mercilessly superimposed, such as in the Soviet Union and in China. Both Soviet and Chinese governments embraced Karl Marx's (1818-1883) ideas about religion. Marx, a philosopher by training, believed religion to be a sinister ploy by the upper classes to control the lower classes. Like many intellectuals high on science in the nineteenth century, he thought religion to be more harmful than helpful to humans. While not famous during his lifetime, Marx's philosophies later became influential, notably in Russia. Vladimir Lenin, Joseph Stalin, and Nikita Khrushchev all shared Marx's view that society was better off without religion; they worked proactively to eliminate it from the Russian consciousness. Each of them seemed to outdo his predecessor in the desire to eradicate faith from culture. While Lenin began the suppression of a once-vibrant Russian Orthodox Church, Stalin's era saw the most deaths resulting from religious persecution. On public television in 1980, Khrushchev famously vowed to show Russia the last remaining priest. The Russian Orthodox Church was devastated during this time. Before the Bolshevik Revolution of 1917, Russia had about 54,000 churches and over 50,000 priests. After the end of the Soviet Union in 1991, there were around 7,000 churches and 7,000 priests.[37] The church was once the heart of the Russian people; at the end of the Soviet era, it had virtually no presence in society. The Marxist ethos had successfully removed Christian influence. In the early twenty-first century, however, Russia's churches began to make a comeback.

Mao Tse Tung was equally brutal on people of faith, although his attacks on religion had less to do with Christianity than with Buddhism, Taoism, and Confucianism—the three traditional religions of China. Chairman Mao led China for nearly 30 years, from 1949 to 1976. Like the Soviet leaders, Mao was an ardent atheist and believed religion to be insidious. Mao Tse Tung was a murderous man, comfortable with the notion that dissidents must be crushed, that rebels must be executed publicly, and conformity must be brutally enforced. Direct and indirect deaths due to his rule are in the millions. It is difficult to understand why Mao is revered in Chinese culture today, particularly given the fact that the Chinese revere ancestors so much—ancestors who in many cases were no doubt put to death by Mao's regime. One wonders if the culture of fear caused people to capitulate in order to survive his dreadful policies. Given the fact that Mao's rule did have positive dimensions— he provided a common voice for China, drove out Western nations, and worked to introduce modern science into China—the negatives are staggering: the re-education camps, the public executions in virtually every village, devastating famines, his blatantly immoral lifestyle, and the cult-like status he engineered for himself.

Secularization became a worldwide phenomenon in the twentieth century. *Secularism,* a zealous policy of enforced secularization, was imposed in the Soviet Union and China as well as other regions of the world. While religion seems to be resurging in Eastern Europe and China, the legacy of forced atheism is undeniable. Western Europe is different; it actually chose to secularize. It was not a sudden decision, as in the case of despotic USSR and China. In Western Europe, the secular spirit slowly, over the course of centuries, gained the upper hand in the culture's social consciousness.

Atheism's heyday seems to have passed us by. A.N. Wilson, in his book *God's Funeral* wrote, "The closing decades of the nineteenth century were the true era of the 'death of God.'" He then envisions a scene where the atheists of the last few centuries come back to earth, astonished by the continuing persistence of faith: "One of the most extraordinary things about the twentieth century has been the palpable and visible strength of the Christian thing, the

Christian idea."[38] Alister McGrath, in his book *The Twilight of Atheism*, argues that disbelief, rather than belief, is what seems to be waning.[39] While religiosity in Western Europe declines, globally it is a different story. People of all faiths continue to practice and pass on their beliefs to posterity, even in the face of terrifying odds and persistent threats. Martyrs of all faiths have given their lives for their beliefs.

It is easy to point to Christian martyrdom in the early years of Christianity while forgetting there were probably more martyrs in the twentieth century than in all previous nineteen centuries combined. It is perplexing why this fact goes neglected, but the omissions are obvious.[40] Christian martyrs are numerous all across the map of twentieth-century Christianity. Historian Philip Jenkins has been particularly helpful in identifying twentieth-century Christian martyrdom in the global South. He brings to attention the fact that while Westerners tend to think about Christian martyrdom as a thing of the past, in the global South those who die for Christian causes go almost completely unnoticed.

Recently the Armenian genocide has come to light in the mainstream media. Beginning in the late 1800s and lasting well into the twentieth century, the systematic extermination of the Armenians in the last days of the Ottoman Empire is egregious. The year 1915 was one of incalculable horror for the Armenians of Turkey as the Young Turk movement "—killed perhaps half of the Armenian Christians in the region."[41] Rapes, beheadings, tortures, and public humiliations were commonplace. It is estimated that nearly two million Armenians may have died during a generation or two, and the genocidal campaign had largely to do with religion. The truth of the matter is that Armenians were guilty of being Christians at the wrong time. The xenophobic Turks believed that in order to purify their land they must exterminate Christians of all kinds. It went beyond ethnic cleansing. Christians, regardless of ethnicity, were almost completely eradicated during the years of World War I (1914–1918). Nestorian Christians call 1915 "The Year of the Sword" as they claim to have lost two-thirds of their population during that time to Turkish killers. The Turkish massacres of Armenians, Assyrians, and Greek Christians lasted well into the 1920s, and few histories of Christianity emphasize these crimes.

The genocides going on in Turkey were part of a larger trend. The first 25 years of the twentieth century were a horrifying time for Christians all over the Middle East as violent pogroms caused their lamps to flicker and die in many places of this formerly Christian heartland. Philip Jenkins uses precisely this imagery in his detailed analysis of the decline of Christianity in that region:

> Whatever the reasons—across the Middle East, Christian communities vanished one after the other, like lights being switched off. Before 1914, Christian pockets were

numerous and widespread, while by 1930, most had vanished or were in the process of disappearing. Asia Minor now became, definitely, Turkey—a Muslim land, freed of virtually all Greeks and Armenians.[42]

In the year 1900, the Middle East was approximately 10% Christian; today it is less than 3% Christian. Iraq, Turkey, and Palestine represent the most dramatic examples of the precipitous decline: all three of them were home to many Christians in 1900. Today, Turkey and Palestine are less than 1% Christian—and that number is declining annually.

The martyrdoms continue, making these regions precarious for Christians. Partly due to the American invasions and the tendency to associate Christianity with the West, the situation for Iraqi Christians has spun out of control, and most have immigrated to Syria or else given themselves up as martyrs—even at the highest levels in the Church: "In 2008, Islamists murdered Archbishop Paulos Faraj Rahho, head of the Chaldean Church in northern Iraq."[43] Nobody really knows how many Christians are left in Iraq, as the Christians in that country are living in hellish conditions and, daily, families are forced to emigrate. The violence continues unabated. On October 31, 2010, 58 Christians were massacred when gunmen walked into a Catholic church during mass and riddled their begging bodies with bullets.[44]

It is a travesty that so many Middle Eastern Christians must uproot and immigrate to the West. Their motherlands, however, offer little more than fear and discrimination. For example, "Today more Assyrians live in the United States, Canada, Western Europe and Australia than in the Church's homeland of Mesopotamia and Iran."[45] Even the highest ranking clergy amongst Middle Eastern Christians are relocating to the West. His Holiness Mar Dinka IV, Patriarch of the Church of the East, reached this conclusion when he moved to Chicago. It is either emigration or martyrdom in Iraq—where he is supposed to be. The Patriarch would be a sitting duck in Iraq.

The final change I would like to briefly address in our section on recession and indigenization during the period 1906 to the present has to do with independence movements in both religion and politics. The twentieth century was a very turbulent time in world politics. Most conspicuously, the bottom fell out of what we know as colonialism during that century. Britain and France survived as the last great global colonial powers well into the twentieth century. Many other European nations had colonial possessions as well. Colonial powers Russia and Japan ended up fighting over territories in East Asia in the Russo-Japanese War of 1904-1905. Japan held considerable colonial power in Taiwan, Korea, and north and northeast China (Manchuria) until World War Two. During that war, Japan set out on an ambitious plan of expansion into China, Southeast Asia, and the Pacific. Their vast colonial hopes came crashing down on August 6 and 9 of 1945—when the American bombs "Little Boy" and "Fat Man" landed on the cities of Hiroshima and

Nagasaki, killing over 200,000 civilians instantly. While the USA is not usually considered a proper colonial power, it did gain several territories in the late 1800s and early 1900s such as Hawaii, Cuba, Puerto Rico, Guam, the Virgin Islands, the Philippines, and others. America has held on to a few of these regions and lost others, notably incorporating Hawaii as a state.

After World War One, independence movements in nations ruled by colonial powers began to gain momentum. Colonialism began to break down in the mid-twentieth century as global liberation movements emerged. Shortly after the Second World War there was a dizzying array of nations proclaiming their independence, beginning with India. India's independence was achieved by remarkably peaceful protests by Mahatma Gandhi and Jawaharlal Nehru. The British Empire came crashing down after its "jewel in the crown"—India—successfully broke away in 1947. Sri Lanka accomplished the same in 1948. Britain abruptly pulled out of Palestine in 1948, leading to many still unsettled problems in that region. In the 1950s, Britain became involved in a dispute with Egypt over the Suez Canal—a 120 mile canal that connects the Mediterranean to the Red Sea, enabling ships to avoid having to sail around Africa. In the minds of many historians, that dispute represents Britain's decline from global superpower status. Egypt worked itself out of Britain's grip in the 1950s, paving the way for numerous African countries to declare independence shortly thereafter. At the height of its power in 1922, Britain was in charge of a full quarter of the world's surface as well as a full quarter of the earth's human inhabitants. "The sun never set on the British Empire" was a famous slogan. This denomination partly explains why English has become a kind of international *lingua franca*. France's once-vast empire collapsed in the 1950s and 1960s, primarily in Indochina (Cambodia, Laos, and Vietnam), the Middle East (Lebanon and Syria), the South Pacific, and various regions of North and West Africa.

Some mistakenly believed that once the European, Christian nations backed out of Asia and Africa, Christianity would wither away and the traditional religions would resurge. Contrary to what anybody could have predicted, quite the opposite happened. It came as a surprise to many in the West that the autonomous churches became much more successful after the foreigners left. As the missionaries moved back to their home countries, the indigenous churches assimilated Christianity more authentically into the fibers of their culture. "Especially in Africa—the African artistic genius is beginning to find its own idiom for the expression of Christian truth."[46]

There is today a growing sense that Christians—no matter the color or continent—truly represent the global body of Christ. In the words of Stephen Neill, there is truly "a sense of international solidarity" among the world's Christians today.[47] Every Sunday, as Americans break the Eucharist bread, it is difficult not to think of Christians in Asia, Africa, and Latin America performing the same symbolic act. As Africa takes its place as the gravitational center of Christianity, Western Christians will have to overcome mental barriers that have for so long privileged Western interpretations as holding primacy. Instead, today, "The West looks eagerly to the East for new insights into Christian theology."[48] In some ways, the West will have to accommodate new theologies—theologies that will appear foreign to modern European "enlightenment" methods of interpretation. Obviously the term "enlightenment" is a self-aggrandizing congratulation of European preeminence, but matters changed in the second half of the twentieth century. The Christian gospel is not in any way dependent on the so-called European enlightenment. Dislocating this bias will not be easy, but Christians from the global South can surely point the way out of this prejudice.

Church historians sometimes refer to the adoption and assimilation of Christianity by a previously non-Christian culture as "indigenous agency."[49] Once the gospel enters the mind and heart of a person, no longer does the missionary have the ability to contain the transformations that may occur. Indigenous agency has led to a marked increase in world Christianity, both in overall adherence as well as in new forms of expression. The worldwide church has gone from being a Western faith to a primarily Southern faith. More than 60% of all Christians today live outside of the traditional Western world. A theologian might stand back and marvel at the shifting Christian geography in the world today as a part of the unfolding plan of God. So be it. One fact is eminent: the Christian church is more diverse today than ever, and the opportunities for Christian witness are far greater today than they were when Christianity was an almost exclusively Western faith.

Conclusion: Many Times, Various Ways

The title of this chapter, "At Many Times and In Various Ways," comes from a verse in the book of Hebrews that claims God spoke to humans throughout history up to the time of Jesus. Is it possible God continued to speak over the last 2000 years? Christians cannot help but look back upon history as a providential story. Interpreting that history, though, is not easy. Difficult questions inevitably arise. Was Constantine a Christian saint or a shrewd politician? Why did Islam have so much success converting Christians? Did God want the Catholic and Orthodox churches to split? Was God pleased or vexed when Luther led half of Christendom away from Rome? Did God celebrate the arrival of the Europeans to Latin America, or was God grieved by the violent disruption that ensued? Why did God allow Marxist ideology to wreak so much havoc in the world? It is almost natural to move from the historical to the theological. If God exists, and if Christ was sent by God, then it seems obligatory that we try to make theological sense of the historical data.

Perhaps we should stand back and ask a fundamental question: Why do history at all? Why select all of these dates and names and line them up in chronological order? What's the point? What is a historian's motive for doing this?

The answer to that question is complex and personal. Historians are not normally in the business of psychoanalyzing themselves. However, more thoughtful historians will at least pay attention to the more critical questions, the "why" questions. Saint Augustine frankly and candidly explained why he participated in the task of history:

> Lord, eternity is yours, so you cannot be ignorant of what I tell you. Your vision of occurrences in time is not temporally conditioned. Why then do I set before you an ordered account of so many things? It is certainly not through me that you know them. But I am stirring up love for you in myself and in those who read this, so that we may all say, "Great is the Lord and highly worthy to be praised" (Ps. 47:1). I have already affirmed this and will say it again: I tell my story for love of your love.[50]

I tell my story for love of your love.

When I was 19 years old, I began my studies in church history. I knew little about my faith background, other than basic, catechetical knowledge. However, as I read Augustine, as I ploughed through Latourette, as I meditated upon Thomas a Kempis, I began to realize I was reading about myself. Augustine's struggles were my struggles. I was surrounded by a cloud of witnesses that went back to the fourth century, indeed, back to the Old Testament patriarchs. Scales fell from my eyes; this was my genealogy.

Can non-Christians take on church history? Of course they can. A big part of history is reconstructing facts, like an investigator trying to piece together the truth of what happened. Eventually, though, one questions "Why?" Why do it? What is the point?

In the chronological approach to church history, we tell a story. Inevitably, however, we have to ask why. Saint Augustine's motive was to bring praise to God. Perhaps other historians have completely different motives. Perhaps not. What is crucial is that we realize we have inherited a story. Moreover, it has been passed down to us. It is our duty to handle it responsibly and carefully. Whatever our motives for doing church history, it is critical that we examine ourselves while we are doing it.

In the next chapter we look at the denominational history of Christianity. Every Christian on the planet is from one denomination or other, whether she or he realizes it or not. Historically, there is no such thing as a "nondenominational" Christian. In chapter two, we look at the three denominational umbrellas that comprise the history of Christianity: Orthodox, Catholic, and Protestant. If you are a Christian, you will fit into (at least) one.

Questions for Analysis

1. Augustine's motivation for delineating history was to bring praise to God. What are some other motivations for "doing" church history?

2. How can Christians possibly determine what is truly and authentically "Christian?"

3. Is the Christian religion strengthened or weakened when governments demand that their constituents follow Christ?

4. Is it inevitable that the rest of the world will become secular like Western Europe has?

5. What makes Pentecostalism so attractive to people?

IN MY FATHER'S HOUSE ARE MANY ROOMS
A Denominational Approach to Church History

"Do not let your hearts be troubled. ...In my Father's house are many rooms. ...And if I go and prepare a place for you, I will come back and take you to be with me. ...You know the way to the place where I am going." John 14:1–4

Introduction

Many Protestant Christians cringe at the thought of being a member of a denomination as if the worst thing a person could do were joining an organized, hierarchical institution. Thus, the rise of "non-denominational Christianity" has become a major phenomenon among Americans, especially young Americans, today. Some Christians have tried to abandon the institutionalization of the church altogether by joining groups that meet in homes, school libraries, or even at Starbucks. Some of my Religion students go down to the beach for a laid back church service and surf in the Pacific Ocean after receiving the Eucharist!

Actually, this denominational phobia is a quite recent development in the history of Christianity. It was only in the 1970s that the nondenominational phenomenon really began to mushroom in America. However, ironically, these "non-denominations" eventually institutionalize if they succeed. They inevitably become established, erect a building, come up with core doctrines, carefully design a mission statement, and ultimately develop a structure for leadership. Within a couple of generations, the group that once met on the beach now has a hierarchy, a set of rituals, a sense of its own history, and a certain protocol for "doing church." The days of hanging out and talking about Jesus while lying on the surfboard become a nostalgic memory. Now the group has to worry about things like "Who is going to teach the children's class?" Or,

"When should we launch the next fundraising campaign?" Or, "What must one do to become a member of our church?"

This scenario has parallels in the New Testament. Christianity, originally a freewheeling sectarian Jewish movement, became institutionalized around the end of the first century. They were forced to come up with creeds, authoritative texts, leadership paradigms, rituals, and all sorts of "denominational" parameters. This cycle continues in the Protestant churches, since new Protestant denominations spring up every year. The Orthodox and Roman Catholic Christians, however, have a long denominational history. One visit to an Orthodox Church and it will become evident how ancient their practices are. I always send my church history students to Orthodox Church services, and they generally have one word to describe what they just witnessed: ancient! Some of them wonder how Eastern Orthodoxy will maintain its relevance in a fast moving, globalizing society like the United States. What my students do not generally realize is that the Orthodox Christians thrive on patterning themselves after the ancient ways. They take pride in the fact that their churches are in continuity with the oldest churches of Christendom—Jerusalem, Damascus, Armenia, and Greece. While Protestants are constantly fearful that their churches might begin to look stale and ossified, the Orthodox churches glory in this ancient ethos with all of its incense, icons, candles, shadows, and esotericism.

The Catholic Church is different from either of the preceding examples. The Roman Catholic Church, like the Orthodox Church, goes way back to the early years of Christianity. However, what makes the Catholic Church so unique is its extremely successful approach to assimilating itself to new cultures. Imagine the size of the Catholic Church. It could easily be considered one of the largest coherent institutions in the history of humankind! Christianity is the largest religion in the world, and the Roman Catholic Church accounts for half of all Christians. The current pope is head of 1.1 billion Roman Catholics worldwide. In other words, about one out of every seven people on the planet is under the authority of the Roman papacy.

The Catholic Church, with all of its rich history and tradition, made major renovations in recent history. In 1962, the Second Vatican Council was convened. Sweeping reforms were introduced. Many people are still disenchanted by what happened. Others, however, warmly welcomed the *aggiornamento*—the radical "updating" of this ancient denomination. It was almost as if this ancient church with an old Latin liturgy and mysterious customs zoomed ahead to catch up to the twentieth century, all during the span of three years, from 1962 to 1965. The changes were enormous, and we will address them in this chapter. For now, suffice it to say that since then, the Roman Church has tried to balance its ancient apostolicity with a modern concern for relevance. They seem to be managing rather well.

The Denominational Approach

The denominational approach is one way to do church history. There are ample books out there on the history of the Greek Orthodox Church, for example. Scores of books come out each year on the Roman Catholic Church. Protestant histories are common. With a brief online browsing session one can find Methodist histories, Presbyterian histories, Anglican histories, Lutheran histories, and on and on.

How does one "do" denominational history? In the most common scenario, a member of that particular community will write the history. In other words, if you are a Lutheran, you will have far greater insight into the Lutheran church than will a member of some other denomination. You will have grown up in the church. You will understand many of the rituals. You will be an "insider" to the history of your movement.

The denominational approach could be called "clan history." It is similar to family genealogy. You understand many of the connections. Evidently, this inside perspective provides advantages. You will know people who can help you answer many of the questions that arise as you organize a coherent narrative. Perhaps most importantly, you have a personal investment into your own denomination's history.

There is a downfall to doing denominational "clan history" however. Generally these histories are written to extol the virtue or glory of one's church. If, for instance, you are a member of the Methodist Church, you will likely have a sympathetic view of your denomination; otherwise you might withdraw your membership. This dynamic is the danger of denominational history. One struggles to remain dispassionate. Personally, I want my church to thrive. I do not want to see it decline or gain a bad reputation. I want to preserve it. I want to see it be a positive force in society. I want people to think good things about my particular group.

Scholars who write denominational histories of their own particular group have to deal with these dual tendencies: first, they obviously know much more about their own denomination than an outsider would, but, second, they struggle to tell both sides of the story. They prefer taking the more positive route when reflecting on their own faith heritage. There are exceptions to this, however. For example, the famous German Catholic theologian Hans Küng has been an outspoken critic of his church for several decades. However, he is widely revered as an able historian. Similarly, the Mormon historian Fawn Brodie published a history of Joseph Smith—the founder of the Mormon Church—in 1945. It presented Smith as an egotistical womanizer. Unsurprisingly, her church excommunicated her. The possibility of unwanted consequences is the danger of researching and writing about one's own denominational history—you can ruffle feathers if you are not careful. Furthermore, if your own people reject what you have written, you can end up with severely damaged relationships.

Allow me to put my cards on the table and reveal that my denominational history is in the Restoration tradition, also known as the Stone-Campbell Movement, located within the larger Protestant umbrella. Sometimes I do write about my own tradition. However, most of the time, I write about denominations outside of my personal background. And trained church historians are obligated to fulfill both of these tasks: first of all, they should cast light on their own particular faith heritage; and second, they must understand the broader context of church history, acknowledging the infinite antecedents that are relevant to understanding Christianity today.

As argued in Chapter One, history is not identical with the past. The past is what actually happened. However, we were not there. So we rely on highly skilled scholars trained in the various historical methods to help us understand the past. Indeed their texts are what we call "history": the art of reconstructing the past. Obviously it is not possible to accomplish this goal perfectly. Every church historian comes from a particular perspective, denominational background, and unique place in the world. You might come from Gary, Indiana. I come from Portales, New Mexico. However, when a young scholar begins to learn how to research history and how to reconstruct the past, hopefully, the unique biases that one brings to the table will diminish, and the historian will do his or her best to be impartial. Credibility is everything when it comes to telling and retelling history. When a person distorts the facts of history, credibility is lost.

As we embark on this denominational approach to church history, I invite you to explore your own faith heritage. Perhaps your eyes will be opened to the connections existing between your particular background and the larger history of Christianity.

Brief Overview

Christianity can be classified into three general categories: Orthodox, Roman Catholic, and Protestant/Independent. About a tenth of the Christian world is Orthodox, making it the smallest of the three. Around half of the Christian world is Roman Catholic, making it the largest. The Protestant and Independent churches added together amount to some 40% of the world's Christians.[1] In other words, among the estimated 2.2 billion Christians in the world, 300 million of them are Orthodox, over a billion are Roman Catholic, and the remainder—around 800 million—are Protestant/Independent Christians.

Orthodox Christianity is generally considered to be oldest of the three because it is rooted in Jerusalem and often still uses the ancient liturgical languages such as Greek (the lingua franca of the Mediterranean region during the life of Jesus) and Aramaic (the primary language of Jesus). Roman Catholic Christianity was originally a part of Orthodox Christianity, and came to represent the Western, Latin-speaking part of the Roman Empire—what we generally today regard as Western Europe. The Roman Catholic Church is by far the largest single Christian denomination in the world today. In the sixteenth century, the Roman Catholic Church had a split triggered by the Reformation that began with Martin Luther's ideas of reform. This separation resulted in a major break within the Western church. Many Christians, especially in northwestern Europe, found Luther's ideas appealing. They began to break away from their associations with the pope in Rome and thus were the beginnings of this infinitely complex form of Christianity known as Protestantism.

Orthodox Christianity

Orthodox Christianity has its origins in Jerusalem, as recounted in the New Testament. It was quickly identified with five major seats of power, known as the Pentarchy: Jerusalem (Israel), Antioch (Turkey), Rome (Italy), Alexandria (Egypt), and, later, Constantinople (Turkey) which in the year 330 was designated by Emperor Constantine as "New Rome." Historically, the Orthodox Churches were prominent in the Middle East, North Africa, India, and Eastern Europe, although there are many Orthodox communities scattered all over the world. Globally, there are approximately 300 million Orthodox Christians, generally organized within a political jurisdiction. For example, there is a Russian Orthodox Church, an Ethiopian Orthodox Church, a Romanian Orthodox Church, and so on. Many Orthodox communities exist in Western Europe and North America because of immigration.

When Western Christians attend Orthodox churches, they often comment on how traditional everything seems. Orthodox Christians pride themselves on maintaining the ancient ways. It is somewhat difficult for Western Christians to understand this phenomenon. Western Christians have had to compete with each other for members, and thus focus on how to bring others into the Christian faith. As a result, Western churches work very hard at becoming more and more relevant to the people around them. Western churches, both Protestant and Catholic, have for a large part of their histories functioned by the rationale that if they were able to entice people to their worship services, then the people who attended might connect with the priest, with a particular member, or with the nature of the worship service. Protestant churches in particular are famous for assimilating to the culture around them. Thus, if the culture is one that seems to appreciate rock music, Protestant

Christianity might introduce rock music into the worship services. If the culture around it seems to want to challenge the patriarchal structures that exist, Protestant churches will introduce female priests and pastors, as they have done. Catholics are also prone to this tendency, especially since the Second Vatican Council in the 1960s, although not nearly as much as Protestants. The Orthodox Christians, however, have functioned in non-Christian, often hostile, lands for so long that Orthodoxy did not always consider how to attract new believers. Orthodox Christianity for hundreds of years has been passed on primarily through birth rates. For example, in Islamic governments, Orthodox Christians were unable to evangelize Muslims because of the prohibitions of Sharia Law. Orthodox Christian worship services, therefore, often seem stale, outdated, focused more upon preserving ancient customs than embracing new traditions. They generally do not view the people around them as "potential converts." Orthodox Christians may respond to religious questions in surprising ways. If you ask a person in Greece what religion they are, the answer seems obvious: "I'm Greek, of course. We all are." There is often very little distinction between the nationality or the particular ethnicity of a people and their Orthodox faith.

Orthodox Christianity prevails in several countries of the world. As with our Greek example, some countries are overwhelmingly Orthodox. Greece, Russia, Serbia, Georgia, Romania, and Armenia are strongly Orthodox countries. There are also several other countries that may not be entirely Christian, but amongst their Christian populations, the vast majority of them will affiliate with their national Orthodox Church such as with Macedonia, Cyprus, and Ethiopia. This is one reason why Orthodox Christians are very uncomfortable with the notion of Christian missionaries coming to their lands. Immediately after the Cold War ended, Catholic and Protestant missionaries began to flood the Orthodox countries in hopes that they could convert them to their respective forms of Christianity. This phenomenon was particularly conspicuous in Russia because of its large population. Communist governments generally suppressed religion, and many people gave up on faith for fear of persecution. However, when the Iron Curtain fell in 1991, new freedoms made inroads throughout Russia and the former Soviet Union satellite states. These new freedoms not only allowed for religious practice among the people, but they also opened up the borders of these nations to foreigners. Many missionaries, both Protestant and Catholic, saw a wonderful opportunity before them. There were huge problems with this approach, however, in the eyes of that small remnant of Orthodox believers who remained faithful through Soviet oppression. In the eyes of the Orthodox, the act of missionizing what they believed to be their people was offensive on three levels. To begin, they believed themselves already to be Christians; second, they thought that the project of evangelizing atheists and secular people was solely the duty of the national church of that country; third, they were highly opposed to a fractured Christianity. As to this third point, Western Christians are quite comfortable with fractured Christianity. It is very common for Catholics and Protestants of all types to live comfortably as neighbors. Most American towns, even if there are only one thousand people within the limits, are very likely to have at least three separate churches—for example a Methodist, a Lutheran, and a Catholic church. Orthodox Christians do not like the brokenness that is so endemic to Western Christianity, particularly Protestant Christianity.

Russia is the heart of the Orthodox family of churches today. Numbers vary significantly in Russia due to the ambiguity of whether one is a practicing Christian or an Orthodox Christian on grounds of being Russian. Nevertheless, the Orthodox community in Russia is around 100 million strong.[2] Ethiopia is the second largest national Orthodox Church with nearly 30 million members. Romania is the third largest national church with nearly 20 million adherents. Greece, Bulgaria, Egypt, and Serbia all have anywhere between 5 to 12 million in their national memberships. Many of the Orthodox churches are located in contexts that were very recently intolerant of religion. Orthodox Christianity in Eastern Europe has only recently emerged from decades of brutality due to the Marxist experiment.

While Orthodox Christianity seems to be enjoying a new era of freedom since the fall of the Iron Curtain in 1991, it must be pointed out that Marxism and Communism took a heavy toll. Soviet restrictions had disastrous consequences in numerous ways. "In 1900, the Orthodox represented 21 percent of the world's Christian population, while the Catholics made up 48 percent....Today, Catholics account for 52 percent of Christians, but the Orthodox just 11 percent."[3] The market share of Orthodoxy is projected to continue its decrease in the twenty-first century.

Another strike against the future fortunes of Orthodox Christians is the very low birthrates in Eastern Europe. Russia, Romania, and Greece all have a 1.4 or less birthrate—in other words, couples in these countries do not have enough children to replace themselves after they die. For a population to remain steady, that number needs to be 2.1. By the year 2100, Orthodoxy may comprise only a tiny sliver in the global Christian pie. Ethiopia is one of the bright spots on this otherwise bleak picture—it has over 80 million people and more than half of them are Christian. Furthermore, the majority of the Christians in Ethiopia are from the Orthodox Church. Considering Ethiopian women generally have six or seven children during their lives, the future of Orthodoxy in that country seems secure.

Overall, Orthodox Christianity may not have a bright future numerically, but its followers are among the most committed. How else could this ancient form of Christianity have survived generations of Islamic jihad, excommunications from other Christians, and merciless oppression by atheistic zealots through the years? As mentioned in the first chapter, Christianity in the Middle East, in Central Asia, and in Eastern Europe has severely declined. Of the three major streams of Christianity, Orthodox Christians have been by far the most persecuted. Lenin, Stalin, and Khrushchev did their best to eradicate religion from Eastern Europe. While we may say they ultimately failed, the fact is they were highly successful in executing faithful Christians and pummeling the institution of the Orthodox Church over the course of several decades. Millions of Christian leaders and faithful devotees were either killed or imprisoned during Communist rule.

Why has Orthodox Christianity remained so changeless to the point of intransigence? There are several theories. To begin, because of the oppressive climate, there were few opportunities for innovations that otherwise may have developed. Second, Orthodox Christians revere the ancient church fathers in a way largely unknown in the West. Even today Orthodox Christians hold steadfastly to the sermons and teachings that came out of the earliest centuries of the church in their liturgies, theological curricula, and monastic cultures. A third possibility is that Orthodoxy has for much of its history existed in volatile contexts and the familiar liturgy of the ancient tradition provided stability in the midst of political turmoil through the generations.

One of the most notable aspects of Orthodoxy is that it has lost very little of its ancient character. Even the calendar of the Orthodox Christians is ancient; many of them still use the old Julian calendar (introduced by Julius Caesar in 46 BC), or else a revised Julian calendar. Whereas the Western world started using the Gregorian calendar in the sixteenth century, the Orthodox lands preferred the ancient method of tracking time. Orthodox Christians are reluctant to change, and their resistance to cultural vagaries is perhaps one of the great attractions to it: in a world of change, the Orthodox Church continues down old paths. Some Protestant Christians in recent years have been attracted to precisely this aspect of the Orthodox Church. Jaroslav Pelikan (1923-2006), the eminent professor of church history at Yale, and Peter Gillquist (born 1938), a former leader in the evangelical Campus Crusade for Christ organization, both converted to Orthodoxy from Lutheran backgrounds. They became convinced that Orthodox Christianity had best preserved the ancient teachings of Christianity. In both cases their conversions were a great surprise since both of them seemed so firmly entrenched in their Protestant institutions.

The Orthodox Churches are structured according to the teaching of Episcopal succession—the form of Christian governance wherein the leaders are ordained by a bishop. There are over 20 autocephalous (self-governing) churches within Orthodoxy, and most of them are organized along national lines. They are united in doctrine, but they vary somewhat in their organizational structures. Each of them has a different primate (highest ranking clergy in a region) rather than one supreme pope as in the case of the Roman Catholic Church. Four of the five patriarchates from early Christianity are Orthodox today. However, the Moscow patriarchate is of particular importance because of its large membership and influence. Orthodox Christians give special honor to the "Ecumenical Patriarch"—the archbishopric of Constantinople—because of its location in the former capital of the Byzantine Empire.[4] However, it would be wrong to think that the patriarch of Constantinople can interfere in other autocephalous churches, as interference is not permitted. He is acknowledged as the "first among equals"; the key to understanding Orthodox polity, though, is to understand that the primates of each national church are all considered equal. This equality in rank among the primates cuts to the heart of the fundamental disagreement between Orthodox Christians and Roman Catholics.

Orthodox Bishop Kallistos (Timothy) Ware writes that the patriarch of Constantinople's leadership is similar to the Anglican Archbishop of Canterbury—he is looked to for guidance and he is considered the head of a communion or family of churches, but there is tremendous freedom in the way each of the national churches function. The Anglican Communion makes its major confessional decisions in a "conciliar" way at the Lambeth Conference every decade or so. Similarly, the Orthodox Churches are "conciliar"—they believe the authority of God comes through the decision-making process of a collective group of leaders. Ware calls it a "highly flexible" system. This approach is different from the Roman Catholic model of authority, a concept that revolves around the issue of infallibility.[5]

It is important to point out that the Orthodox Churches do not consider themselves a branch or a wing of Christianity. They consider themselves to be the authoritative church on earth today. They believe they are a continuation of the church that was established by Christ and his apostles and has continued down to the present day. While they respect the Roman Catholic Church and long for a reunion with them, they ultimately believe the Roman Church has withdrawn from true Orthodoxy—which literally translates to mean "correct belief and worship." Interestingly, Orthodox Christians believe the Protestants are misguided, not primarily because they splintered off from the Roman Church, but because their origins are in a church living in schism. Orthodox Christians agree that the Roman Church is rooted in the apostles, yet they believe it to be a church living in rebellion. The Orthodox Churches are highly involved in the ecumenical movement to repair Christian divisions, but make no mistake—they believe themselves to be the most authentic form of Christianity.

Orthodox Christians consider themselves the "church of the seven councils." The seven councils were a series of high-level church gatherings that took place between the years 325 and 787 in the Byzantine Empire; the host cities of all seven councils are today in modern-day Turkey:

- Nicea I (325)
- Constantinople I (381)
- Ephesus (431)
- Chalcedon (451)
- Constantinople II (553)
- Constantinople III (680)
- Nicea II (787)

These councils are what largely formulated Christian doctrine in the first seven centuries of the faith. We must keep in mind that the Latin-speaking West and the Greek East did not officially split until 1054, thus the church of the Roman Empire was united in doctrine for the entire first millennium.

Other Christian movements were condemned at these councils, notably at two: Ephesus in 431 and Chalcedon in 451. The Council of Ephesus in 431 condemned a bishop of Constantinople by the name of Nestorius. Nestorius refused to recognize the Virgin Mary as being "the mother of God." Here he disagreed with the majority of the church fathers who claimed that Mary was "theotokos," meaning "God-bearer," or, "mother of God." The famous Hail Mary prayer to this day even declares Mary "Mother of God." Both Orthodox and Catholics protect this doctrine. Nestorius refused to agree. He preferred to call Mary the "Mother of Christ" but not the "Mother of God." His descendants in the faith still exist today and are known as "The Church of the East." They were called the Church of the East because they were located mainly east of the borders of the Roman Empire. This group of Christians also goes by the names "Nestorians" or "Assyrians." They disappeared from the radar of Byzantine Christianity due to their location outside Byzantine territory. After this council, Nestorius' followers fled to Persia and made a home for themselves in the Persian Empire. There are around 400,000 Nestorians in the world today, located mainly in Iraq, Iran, and Syria although many of them have fled to the Western world for security. They continue to revere Nestorius as a saint. There have been extensive talks in recent years to mend the differences between the Eastern Orthodox and the Assyrian Church of the East.

The second council in this context is the Council of Chalcedon in 451. This important council accomplished two things in particular: first, it declared the Pentarchy—meaning the five ruling bishops of Rome, Constantinople, Alexandria, Antioch, and Jerusalem—to be the highest authorities in Christendom; and second, it represents one of the most important schisms in church history.[6]

Where did the notion of the Pentarchy come from? Rome, Constantinople, Alexandria, and Antioch were four of the greatest cities of the Roman Empire. Jerusalem's importance came from its being the mother Church—where Jesus Christ's death, burial, and resurrection took place. In 451 the Council of Chalcedon declared the five patriarchates to be the ruling entities of Christendom; however, Rome and Constantinople were considered higher in honor. From early church history, Rome has enjoyed a kind of privileged status, mainly because of its connection to the apostles. Traditionally, the church at Rome was founded by Peter, and both Peter and Paul were martyred there. The Church at Rome was, and is, linked to Peter, the apostle with perhaps the greatest standing in the early centuries of the church. Rome was also viewed as important because it was the seat of the Roman Empire until around 330—when Constantine moved his capital east to Constantinople. Eastern Orthodox Christians see the bishop of Rome as an essential part of the church since Rome is part of the Pentarchy. However, in the minds of the Orthodox, the pope needs to return to the true, original, Orthodox family. Orthodox Christians believe the Roman bishop is necessary for them to begin making decisions together again in the form of ecumenical councils. Orthodox Christians believe the authority of the church comes from the Holy Spirit, and the Holy Spirit communicates with the people not through one man (such as the pope), but through the collectivity of voices in the councils. Therefore, Orthodox Christians believe the last fully ecumenical council occurred in the year 787, for that is the last time Rome was represented, and was still in full communion with them. In the minds of Orthodox leaders, a genuinely ecumenical council can only occur when Rome returns to the Pentarchy—to Orthodox Christianity.

In 1870 at the First Vatican Council, the Roman Church declared the pope to be infallible, meaning his decisions on matters of faith were without error. This decision cemented a long-standing fracture, and has posed a major obstacle for the union of the worldwide church ever since. The Orthodox Churches still believe all five patriarchs to be necessary for a united Christendom. Hopes for reunion remain scant since the doctrine of papal infallibility was dogmatized in 1870. They believe the bishop of Rome made a huge mistake by essentially bypassing the other members of the Pentarchy. The Orthodox Churches to this day consider the bishop of Rome to be in a place of "primacy" but not "supremacy."

Another reason for the significance of the Council of Chalcedon in 451 is that it represents one of the great schisms in Christian history. There was a large group of Christians who disagreed with the Chalcedonian decisions. North Africa and Syria became the heartland for these "Non-Chalcedonian" or "Monophysitic" Christians. They became known as "Monophysites" (meaning "one nature") because they were uncomfortable with the language used at the

Council of Chalcedon. Their particular viewpoint was that Christ had only one nature, and it was divine. The Chalcedonian, or majority position, held that Christ had two natures: one divine and one human, but they were unified. The Chalcedonian Creed claims to understand Christ to be "...begotten in two natures without confusing the two natures...without dividing them into two separate categories."[7] The Monophysites believed it was senseless to say Christ had two natures—he was either human or divine. They believed that while Christ's human side did exist, it was dissolved into his divinity. His essence, his very nature, was therefore fully divine, not partially divine.

Some of the Monophysites lived within the Byzantine Empire, so they did not disappear from the Byzantine records as completely as the Assyrian Church of the East (Nestorians) did. There were repeated efforts to bring these Monophysitic Christians back into the fold. Linguistic differences and politics played roles in the controversy as well, so it cannot be reduced to theology. The Egyptians and Syrian Christians were not primarily Greek in culture and language. Over time, they were joined in their views by Armenia, some South Indian churches, Ethiopia, and Eritrea. Today, these Christians constitute the "Oriental Orthodox Churches." There are around 50 million Oriental Orthodox Christians in the world today. They are in communion with each other, and have been involved in extensive dialogues with the larger Eastern Orthodox Churches in recent decades.

The year 1054 is the date usually used to designate "The Great Schism" as church historians call it. The famous event transpired at the Hagia Sophia in Constantinople (Istanbul) in modern Turkey, arguably the greatest Church in the history of Christendom. A Roman Catholic Cardinal named Humbert and two other papal legates were sent from Rome to try to settle several disputes on the matter of liturgy. The discussions quickly soured and Cardinal Humbert walked up to the sanctuary of that great church, placed a Bull (official letter) of Excommunication on the altar, and then walked out. The Cardinal shook the dust off his feet—a formal gesture of repudiation, and said, "Let God look and judge."[8] In the papal bull he cited the *filioque* as grounds for excommunication of the patriarch of Constantinople. An Orthodox deacon ran after him and begged him to reconsider. Humbert refused. This event marks the official division between Eastern Orthodox and Roman Catholic Christianity.

Many little steps led up to this decisive moment. The problems sprang out of various realms: political, cultural, social, and theological. One serious problem was the issue of language. Linguistically, the East and West were becoming distinct by around the year 500. Byzantines and Westerners had literally stopped speaking each other's language, thus triggering many unnecessary misunderstandings that would have been untypical in a bilingual culture. In the time of Christ, the "Greco-Roman" civilization was diverse and multi-lingual; almost everyone knew Greek, Latin, or both. It was also a united empire: first Greek, then with Roman conquest became "Greco-Roman," a fusion of Greek and Roman culture, language, and ethos. This relative cohesion began to split, however, in the late 200s. Theoretically it was still united; it was ruled, however, by two different emperors, an Eastern one and a Western one. Constantine complicated things when he consolidated control of the empire in the early 300s and based his capital, New Rome, on the Eastern side. He called his new capital "Constantinople." It was probably a sound decision, since the western portion of the empire fell into disarray due to the Germanic invasions that began during the mid-third century. As a result, the locus of power in the Roman Empire moved east. In the 600s, though, Islam began to spread, capturing huge territories, including much of the Mediterranean region such as North Africa, the Middle East, Turkey, and Spain.

The net result of this slow division in the once-united Roman Empire was that the Church became divided along cultural lines: one Latin Catholic and one Eastern Orthodox. While it is tempting to focus on sociological reasons for the split between East and West, it is important to emphasize the theological differences that divided them. Most Roman Catholic and Eastern Orthodox scholars see the theological differences as important as cultural ones. Indeed, at the very core of all of the debates, over the course of centuries, were two theological matters: first, there are claims of authority by the pope at Rome; and, second, a peculiar doctrinal issue characterized by one compound Latin word: *filioque*, which translates, "and the son." How could one little, though highly controversial, word divide entire civilizations?

The Constantinopolitan Creed of 381 has a section within it wherein the Holy Spirit is defined: "...the Holy Spirit, the Lord and life-giver, who proceeds from the Father."[9] The Western Church inserted the *filioque* afterwards, however, making the Creed to read, "...who proceeds from the Father *and the Son*." The addition began in the 500s in Spain; it then spread to France and Germany. It was not really an irreparable issue until Charlemagne's time in the 800s, as his court condemned the Eastern Church for not changing the Creed.[10] The Orthodox Church disagrees with the use of the *filioque* clause because it was never passed by an ecumenical council. The central issue here was one of authority. Charlemagne wanted the Greek East to accept his decisions. Besides, by the time of Charlemagne, the Western Church had grown accustomed to the addition to the Creed. Interestingly, the pope at the time—Leo III, the one who crowned Charlemagne—tried to patch matters up, but ultimately he caved in to political pressures. Thus, the *filioque* was adopted by the Roman Catholic Church without a council, and this is precisely why the Orthodox Christians were offended. Since the time of Charlemagne, this theological divide remains a sticky point in the complicated relationship between Eastern and Western Christianity.

The last of the great seven ecumenical councils was at Nicea in 787. The major decision of that council was to restore the use of icons in the churches and in worship. The Orthodox Church commemorates the triumph of icons each year with the celebration of "Orthodox Sunday." However, clearly, by that time the Catholic-Orthodox divide was developing, and the Second Council of Nicea was the last time that Orthodox and Catholic Christians met *as one church*. After 787, the two churches never came together for another ecumenical council. This fracture remains to the present.

Thus, the *filioque*, the crowning of Charlemagne, and the notion of authority—who can change a creed and by what authority—were the issues that effectively separated the Orthodox from the Roman Catholics. In the year 1054 the Catholic-Orthodox split became official due to the mutual excommunications. In 1204 the split became complete and penetrated into the minds and the hearts of the common folk due to the Latin Crusaders' attack of Constantinople and the establishment of a Latin kingdom in the heart of the Greek East. The great divorce between East and West evolved over the course of centuries.

Authority and the *filioque* were the largest and most conspicuous issues at the heart of the Great Schism in 1054, but there were many other smaller matters that contributed to the divide. For example, the Orthodox Church allowed its priests to marry (though not their bishops) while the Catholic Church was generally opposed to a married clergy. Orthodox Christians were much more rigid in their fasting than were Catholics. They still use regular, leavened bread in the Eucharist, while the Western Church uses unleavened bread. These may seem trivial matters, but they further compounded the depths of the schism.

Orthodoxy today is like stepping back in time. When Westerners attend their churches, they are typically struck by some of the seemingly awkward practices, although most of these practices date back to the early centuries of Christianity. It is just that they have been dropped in the Western traditions. Orthodoxy reveres the ancient creeds and believes they should not be changed. They walk around their church buildings holding icons in the air, following their priest who normally leads the procession. The women often cover their heads inside the church. They burn candles and incense and their priestly vestments have scarcely changed over the course of hundreds of years. The lighting is normally dim, which provides a deep sense of the holy inside the church. The liturgies are ancient and worship is extremely formal, performed almost entirely by the priest and the choir. The priest is aloof during worship, by Western standards. The altar is separated from the worshipers by the icon screen—known to the Orthodox as the "iconostasis."

Perhaps the most common site in an Orthodox church is the presence of numerous icons. Icons are at the very heart of Orthodoxy. Worshipers kiss them, bow to them, burn incense to them; they are treated reverently, as if they were actual people. Icons are created only by faithful Orthodox Christians and are produced in a liturgical setting, accompanied by prayer and often by fasting. Icons cover the interior of Orthodox churches, particularly older churches. Many Orthodox Christians have given their lives through the years to protect icons, particularly during the age of iconoclasm in the 700s when the Byzantine government tried to eradicate all icons from the churches. The period of iconoclasm had a lot to do with the expansion of Islam, as most Muslims were highly offended by icons. Islam prohibits its members from showing reverence to depictions of humans or animals as they believe this to be idolatrous.

Orthodox architecture, often dominated by domes, is yet another indication of the conservative nature of Orthodoxy. This form of architecture dates to early Christian times and was adopted by the Islamic world—which is why Muslims tend to prefer the Byzantine style for mosques. The inside of an Orthodox church is arranged according to ancient practice. One enters the building from the porch and comes to the narthex—a lobby of sorts where it was common for the catechumens (people preparing for conversion to Christianity) and penitents (those making penance for sins committed) to stand and listen to the liturgy. The next room one encounters is the nave, where the worshipers stand during the "Divine Liturgy." (Catholics call their gatherings "the mass," and Protestants generally refer to their gatherings as "worship" or "church service.") Some Orthodox churches in the West allow the people to sit during services, but in traditional Orthodox contexts, it is believed that people should only stand before God, in order to show respect. While standing during an Orthodox liturgy, the iconostasis up front dominates the scene. It is covered with icons and has windows and doors on it that are opened occasionally during the worship service. The altar, where the Eucharist is prepared, is behind the iconostasis, in the room known as the sanctuary. The sanctuary is generally only for clergy or perhaps their assistants who help them prepare the Eucharist for the people.

The Sacraments are known in Greek as "the mysteries." The mystery of the Sacraments is that they are outward and visible signs of inner, spiritual grace. Orthodox Christians have the same seven Sacraments as Catholics:

1. Baptism
2. Chrismation (Confirmation)
3. Eucharist
4. Repentance (Confession)
5. Holy Orders

6. Holy Matrimony
7. Anointing of the Sick

Water, bread, wine, and oil—these are the outward signs of inner grace. Orthodox Christians differ from Roman Catholics in several ways when it comes to the Sacraments, for example, they practice Baptism by threefold immersion; they use leavened bread for the Eucharist, rather than unleavened bread; and they have a face-to-face Confession, rather than from behind a screen. Often, Confession occurs in front of the entire congregation at the front of the church before the Divine Liturgy so that the person can be absolved from sin and can participate in the Eucharist more confidently.

A final word about Orthodox Christians has to do with their views on the authority of scripture. Orthodox Christians believe strongly in the inspiration of scripture—that God has inspired the biblical writings. However, Orthodox Christians do not share the Protestant view of "sola scriptura"—that Christians are free to interpret the Bible on their own. In Orthodoxy, Christians are part of a larger tradition consisting of the church fathers, the liturgies, icons, canon law, the councils, and the presence of the Holy Spirit in the lives of the faithful today. In other words, while Christians are free to read the Bible and meditate upon it, the scriptures are only a part of the faith. Indeed, Orthodox Christians point out the church chose the scriptures. The scriptures did not choose the church. I once heard a very helpful analogy from an Orthodox priest. He said that America existed first, and later the people of America authored a Constitution to guide them. Similarly, he argued, the church was first, and later they developed a text to help steer the church in the right direction. It was the early church that negotiated which texts should comprise the present-day canon. The scriptures did not fall out of the sky; they were written by men and chosen by church leaders. The inspiration of the scriptures came from the Holy Spirit, and the Holy Spirit worked in the lives of men who decided which texts should be faithfully preserved. This is all very different from Protestant Christianity, which argues that Christians are free to interpret the Bible on their own, and that each interpreter has the right to live out the text according to how he or she perceives it. Orthodox Christians believe strongly that while one may interpret the Bible, one must not stray outside of the bounds of the historical traditions of the church that have been preserved for two thousand years.

Roman Catholic Christianity

One is hard-pressed to overstate the significance of the Roman Catholic Church; it is the largest organized religious institution in the world. There are well over a billion Catholics alive today, widely distributed across the nations of the world and organized into more than 2,000 dioceses.[11] There are more than twenty countries in the world that have a Catholic population of over 10 million. About 17% of humanity is Roman Catholic. Almost 70% of the Catholic Church is located in the "global South" where birth rates are higher, so the future of the Roman Church appears very bright.[12]

The word *catholic* comes from a Greek word meaning "complete" or "entire." When speaking of the Roman Catholic Church we are talking about three concepts: first, a church; second, a church that is led by the bishop of Rome; and, third, a church that encompasses Christians from all across the entire globe. The word *catholic* is also an adjective, indicating something very broad and wide-ranging. In the English language, however, the word is used today almost exclusively to refer to Roman-based Christianity.

The Roman Catholic Church is very diverse. The largest Catholic block in the world is in Latin America, home to the two largest Catholic countries: Brazil and Mexico. Brazil and Mexico have a whopping combined total of 270 million Catholics. Latin America is home to 42% of the world's Catholics (approx. 500 million).[13] The second largest Catholic block in the world is in Europe, where around 26% of the world's Catholics live (approx. 300 million). Africa is home to the third largest continental block of Catholics, encompassing around 13% of the global Catholic population (approx. 170 million). The Catholic Church, like many of the Protestant churches, is growing fantastically on the continent of Africa. Asia is home to around 10% of the global Catholic Church (approx. 120 million), due largely to the Philippines which contains the world's third largest national Catholic population. The United States is home to the world's fourth largest Catholic community; North America as a continental block contains around 7% of the world's Catholics (approx. 75 million). Oceania is a sparsely populated region of the world, but the Catholic presence there is strong, comprising about 1% of global Catholicism. There are small Catholic communities scattered throughout the Islamic world.

The most important difference between Catholics and non-Catholics is the issue of authority. The litmus test boils down to the pope. If you are a Catholic, you consider the bishop of Rome the authority in all matters of faith and religion. If you do not hold to this principle, then you are probably not Catholic.

The Roman Catholic Church is headed by the bishop of Rome. The current pope, Benedict XVI, is part of a long tradition dating back to early Christian times. The Roman Catholic Church believes Peter was the first pope. Catholics emphasize the significance of Peter, pointing to their belief that Jesus established his church on earth and essentially put Peter in charge. The Roman Church cites several scriptures in support of this such as Matthew 16:18–19. In that passage Jesus says he will give the "keys of the kingdom of heaven" to Peter, thus officially ordaining Peter to a position of authority. The Roman Church believes this all-important scene recorded in Matthew essentially means that whoever is in the position of the bishop of Rome has jurisdiction over the entire ("catholic") church. This issue is quite controversial since obviously the Protestant and Orthodox churches interpret this passage very differently. Nonetheless, the Roman Catholic Church, to the present day, believes this biblical reference to be paramount. It is the basis by which the Roman bishop claims jurisdiction over all of Christendom.

While the Roman bishop is the supreme head of the church, there are numerous levels of authority. The Catholic hierarchy is massive, and it is all based on the notion of apostolic succession, also known as episcopal succession. Apostolic succession is not unique to the Roman Church: the Orthodox Churches and many Protestants such as the Anglicans share this understanding. Apostolic succession is the idea that the Lord Jesus ordained his apostles for leadership in the church. The apostles ordained leaders as well. And those that the apostles ordained also ordained others during their lives, and on and on through the ages down to the present time. In other words, whoever is an ordained clergyman today is a part of a long chain—a long line of succession that goes all the way back to the Lord Jesus himself, the King of Kings.

The Roman Catholic Church is a colossal organization of over a billion members. Imagine running a company that oversees a population roughly equivalent to three times the population of the United States of America, or, roughly the population of India. The church is served by over 1.5 million full-time workers all across the world.[14] There are many offices in the Roman Catholic Church, although the most significant are the cardinals and the bishops, which are not necessarily distinct. Most of the cardinals are also bishops. Cardinals are quickly recognizable due to their blood-red colored vestments that signify their willingness to die for the faith. They are organized into the College of Cardinals which serves as an advising apparatus to the pope. They are also entrusted with the vital task of electing each new pope. The Roman Curia (court) is the administrative cabinet of the Holy See and advises the pope. The pope used to be a political leader in what we know today as Italy, ruling over the Papal States. Since the late eighteenth century, however, the pope has played only a minimal role as a political leader. While today the pope is the political leader of the State of Vatican City, it is only a small enclave in the city of Rome with less than 1,000 people in it; thus the pope's leadership is almost exclusively that of being spiritual head of the Roman Church.

The universality or, the "catholicity," of the Roman Church is held to be one of the great benefits of membership. Recently, I asked one of my students why she liked being Catholic.[15] She provided some answers that are no doubt shared by a vast number of Roman Catholics:

- She said she loves the fact that wherever she goes in the world, in all probability there will be a Catholic Church there. The mass will be similar to what she has experienced all her life, and the biblical readings will be the same ones read in her home parish. The Roman Church, like most Orthodox and many Protestant churches, follows a set lectionary wherein the Bible is divided up into various readings over the course of three years: A, B, and C.

- She said she appreciates the fact that her priests are not married. She believes being single provides the priest the freedom and time to minister effectively to a body of Christians. She believes that by being single, Catholic priests "give their entire life to God and the church."

- She likes how Catholic churches are, by and large, open to the public. They always expect worshipers or explorers to come by, and thus they leave their doors open much of the time for burning candles, or for prayer and meditation. She enjoys knowing that she can usually attend mass whenever she needs, as many Catholic churches have daily masses.

- She is proud of the lay participation in the Catholic Church. Laypeople are able to participate and lead various ministries.

- She is thankful that the church has a definite figurehead. She believes the pope keeps the church unified. While Orthodox churches are organized nationally and Protestant churches are extremely divided into thousands of groups, she knows that Catholics are all under the authority of one man—a "president" of sorts.

- She likes that the Catholic tradition is interpreted in broad and diverse ways, allowing room for charismatic Catholics as well as extremely conservative ones. Some Catholics prefer the mass according to the old Latin Rite, whereas some have adopted extremely innovative approaches to worship, such as in the Philippines with the *El Shaddai* movement—a Pentecostal group that manages to stay within the fold of Roman Catholicism.

Similar feelings were reflected in a recent posting on one of the most widely read Catholic news Web sites.[16] In a series of articles called "What I Love about the Catholic Church," Father Dwight Longenecker outlines a number of reasons why the Catholic Church is appealing to its members. We can summarize his points by highlighting the four core reasons he is committed to being Catholic:

- Diverse membership: rich or poor, brilliant or dull, French or Indian, the Roman Catholic Church is open to all people.

- Local, yet global: go to one Catholic Church, and you will get a sense of the universality of the institution.
- Theologically diverse: the Roman Church has mystical traditions that look very much like Eastern religions, but there is also a "folksy" dimension to the Church.
- Socially conscious: the Roman Catholic Church has "at every place and in every time been subversive."[17]

Obviously, this unscientific sampling is subjective, but in this case the two subjective perspectives share much in common, illustrating why the Roman Catholic Church appeals to its devotees.

Catholics are part of a long tradition that has been preserved by faithful members throughout the centuries. As discussed in chapter one, the Roman Catholic Church and the Eastern Orthodox family of churches were two sides of the same coin until the major split of 1054. However, the two churches were evolving in different directions from early on in Christian history. By 1054, there were two rather distinct Christian cultures in the Greco-Roman area of influence: a Latin West and a Greek East. The Roman Catholic Church, therefore, reveres many of the same saints as do the Eastern Orthodox prior to the separation.

While Eastern Orthodox Christians tend to emphasize the significance of the ancient holy fathers, Catholics are more likely to revere the entire tradition and summation of all twenty centuries of Christian teaching. Catholics call this legacy the *magisterium*. They believe that the councils, the doctrines, the popes, the scriptures, the canons, the theological writings of the church fathers, and the apostolic succession all combine to comprise an entire corpus of authority that is effectively preserved in the authority of the Bishop of Rome. Catholics are so devoted to their pope—which they call "the Holy Father"—because he represents a concept much greater than himself. He represents a tradition with all of its various components. This vast collection of documents, practices, traditions, and figureheads—the *magisterium*—is precisely what Catholics believe gives their faith tradition its legitimacy and authority.

The greatest theologians in the history of the Roman Catholic Church were Augustine (354-430) and Thomas Aquinas (1225-1274). Augustine is venerated as a saint in both the East and the West since the Orthodox and Catholic churches were still united during his life. Aquinas is revered mainly in the West since he came along after the split of 1054. Both of these theologians wrote in Latin. Thus, they are more closely affiliated with the Western, Roman tradition of Christianity. Augustine wrote a famous autobiography entitled *Confessions* that is one of the more influential books in the history of Western civilization. It is a marvelous example of autobiography, a genre of literature that Augustine indelibly influenced in this candid work. Augustine tells us in that work that he lived a sinful, lascivious life prior to turning to Christ. In sometimes vivid detail he discloses his sexual indiscretions and other failings in light of the Christian standard of truth, which he eventually reasons is correct. Augustine was clearly one of the brilliant intellects in Western civilization, yet his *Confessions* reveal a vulnerable, endearing personality of early-Medieval Christianity. His impact on Latin Christianity is profound. Both Protestants and Catholics rely heavily on the theological foundations he built with his writings. Augustine still receives widespread attention from scholars of Christianity.

During Augustine's life, the Germanic Goths were in the process of conquering Rome, and Augustine struggled to comprehend the meaning of this invasion. The god of the Roman Empire seemed unable to thwart the gods of the invading culture. Augustine argued in his masterful *City of God* that all human institutions would eventually become subject to the Christian God, however. The book was particularly poignant for Augustine's audience in the Western, Latin side of the Roman Empire because as he was writing, the Visigoths sacked Rome (in 410), causing many to question the Christian God.

In some ways the Protestant Reformation was an attempt to recover the theology of Augustine. Luther and Calvin were very familiar with Augustine and considered him the epitome of Christian orthodoxy. Fundamental to Augustine's thinking was the idea that humans cannot save themselves, only God can save them. Augustine was uncomfortable with the notion of "free-will"—the idea that humans can become righteous enough to achieve salvation on their own effort. Augustine took a rather dismal view of human nature, arguing that the only way one can achieve salvation from sin is through God's intervention. Humans are completely unable to save themselves according to Augustine; salvation is entirely the gift of God.

Aquinas is often considered the most important theologian of the Medieval Catholic Church because he shaped Christianity considerably with his "scholastic" methods. Scholasticism was a philosophical movement in the twelfth to fourteenth centuries that tried to reconcile the early church fathers with the Greek philosophies of Aristotle. Aquinas' legacy is that he provided a framework for merging faith and reason—a tradition that remains to the present in the Western church. While Aquinas believed in the importance of non-Christian approaches to human understanding, by no means did he think they were complete. Only God's revelations can offer completeness of knowledge. Human understanding without God's revelation is destined to crumble. Perhaps most importantly according to Aquinas, humans will never be able to understand God apart from revelation. In other words, God must communicate to humans directly in order for humans to have any notion of what is real and true.

For these reasons, Aquinas held the Christian scriptures and the entire Catholic *magisterium* in the highest regard. While some may try to prove God through reason, ultimately they will fail unless they have the Christian scriptures and the interpretations of the Roman Church. The Roman Catholic commitment to Augustine and Aquinas is expressed eloquently in the writings of Joseph Ratzinger, the current Pope Benedict XVI.[18] Pope Benedict is a great admirer of both of these theologians. He has referred to them often in his speeches and writings. While Augustine provides a voice for understanding Christianity in the increasingly secular society of Western Europe, Aquinas provides vast resources for merging faith, or revelation, and reason. Benedict XVI is acutely aware of the declining status of Christianity in his Western European culture, and he has used Augustine and Aquinas as resources that are as relevant today as ever.

We now address the great councils of the Roman Catholic Church. The Roman Church, as pointed out, was in full communion with Orthodox Christianity prior to 1054. However, after that year the Latin Church continued to hold councils. Between the years of 1054 and the Protestant Reformation of 1517, there were ten Roman Catholic councils, dealing with everything from clerical celibacy—passed in the year 1123 at the First Lateran Council—to whether the pope was subject to the decisions of a general council. The Avignon crisis had caused a lingering problem in the Roman Catholic Church: which is more authoritative, the pope or a council? This issue was not fully resolved until the First Vatican Council of 1869-1870 and the promulgation of papal infallibility.

The Roman Catholic Church recognizes 21 councils over a period of 1700 years: from the First Council of Nicea (325) to the Second Vatican Council (1962-1965). It is important to point out that since the Protestant Reformation, there have been only three Roman Catholic councils: the Council of Trent (1545-1563), the First Vatican Council (1869-1870) and the Second Vatican Council. The Council of Trent was invoked in order to deal with the major split happening in the Roman Catholic Church during the sixteenth century. Protestantism is discussed below, but for now it is sufficient to say that the Council of Trent was first and foremost a rejection of the Protestant Reformation. During that council, the Roman Church essentially hardened its position in many areas of doctrine—many of those decisions are still in place today. The Council of Trent rejected Luther's idea of "sola scriptura" or "scripture alone." The Council concluded that scripture and tradition were absolutely necessary, hearkening back to the idea of the *magisterium*. The Council also declared the following:

- Only the clergy can properly interpret the Bible;

- Only the Latin Vulgate—the Latin translation of the Bible—is to be allowed in the churches (Luther had introduced a German Bible);
- There are Seven Sacraments (not only two—Baptism and Eucharist—as Luther held): Baptism, Confirmation, Eucharist, Penance, Holy Anointing, Holy Orders, and Marriage;
- Laity must not take the Eucharist wine;
- Purgatory, relics, and indulgences are important aspects of the faith;
- The "Index of Forbidden Books" was created to prohibit Catholics from reading heretical material such as the widely distributed Protestant writings.

The Council of Trent was thus an attempt by the church to hold fast to the historical faith as it had been passed down. The vast and sweeping reforms proposed by Luther were adamantly rejected, although many of his reforms were adopted into the church hundreds of years later.

The First Vatican Council took place from 1869 to 1870 as a conference to finally establish the pope as the final authority. It was called by Pope Pius IX in order to officially ratify the idea of papal infallibility as dogma—that in regards to matters of faith, the pope speaks without error. The doctrine of papal infallibility passed at the council, and was a disturbing innovation to non-Catholics. Not even all Catholics accepted it; those known as "Old Catholics" are located primarily in Switzerland, Austria, and Germany. They are a small denomination and do not consider themselves to be in communion with the Roman Catholic Church. Their episcopal line of succession and ordination are in accord with the ancient Roman Church; they simply broke away from the majority at that council. Old Catholics, like the Orthodox Churches, emphasize the conciliar approach to authority—that the council is more authoritative than the pope. They also agree with the Orthodox Churches that the only official councils are the first seven. They give the papacy a "primacy of honor" just like the Orthodox do, but they do not believe in the infallibility of the pope. They do not believe in mandatory celibacy either. Most Old Catholics even allow women to be ordained. They are ecumenically inclined and are a member church in the World Council of Churches.

Vatican I, as the First Vatican Council is popularly known, has become linked to the doctrine of papal infallibility. The council declared that when the pope speaks *ex cathedra*, or, "from the chair," his teachings are guided by the Holy Spirit and thus are considered authoritative and free from error. This doctrine has often been mistakenly assumed to mean that the pope is without sin. Rather, the teaching of papal infallibility has nothing to do with the personal morality of the pope. The doctrine itself means that when the pope speaks officially on matters of faith, his teachings are completely reliable and can be trusted as if they were from God. Some historians, for example, Hans

Küng, understand Vatican I and the doctrine of papal infallibility as an unfortunate reaction to what was going on politically in Italy during that time.[19] The Papal States—traditionally a state in Italy ruled by the pope on a spiritual and political level (known as the "temporal power" of the pope)—was captured from the papacy along with the city of Rome in 1870. The Kingdom of Italy easily conquered Rome in that year and annexed it. Vatican City was created decades later in 1929 in order to give the papacy its own political jurisdiction.

The legacy of Vatican I is clear within Christianity today, albeit with mixed reactions to it. Many Catholics are strongly in support of the doctrine of papal infallibility. However, other Christians find it to be a severe impediment to Christian reunion. Vatican I, like the Council of Trent three hundred years earlier, represented a defiance that offended other Christians during its time. The relationship between Catholics and non-Catholics remained cold throughout the better part of the twentieth century. That all began to change, however, in the 1960s with perhaps the most important council in the history of the Roman Catholic Church: Vatican II.

Vatican II, or, the Second Vatican Council, was very different from all of its predecessors. It was called by Pope John XXIII and lasted from 1962 to 1965. John XXIII's legacy is huge, as he has been called "The most significant pope of the twentieth century."[20] This pope was no Pius IX, who was often seen as a traditionalist, reactionary pope. On the contrary, John XXIII called for aggiornamento—a sweeping renovation of the Roman Catholic Church. His vision was that the church needed to open up the windows of the cathedral to let some fresh air blow in. He was an older, peaceful man, and set his sights on bringing the church out of its medieval past and into the ecumenical mainline of Christianity.

"Good Pope John" XXIII, as he was often called, reigned from 1958 to 1963. He is chiefly known for calling the Second Vatican Council and thus spawning a new era in Roman Catholic history. His call for a Second Vatican Council was completely unforeseen in the church, as many had considered him to be a "caretaker pope" since he was already in his late 70s when he took over the office. His call for aggiornamento (literally "bringing up to date," or "renewal") was taken seriously by the bishops at Vatican II. Many were grateful for his vision of renewal, while many traditionalists thought the reforms were far too much, far too soon.

John XXIII represents a major pivot in the Roman Church. Shortly after becoming pope, it was clear things were going to be different in his papacy. Almost immediately upon taking office, he removed the expression "treacherous Jews" from the traditional Catholic prayers on Good Friday. Most notably, he tried to make reparations with Jews with his famous expression to a Jewish delegation from the USA, "I am Joseph, your brother!" He extended an olive branch of peace and goodwill to Christians as well as to other religious adherents; this conciliatory spirit was formally ratified in the Vatican II document *Nostra Aetate*.

John XXIII called the Second Vatican Council in 1959 and after extensive preparation it opened in 1962. He died in 1963, but it continued for two more years under a new pope. Without the unique personage of John XXIII, Vatican II would not have happened. The results of the council represent a major turn from what had existed in the Roman Church immediately preceding it. Here are some of the major changes that occurred[21]:

- Recognition of other Christians as true Christians;
- Desire to have good relations with non-Christians;
- An emphasis on reformation in the Roman Church;
- An encouragement for the laity to focus on the Bible—something that was generally untypical in the Roman Church up to that point;
- Vernacular (common, local) language would replace Latin in the liturgy;
- The priest would face the congregation during the liturgy;
- Admission of laity to the study of theology;
- Recognition of human rights and freedom of religion;
- Recognition of historic Catholic anti-Semitism;
- Recognition that salvation is not limited to Roman Catholics;
- An emphasis on the collegiality of all bishops; and
- The office of the deacon was brought back for men and the law of celibacy for deacons was abolished.

Hans Küng, a theologian and priest who attended the council, argues however that there were some down-sides to the Vatican II, preventing it from the successes it could have achieved:

- John XXIII died fairly early on during the council, preventing the full measure of reform that could have happened. He was succeeded by Paul VI who reigned from 1963 to 1978. While Paul VI was relatively open, he was not as progressive as John XXIII;
- Cardinals from the Roman Curia supervised many aspects of the various sessions, impeding progress because of their generally conservative stance;
- Infallibility remained on the books, frustrating many bishops;
- Celibacy was upheld; and
- Contraception was condemned.

Küng argues that by 1967, only two years after Vatican II ended, it was becoming clear that the papacy was showing signs of returning to the old ways of thinking.[22] For example, in the 1968 papal encyclical *Humanae Vitae*, the Church declared artificial birth control as against the teachings of Christianity. Most Roman Catholic members, however, rejected this teaching. Küng writes,

> *Humanae Vitae* was the first instance in the church history of the twentieth century when the vast majority of the people and clergy refused obedience to the pope in an important matter.[23]

Many Catholics, especially in the West, ignore the pope's prohibition of artificial birth control.

Today the Roman Catholic Church conducts a ministry unparalleled in human history, the scale of which is mindboggling. Theologically, the Catholic Church tends to reflect the vision of its popes, and the last two popes—John Paul II and Benedict XVI—are known to be conservative. The current pope has brought back older Roman Catholic practices, for example, a more rigorous fast before the Second Vatican Council[24] Pope Benedict has also urged Catholics to resurrect the Latin mass that fell into disuse after Vatican II.[25] Furthermore, Benedict has revived one of the most controversial teachings in the last millennium of the faith: indulgences—the precise issue that spawned the Protestant Reformation.[26]

Protestant Christianity

Protestant Christianity is a more recent development in the 2000-year history of Christianity. It sprang out of a series of theological controversies in six-teenth-century Germany involving a Roman Catholic monk by the name of Martin Luther (1483–1546). Following a pilgrimage to Rome in 1510, Luther became rather disillusioned with the church and began to think seriously about reform.[27] Luther nailed a list of 95 grievances on the Wittenberg castle church door in 1517. His chief complaint in the theses had to do with the church's teaching on indulgences. Essentially, the church taught that if you paid money, you could reduce a person's time spent in Purgatory. Luther eventually came to the conclusion that it was all an extravagant scam. He came to see the notion of selling indulgences as blasphemous and utterly devoid of truth. Luther's defiance was a real threat to the finances of the church. If he were to succeed in convincing others that the sale of indulgences was illegiti-mate, then he could potentially dam the flow of money that went to Rome from northern Europe. This is indeed what happened.

This was a watershed moment in the history of Christianity. The 95 *Theses* were promptly condemned by the Roman hierarchy. Others, however, found them to be important and timely. The theses proved to be highly motivating to all classes of people, from peasants to princes, and many rallied behind Luther. Luther's followers multiplied, and his isolated "protest" in eastern Germany developed into a vast array of Christianities that permeate the world today. These various and diverse movements are known collectively as "Protestantism," although most Protestant denominations are separate units, independent both on theological and structural grounds.

One is hard-pressed to overstate the significance of the Protestant Reformation in sixteenth-century Europe. Not only did it give birth to a new dimension of Christianity, but it affected the intellectual and political climate of Europe in profound ways. Something extraordinary happened in the aftermath of the Reformation. It suddenly opened up the door to new ways of thinking. People were astounded that Luther had challenged the sacred institution of the church and had actually gotten away with it. Prior to Luther, schismatics were severely punished or even burned at the stake. These teachings continued, to be sure, but Luther's successful break with the larger church signified a changing Europe. Luther's Reformation caused people to think outside of what was considered the norm for the times. The net result was innovation in many spheres of human activity—political, social, intellectual, and technological among many others. This revolution in the Western church was an important link in the chain leading to the so-called European Enlightenment.

One of Luther's central concepts was the notion of Christian freedom, which he wrote about at length, arguing that Christians are not under God's law, but they freely serve God because they have been set free in Christ. This idea was contagious, ultimately opening the way to the notion that people could govern themselves, paving the way for democratic ideals. Protestants and Catholics began to divide, and Protestants began to divide from other Protestants. The situation of the churches inevitably affected the political sphere. The "Holy Roman Empire"—a once sacred institution that was the backbone of European society—was called into question in this context. Indeed the united empire swiftly began to fragment, eventually resulting in the birth of distinct nation-states.

Sweeping changes were introduced in the religious sphere. Luther's protest began to crack apart the united "Roman" Church that governed Western Europeans in all matters of faith. The Roman Church began to be challenged in previously unthinkable ways to the point that it largely ceased to exist in many locations such as England, Scandinavia, and several other parts of Northern Europe. If it did exist in those contexts, it was only as a small minority, even a persecuted minority.

Various forms of Protestantism began to emerge shortly after Luther. It is almost as if there had been a dam, and Luther punched a hole in it. Eventually, other holes were punched, and the once impenetrable institution of the Roman Catholic Church was increasingly being seen as vulnerable. Ulrich Zwingli, who was actually protesting against the church on different issues at the same time as Luther, initiated a series of reforms in the city of Zurich, Switzerland. John Calvin presided over the city of Geneva and it became a well-known Protestant city. He produced copious amounts of writings devoted to reform. John Knox was another reformer during this time that was heavily influenced by John Calvin; he took the new Protestant teaching to Scotland. Philip Melanchthon, a colleague to Luther in Wittenberg, systematized Luther's writings and built a coherent framework for what would become Lutheran theology.

Political leaders got involved in the protests as well. The word *Protestant* actually derives from a group of princes in Germany who sided with Luther and protested against the church's banning of Luther's writings. This alliance of princes eventually became known as the Schmalkaldic League and protested the interference of the church in their lands. We can see the intimations of independent city-states reflected in their decisions. Some historians have argued that their alliance was less about theology and more about economics. They saw the advantages by not having to patronize Rome with constant payments. The argument has also been made that they were offended by Rome's persistent meddling in their affairs. There were highly complex power structures at play. For example, "Some historians feel that the Protestant Reformation was basically a revolt of the Teutonic [Germanic] peoples against a Latin culture."[28] Whatever the case, these protests led the Holy Roman Emperor to declare war against the Protestant alliance in the 1540s. England became involved in all of this contention as well when in the 1530s King Henry VIII opted to put all of the church lands, properties, and clergy under his own authority rather than the pope's. Thus began a series of wars that wracked Europe for over a hundred years. Only in 1648 at the Treaty of Westphalia in Germany did Europe essentially declare a truce based on the notion of *cuius regio, eius religio*. This famous phrase finally brought peace to Europe. When translated, it means "Whose realm, his religion." In other words, if your king is Protestant, then you live in a Protestant land. The Treaty of Westphalia, also known as the Peace of Westphalia, set in place a trend in Western Europe that continues: southern Europeans tend to identify with the Roman Catholic Church and northern Europeans, at least nominally, largely identify themselves as Protestants.

The term Protestant is difficult to define. In this book, we are operating by the assumption that any Christian in the world will fall under one of three categories: Orthodox, Catholic, or Protestant. In other words, if a person is not Orthodox or Catholic, he or she is a Protestant. Protestant denominations are many and various. There are thousands of them. There is no Protestant pope or Protestant patriarch. When speaking of Protestantism, we have in mind a vast number of denominations, networks, and independent groups that do not follow the Orthodox way, nor do they give their allegiance to Rome. Protestantism is terribly complex. There are some Protestant churches that appeal to Catholics; for example, some "high" Anglican churches have retained a Catholic ethos. Other forms of Protestantism take an entirely different approach to the interpretation and exercise of their beliefs. For example, there are independent forms of Protestant Christianity in Africa that are truly indigenous, with hardly any connection to Europe whatsoever. They may have originated with a Western missionary or perhaps with an African who was influenced by Westerners, but they have evolved through the years to the point they have little in common with the historic Protestant denominations of Europe or America. Protestantism is a catch-all term for all of those not affiliated with the traditional Orthodox or Roman Catholic movements. In many ways, Protestants have more in common with Roman Catholics than they do with the Orthodox churches, since Protestantism, historically, shared so much in common with Roman Catholicism: similar culture and heritage, they come from the same offshoot dating back to 1054, a shared historic reliance on Latin rather than on Greek, and a "Western" worldview as opposed to an "Eastern" worldview. Protestantism is best considered an offshoot of Roman Catholic Christianity, while Roman Catholic Christianity can be seen as developing out of the ancient Orthodox churches.

While in many ways Protestantism's spectacular diversity seems overwhelming, there are some core convictions of most Protestants that can be discerned if we stand back and take a broad purview of this massively complex movement in Christianity. What follows now is an outline of some of the qualities that constitute what may be called a Protestant ethos within Christianity.

First and foremost, Protestants generally consider the Bible the sole authority in matters of faith, or, as Luther famously put it, *sola scriptura*, or, "scripture alone." Neither Catholics nor Orthodox Christians share this belief. Both Catholics and Orthodox Christians argue that the scriptures are one source for authority but not the only one. Luther and other Protestants argued that when religious leaders offered teachings different from the Bible, they had to be questioned. Therefore, Luther's principle of *sola scriptura* has been characterized by some as a "dangerous idea."[29] When the scriptures get translated into the language of the masses, the masses begin to take more ownership of their faith. For most of Roman Catholic history, the church relied on the language of Latin for ecclesiastical matters, and very few people could understand that language. It had become essentially a language of the elite, trained clergy. When the scriptures were translated into the vernacular, the people were empowered. In fact, Martin Luther translated the Bible from Latin into German. After Luther completed his task, other scholars translated the Bible into other European languages. Now, the common people could search for themselves what the Bible stated and compare it against what they were hearing from the religious leaders. Immediately there was a climate of investigation and, perhaps, distrust. One of the primary reasons Luther rebelled against the Catholic Church was because he did not find the idea of indulgences in holy writ. Thus, indulgences had to be jettisoned. Similarly, Luther came to question the whole idea of Purgatory since it is not apparent in scripture either. Protestants came to believe that the litmus test of any teaching was whether or not it had confirmation in the written word. If a matter is discussed in the Bible, it must be taken seriously. If issues outside the biblical canon are being preached from the pulpit, they must be questioned. This concept is perhaps the key idea that gave birth to the Protestant Reformation and triggered the thousands of Protestant and Independent Christian groups in existence today.

A second key characteristic in Protestantism is "the priesthood of all believers," which for Protestants means a strong emphasis on the laity. Due to the empowerment of the common person in the principle of *sola scriptura*, the Protestant churches, early on, developed a reliance on lay participation that was uncommon in Orthodoxy and Roman Catholicism. Based largely on the biblical book of First Peter, Luther reasoned that all Christians are priests; the priesthood is not an office reserved to a select few who have particular credentials. This teaching comes with profound implications. The Protestants immediately had to deal with a cacophony of voices, claiming to be authoritative simply because their views could be supported by scripture. The problem with this understanding is obvious: if everyone is a priest, then who is the laity? A nation of priests means there is a conflict of viewpoints since no two people will want to lead in the exact same way. No two people will interpret the Bible identically. As a result, the Protestant movement almost immediately splintered off in hundreds of directions with new denominations being established all along the way.

This Protestant tendency to splinter and proliferate continues apace in Christianity today; new Protestant denominations are born virtually every week. Perhaps the best example of Protestantism's "priesthood of all believers" teaching is illustrated in the African phenomenon known as the AIC—the African Independent Churches. There are thousands of these churches in Africa, and they are radically different from each other. One new denomination will rise up due to some person's prophetic experience, and then a few of his followers will decide to establish their own movement, and so on. There is no end in sight to the proliferation—it just keeps on splintering and morphing into new religious movements. Consequently, theology changes each time a new AIC is born. This dynamic reflects the natural outworking of "the priesthood of all believers"—virtually any interpretation of Christianity is acceptable since every person has equally valid claims to authority. When there is no singular, centralized authority, there ends up being an infinite number of authoritative claims.

For example, one denomination in Zimbabwe known as the *Vapostori* (apostles) was founded in the 1930s by a shoemaker who claimed he died and was resurrected. This shoemaker, Johane Masowe, believed God ordained him as a new John the Baptist. He began a prophetic ministry of preaching, healing, exorcism, and tongue-speaking that has grown large and expands across sub-Saharan Africa. One of their unique beliefs is that they reject the authority of the Bible. They believe that the Bible incorrectly freezes God's ability to work through the vibrant, uncontained power of the Holy Spirit. Thus, they prefer authority from their prophets and relegate the scriptures to marginal status. Inevitably, they continue to proliferate each time a new prophet comes along with a new and authoritative word of prophecy. While this recipe for diversity may appear bizarre or haphazard, this is precisely how Protestantism has always functioned. Martin Luther was simply a new prophet, claiming his interpretation of the Bible and the faith of Christianity was superior to the entire history and structure of the Roman Catholic Church. If we go further still back in time, we will see that the bishop of Rome broke away from the other Orthodox patriarchs because he believed his interpretation of the Christian faith was superior to their interpretations. Luther's "priesthood of all believers" idea has serious implications—it leads to theological relativism. Is this or that prophet authoritative? It depends on the person being asked.

The net result of "the priesthood of all believers" is increased lay participation, like a democratization of the church. After Luther's initial protest, Protestantism almost immediately started incorporating variant church practices like congregational singing (not practiced in Catholicism at that time), increased leadership opportunities for the laity, and higher rates of biblical literacy. When people realized their interpretation of the Bible was more or less valid, and when the authoritative structure of the institutionalized church began to unravel, people began to step up and fill the gap. Within only a few years of Luther's death, a vast number of Protestant movements emerged, each with leaders claiming authority. For example, Luther's movement was not even the only version of Protestantism in his own town of Wittenberg; there was another important Protestant leader named Andreas von Karlstadt who was a colleague of Luther's at the university. Luther and Karlstadt were both convinced Protestants, but they differed in how the Reformation should be carried out. Eventually, Luther won this ideological battle and Karlstadt ended up preaching and teaching in Switzerland. Luther was convinced that his own views of Christianity were superior not only to the papacy's views but also to the other Protestants. Luther became the chief prophet of Protestantism in his realm. Other Protestants, however, became important in other parts of Western Europe such as England, Scotland, Switzerland, Italy, and Holland.

A third key teaching of Protestantism is "justification by faith." One of the most important innovations of the Protestant reformers was their emphasis on a personal understanding of God's plan for the individual. Luther believed it was incumbent upon a person to understand God's revelation through scripture. Luther wanted to cut through all of the institutions and bureaucracies and get to the heart of the matter. More specifically, he believed they could be found in the teachings of Saint Paul. Luther believed not only in *sola scriptura*, but also in *sola fide*, or "faith alone." Massive implications came along with this teaching. Alister McGrath, one of the important scholars of Protestantism today, summarizes these implications well:

> So why did this doctrine play such an important role in the first phase of Protestantism? ...The answer to this question is complex and nuanced and relates particularly to the emergence of the idea of the "individual." ...The doctrine of justification made a powerful appeal to this emerging sense of individual identity. One's relationship to God was a *personal* matter, involving the creator and the creature. ...Luther's doctrine of justification by faith was widely understood to mean that the individual relates directly to God, without having to involve the institution of the church or its priests or rites. The doctrine resonated profoundly with the notion of a privatized, personal faith. ...This individualist understanding of the doctrine of justification became so influential that second-generation Protestants felt the need to restore the balance and remind their followers of the corporate dimensions of faith.[30]

Indeed there were many Christians who felt Luther had not gone far enough in his reform. Many of the lower classes felt betrayed by Luther in 1524 and 1525 when he turned his back on them after they had launched an all-out revolution known today as the Peasants' War. These peasants all over Germany, Austria, and Switzerland started a revolution, believing the current order had to be jettisoned in favor of a completely new conception of Christendom. It backfired. It is estimated that perhaps as many as 100,000 German peasants died in the ensuing battles.[31] Luther strongly condemned the peasants in a famous work with the acerbic title *Against the Robbing and Murdering Hordes of Peasants*. There is no doubt that Luther contributed to this rampant bloodshed. He wrote, "Smite, slay, and stab, secretly or openly, as if among mad dogs, lest the whole of the land be ruined."[32] At one time, Luther had been considered the hero of the peasants, the instigator of a new world order, and the leader toward social justice among the peasants who saw him as a way out of perpetual subservience. After the bloodbath, it was clear to Luther that "...this new approach was dangerous and ultimately uncontrollable."[33] Only then, Luther "...tried to rein in the movement by emphasizing the importance of authorized religious leaders, such as himself."[34]

Sola scriptura, the priesthood of all believers, and justification by faith (*sola fide*) were the three most important ideas spawned by the reformers in sixteenth century Europe. These ideas have been interpreted in a whole host of ways through the years. Perhaps the most important Protestant thinker since Luther was John Wesley (1703–1791). Wesley took all three of these ideas very seriously; however, his focus was on different ideas from Luther. Most importantly, Wesley believed that any true Christian should have a personal crisis point, a "born again experience," or a direct experience of God through the Holy Spirit. True Christians have to make a choice. Should a person remain worldly, or should a person become holy, transforming his or her life through the power of the Holy Spirit? Wesley was not the first Christian to introduce the idea that the Holy Spirit will enter a person when he or she takes on Christ as personal Lord and Savior. However, his emphases were new; they were more about feeling God's presence and experiencing God personally. Wesley went much further than Luther here. Luther argued that a person was saved solely by faith. Wesley agreed, but he argued that a person did not quite know if salvation had come unless he or she had experienced God directly.

Wesley's debt to Luther was obvious; in fact, he accredited Luther with actually causing his born again experience. It was in London that Wesley was listening to someone read Luther's commentary on the book of Romans, in particular the doctrine of justification by faith. Reflecting on that experience, Wesley said that as the teachings of Luther entered his ears, he felt his heart become "strangely warmed." Wesley's impact on Protestant theology is unmistakable. His powerful idea that humans should experience God has become widely adopted in world Christianity today. While the roots of this teaching are in scripture, and interpreted afresh by Luther, it was Wesley who made it integral to the Protestant way of thinking.

Protestants now comprise roughly 40% of the world's Christians. Catholics still have the edge with around 50% of the world's Christians. Catholics planned ahead better, expanding their political and religious empire as early as the 1400s with the colonial expansion to the Americas. Protestants arrived late on the scene; they did not pour their resources into Christian missions until the 1700s. Those centuries proved critical as Catholicism gained huge numbers of converts worldwide, most obviously in Latin America—the heartland of the Roman Church today. It was not until fairly recently that Protestantism began to be a truly global phenomenon. Philip Jenkins points out the changing face of Protestant Christianity:

> In 1800 perhaps 1 percent of all Protestant Christians lived outside Europe and North America. By 1900 that number had risen to 10 percent. ...Today, the figure stands around two-thirds of all Protestants.[35]

Clearly, for Protestants, the big payoff occurred in the twentieth century and continues today.

A still more recent type of Christianity is a development that came out of Protestantism in the twentieth century known as "Pentecostalism." Most scholars do not separate Pentecostalism from the larger understanding of Protestantism, although Pentecostalism does emphasize some aspects that mainline Protestantism generally does not. Like Wesley, Pentecostal Christians place tremendous stock in personal experience. These Christians believe strongly in the ongoing presence and extremely active role of God's Holy Spirit in the life of the Christian. As a result they emphasize miracles in a unique way. Pentecostal Christians believe the miracles witnessed on Pentecost Sunday in the book of Acts are still with us: casting out demons (exorcism), speaking in tongues, and immediate healing through prayer.

While Pentecostal types of Christianity are as old as Christianity itself, the modern Pentecostal movement is usually dated to 1906 in the city of Los Angeles, California, when an amazing revival on Azusa Street occurred. By the end of that century, around 500 million people, or one out of twelve people on the planet, were impacted by the Pentecostal movement. Today, it is estimated that approximately 30% of all Christians could be considered Pentecostal, although that figure is hotly debated. Part of the problem is that Pentecostal forms of Christianity have been adopted by members of all kinds of churches. Many Protestants as well as Catholics exhibit some of the Pentecostal characteristics in their worship services. Scholars often try to make a distinction between "Pentecostal" and "Charismatic," albeit with difficulty. Essentially, a charismatic Christian is one that remains a part of another denomination (Roman Catholic, Baptist, Presbyterian, for example) but incorporates elements of Pentecostal faith into his previous understandings. Many Latin American Catholics today, for example, could be considered charismatic because they worship in a much more lively fashion than traditional Catholics do, and they emphasize the power of the Holy Spirit—particularly in healing—in a way uncommon in the traditional Catholic churches. Nevertheless, they continue to define themselves as Roman Catholics. A true "Pentecostal" Christian, however, is someone who is a member of a group that openly declares itself Pentecostal. For example, in America, the denomination known as the "Church of God in Christ" is the largest Pentecostal denomination in that country. It overtly identifies with the Pentecostal movement that began in Los Angeles in 1906. There is, however, much overlap, and one is hard-pressed to disentangle the two terms charismatic and Pentecostal.

In the last couple of centuries, Protestant Christianity was shaped a great deal by its relationship with the United States of America. Indeed, historically and currently, the USA is a Protestant land. Well over half of Americans are Protestants while only about 25% of Americans are Roman Catholic. North America was settled largely by Protestants from England. Catholic Spain and Portugal settled what we know today as Latin America, and Catholic France settled what we know as Quebec. America has made an indelible impact on Protestantism, and Protestantism has made an indelible impact on America. The United States is the third-largest nation in the world today (after China and India) by population, and the USA has been a global superpower since at least the mid-twentieth century. These factors are important because the USA, like the British Empire before it, had a tremendous impact on world affairs. The USA sent missionaries all over the world during the twentieth century, carrying very American forms of Protestantism with them. America continues to be a beacon for Protestant Christianity today through its colleges and seminaries. Many Christians from all over the world study in American institutions of higher education today, and most of these institutions were indelibly impacted by Protestantism in their histories.[36]

As the most significant economy in the last half of the twentieth century, the USA was also able to export its very Protestant outlook to the rest of the world through commerce. Some social scientists have coined a term—globalization—which in many ways encapsulates the point here. American industry, education, politics, and culture have deeply impacted places as far away as South Korea. Protestantism is enmeshed into the American spirit. Indeed, a famous, pioneering book on this topic was written by sociologist Max Weber in 1904. In *The Protestant Ethic and the Spirit of Capitalism*, Weber argued that Protestantism gave birth to capitalism in Europe. He claimed that Protestant theology fostered a unique work ethic, ultimately giving rise to capitalism and the profound industrial revolutions that occurred in the Western world over the last two centuries. America, a country with unmistakably Protestant roots, epitomizes this capitalistic spirit, and the Protestant ethic continues to permeate and influence world affairs.

It is notoriously difficult to define Protestant Christianity, due to its constant tendency to splinter off, update its theology, morph into new Protestant movements, and plant itself into new contexts. The genius of Protestant Christianity is its greatest challenge—change. Protestant theology is constantly changing, constantly reinventing itself, and constantly reforming—a Latin phrase known as *semper reformanda*. Theologian Paul Tillich (1886-1965) referred to this as the "Protestant Principle." Taking the notion of *sola scriptura*, Protestants are constantly engineering new interpretations of the Bible in order to better understand the nature of God. The problem, however, is obvious. To whom does one turn for authority? It is a stalemate, a gridlock from which Protestant theologians have never been able to fully escape. Some Protestants are grateful for this freedom to innovate, freedom from authoritative power structures, and freedom to constantly reform. Others decry the Protestant Principle, wondering why Protestant Christianity has allowed itself to proliferate into hundreds of thousands of denominations. In many ways, Protestant Christianity is a fractured form of the faith, yet that fracture is precisely the reason it captures the minds of new generations. Protestant Christianity, by its very nature, empowers new leaders by giving them the authority to interpret the Bible and reform the institution of the church.

Protestant Christianity is diffuse. The two largest Protestant denominations in the world today are the Anglican (originated in England) Communion of churches and the Assemblies of God. Both of these denominations have well over 50 million adherents in many different countries. The official title of the leader of the Anglican Communion is the "Archbishop of Canterbury." The Assemblies of God is a world Pentecostal denomination with churches all over the world. Historically it emerged out of the Azusa Street Revival in Los Angeles in 1906. By and large, however, Protestant denominations, like Orthodox denominations, are organized nationally. For example, the Evangelical Church of Germany, the Southern Baptist Convention (USA), the Methodist Church of New Zealand, the Pentecostal Church of Chile, and the Presbyterian Church of Korea are all national denominations with membership in the World Council of Churches. All of these churches vary considerably in their theology, creeds, and doctrines. Virtually any nation in the world that has a significant Christian presence will have many Protestant denominations that are registered with the state.

The question remains: What, then, is Protestantism? Perhaps it would be best to clarify what Protestantism is not. It is not Roman Catholic and it is not Orthodox. For better or for worse, Protestantism is an umbrella term that embraces thousands of different manifestations of the Protestant teachings identified above.

Rampant Protestant proliferation begs the question, "Should Christians unite?" After all, Jesus prayed in the garden shortly before his arrest and execution that "...all of them [his disciples] may be one, Father, just as you are in me and I am in you (John 17:21)." This question is loaded and requires complex answers. However, let it suffice to say that most Protestants do not see a need to unite all of Christianity into one huge mega-church, although some have indeed pined for that in the past. Rather, Protestants are generally concerned with representing Christ in their own areas of the world. Some Catholic and Orthodox Christians criticize this aspect of Protestantism. They say Protestantism seems too eager to divide the body of Christ. Where you have one Protestant, you can generally count on having more in the future due to their tendency to create new movements. So be it. Thus is the nature of

Protestantism. Perhaps a more theological question would be, "Is it wrong for Christians to remain divided?" Unfortunately, we simply do not have a clear answer to that question. It is productive, however, to realize that Christians are, in the words of the apostle Paul, the body of Christ. While there is room for variety in the body, there seems to be a need for Christians to communicate with each other across denominational lines. Whether that results in outright church mergers, or in churches that live in partial communion with each other, will be up to the leaders of those denominations themselves.

Conclusion: Many Rooms

The title of this chapter is "In My Father's House Are Many Rooms." Historically, most Christians interpreted this passage from John 14:2 as a word of comfort from Jesus to his apostles on the night before his crucifixion and death. Here is that passage in its context:

> Do not let your hearts be troubled. Trust in God; trust also in me. In my Father's house are many rooms; if it were not so, I would have told you. I am going there to prepare a place for you. And if I go and prepare a place for you, I will come back and take you to be with me.

This beautiful passage offers bountiful hope to the believing Christian. However, it can also be interpreted in a larger sense: God's house has many rooms, and many different people will go there at the end of days. The question for the ages is "How many rooms?" Or perhaps more precisely, "How many people will be there?" Much ink has been committed to answering such questions. "Who will go to heaven?" "How open is God's house?" "Is there room in God's house for members of all faiths?" Of course this side of heaven there is no complete explanation. It is a matter to be settled outside of human space and time. For now, humans must tenaciously cling to hope.

In a denominational approach to history, we begin to see the beauty of the various church traditions and understand how the past has shaped our denominations today. We learn that all denominations have their roots. In fact, all Christian branches come from the same tree—Judaism. Since the Protestant Reformation, the tree branches have become extensive and tangled. We could say the Christian tree now looks a lot more like a massive sequoia than the sapling that emerged in the first century.

Church historians have their biases. All of them do. Even so, the duty of the trained scholar is to tell the story with integrity. It is important to point out the good and the bad. It is important to know that sometimes "the good" will vary depending on perspective. For example, recent Protestant growth in Latin America is seen as a positive development in the eyes of most

Protestants. Roman Catholics, however, might view this development as regrettable.

Questions for Analysis

1. Why do Westerners know so little about Eastern and Orthodox Christianities?

2. Why do you think the Roman Catholic Church has succeeded to the point of being the world's largest religious institution?

3. Is the Protestant Principle an ingenious innovation or a perpetual failing?

4. What are some of the reasons Christianity remains a divided faith? What would have to happen for unity to occur? How might a Christian work towards unity with other Christians?

5. There is an old joke that says people are going to be quite surprised to see who is in heaven. Who do you think will be there? Jesus said there are "many rooms." I suppose the Christian might ask: How many rooms? What kind of rooms? Are the rooms connected to each other?

CHAPTER THREE

AND THE LORD ADDED TO THEIR NUMBER DAILY

A Sociological Approach to Church History

"Peter replied, 'Repent and be baptized, every one of you, in the name of Jesus Christ for the forgiveness of your sins. And you will receive the gift of the Holy Spirit.' ...Those who accepted his message were baptized, and about three thousand were added to their number that day. ...And the Lord added to their number daily those who were being saved." Acts 2:38, 41, 47

Introduction

I was 19 years old, sitting in my dorm room at Lubbock Christian University when I received a phone call from one of my old high school buddies. He was distraught and needed to talk matters out. He had just experienced one of the most catastrophic events of his life: his father had rejected him. My friend is a Mormon. Young Mormon men are encouraged to go on a two-year mission in a foreign field. It is considered shameful to abort a mission. He had not yet left the country, but he began to have serious doubts during his training. Ultimately he backed out and had to face his devastated parents. A deep rift occurred, but fortunately those wounds have been healed. At the time, however, my friend was deeply shaken.

Mormons are some of the most successful missionaries of all time. They take seriously the command of Jesus to "Go into all the world and preach the gospel to all creation" (Mark 16:15). Probably most Americans have experienced two young men—known as "elders"—ringing the doorbell and offering to discuss the Book of Mormon and the beliefs of The Church of Jesus Christ of Latter-Day Saints (their formal denominational title). Are Mormons Christians? Many scholars of Christianity say yes, in spite of some unique doctrines.[1] Their uniqueness, in some respect, has proven to be a divisive issue in America, notably in the political arena. In 2011 presidential candidate Mitt Romney came under fire from leading evangelicals because of his Mormon faith.

Whether accepted as authentically Christian or not, it cannot be denied that Mormons "go into all the world" witnessing for their faith. Their dogged commitment to a higher cause is admirable. Moreover, they have been rewarded for their tenacity with remarkable success in bringing people into the fold.

One prominent sociologist, Rodney Stark, famously calculated that Mormons have had approximately the same rate of growth as the early Christians did in the first few centuries after Christ.[2] Claiming that the LDS "has sustained the most rapid growth of any new religion in U.S. history," he estimates they will likely reach 265 million members by the year 2080.[3] Stark's research has prompted him to make the fascinating projection that we are on the threshold of an "incredibly rare event: the rise of a new world religion." Mormonism just might become:

> ...the first major faith to appear on earth since the prophet Muhammad rode out of the desert (whereas the Latter-day Saints gained strength initially by riding back into the desert). ...Mormonism will soon achieve a worldwide following comparable to that of Islam, Buddhism, Christianity, Hinduism, and the other dominant world faiths.[4]

How could a bona fide scholar make such claims? Is not religion an inherently biased field of enquiry? Are not religious statistics simply geared to propagate religious teachings? No. Not necessarily. Certainly, statistics can become abused when it comes to religion, but a scholar who has been trained in methodology knows the difference.

We can illustrate by discussing Rodney Stark himself. Recently, one of my colleagues at Pepperdine asked me to join his sociology of religion class because he was planning to conference call this living legend for a class discussion.[5] Stark was gracious and answered many questions from the undergraduates. One of the students asked whether Stark is religious. He danced around the question at first but then said for most of his life he was agnostic. During the last several years, however, he has gravitated towards Christianity. Curious, I went online to investigate further and found an interview with Italian scholar Massimo Introvigne in 2007. In that interview Stark unpacked his personal religious position:

> *Introvigne:* Finally, a personal question. After reading your last book, *Discovering God*, many readers probably ask themselves where exactly does Rodney Stark stand with respect to faith, Christianity, belief.

> *Stark:* I have always been a "cultural" Christian in that I have always been strongly committed to Western Civilization. Through most of my career, however, including when I wrote *The Rise of Christianity*, I was an admirer, but not a believer. I was never an atheist, but I probably could have been best described as an agnostic. As I

continued to write about religion and continued to devote more attention to Christian history, I found one day several years ago that I was a Christian. Consequently, I was willing to accept an appointment at Baylor University, the world's largest Baptist university. They do not require faculty members to be Baptists (many are Catholic) and I am not one. I suppose "independent Christian" is the best description of my current position.[6]

There is a yawning chasm separating the scholar who is trying to figure out facts from the practitioner who is trying to win converts. The scholar has been granted a doctoral degree because he or she has demonstrated an ability to discern the difference between propaganda and factual information. The enthusiast is more focused on improving or expanding a particular ideology. These are two different enterprises. All scholars have beliefs. The lines separating objectivity from hidden or unconscious subjectivity are not always clear. For instance, a political scientist may have a conservative proclivity that comes out in her research repeatedly. Conversely, an atheist psychologist might automatically dismiss the possibility of supernatural phenomena. Admittedly, the social scientist or religious studies scholar will never reach the point of absolute objectivity. However, one person's research can certainly be understood as more objective than another's. Scholarly merit is determined through scholarly consensus and peer review. That is how the sciences operate. It is not a perfect system, but it is the best we have. The scholarly community considers one person's work, and eventually a consensus emerges whether to accept the work as useful or reject it as flawed. It is a great victory to have one's work published in a scholarly journal; it is evidence that the ideas are being taken seriously.

During my PhD program—which took place in a secular department of religious studies—I was different from the other students in that I was also employed as a Christian pastor. Most of the people with whom I studied and worked either kept their religion private or they were irreligious. Unlike a department of Christian theology or a seminary, religious studies programs are not considered the proper path for ordained ministry in the churches. Religious studies is a field that attracts people who enjoy *investigating* philosophy, worldviews, anthropology, gender issues, and socio-cultural trends. However, these people are not necessarily concerned with propagating their own religion, if they had one. It is not that they are hostile to religion (although one does encounter that occasionally). They are simply more interested in religion as a human phenomenon. As a biologist would study cellular growth or a geologist would track plate tectonics, religious studies scholars try not to allow metaphysical questions or assumptions into their research.

The Germans have a word for this discipline: *religionswissenschaft*, which translates as "the science of religion."[7] It is the attempt to study religion objectively, without allowing one's personal faith background to cloud the data. Church historians also work for objectivity, although some are openly confessional—using history to bolster their faith claims. This enterprise is a noble enough enterprise as long as it is clear at the outset what they are up to. It is important for historians to show their cards, so their audience has some idea of what to expect. It would be intellectually dishonest to cast oneself as an objective historian while covertly recruiting the reader towards a particular religious faith. Absolute objectivity is of course unrealistic, but most academics genuinely strive to attain it.

Similarly, sociology is a field where personal religious faith is supposed to remain at bay. It would be inappropriate for sociologists to consciously allow their personal faith to direct their findings. This would compromise the nature of scientific discovery.

The Sociological Approach

The title of this chapter sounds rather mathematical: the Lord "added" to their "number." Sociologists are in the business of counting, thus a natural question here would be "How many were added?" and "What was their number at that moment in time?" These are precisely the questions Rodney Stark asked in his influential studies on the growth of early Christianity.

When attending scholarly conferences, I like to listen to sociology of religion presentations, but occasionally I get overwhelmed by the mathematics. Some sociologists are intensely focused on employing *quantitative* methods in their data gathering. Interpreting the data is where it gets even more complicated, a task generally characterized as *qualitative* analysis. There are longstanding debates in sociology about objectivity, measurement, and theories of knowledge. In general, though, sociological research employs a combination of quantitative and qualitative approaches to the material under investigation.

Sociology is a massive field of inquiry. At its most fundamental level, it is the study of society. There are numerous methodologies that are properly considered sociological. Common to all of them, however, is the attempt to count, measure, and interpret. There is almost always a mathematical component to sociological research because the whole point is to measure something. However, in order to generate quantitative results, sociologists have to be creative in their research. There are innumerable ways to gather data, such as through interviews, comparing one's research with the conclusions of other studies, or developing an entirely new instrument. An instrument can be a scale, scoring system, index, test, or some other form of quantitative measurement. The goal of a sociologist is to be empirical. The problem, however, is that humans are highly complex animals. Thus, sophisticated qualitative methods are critical as well, in order to determine how exactly a particular human phenomenon can be accurately assessed and, ultimately, measured.

Sociological techniques have been borrowed by scholars of religion for some time, but the two disciplines formally converged in the work of three scholars in the late nineteenth and early twentieth centuries: Karl Marx, Emile Durkheim, and Max Weber. Marx (1818–1883) has become famous, or perhaps infamous, for his statement that religion is the opium of the people. As a materialist, Marx had little regard for religious claims, especially supernatural ones. Religion perpetuates the status quo. It keeps people dull and silent when in reality they need to take action in order to achieve greater social equality. For Marx, the capitalist system is inhumane since it funnels wealth towards those who are already rich. Religion stifles social change because it encourages people to accept their circumstances rather than rise up in protest. People thus long for heaven rather than try to achieve social progress in the here and now.

Marx's claims are easily critiqued today. For example, rather than dulling people, religion often incites the masses to take action. Jesus was a revolutionary whose ideas have overhauled civilizations. Rather than quieting the masses, violent protest frequently breaks out in the name of religion. Another glaring problem with Marx's theory is that social progress is often linked to religious ideals. There are many examples to illustrate this phenomenon, such as in the sermons and activism of Martin Luther King, Jr. in the United States civil rights movement. We could discuss the anti-apartheid work of Archbishop Desmond Tutu in South Africa. We could highlight the social activism of Roman Catholic journalist Dorothy Day. Germany's Martin Luther, the leader of the Protestant Reformation, is perhaps the most obvious example of a devout Christian who transformed society through his religious convictions. In spite of all this evidence to the contrary, Marx's theory of religion has proven tenacious. No general theory of religion is complete without a serious consideration of Karl Marx's key ideas.

In 1912 Frenchman Emile Durkheim (1858–1917) authored a classic text in the sociology of religion entitled *Elementary Forms of Religious Life*. Durkheim wrote at a time when scholars were fascinated with the concept of totemism—the idea that pre-modern tribes connected their own clan identities to a totem, usually an animal. He claimed that these societies required great uniformity, and the clan animal helped to unite them under one banner. This animal became highly important to the clan and took on religious significance. Communal relationship with the animal was upheld through various taboos (forbidden acts), rituals, and symbols. These beliefs and practices became the realm of the sacred. Durkheim believed this theory could explain the origin of religion. Humans must conform to their society's beliefs and practices, or else they become ostracized. However, as human societies evolve and become ever more complex, individuals develop more autonomy. This dynamic particularly resonates when humans come into contact with other religious systems. Australian Aborigines, the people Durkheim studied, were isolated and unaware of other belief systems. However, in time, all societies encounter other societies and thus have to modify their views. Parochial belief systems do not hold together for long when confronted with radically new ways of thinking. In Durkheim's view, societies inevitably become more pluralistic and universalistic in order to accommodate the new ideas coming from outside the group.

Max Weber (1864–1920) wrote extensively about religion. He wrote prolifically about the religions of India, Chinese religion, Judaism, and Christianity. Two of his works are considered classics in the field: *Sociology of Religion* (1920), and his tour de force *The Protestant Ethic and the Spirit of Capitalism* (1905). Weber's Protestant ethic idea is one of the most durable and influential theories in the field of church history. It warrants further examination.

Max Weber's writings were deeply affected by economics and social theory. Moreover, in 1904 and 1905 he published a classic study that brilliantly integrated economics, sociology, and religion. It has been more than a century and the book is still cited regularly in the humanities and social sciences, a rare occurrence for a book that old.

The general theory behind *The Protestant Ethic* is not terribly complicated. Weber claims that Protestant Christianity contributed greatly to the rise of capitalism. Protestants were largely responsible for developing and improving upon the nascent capitalism emerging in Europe in the aftermath of the Reformation. Weber reasoned that Protestant Christians tend to be more materialistic than other religious groups. To understand the reasons for this phenomenon, we have to look no further than the two great figureheads of Protestantism: Luther and Calvin.

Martin Luther, the progenitor of Protestantism itself, claimed that all humans are fundamentally equal before God, even peasants who work the land. This interpretation was very different from the Catholic ethos of that time. Luther asserted a doctrine known as the priesthood of all believers. He held that all Christians are priests; therefore, the work of a priest is no better than the work of a farmer. Furthermore, priests are not the only ones who are called to their work; rather, every human being is called to a vocation (from the Latin word *vocare* which means *to call*). Almost singlehandedly, Luther changed the understanding of what it meant to have a vocation. All work is for God. Your work is your calling. By expressing yourself through your work, you are praising God. The connection between human work and the divine realm was no longer limited to the clergy. Now, everyone is a priest, just with different jobs, different callings.

Furthermore, Protestants tend to work very hard because of this calling from God that they experience. No longer do they labor simply to please a landowner; they now work to please God because he calls them to a task. People work harder when they perceive themselves to be working for God rather than for man.

However—and this is key—these Protestants tended not to spend their earnings because of the important Christian virtue of self-denial. Wasting money is irresponsible. Even church leaders must be careful to guard against extravagance. They should be dutiful stewards of the Lord's treasury. Ostentation should be avoided in all things. Besides, God is not met in the icon or sculpture. Since every person is a priest and has direct access to God, why would icons and sculptures even be necessary? This idea explains why Protestants still tend to be uncomfortable with the veneration of images. It also explains why Protestant church buildings are generally much more humble than their sumptuous Catholic and Orthodox counterparts. This simplicity becomes even more noticeable inside the church buildings. Protestants are comfortable with four white walls, some pews, and a pulpit. Catholics and the Orthodox prefer candles, icons, engravings, vestments, décor, sculptures, and ornate altars.

Charity for the poor also took on new meaning in a Protestant worldview. If one's vocation is his opportunity to worship, then beggars are essentially turning their backs on God. Laziness becomes an effrontery to the one who called us to participate as co-creators. Why would one squander the opportunity to work for, and with, God?

This combination proved congenial for budding capitalism. People worked zealously as if working for God, made their money, and then refused to spend extravagantly on themselves, on their churches, or even on charity. Work hard, spend little. It is the perfect formula for acquiring capital.

John Calvin enters the scene here. Weber believed Calvin's understanding of predestination was critical in the rise of capitalism. Essentially, Calvin argued that all humans have been predestined by God for eternal life in either heaven or hell. God alone knows the destiny of all human souls. Calvin received deep assurance in this doctrine because a person cannot "lose" his or her salvation. All of us have been predestined by God.

The natural question is: "What if I think I am saved and then on judgment day I find out I'm not?" Calvin responds, "Rest assured, if you live like a good Christian, then you are obviously saved. If you live like a scoundrel, you are obviously condemned." This all brought deep satisfaction to Calvin, but some of his followers became unsettled! The outcome was that Protestants worked indefatigably to prove to themselves that they were indeed part of the elect. In brief: work hard, spend little, and accumulate loads of capital. It is a perfect recipe for capitalism.

This approach was all very different from Roman Catholicism, where you get saved by following the prescriptions of your priest. The clergy has been divinely appointed, through the law of apostolic succession, to speak authoritatively on matters pertaining to faith and salvation. Thus, in Roman Catholic Christianity, the laity is beholden to the clergy. The clergy essentially has the power of salvation in its hands. Do what the priest says and you'll be fine. After all, according to the teachings of the church, the priest essentially works on behalf of Jesus Christ. While Christ was on earth, he gave the "keys of the kingdom of heaven" to Peter, saying "Whatever you bind on earth will be bound in heaven, and whatever you loose on earth will be loosed in heaven."[8] This idea has been enshrined in Roman Catholic teaching for centuries, and serves to legitimate the clergy. Since Peter was given the keys to heaven, his successors hold the keys as well. Thus, today's pope—the Bishop of Rome (where Peter presumably lived in his later years)—holds the power to save a person's soul. And since every parish priest in the Roman Catholic hierarchy receives his authority from the pope, then he also shares in that divinely appointed task of offering salvation, through Christ, to humankind.

Luther and Calvin said, "no way". You are saved purely by God's divine grace. No one else can do this for you. Thus, for Protestants, it was a relief in one sense because the clergy could no longer deny people salvation. The downside, however, was that salvation is now in your own hands. You have to take extra care to convince yourself—and others—that you are indeed one of the "saved." The only way to ensure your own salvation was to work, and to work hard, in order to show yourself and everyone else that you were truly elected. Thus, people were not simply working to earn money; they were working to validate their salvation! Of course each person was either saved or condemned according to the doctrine of predestination. Even so, each person was obliged to prove he was saved through his life, conduct, and labor. Consequently, the man who works extremely hard, and earns ample income, is undoubtedly saved. Prosperity = evidence of one's salvation.

According to Weber, all of these hard-working, frugal people were the seedbed of modern capitalism. Furthermore, it spawned a radical change in the intellectual landscape of Europe. Jesus taught that excessive money was a problem, a temptation that could kill and destroy. It was the rich who were verbally attacked by Jesus, not the poor. With these changes the Reformation brought about, however, the former vice had become a virtue. Previously, the accumulation of wealth was perceived as threatening one's salvation. Jesus warned against wealth, "Truly I tell you, it is hard for someone who is rich to enter the kingdom of heaven. Again I tell you, it is easier for a camel to go through the eye of a needle."[9] Similarly, the apostle Paul taught "the love of money is a root of all kinds of evil."[10]

Perhaps no one has articulated the Protestant ethic as articulately as the famous American Benjamin Franklin.[11] Thrift, investment, self-denial, hard work, and the wise use of time and money. "Time is money." "A penny saved is a penny earned." "Early to bed and early to rise, makes a man healthy, wealthy, and wise." "Waste nothing." "Lose no time. Be always employed in something useful. Cut off all unnecessary actions." These statements illustrate this new ethic, or, as Weber would call it, "The spirit of capitalism." Others have called it an "inner-worldly asceticism." You deny yourself. But you work hard. The "other-worldly asceticism" of the Roman Catholic monks became re-appropriated by Protestants. The difference was that the Protestant ethic was for everybody, not just a select group of holy celibates.

A few years ago the Dutch banking company called ING aired an advertising campaign that epitomizes the Protestant ethic and the spirit of capitalism. The campaign was based on a succinct motto: Save your money! I would be willing to bet that the person who made the decision to air that campaign has Protestant roots!

In fact, save their money is exactly what these frugal individuals did. Moreover, they also reinvested their money. As anyone knows, when you save, you earn interest. Capital accumulates, and it gets reinvested, and soon there is more capital, which gains more interest. What is fascinating about Weber's theory is that this dynamic was happening in the working classes; it was not simply a scheme by the wealthy aristocrats.

Importantly for Max Weber's theory, this process happened in one place, and in one time in history: in Western Europe. More specifically, these patterns evolved most clearly in *Protestant* Western Europe. Weber then took a global survey of other cultures, arguing that Protestant Western Europe offered a unique context that fostered these new developments.

Capitalism did not arise in China.[12] Weber went to great lengths to explain why. China had been long ruled by its emperors who controlled an aristocratic class of Confucian elites, a system Weber described as "patrimonial officialdom."[13] The great goal of the upwardly mobile in Chinese society was not to attain wealth but social status, which did not necessarily include great materialistic gain. The goal was to enter the realm of the ruling elite. It was extremely competitive. This competiveness for status fostered large-scale mistrust. The elite ruling class, representing the emperor, held sway over local village leaders and stifled economic progress because of a vast disconnect between the massive centralized bureaucracy and the village worker. In addition, a traditional reverence for humility—as evinced in the religions of Taoism and Confucianism—encouraged a life of simplicity. The accumulation of wealth was unbecoming. Weber argued that this combination of patrimony, ambition for status, and esteem for simplicity failed to produce the spirit of capitalism. For all these reasons, Chinese civilization remained economically static, but content.

Similarly, capitalism was prevented in the religions of India because of the caste system led by the Brahmins and the Kshatriyas.[14] People deserve to be low caste or outcastes based on how they lived in previous lives. Great discipline (through yoga, which means "union") is required to help one escape the cycle of rebirth, samsara. Buddhism and Jainism were both almost entirely focused upon asceticism or self-denial. Most people realized they did not have the wherewithal to achieve moksha, so they gave money and goods to the monks to keep the system in good order and to improve their lot in the next incarnation. While India did achieve some great breakthroughs such as the number zero, thriving crafts and trade, and low taxes, the caste system was highly restrictive. Essentially it prevented people from interacting with one another in any significant way. Commerce between castes became complicated. The concept of ritual pollution prevented lower castes and outcastes from interacting with elite castes. This restricted trade partnerships. In addition, the ultimate religious pinnacle one could reach was to withdraw from this world in order to achieve a mystical, ecstatic union with one's god, or with ultimate reality itself. This interpretation had the effect of tainting the whole notion of secular work. Physical labor became a profane, necessary evil. The realm of the sacred, the spiritual quest, was the highest pursuit for man (yes, reserved for Brahmin men). Capitalism could scarcely thrive in this context.

Judaism did not produce capitalism either.[15] The main reason was because after the diaspora—the dispersion of Jews out of their homeland and around the world—they tended to adopt an *outcaste* mentality. They often withdrew from the larger communities of which were a part. This self-isolation led them to remain strangers wherever they settled. According to Weber, Jews, who often exhibited remarkable prowess in business and trade, had two standards, one for Jews and another for everyone else. In fact the Torah commanded this dichotomy in Deuteronomy 23:19–20.

> Do not charge a fellow Israelite interest, whether on money or food or anything else that may earn interest. You may charge a foreigner interest, but not a fellow Israelite, so that the LORD your God may bless you in everything you put your hand to in the land you are entering to possess.

This attitude, though, bred resentment. Jews eventually came to be associated with usury by non-Jews. While Jews may have prospered as a community, capitalism as a social economic system could not flower with this mentality.

Protestants, however, were different from their Jewish forebears in this important regard. They did not play favorites with their own, at least not nearly to the extent that Jews did. Protestants attempted to remain neutral in loans and other business dealings. As a result, this institutionalization of trust, in the form of capital lending and business dealings, stimulated widespread social confidence. The net result was that the central tenets of capitalism were unleashed. Business and trade flourished like never before, bringing about the dawn of modern capitalism as we know it.

It has been said that Weber "stood Marx on his head." In other words, religion is not a mere *reflection* of social structure and economic forces. Rather, religion is precisely the reverse! Religion, in this case Protestantism, ushers in a revolution of massive force. Protestantism led to a vibrant commercial culture with its markets, rational book-keeping, separation of home and business, and all that defines capitalistic societies today.

We must point out that Weber has his detractors. For example, Rodney Stark offered a thoughtful critique of Weber's thesis, essentially arguing that capitalism arose in the trade guilds of medieval (therefore Catholic) Europe. Stark does not dismiss Weber altogether. He is in perfect agreement with Weber that Christianity's understanding of a supremely rational creator and a rational universe allowed for alchemy to evolve into chemistry and astrology into astronomy. At the heart of the entire modern Enlightenment pursuit is a core conviction that God's created order is coherent and meaningful. It is good and right that God's most rational creatures explore it, most notably through the avenue of modern science. Stark, though, asserts that modern science is here because Christianity created a social climate that allowed the scientific pursuit of truth to take root.

Rodney Stark argues that it is a mistake to think of Protestants as the inventors of capitalism. This approach to life was happening in southern–Catholic–Europe *centuries* before it occurred in northern, Protestant Europe. Stark highlights Augustine and Aquinas as the great architects of what became modern capitalism, particularly with their emphases on property, interest, and most of all, the accumulation of profit. He also points out that all important revolution brought about by Constantine. Christianity became the religion of the powerful rather than simply the pious. Constantine unleashed a new Christianity with all of its profitable materialism embedded in a massive culture like the Roman Empire. Effectively, Constantine made Christianity a religion for a grand society—a proper church with buildings, priests, treasuries, and a national defense—rather than an insular sect that had to keep its humble head down.

Thus, for Stark, capitalism is rooted in *Christianity*, not in Protestantism. To trace the history of capitalism, we must go beyond Protestantism into the Orthodox and Catholic background. In that medieval world, we will find the archetype for modern banks. Modern banking arose out of the medieval abacus schools as the error prone Roman numeral system was replaced by the Hindu-Arabic one. In the medieval, Catholic world we discover highly sophisticated developments in manufacturing that completely revamped industries such as wool-making in Flanders and England. Indeed, Protestantism accelerated the rise of capitalism, but the roots go back to northern Italy's city-states and even further back to the church fathers—none of whom were Protestants.

To conclude our discussion of Weber, we should note that one of the great confirmations of Weber's theory is the New World. The Protestant New World—the United States and Canada—developed more rapidly than the Catholic one, Latin America. Perhaps all one has to do is look at this laboratory in the Americas to test Weber's thesis. Based on the history of economic development in these two cultural blocks, it seems Weber got it right. North America's Protestant ethic created the most fiercely capitalistic society on earth. For several centuries, Latin America languished in economic development and is only now adopting capitalistic structures in earnest.

To focus on whether Weber's theory is true or not is to miss the point. The great contribution of Weber is that he, in contrast to Karl Marx, saw religion as central to the development of societies and human institutions. Marx's argument that religion is simply a by-product of the materialistic struggle seems paltry after reading Weber. Religion is enmeshed within virtually any social institution or movement. Religion plays a critical role in the historical development of society. Weber's writings force us to recognize this principle.

As witnessed in the previous discussion of Weber's analysis, it can be seen that sociological studies of religion are absolutely crucial for the historian of religion. Durkheim and Weber, and those who followed in their methodological wake, changed the field of church history fundamentally. Through their case studies, they help us to understand larger trends within Christianity, or the history of any religion that they set their sights on. In the words of esteemed sociologist of religion Werner Stark,

> Without the work of the historian of religion, the sociologist would be helpless. Yet neither can substitute for the other; whereas the former is interested in longitudinal lines of development, the latter tries to cut through these lines vertically. It is the sociologist's hope that his categories will prove fruitful for the organization of the historian's material.[16]

Indeed, the historian of religion is deeply indebted to sociological analyses. Sociology is a great informant for the church historian. Without these case studies in our purview, the historian would be scarcely prepared to argue larger, more general interpretations on the history of a movement. In this case, that movement is Christianity.

Brief Overview

Christianity is the largest religious institution in the history of humankind. In addition to having more devotees than any other religion, it is also the most global, most diverse, and perhaps most influential religion in history. Several of the world's cultural blocks are today, at least in name, largely Christian: North America, Latin America and the Caribbean, Eastern and Western Europe, sub-Saharan Africa, Oceania, and parts of Asia. The enormous size and global influence of the Christian faith emphasize why Christianity must be understood as a global reality.

How did this happen? How did a tiny Jewish sect grow to become so large, so powerful, and so attractive to so many throughout the centuries?

Rather than investigating a man, a movement, or an epoch, our purpose in this chapter is to back up and see the bigger picture of Christian history. Gazing at this big picture causes us to ask a question: How did it happen? Using sociological tools such as databases, case studies, social trends, and statistical projections, we shed light on how the marginal Jesus movement grew throughout twenty centuries to become the world faith it is today. We also discuss why it continues to recede in the Western world.

So far in this chapter we have discussed the sociological approach, introduced foundational figures in the discipline, and examined one of the more significant sociological analyses in the field of church history: Weber's so-called Protestant ethic and its influence on the spirit of capitalism. The body of this chapter, however, is an attempt to understand the numbers and interpret them. The social sciences have provided a great deal of information regarding the growth and spread of Christianity. Drawing on this data and some key interpreters, we investigate what these numbers may be saying to us historically and, perhaps, theologically.

First, we look at general statistics that illustrate the growth of Christianity. Second, we point to pivotal moments in the 2000-year history of Christianity. Third, we discuss current trends in Christianity that shed light on future possibilities for this religion. In this third section we give special attention to the phenomenon of secularization—a sociological concept that has become central to the discussion of Christianity in the Western world.

Christianity: The Largest Religion in the World

There are around seven billion people in the world right now. One-third (33%) are Christian, one-fifth (21%) are Muslim, one-eighth (13%) are Hindu, and one-seventeenth (6%) are Buddhist. These are the only religions in the world that are statistically significant; in other words, these are the only religions that contain more than 1% of the world's population. Judaism, Sikhism, Baha'i Faith and all other religions in the world each amount to less than half of 1%.[17]

These statistics may be surprising because the world is often thought to be a religiously diverse place. Actually, the world is not as diverse as one might think. When we combine Christianity and Islam, two faiths that trace their roots to Judaism, we see that over half of humanity (54%) is either Christian or Muslim. Cultural geographers point out that these two religions prevail over 70% of the Earth's inhabited territory.[18] Christianity and Islam are, truly, world religions. Though Christianity is more diverse and more global, both of these religions are very widespread.

It is important to point out that people rarely switch religions. When this change of a belief system does happen, it is newsworthy and can deeply impact the future demographics of a particular region of the world. It has been estimated that over 99% of people in the history of humanity practiced the religion their parents modeled for them.[19] While it is fairly common for people to convert to new doctrines or take a fresh perspective on their own faith, outright conversion to an entirely different religion is very rare indeed. People may shift from one form of their religion to another—for example from Presbyterian to Pentecostal—but these are not considered changes in *religion*. They are better characterized as changes in *emphasis* since the core beliefs remain relatively unchanged. Those who deny the religion of their parents and make an outright conversion to another are, historically, exceptional.

Religions tend to be associated with countries or regions of the world. People in India tend to be Hindu. People in Latin American tend to be Christian. People in the Middle East tend to be Muslim. This is not a hard and fast rule, but it certainly reflects a general tendency. A good example is the United States of America. Around 80% of Americans *explicitly* consider themselves to be Christian. When we combine all Jews, Buddhists, Muslims, Hindus, and other world religions in America, the total percentage is only 4.7% of the U.S. population.[20] Statistically speaking, America is a strongly Christian nation.

Imagine if by the year 2100, America was 50% Muslim. That would be highly unlikely. It is significant to point out, however, that this type of transformation has happened in human history. While rare, it will probably happen again. Why? In a word, the answer is proselytization—the concept of consciously attempting to convert someone else to one's own faith. Christians call this "evangelism" or "missions."[21]

General Statistics on the Growth of Christianity

While Christianity is the largest faith today, it may not necessarily hold this place forever. Nor, obviously, has it always been the religion with the most believers. Christianity's rise to global prominence can be traced through quarterly estimations, using the years 500, 1000, 1500, and 2000 as a guide.[22]

It began as a Jewish sect shortly after Christ's death in the first century A.D. Through the work of Paul and others it morphed, surprisingly, into an inclusive religion regardless of ethnicity. Missiologist Andrew Walls has called this diversity the Ephesian Moment, "the social coming together of people of two cultures to experience Christ." Walls cites Ephesians 2:22 as the rationale for why there could be only one Christian community, instead of two: "In union with him [Christ] *you too are being built together with all the others* to a place where God lives through his Spirit."[23] Had the Ephesian Moment not occurred, Christianity would have remained, in all likelihood, an ethnic sect. With the Ephesian Moment, though, a new frontier opened. Gentiles were in, and they swiftly appropriated this originally Jewish movement.

By the year 500 there were approximately 43 million Christians alive, which would have been about 20% of the world's population.[24] Rodney Stark argues for a sudden spike in Christian adherence between the years 250 and 300. In the year 250, Christianity was the religion of only 2% of the Roman Empire. In the year 300, Christianity claimed around 10% of the empire. By 350, well over half of the Roman Empire was at least nominally Christian. He writes, "40 percent per decade (or 3.42 percent per year) seems the most plausible estimate of the rate at which Christianity actually grew during the first several centuries." As noted earlier, this is remarkably similar to the average growth rate of the Mormon Church over the last century.[25]

In the year 1000, still, approximately 20% of the world was Christian. In spite of successful missionary campaigns into northern Europe and Central Asia, all the gains had been offset by mass Christian defections to Islam, particularly in the Middle East and North Africa.

In the year 1500, Christianity's world market share had not changed much and was hovering right around 20%. Matters would soon change, however.

The year 1500 marks a period of major Christian expansion, particularly in the voyages of the Spanish and Portuguese to the Americas. Subsequent European empires established bridgeheads all over the world. From West Africa to East Asia, Christian Europeans—and later Christian North Americans—were sent out by the thousands in the name of Christianity and commerce. During the nineteenth and early twentieth centuries, Britain rose to become the unrivaled superpower in the world, on land and on sea, and it opened up many opportunities for British missionaries: safe travel, military protection, an English-language infrastructure, and unprecedented access to the peoples of these lands.

The era of European colonialism did not yield an immediate harvest, however. In the year 1800, Christianity was the religion of about 23% of the world's population.[26] In other words, from 1500 to 1800, Christian growth was mild. However, as Stark has shown, exponential growth eventually pays handsome dividends. By 1900, this number had increased to around 33%, where it has remained for over a century. Approximately one-third of humanity was Christian by 1900, when the modern heyday of Christian missions ceased.

Thus, the years 1800 to 1900 represent a second important spike upward in Christian adherence. The first spike—around the year 300—was a result of, in Stark's words, "the rather extraordinary features of exponential curves."[27] The second spike had much more to do with Christian missions and proactive evangelization campaigns to convert non-Christian peoples to the faith.

So what about the future? Will Christianity grow? Will it die? Either scenario is possible.

Christianity: A Religion That Is "Moving South"

Christianity's center of gravity has shifted in recent years. This phenomenon has caused a splash in the academic study of religion. The changes are astonishing. Christianity—by far the largest religion in the world today—has moved South. No longer is Christianity primarily a Northern or Western faith. The majority of Christians today live in the global South.

What is meant by that expression the "global South?" What scholars usually have in mind are Asia, Africa, and Latin America. Historically, other expressions have been used such as the Third World, the two-thirds world, or the developing world. The preferred term today is the global South.[28]

Christianity's demographics changed radically in a short period of time, and few scholars were aware of the massive implications of these changes until quite recently. The watershed moment took place around 1980. For many centuries prior to 1980 over half of the world's Christians lived in Europe and North America. After 1980 the majority of the world's Christians lived in Africa, Asia, and Latin America.[29]

Another key statistic illustrates Christianity's move to the global South.[30] In 1900, 82% of the world's Christians lived in Europe or North America; only 18% of the world's Christians were outside the Euro-North American block. In the year 2005, only 39% of the world's Christians lived in Europe or North America. During that century, Christianity's heartland moved south to the point that over 60% of the world's Christians now live in Asia, Africa, or Latin America.

How did this shift to the global South happen? The most obvious answer is Christian missions. In modern times, there were two great waves of Christian missions: the Catholic wave in the 1500s and the Protestant wave in the 1800s. During these periods, Christian missionaries from the West launched massive, expensive, and focused campaigns to take the gospel to non-Western nations. Millions of people accepted the Christian gospel and themselves became missionaries to their own peoples.

Herein persists one of the great misconceptions of Christian missions. It is all too easy to think that Western missionaries "won" entire continents over to Jesus Christ. Without minimizing the heroic deeds of these Euro-North American missionaries, the people who received them deserve equal credit for spreading the faith. The mass movements that occurred during the great expansion of Christianity could not have happened without indigenous agents. How could missionaries even communicate with people of different cultures unless someone accepted them, protected them, fed them, taught then the language, and introduce them to others?

Western missionaries often arrived to these lands with few language skills, and local people had to help them in the very basics of survival. Upon arriving to these foreign shores, Europeans and North Americans needed guidance on how to survive: which plants could be eaten, how to find fresh water, with whom to trade, how to act appropriately, how not to offend people. A few key locals would eventually "accept" Jesus Christ as their lord. These converts then explained Christianity to their people. And in many cases it made sense to them.

Once Christianity took root, it often indigenized, shedding much of the cultural assumptions brought by missionaries. Naturally, many of the indigenous social and cultural norms became interwoven with Christian teachings. The mission churches were often very different from the churches back home in the USA or in Europe. Nevertheless, they were clearly attempting to be Christian churches. Looking back, we can say that the Western missionaries to the global South were successful. They planted Christianity while locals made it their own, resulting in thriving churches comprised of hundreds of millions of people all over the global South.

Alongside Christianity's historic, geographical shift is the *changing Christian ethos*—the way the world's Christians prefer to live out their faith. If present trends continue, the world's Christians will continue to embrace Pentecostal, charismatic forms of the faith. And this change in Christianity's ethos is directly linked to the indigenization of the faith. Pentecostal Christianity is growing apace in the world right now. One influential scholar, Paul Freston, writes:

> Within a couple of decades, half of the world's Christians will be in Africa and Latin America. By 2050, on current trends, there will be as many Pentecostals in the world as there are Hindus, and twice as many Pentecostals as Buddhists.[31]

Indeed, Pentecostal Christianity is one of the fastest growing religious movements in modern times. Harvey Cox is another scholar who has noticed these
changes in the global church. His important work *Fire from Heaven: The Rise of
Pentecostal Spirituality and the Reshaping of Religion in the Twenty-First Century*
attempted to make sense of these new developments.[32] Both of these scholars
recognize that Christianity is undergoing seismic changes that will have
inevitable consequences. Most notable among the changes are:

1. Christianity is receding from Europe—its center of gravity for a millen-
    nium;
2. It is gaining ground in the global South;
3. Its changing ethos is reflecting the customs, beliefs, and worldviews of
    its host cultures in remarkable ways.

The Future of Christianity

Major changes are going on in Christianity today—changes that will impact the
future of this religion forever. This trend is not altogether surprising. Christianity has always morphed, reformed, and spread to new places. For example,
Christianity in Norway in the 1300s was very different than Christianity in
Zambia in 2000. While the Christians in those places in those times held
many of the same principles, they varied considerably in how to practice the
faith, and how to interpret the Bible. The genius of Christianity is its adaptability, its lack of borders.[33] It is always changing: geographically, theologically,
liturgically, and socially. Religions are never stagnant; like cultures they defy
rigid categories and definitions. Christianity has proven to be particularly
adept at finding its way into new people groups.

Historian Lamin Sanneh often points out that the reason Christianity has
succeeded in adapting is because it is based on a person, Jesus. In Christianity,
God reveals itself as a human being. This personification is very different from
other religions. In Islam, for example, God reveals itself through text. Thus, in
Islam, a person must understand God's words, the Quran, to understand
God's revelation. Christianity is different. While one may or may not read and
understand a text, the key is to know the man Jesus. The text can help with
that task, but by no means is the text equated with the revelation. Knowing
Jesus is far more important than knowing the texts about him. In Islam, the
text remains most critical to the faith. Therefore, Muslims must learn at least
some Arabic. Christians, however, do not have to learn a particular language.
They have to learn a man.

Christians in the global South are continually being introduced to this
man Jesus, in many cases for the first time. China, for example, is witnessing
an epoch similar to what happened in the book of Acts. Many people are
hearing—for the first time—about the life, the teachings, and "the way" of Jesus

of Nazareth. This development is fascinating and unpredictable, especially considering it is coming in the wake of one of the more punishingly atheistic epochs in recorded history.

Today, the notion of Christianity moving south is attracting more scholarly attention because the implications are huge. Christianity is the religion of one-third of the human race and the likelihood of this changing anytime soon is small because of higher fertility rates in the global South. Many Western nations have fertility rates that are in decline or soon will be such as in Germany, Denmark, the U.K., France, and Italy.[34] Eastern European nations are in steep decline—the governments of Russia, Bulgaria, Romania, and Ukraine have launched national baby making programs that reward mothers of multiple children. Some have even referred to the extremely low fertility rate in Eastern Europe as an auto-genocide.[35]

Westerners commonly perceive the future of Christianity to be dire due to these once strongly Christian nations becoming less populated. However, the statistic that is rarely given attention is that Christianity is growing rapidly in other places—where the birth rates are high. Most Latin American countries easily replace themselves. African birth rates are the highest in the world. It is not uncommon for African women to have six children on average, which is indeed the case in several African nations such as the Democratic Republic of the Congo, Ethiopia, and Angola. Overall, because the high fertility of the global South offsets the low fertility of the global North, Christianity will continue to remain the largest religion in the world.

According to today's fertility trends, Islam and Christianity will continue to grow their world market shares. Hinduism, Buddhism, and other religions will likely shrink in terms of global percentage. While Hindus constitute 13% and Buddhists 6% of the global population, these numbers will almost inevitably decline.

Fertility rates combined with compounding growth are critical concepts for understanding future demographic trends. In other words, there comes a point where a religion's market share inevitably declines unless it manages to gain numbers by extraordinary fertility rates or by large numbers of conversions— which is rare. As numbers compound, the likelihood of percentage growth in minority religions rapidly declines. For example, well over two billion people in the world are today Christian and well over one billion are Muslim. It will become increasingly difficult for religions such as Hinduism, Buddhism, Sikhism, and Judaism to claim greater market share in the future because of the compounding numbers of these two gigantic religions. Unless the minority religions are able to claim a higher fertility rate than Christianity and Islam, their percentage of the world population will decrease in all likelihood. There are other variables involved such as the age of the women when they have children (cultures with younger mothers will multiply quicker), life-expectancy, and success at converting others to their faith. However, even when those variables are considered, the staggering growth that results from compounding numbers becomes a statistical juggernaut.

Some scholars comment that Islam is growing much more rapidly than Christianity; this conclusion is premature, however. There is little reason to assume that Muslim nations will have higher fertility rates than Christian nations in the global South. Many of the theories that claim Islam is rapidly gaining ground on Christianity neglect the paradigm shifts in Christian demography.

While Buddhism, Christianity, and Islam are missionary religions, they grow mainly because of fertility. It is significant to point out, however, that there *have* been watershed moments in history when entire people-groups converted to one religion or another, but they are exceptional. How will this dynamic play out in the future? Nobody knows. Religious growth is uncontrollable and unpredictable; the history of Christianity showcases this principle remarkably well. Only in retrospect can we discern what events were decidedly pivotal in the history of the Christian faith. We can home in on four dates that proved epochal in four different parts of the world.

First, the year 312 marks Constantine's victorious Battle at the Milvian Bridge in Rome, which he accredited to Christ. Shortly thereafter, Constantine began to show favor for this previously illegal religion, issuing the Edict of Milan in the year 313. That Edict represented a pivot in the history of Christianity—from illegal to legal status.

Second, the year 988 was when Prince Vladimir of Kiev converted to Christianity and began Christianizing the people of the great Russian land mass.

Third, 1492 marks the year Columbus's discoveries had the effect of initiating a massive campaign to Christianize the people of the Americas.

Finally, 1807 is the year the Slave Trade Act passed in the parliament of the United Kingdom. Led by a devout, evangelical Protestant Christian named William Wilberforce, this monumental act marked what would become a vital link between England and sub-Saharan Africa—the next heartland of Christianity. The Atlantic slave trade began its long decline in that year and the African continent became a popular destination for British missionaries.

Throughout history, Christianity was usually transmitted by isolated Christians who might travel in pairs across long, lonely stretches of land to win a handful of souls to Christ. The remains of dedicated missionaries litter the world's crust from California to Japan, all in the name of bearing good news—the gospel—to new people-groups. In the vast number of cases, missionaries converted only a family or two, and perhaps started a small Bible study or humble worship assembly. However, as mentioned earlier, it was local people who did most of the recruiting and the converting of their own compatriots to the newfound faith. The role of the missionary as a seed-planter and nurturer should not be minimized, however. In the past and still today, missionaries play a strategic part by building on the work of their predecessors, faithfully serving their God in the best way they know how—by teaching stories of the Bible, administering the sacraments, reaching out to the needy, and offering their lives to the people they love and serve.

Today, Christianity is witnessing the fruits of the labors of those missionaries. The Christian faith has taken root in those lands where missionaries worked and died. As a result, the nature of Christianity is changing dramatically. We are today eyewitnesses of a universal, transcultural, multi-lingual religion that spans the entire breadth of the world's surface. Of this phenomenon, historian Stephen Neill wrote in 1964:

> It is only rarely that it is possible, in the history of the Church or in the history of the world, to speak of anything as being unmistakably new. But in the twentieth century one phenomenon has come into view which is incontestably new—for the first time there is in the world a universal religion, and that is the Christian religion.[36]

Christianity, in this sense, may be considered the first *world* religion.

The four largest religions in the world today are Christianity, Islam, Hinduism, and Buddhism. Hinduism has never really been a missionary religion, and its growth is through fertility alone. The great era of Buddhist expansion to new lands is over, and its market share of the world's inhabitants is in decline. Conversions to Islam are isolated. Islam is growing today, but that is almost wholly through fertility rates.

Christianity is different. As many in the Western world walk away from the Christian faith, this trend is offset by people actually converting from non-Christian to Christian in other parts of the world—most notably in China. Globally, one out of every five people lives inside the border of China. After decades of insularity, the great walls are falling, and this could affect religious demographics significantly. While it is too soon to predict just how eager the Chinese people are for Christ, the opportunities for Christian growth are obvious. If a major movement of Chinese Christians were to occur, it would alter the face of Christianity. At this stage, educated estimates of the number of Chinese Christians range between 5% to 10% of the population.[37] In other words, 100 million Chinese citizens might be Christians.

The Christians of China are known to be majority Protestant, and generally evangelical. While most of them are recent converts, they are proving to be skilled missionaries. What is most striking is their zeal, even in the face of government opposition. A cover article for the *New York Times* recently reported a congregation in Beijing that raised the eyebrows of the governing authorities when they raised $4 million for a church building. The police raided, evicted them from their meeting place, and took the leaders into custody.[38] Some highly ambitious Chinese Christians have decided to mission-ize the Middle East. One group, known as the "Back to Jerusalem" movement, describes itself as "God's call to the Chinese church to complete the Great Commission."[39]

The cross-cultural transmission of the faith is more creative and ambitious than ever. Christians are spreading their faith through mission work, litera-ture, and all forms of high-tech multimedia. The phenomenally successful *Jesus Film* (1979) has been labeled the most watched motion picture of all time according to the *New York Times* and the British Broadcasting Corporation (BBC).[40] Created by Campus Crusade for Christ founder Bill Bright, the *Jesus Film* has purportedly been viewed six billion times in over a thousand lan-guages. The official website claims that since 1979 over 225 million people have made decisions to follow Christ because of the film's impact on them.[41] If these statistics have credibility, then this film is easily one of the most effective evangelistic tools in the history of Christianity.

Secularization

A few words must be said here about secularization—a concept that is com-monly applied to the Western world, Western Europe in particular. Western Europe was for centuries linked to Latin-based Christianity—first for the Roman Catholic Church and after 1517 various Protestant forms of faith. Secularization has destroyed that link—at least for the time being. Even so, in many ways, Western Europe seems bathed in Latin, Roman Christianity.

Statistically, Western Europe is Christian. In every single Western Europe-an nation, Christianity is the majority religion. Overall, Western European Christians are 63% Catholic, 36% Protestant, and less than 1% Orthodox. Only a small percentage of Western Europeans explicitly identify themselves as members of non-Christian religions. A small, but growing, percentage claims to be "non-religious"—around 15%.

While Western Europe is, at least statistically speaking, still Christian, it is certainly not the center of Christianity anymore. In 1900, eight of the world's top ten Christian-populated countries were in Europe: Britain, Germany, France, Spain, Italy, Russia, Poland, and Ukraine, although the latter three are in Eastern Europe.[42] There was little doubt, however: Europe, clearly, was the axis mundi for the Christian faith.

Today, the situation is completely different. In 2005, Germany was the lone Western European nation still on that list.[43] Western Europeans do not attend church much these days. In 2006, Pope Benedict went to his native Germany—a country where less than 15% of the population attends Mass—and warned "[W]e are no longer able to hear God ...God strikes us as pre-scientific, no longer suited for our age."[44] Perhaps Philip Jenkins said it best:

> Europe is demonstrably not the Faith. The era of Western Christianity has passed within our lifetimes, and the day of Southern Christianity is dawning. The fact of change itself is undeniable: it has happened, and will continue to happen.[45]

Why did this dynamic occur? Why did Western Europe, apparently, get up and walk away from faith? These are big questions, and many historians, theologians, and social scientists are still trying to answer them.

Many have argued that secularization is rooted in the social shocks brought on by the Protestant Reformation. One of the most important consequences of the Reformation was the rise of national identities. Luther paved the way to nation-states by undermining religious authority and triggering a long period of violence and instability. In 1648 the Treaty of Westphalia stopped the bleeding of the Thirty Years' War with the dictum: *cuius regio, eius religio*, "whose realm, (use) his religion." If your king is Catholic, be Catholic. If he is Protestant, follow his lead. It may have stopped the war, but it did so at the expense of religious conviction, suggesting a sort of religious relativism. Are Catholics or Protestants the true Christians? Well, it depends on where you live—not too satisfying for the seeker of truth.

In histories of Christianity, the Treaty of Westphalia is generally treated as a documented beginning for European secularization. Today, however, the concept of secularization is much more complex. It has come to be understood as a cultural movement that marginalizes faith. It challenges the assumption that religion is good for society. Like the Treaty of Westphalia, secularization is essentially a living argument that religions need to back off in order for society to be free and peaceful. Perhaps more than anything else, it is an erasure of the distinction between the sacred and the profane. Religious holidays become downplayed, sacred places lose their religious quality, and the influence of the clergy becomes drastically reduced. It is common today to visit Western Europe and see churches turned into pubs, stores, warehouses, even mosques.

Why did this religious diversity happen? There are many answers, but we can highlight the most obvious:

- *Nationalism*: the nation-state supplanted the role of the pope. People began to identify with the ruler of the land rather than the authorities of faith, due to *cuius regio, eius religio*.
- *Urbanization*: people moved to the cities. There was a breakdown in the old agrarian structure of society. In the city, people are anonymous. There is less accountability. Individuals choose how they want to be-

lieve rather than how their community expects them to believe. Quite naturally, this also affects behavior.

- *Individualism*: Luther's legacy persists—a deep questioning and a need to return to the sources (*ad fontes*). Nothing is true except for what I can independently confirm to be true. Religious authority takes a beating.
- *Scientific advance*: experimentation takes precedence to religious tradition. There results an erosion of confidence in religious texts, clergy, and institutions. Truth is determined by demonstration and experimentation, not by conformity to social codes or religious norms.
- *Religious pluralism*: the Italian circumnavigators and Catholic missionaries began to encounter people from vastly different cultures in Latin America, Africa, India, and China. These people did not have Christianity, and some of them seemed to be doing fine without it.

These are some of the larger, contextual pieces of a puzzle that still confounds scholars. However, it is far from a complete picture. For example, sociologist Peter Berger, in his classic book *The Homeless Mind: Modernization and Consciousness*, persuasively argues that Westerners are discontent because of mass bureaucratization. Many of them no longer feel connected to their families due to migratory trends. Humans who change contexts are in many ways socially homeless, living a confused existence, "A world in which everything is in constant motion."[46]

What is the net result? The result is that religion in the Western world is in serious crisis. "The age-old function of religion—to provide ultimate certainty amid the exigencies of the human condition—has been severely shaken." Berger provides a label for this predicament: "social homelessness."[47]

The reality of the basic premise of the secularization thesis is undeniable—Western Europeans do not go to church like they used to, and most of them know little about Christianity. However, what does this trend in Europe mean for the future of Christianity? Scholars do not really know. Are Western Europeans actually less religious, or are they simply avoiding the institutional structures of religion? Every single Western European nation has secularized, and consequently church participation has fallen precipitously. There are several other key indicators to illustrate the secularization thesis:

- Policy making takes place separate and apart from the churches;
- Schools are not in the hands of the clergy;
- Charitable, benevolent welfare is largely in the hands of the state;
- Hospitals are not controlled by the churches;
- Church attendance is, in most cases, under 10% of the population in Western Europe.[48]

The question persists, however: Why? Some scholars tend to think in Marxist terms: when the needs of the people are met, religion will simply wither away. While there is credibility to this view, there are also numerous counterexamples. The United States remains a vibrantly religious culture but is economically on a par with Western Europe.

The long decline of religion in Western Europe continues. It is evidently a cultural juggernaut. Attendance rates are at their lowest in history, and there is little evidence to suggest a turnaround. In the late twentieth century, about 40% of Western Europeans claimed they "never" attended church.[49] Grace Davie, a noted scholar of secularization in Western Europe, writes: "An ignorance of even the basic understandings of Christian teaching is the norm in modern Europe, especially among young people."[50] A study in 2011 claimed religion may soon go extinct in nine countries.[51]

There are some creative theories, however, such as Graeme Smith's, which call the secularization thesis into question. Smith argues a fascinating idea—that secularization is simply Christianity in disguise. He writes:

> [S]ecularism is not the end of Christianity. Rather, we should think of secularism as the latest expression of the Christian religion. ...Secularism is Christian ethics [without] its doctrine. It is the ongoing commitment to do good, understood in traditional Christian terms, without a concern for the technicalities of the teachings of the Church. ...Secularism in the West is a new manifestation of Christianity, but one that is not immediately obvious because it lacks the usual scaffolding we associate with the Christian religion.[52]

Graeme Smith is not alone in this claim. Anthropologist Jonathan Benthall argues a highly nuanced thesis that says, essentially, religion never went away. For all this talk about Europe secularizing, religiosity is universal and intrinsic to our species, and nothing has changed that. Humanitarian movements, strikingly similar to Christianity's prophetic voice of justice, are clearly a modern outworking of religious tendencies. In other words, religion is not receding in Western Europe; it is being reinvented.

Benthall argues that religion is very difficult to define. If we define religion as Christianity, Judaism, or Islam, then sure, religion seems to be less prominent in Western Europe. However, if the definition of religion is opened up to include concepts such as social justice, environmental activism, charity, and civility, then religion in Western Europe has merely adapted itself to suit a scientifically advanced context created by modernization and scientific methods. While miracles may have been expelled in this worldview, the longing to heal people through medicine has not. Both of these approaches are rooted in a deep and abiding human orientation towards religion.[53]

Grace Davie argues that while Western Europeans tend not to *belong* to a church, they still *believe* in many identifiably Christian teachings. Her idea has become known as the "believing without belonging" thesis.[54]

Dietrich Bonhoeffer (1906–1945), while awaiting execution in a Nazi prison, famously wrote about the future of Christianity in Europe. Bonhoeffer foresaw a secular future for Europe. He was partially reacting to how his fellow countrymen could have possibly allowed Hitler's rise to power—in a supposedly Christianized Germany. Bonhoeffer struggled with the meaning of Christianity as a religion. In his view, the future of Christianity in Europe was a "religion-less" Christianity.[55]

> Hasn't the individualistic question about personal salvation almost completely left us all? Aren't we really under the impression that there are more important things than that question? I know it sounds pretty monstrous to say that. But, fundamentally, isn't this in fact biblical? Does the question about saving one's soul appear in the Old Testament at all? Aren't righteousness and the Kingdom of God on earth the focus of everything?[56]

Bonhoeffer envisioned a Christianity that was a lifestyle more than it was an institution. Even the doctrine of God should be revisited at a time when Christianity has, in Bonhoeffer's terms, "come of age": "God as a working hypothesis, as a stop-gap for our embarrassments, has become superfluous."[57]

If Bonhoeffer was right, then perhaps Christianity as an organized religion in Western Europe will indeed cease to exist. Maybe the Christianity of the future will be a Christ-like ethic, a sensitive and humane treatment of others, with compassionate social institutions, but without rituals, clergy, and build-ings? Perhaps the future of Christianity will be kindness, love, and justice, without the constant prodding of the church?

While Western Europe continues to secularize, we would be remiss if we did not point out that there are faithful remnants scattered about the land, bearing a witness for a somewhat ghostly Christian past. In addition, immigra-tion and reverse missions have led to new churches that are growing. London has several megachurches, and most of them are either African or Caribbean. Kiev, Ukraine, is home to the Pentecostal megachurch Embassy of God, led by Sunday Adelaja, a young Nigerian-born pastor. This church has now expanded to 35 countries.

There are thriving traditional churches as well such as Holy Trinity Brompton, where, in the 1990s, Nicky Gumbel transformed the Alpha Course into a worldwide phenomenon for introducing the Christian faith to non-Christians—kind of ironic in a historically Christian city like London. Indeed, Gumbel recognized that his fellow Londoners had almost no idea about even the very basics of the Christian faith.

While the vast majority of Western Europeans do not attend church any-more, there are still bastions of Christian witness. For example, the World Council of Churches, based in Geneva, is the hub for the largest Christian network in the world, and the flagship for the interdenominational ecumeni-cal movement. Pentecostal churches are popping up all over the region, as they are in many corners of the globe. Immigrant churches (and mosques) are full and growing, with few signs of becoming secular like their native counterparts. Thus, in many ways the ancient Christian faith is still alive in former Chris-tendom.

Nevertheless, there is no way to predict what will happen in Western Eu-rope. For all the talk about the rise of Christianity in the global South, it is perhaps just as likely that Christianity may, one day, rise up again in Western Europe, perhaps only in a different guise.

We cannot predict what will happen globally, either. Religions die, they flourish, and they pulsate back and forth, assimilating aspects of new and old cultures. For all we know, there might be a new religion on the horizon that will take the world by storm at some point in the future. Perhaps the bizarre religion of "Chrislam"—a fusion of Islam and Christianity that has occurred in parts of Nigeria—is not altogether surprising considering the religious strife in a country that is about half Muslim and half Christian.[58]

Whatever the case, we do know this: Christianity is rather young, only 2000 years. For those two millennia, it has grown, albeit in a punctuated way. In the beginning, it was a Jewish sect, marginal to another religion. Today, it claims the devotion of one out of three humans on the planet. Its rise has been gradual, and its future appears secure if history is in any way a useful measur-ing stick.

Conclusion: And the Lord Added

Contemporary Christian songwriter Matt Redman, from Britain, was well positioned to write his 2005 award-winning song "Blessed Be Your Name." The song's lyrics are powerful, but the final refrain is particularly relevant here:

> You give and take away...
> My heart will choose to say
> Lord, blessed be Your name

Redman probably understands more than most how quickly and thoroughly Britain has secularized. Christians are a marginal group on the island today. Christianity has a glorious past in Britain: Columba, Augustine of Canterbury, Wilfrid, Thomas Becket, Julian of Norwich, Margery Kempe, John Wesley,

George Whitefield, William Wilberforce, John Henry Newman, Charles Spurgeon, Catherine Booth, and on and on we could go. However, the Lord gave, and the Lord has taken away.

This chapter's title, "And the Lord Added to Their Number Daily" must be corrected with Job's declaration when his life fell apart:

Naked I came from my mother's womb,
And naked I will depart.
The LORD gave and the Lord has taken away;
May the name of the LORD be praised.[59]

If God is in control, as virtually all Christians believe, then why in the world would he allow Christianity to collapse like it has in Britain? Just a century ago Britain was ablaze with Christian excitement. Their missionaries were sailing all around the world, evangelizing new cultures. The British became famous for their missions. Robert Morrison and Hudson Taylor famously evangelized China. William Carey and Amy Carmichael built important missions in India. David Livingston worked indefatigably in Africa. Henry Venn was one of the greatest missionary statesmen of all time, giving his life to organizing transcontinental missions and helping indigenous leaders rise up all over the world.

...But the Lord has taken away. The fires have cooled. Perhaps a better analogy for Britain today would be a valley of dry bones.

Matt Redman is one of a small group of British Christians who are trying to breathe life into those bones. While everyone from the BBC to the pope declares Britain a secular society, Redman swims against the flow, writing Christian music, planting churches in his secular homeland, and writing books aimed at reversing these discouraging trends.[60] Is it a losing battle? No, I don't think it is. Let me explain why.

In 2010, I was at a conference in Nairobi, Kenya. There were some excellent speakers at this conference, held at the Nairobi Evangelical Graduate School of Theology. After each session, like at all conferences, people stand around and drink coffee and tea and eat snacks. I happened to come upon a conversation between two East African pastors. They were strategizing for some upcoming mission work. They allowed me to stand there and listen as they discussed their approach to "evangelizing the natives." The conversation surprised me because I had always been taught that Africa was the place that needed missionizing. Western nations are the ones who are supposed to take the gospel to *them*! Things have changed. Africans are now strategizing how to get the gospel back into Western society. As Matt Redman sang, "You give and take away. Lord, blessed be your name." These people who were the "indigenous" 100 years ago have now become the missionaries to the "natives" of

Britain who have little knowledge of the gospel. The Lord took away, but he also gave.

That conversation was hopeful with a slight tinge of discouragement. All of my ancestral roots trace back to the British Isles. My people were Christian for centuries. However, my forebears have decided to go in a different direction. Where? I do not think they know. Perhaps ...just perhaps ...the people my ancestors evangelized—Africans, Asians, Caribbeans—will reignite a Christian passion in Britain. There are reasons for hope. For example, some of the more noteworthy pastors in Britain today are Africans.

- Matthew Ashimolowo is a Nigerian pastor of the Kingsway International Christian Centre in London, a megachurch with 10,000 attendees each Sunday.
- Bishop Eric Brown oversees The New Testament Church of God, a black denomination in Britain with 30,000 members.
- Rev. Joel Edwards, from Jamaica, is also a pastor in the New Testament Church of God. For over a decade he was the General Director of the Evangelical Alliance in the UK, representing over a million evangelicals.
- Bishop John Francis founded Ruach Ministries in the UK. He ministers to 5000 Londoners each Sunday and conducts televangelism in Britain and the USA.
- Rev. Ermal Kirby is one of the highest ranked clergy in the Methodist Church in the UK. The London district of the Methodist church has 22,000 members today; over 60% of them are ethnic minorities.[61]
- Most Rev. John Sentamu, Archbishop of York, is the second highest ranked clergyman in the Anglican Church after the Archbishop of Canterbury. He was born in Uganda.
- Bishop Wilton Powell pastors The Church of God of Prophecy, one of Britain's oldest black Pentecostal churches. With 25,000 members they have had great success in addressing social ills within the UK's black communities.

The empire is striking back. While many discuss the rise of Islam in Europe, there is another force rising in Europe as well—Christians from the lands of the old European colonial empires. Will it be enough to stem the forces of secularization? Only God knows. After all, it is the Lord who adds to their numbers.

Questions for Analysis

1. What are some ways that a Christian scholar can do social scientific scholarship? Is it ever possible to be "objective" in one's scholarship? For that matter, is it possible for non-Christians to be impartial in their scholarship of Christian topics?

2. In your opinion, what would it take to re-Christianize Western Europe? What methods and techniques would be employed? What would effective missions to Europe look like?

3. If Weber is correct, should Protestantism be proud of its accomplishment of ushering in the age of capitalism? Why or why not?

4. Why would God allow Christianity to die out in places, such as in the Middle East and in Western Europe?

5. Is it possible that a new way of being religious is rising in Western Europe? Could Benthall be correct that religion is being reinvented in Western Europe today?

CHAPTER FOUR

GO AND MAKE DISCIPLES OF ALL NATIONS
A Geographical Approach to Church History

"Then Jesus came to them and said, 'All authority in heaven and on earth has been given to me. Therefore go and make disciples of all nations, baptizing them in the name of the Father and of the Son and of the Holy Spirit, and teaching them to obey everything I have commanded you. And surely I am with you always, to the very end of the age.'" Matthew 28:18–20

Introduction

Ethiopia was unimaginable for me.[1] The whole experience is cloudy, like a dream. Upon return, people asked about the trip, and I had no words. I encountered the strangest sites I have ever seen in Ethiopia. I had never entered a culture so *...foreign*. Part of the problem was that I had no context to situate my experiences and observations. I knew almost nothing about this remote corner of Africa until graduate school when I started researching ancient forms of Christianity. Ethiopia kept popping up in my studies as one of the most ancient national churches in the world. In fact, it is usually recognized as the second oldest after Armenia, dating to the early 300s. To visit Ethiopia is to step back in time. Indeed "Lucy" is housed there, the oldest hominid ever discovered. Lucy alone took me back 3.2 million years!

For Christians, Ethiopia is a feast for the eyes and soul: the isolated monasteries of Lake Tana permit only men to visit so as not to tempt the resident monks. These monasteries are home to ancient manuscripts, colorful and well-preserved icons, remains of Ethiopia's revered emperors, and, purportedly, secret treasure. I witnessed monks traveling from one island monastery to another on papyrus boats, the preferred method of travel since the pharaohs. I explored the royal compounds of Gondar—the African Camelot—with its Italian influence, medieval-like buildings, and sizeable population of Ethiopian Jews.

In the city of Axum I exchanged holy kisses with the priest who guards the Ark of the Covenant. Yes *that* Ark. Ethiopia claims to be in possession of Solomon's Ark after it went missing from the Jerusalem temple when the Babylonians swept through in 587 B.C. They are so convicted of this belief that every church contains a *tabot*—a replica of the ark—inside each of their churches. A hallowed Ethiopian text, the *Kebra Nagast*, describes how the Ethiopian people were grafted in to the people of God. It recounts a romantic relationship between Queen Makeda of Sheba and Solomon. It chronicles how the Ark eventually arrived to Ethiopia through the influence of Solomon and Makeda's son, Menelik. According to the Ethiopic Church, the Ark is now housed in the Chapel of the Tablet at the Church of Our Lady Mary of Zion in Axum. Whether it is there or not, the possibility is most intriguing. Ethiopians believe the Ark makes their land holy. They consider themselves heirs of all God's covenants in the Hebrew Bible.

Axum is a proud city. It is the seat of the old Axumite Empire, one of the great civilizations of antiquity. Its heyday was the first to tenth centuries A.D. Ethiopians think of Axum as the spiritual center of the country. The city is a UNESCO World Heritage Site for good reason: ancient tombs, giant stelae mysteriously fashioned from granite, ancient monasteries, even the Queen of Sheba's palace and huge bath is there.[2] The Ezana Stone, Ethiopia's own Rosetta, rests there. This tri-lingual monument describes the conversion of King Ezana to Christianity in the 300s A.D. Narrated in Ge'ez (ancient Ethiopic), Sabaean (Old South Arabian), and Greek, it gives glory to God for Ezana's military victories.

Nothing, however, prepared me for Lalibela—home of the twelfth-century rock-hewn churches.[3] These thirteen cruciform sanctuaries are etched down deep into granite. I still cannot fathom how they managed to do it. They say God sent angels to assist in the task.

The roofs of the churches are ground level. One has to descend many stairs to enter. Solemnity, mystery, and rich history permeate Lalibela. The churches were designed as a New Jerusalem since Saladin and his Muslim forces captured the holy city in 1187. Lalibela was built shortly thereafter. Old Testament names have been applied to nearly everything there. Europeans scarcely knew of the site until the late nineteenth century. Only a handful of Portuguese explorers saw the majestic churches before then. The priest Francisco Alvares laid eyes on them in the 1520s but considered the sights so fantastical that he doubted whether anybody would believe his descriptions:

> I weary of writing more about these buildings, because it seems to me that I shall not be believed if I write more. I swear by God, in whose power I am, that all I have written is the truth.[4]

Cameras do no justice to the beauty of this magnitude; nay, cameras are inappropriate inside these houses of God.

Comprised of labyrinthine tunnels and grottos, one stumbles upon hidden crypts, monk corpses, and secret chambers every few feet. Inside one church I witnessed an exorcism as a priest rubbed a large, golden cross over the body of a young lady. She shrieked and convulsed as incense enveloped her. In the background, monotone chants accompanied by primitive Ethiopic instruments hypnotized crowded rooms. In one vault I witnessed an enclave of monks involved in a pious ceremony that erupted into clanging and shouting at the end. My guide, a twenty-something Lalibelan, assured me there was nothing to fear. The monks seemed to take little notice of me hunched down among them, buried in their rancid-smelling habits. I was told their holiness prevents them from proper hygiene; it is a luxury to be avoided. These ascetic men live for God and little else. My guide was perplexed why I would want to sit with these entranced, unkempt holy men chanting magical words from the distant past. As I sat and studied their half-conscious faces I thought to myself, "This is why I study church history."

The rock-hewn churches were not designed for large masses, but rather for an intimate encounter with the great God of earth and rock. Separated from the world, these churches allow very little natural light. Everything one observes is muted, transporting the worshiper to higher, more mystical realms. The boundary separating sacred and profane emerges vividly. Descending into the churches, the old life of photographs and tourist talk collapses into timelessness and holy confusion.

Emerging, I wondered how a place could have become so strangely isolated from the larger world. I was told, for example, that of the fifteen thousand people living in Lalibela, nearly one-tenth are priests. I also wondered why so many people seemed content with their unemployed status, sitting and chanting all day every day, neglecting themselves, completely devoted to God. Christ becomes their sole purpose.

Lalibela evoked a strange reaction within me. I wanted these people to be *less* religious. They were living in abject poverty with nothing to do other than pray and chant. My unconscious Protestant proclivities were now exposed. I never knew I fit the mold of Max Weber's thesis so perfectly. In my view, these people should understand that all people are priests, no matter their occupation! Like Luther, I saw the biblical precept of "the priesthood of all believers" with absolute conviction. One does not have to chant and pray all day to be acceptable to God. We worship a God of grace. He favors those who love him and serve others. These monks are in the business of serving themselves and their own aspirations for heaven!

While engaged in this accusatory line of thinking, I realized my own conditioned pattern of thinking. Here, an American in Ethiopia. My homeland is the land of vast capital with compounding interest, 401K plans, bountiful business opportunities, and extravagant wealth. Ethiopia is the antithesis of that. These people do not think like me. Who is Luther to them? They do not care to lay up for themselves treasures on earth. They lay up treasures in heaven. My accusations turned to shame. I was in the presence of pure holiness. What a beautiful experience to sit with people striving to cultivate a life of complete submission to Christ. Why worry about the vagaries of the stock market when Christ taught "tomorrow will worry about itself?" Jesus warned, "The pagans run after all these things" such as nice clothes, fine cuisine, and lucrative investments.[5]

At some point, my theological reflection turned back to academic observation. I realized that Ethiopia is a society well-preserved by geographical factors. First off, it is hemmed in by high mountains. The rugged terrain explains why the Italians could never fully defeat them. Mussolini consolidated most of Ethiopia, but not all of it. Ethiopia is sometimes referred to as the only African nation that was never dominated by a Western power.

There are other reasons for Ethiopia's isolation. It is today a landlocked country, severely restricting the influx of products, ideas, and cosmopolitan culture so common in most ports of the world. Ports enable a nation to flourish simply by taxing incoming products. However, becoming overly dependent on a port is a move that can backfire. For instance, the old Ethiopian capital of Axum declined rapidly in the seventh and eighth centuries when Arabs took control of the ports and cut off trade routes during the rapid expansion of Islam.

Ethiopia is also somewhat isolated theologically. It became disconnected from much of Christendom when it rejected the conclusions of the Council of Chalcedon in the fifth century. It was not alone in this decision, as this was the position adopted by the powerful Coptic church of Egypt. However, its impassability prevented the level of interaction one might expect between two sister churches. This isolation may have been Ethiopian Christianity's saving grace. As Islam continued to expand and gain influence in Egypt, Somalia, Yemen, and Sudan, Ethiopia became something of a Christian island in a sea of Islam. The Ethiopian Orthodox Church did not become formally autonomous until 1959 when the Egyptian patriarch granted autocephaly. By that time, Ethiopia's Christian population was three times the size of Egypt's. Roles had switched. Coptics were a persecuted minority but Ethiopia's Christians easily outnumbered its Muslims. It is still this way. Ethiopia is around 55% Christian (compared to 34% Islamic), and the Christian culture is extremely active.

As early as the ninth century, the Red Sea was an Islamic sea, and Ethiopian Christianity, clearly, was vulnerable. Instead of looking outward with visions of evangelism, it was forced to look inward, steadfastly preserving the old ways, even looking back to Judaism for solidarity and meaning. Even today the Ethiopian Church emphasizes its Jewish roots: a heavy emphasis on the Old Testament, dietary restrictions, Sabbath observance (in addition to Sunday worship), and a profound Jewish self-understanding. While much of church history is spotted with anti-Semitism, Ethiopian history exudes an unyielding drive to connect with Jewish themes.

The Geographical Approach

So where does geography fit into this discussion? Ethiopian Christianity is a rich, multidimensional example of how geographical factors can impact church history. For example, because of Ethiopia's geographical isolation, Christianity has been preserved against all the odds. Geography is precisely what prevented Ethiopia from being fully colonized, as happened with virtually every other civilization in Africa, allowing for an indigenous kind of Christianity to survive into the present. For centuries, empires tried in vain to capture this fiercely independent stretch of land roughly twice the size of France.

When Africans establish independent churches, they often include the word "Ethiopia" in the title—kind of a "shout out" to its indigenous character. For example, in nineteenth-century South Africa an "Ethiopian Movement" emerged as a critique of the white man's control of Christianity. Based on the passage Psalm 68:31, Ethiopia's reputation resounded throughout the continent: "Ethiopia shall soon stretch out her hands unto God." Ethiopia's fiercely independent form of Christianity became heralded even amongst Africans who knew little about the Ethiopian Orthodox Tewahedo tradition, and had never even visited the inaccessible land. With colonialism and imperialism surrounding them, Africans were inspired by this one place that seemed to thumb its nose at Europe and everyone else. Ethiopia represented freedom, strength, indigenousness in a world where, to quote Nigerian novelist Chinua Achebe, "Things Fall Apart." Indeed Africa was falling apart. It was becoming "owned" by foreigners. One nation stood firm and proud: Ethiopia.

Not only did Ethiopia's geography keep certain peoples out, notably Muslim and European invaders, but they also kept certain traditions in, such as the heavy emphasis on Judaism. I think most students of Christianity scratch their heads when they realize just how little Christianity and Judaism interact these days. Few Christians have ever darkened the door of a synagogue, but Ethiopia's isolation kept many Old Testament beliefs and practices intact.

It is a well-known principle in religious studies that geography has a unique ability to shape faith. Religions evolve or stagnate for geographical reasons. For example, Hinduism is the religion of India, largely because of the mountainous buffer hemming it in. Shintoism is exclusively the religion of

Japan; the islands prevented the cross-pollination of ideas for centuries. Only later did the Chinese religions and Buddhism enter. This phenomenon occurs with frequency in world religions.

Why did Christianity spread? It has much to do with geographical factors combined with political ones. The *Pax Romana* allowed Christians in the Roman Empire to travel relatively easily in the first few centuries of the faith. Christianity had a difficult time penetrating Asia because of the huge mountains and vast steppes that made travelers vulnerable. Water provides a wonderful facilitator for religions to travel, but the technological capabilities have to be advanced enough. It took Europe many centuries to build a ship strong enough to handle the Atlantic Ocean, but when technology was up to the task, Latin America became Christianized in short order.

It is also common for geography to inspire religious belief. In Romans 15 the apostle Paul tells of his aspiration to evangelize Spain—the extreme limit of "the West" in his understanding. We do not know if he ever made it, but we do know that for two millennia Christian missionaries have been among the most notable adventurers, intensely motivated by their desire to take the gospel "into all the world."[6]

Christianity is chock-full of examples of those who risked life and limb to scale mountains, sail seas, trudge thousands of miles to bring the message of Jesus. Every form of Christianity has its heroes. The Nestorians have Alopen, the first recorded Christian missionary to reach China. Alopen likely traveled 4,000 miles by foot on one of the Silk Roads in the seventh century. The Eastern Orthodox traditions have many heroic missionaries. Cyril and Methodius may be the most famous for their evangelization of the Slavic peoples in the ninth century. The heartland of Eastern Orthodoxy is Slavic including the peoples of Russia, Ukraine, and the Balkans. The list of Roman Catholic missionaries is equally extensive, and Francis Xavier may be the most prolific name on it. In the sixteenth century he co-founded the Jesuits and worked extensively in the Far East. Protestant missions began in earnest in the eighteenth century. British missionaries in particular became famous due to the global presence of their empire, enabling their geographic horizons to become unusually expansive. David Livingstone in Africa, Hudson Taylor in China, and William Carey in India are among the most important.

While some postcolonial scholars lament the age of European hegemony, there can be no doubt that the era proved highly productive for Christianity as a whole. Geography and politics, combined with religious fervency, led to a jump in global Christian adherence—from about 20% of the world's population to around 30% during the high tide of European dominance. Indeed Christianity's global market share hovered around 20% from the years 400 to 1800. During the nineteenth century, however, Christianity experienced a boom. By the end of that century Christianity's market share was over a third of humankind. It is undeniable that British control of the seas, combined with the largest empire in human history, provided a congenial atmosphere for Christianity to travel, preach, and extend its influence. Many Christians lament that Christianity spread globally because of colonial protection. However, for better or for worse, it is a fact.

Historians argue about the collusion of Christianity and colonialism. For example, Edward Said and other leading postcolonial scholars claim Christianity was simply the handmaiden of European empires. However, it is clear that colonial administrators frequently opposed the work of missionaries, particularly in the case of Britain. Missionaries were a threat to commerce. In the minds of more entrepreneurial colonists, missionaries unnecessarily complicated relations by trying to get natives to change their beliefs. Religion touches nerves. Missionaries were challenged often by both sides: by natives and by British magistrates. Nevertheless, wherever one lines up on this complex debate, it is undeniable that Christianity grew substantially during this era.

Christianity grows when the geographical reach of a Christian empire grows. Globalization, for example, has launched American Christianity—with its values, language, and customs—into foreign parts. Geographical phenomena are not nearly as restrictive as they once were. Mountains, valleys, vast plains, oceans, and rushing rivers are no match for the Internet. Evangelists can fly to remote lands, conduct services electronically, or even take up collections through PayPal. We are in a world different from the one of Livingstone in the nineteenth century. Although he drove himself to death looking for the source of the Nile, that task can be done quickly and easily today with a helicopter. Boniface axed his way through the dense Black Forest to evangelize the Germans in the eighth century. Today, however, people can evangelize entire people groups through chat rooms, Skype, and Facebook. Christianity's geographical limitations are virtually non-existent today. The World Wide Web is indeed worldwide.

Christianity's great strengths have always been its fluidity, its adaptability, its borderlessness. In 2010 I published *The Changing World of Christianity: The Global History of a Borderless Religion*.[7] I had a hard time deciding on a title, but the more I observe trends in Christianity, the more I become convinced that no word better explains the innermost essence of Christianity: borderlessness.

We return once again to geography, a critical component in understanding how Christianity came to be the largest religion on earth. In particular let us return to Acts chapter 8, featuring Philip and the Ethiopian eunuch. What appears to be an incident about the conversion of a Gentile is actually a passage about geography. The genius of the Ethiopian passage is that "good news" is for all people, even *Ethiopians*. As Peter said in Acts 2, the gospel promise "is for you and your children and for all who are *far off*."[8] In all likelihood, the Ethiopian represents geographical distance for Luke, the author. Gay Byron's brilliant study of Blackness explains:

> Although travel and tourism were common activities in Greco-Roman Egypt, very few ancient geographers or historians were able to travel to Ethiopia. Therefore, many of the geographical descriptions and historical summaries about Ethiopia serve more to stimulate the literary imagination of the reader than to record actual events. The most characteristic feature of Ethiopia in early Greek writings is its remote geographical location. As reflected in the minds of the elite Greco-Roman authors, Ethiopia represented the "end of the earth" (*eschatou tes ges*). Both Homer and Herodotus identified Ethiopia as a region in the southern part of the world far removed from the center of Greek culture. But Ethiopians were found not only in the southern part of the Greco-Roman world; they could also be found in the East and in the West. Homer claims that these dark-skinned remote people lived either toward the setting sun or toward the rising sun. This statement seems to have been the genesis for the widespread confusion among the ancients regarding the exact geographical location of the Ethiopians.[9]

If Byron is correct, then the borderlessness of Christianity has profound implications.

Christianity was never intended to be a faith for a particular ethnicity. It is for all. This important element distinguishes Christianity from other religions. Hinduism is for Indians. Judaism is for Jews. Islam is for those willing to enter the realm of the Quran—the language of Arabia. Christianity, however, according to the apostles and New Testament writers, was for all tribes and tongues. From the very beginning of the New Testament to the very end, the writers are intent on teaching the message of Christ is for all people everywhere. Indeed from the genealogy of Jesus, which emphasizes his Gentile ancestors, to the book of Revelation, we are told repeatedly that the gospel is for all human beings everywhere. In Revelation chapter 7 we are privy to a vast, inclusive, heavenly multitude. In the words of John's Apocalypse,

> There before me was a great multitude that no one could count, from every nation, tribe, people, and language, standing before the throne and before the Lamb. They were wearing white robes and were holding palm branches in their hands. And they cried out in a loud voice: "Salvation belongs to our God, who sits on the throne, and to the Lamb!"[10]

Geographical boundaries fade away in light of the gospel.

Luke seems convinced on this issue. In the book of Acts he goes to great lengths to argue the borderlessness of the Christian gospel. He hearkens back to the prophet Joel to emphasize "In the last days, God says, I will pour out my Spirit on *all* people." It seems Luke almost pulls out a map to make his point in this particular text, reminding us that Christ is for "every nation under heaven."[11] Luke wants his readers to clearly, unmistakably understand that this new faith was not linked to ethnicity. Jesus Christ transcends all manmade boundaries. In Acts 2 Luke is radically inclusive in his list of people-groups that participated in the founding of the Christian church:

> Parthians, Medes and Elamites; residents of Mesopotamia, Judea and Cappadocia, Pontus and Asia, Phrygia and Pamphylia, Egypt and the parts of Libya near Cyrene; visitors from Rome (both Jews and converts to Judaism); Cretans and Arabs.[12]

Luke asks "What does this mean?"[13] Hint: He knows exactly what this means.

How could Christianity be so radical as to include virtually everybody, all tribes and nations and languages? Answering that very question may be the point of Luke's Ethiopian Eunuch story. Some scholars have even pressed the issue further by calling attention to the Ethiopian being a "eunuch," or, a castrated man. Jack Rogers writes,

> The repeated and direct involvement of the Holy Spirit, the significant reference to the liberating prophecies of Isaiah, and the fact that the first Gentile convert to Christianity is from a sexual minority and a different race, ethnicity, and nationality together form a clarion call for inclusiveness, radical grace, and Christian welcome to all who show faith.[14]

Whether Luke intended this reading or not, his larger intent is unmistakable: the story of Jesus is for everybody. There are no exceptions. It is no wonder that Christianity has assimilated well into the geographical edges of the world. Christ is for all of us. I imagine Luke would be very pleased to see the border-lessness of Christianity two thousand years after his recorded events.

Brief Overview

We now embark on a geographical overview of Christianity's global expansion. The title of this chapter is "Go and make disciples of all nations." It is based on Jesus' injunction in Matthew 28, immediately before he ascended into heaven. A geographical survey of church history illustrates just how faithful they were to his request.

The chapter is organized into eight geographical sections: the Middle East, Eastern Europe, Western Europe, Latin America and the Caribbean, North America, Asia, Africa, and Oceania. These are the eight cultural blocks of the world. Christianity is the largest religion in six of them. The two exceptions are the Middle East and Asia. The chapter's narrative, combined with maps and statistics, will provide a bird's-eye view of Christian history, specifically how Christianity came to be the religion of over two billion people.

Middle Eastern Christianity

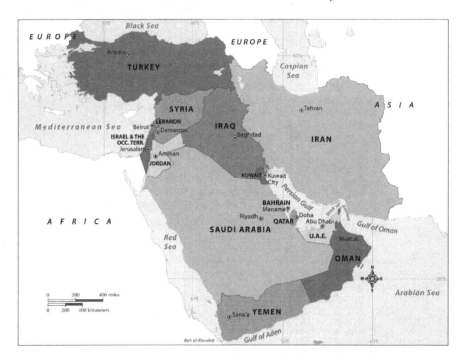

For Christians, the Middle East is holy. The city of Jerusalem is especially holy. Each year, many Christians embark on pilgrimage to "the Holy Land," where Jesus walked and taught. According to Christian theology, Jesus lives in the hearts of his followers through the presence of the Holy Spirit. However, there is something uniquely sacred about Jerusalem, the city where Jesus died and resurrected, and where the church was born.

Christianity began in the Middle East—the land of the apostles, the prophets, and the savior himself. In geographical terms this cultural block consists of fourteen countries: Iran, Iraq, Saudi Arabia, Turkey, Syria, Lebanon, Israel and the Occupied Territories, Jordan, Kuwait, Yemen, Oman, United Arab Emirates, Qatar, and Bahrain. There are around 300 million people in the Middle East, and 93% of them are Islamic. For centuries, Christianity was the dominant religion in the region, but the rise of Islam precipitated a long decline. Today, only 2% of the inhabitants of the Middle East are Christian, roughly equivalent to the percentage of Jews. The Middle East is home to around seven million Christians; 58% Roman-Catholic, 29% Orthodox, and 13% Protestant. Since Islam has a much higher fertility rate than Christianity, the small community of Christians will decline further. Nevertheless, in spite of Christianity's near disappearance in the land of Jesus, the Middle East will forever remain the birth land and cradle of Christian civilization.

Westerners misunderstand the Middle East. One writer put it this way, "The Middle East is perhaps the most difficult region of the world for Westerners to comprehend."[15] There are several reasons for this lack of understanding. First of all, the Christian world and the Islamic world have struggled mightily for centuries. Second, Westerners rarely travel to the Middle East because of political instability leading to travel warnings. Third, for much of recent history, the region has been at war.

Today, the heart and soul of the Middle East is Islamic. Throughout history, the Islamic notion of a religiously homogenous land rewarded Muslim integration and crippled Christian presence. The backbone of Islamic society is Sharia law, a marriage between religion and politics. An Islamic society is usually a Quranic society. To Westerners, Muhammad is reminiscent of the Old Testament prophets, who blended religion and state. Muslims adopted this approach. To be a faithful member of society is to be faithful to the religion. A good citizen is a good Muslim. The modern Western model is very different; church and state are separated.

The Arab Spring, begun in 2010, has destabilized the region in unprecedented and unpredictable ways. Could the Middle East become a democratic culture block along the lines of Western Europe or North America? It is highly doubtful because of the central role of the Quran in the history of Islamic civilization. There are enormous implications when societies use a particular text as a foundation. Western society has been shaped by the Bible; Islam has taken a Quranic trajectory.

The story of the Middle East is the story of Christianity's extravagant growth and steady decline. Why did this happen? Why has Christianity gone nearly extinct in the land of Jesus? There are several ways to answer these questions, but the beginning and end of the discussion is Islam.

Muhammad died in the year 632. One hundred years later, Islamic rulers were firmly in control of the Middle East. Some Christians were not sure whether Islam was a Christian sect or an independent religion. For example, prominent Christian theologian John of Damascus (676–749) argued that Islam was a Christian heresy. After all, Islam adopted much of the Judeo-Christian worldview: monotheism, a similar social ethic, and a shared historical consciousness rooted in the biblical patriarchs. In time, however, it became clear that a new movement was evolving.

Islam's terrific growth was achieved by a method of governance known as *dhimmitude*. Under the *dhimmi* system, non-Muslims were required to pay much higher taxes, were given second-class status, and their religious freedoms were restricted. While Christians were allowed to worship, they were not able to construct new churches or evangelize. Conversion to Islam was welcomed and rewarded, whereas defection from Islam could mean a death sentence. Demographic trends worked against Christianity. Christian men could marry only

Christian wives; however, Muslim men could marry up to four non-Muslim wives, as long as the women were monotheists. Children of mixed faith marriages were required to be raised Muslim. In short order the number of Christians declined.

Another issue was language, one of the supreme differences between Christianity and Islam. Central to Islam is the belief that Arabic is God's language. The process of transmission is quite clear in Islam: God spoke to the archangel Gabriel; Gabriel spoke the words of God to Muhammad; Muhammad—who was illiterate—spoke the words to his scribe Zaid; and Zaid wrote down the words. Muslims believe in an unbroken chain of oral transmission from God to the Quran, free from error.

Christians consider the Bible to be inspired but there is little consensus beyond this basic agreement. Christians think of the Bible as God-breathed but with room for human influence. The point of Christianity is that Jesus is the Word made flesh. He walked among us. God's message was revealed throughout the centuries by prophets. However, in Jesus, the Word of God became human. God's revelation was no longer confined to commandments in written or oral form. To Christians, God is most clearly understood through the life and teachings of Jesus Christ.

We come to a major divide here between these two behemoth religions. The distinction is vital. For Christians, God's primary revelation came in the form of flesh. In Islam, God's primary vehicle for revelation is "the recitation," or, the Quran. For a Muslim, when you recite the Quran, you are reciting, verbatim, the words of God.

There are many other differences between Christianity and Islam. Some of them are subtle. For example, biblical stories are retooled in the Islamic rendition. In Genesis, Abraham goes to offer his son Isaac to demonstrate his faith in God. In Islamic tradition, Ishmael, Abraham's firstborn, replaces Isaac in the story. Ishmael is revered in Islam as the father of the Arabs and the ancestor of Muhammad.

There are other differences that may seem subtle at first but in context are quite significant. Muslims revere Jesus as one of the five great prophets of all time, along with Noah, Abraham, Moses, and Muhammad. The Islamic interpretation of Jesus, however, is entirely different. While Jesus is deeply revered, he is not God. He did not die on a cross. It was probably Judas who was killed on the cross. God would not allow such a despicable death for the Son of the Virgin Mary. (Muslims also believe Mary was a virgin when she gave birth to Jesus.) Muslims believe Jesus will usher in the Judgment Day in almost exactly the same way Christians anticipate. To insinuate Jesus was the son of God however is a grave sin in Islam because it begs questions that could compromise the *absolute* monotheism presupposed in Islam.

I often tell my students if one wants to peer into the world of early Christianity, it is of great benefit to understand Islam. Practices of the Islamic community today transport us back to early Christianity: regulated and prostrated prayers, domed buildings, and myriad customs prominent in the Middle East. When traveling in the Middle East I was amused by some of these "Islamic" customs that are rooted in early Christianity and even in Judaism: washing the feet after a journey, slaughtering animals immediately before meals, anointing visitors with oil, segregation of men and women, and reclining around a table while seated on the floor. I once heard an Assyrian Orthodox priest observe that if you want to understand the Islamic approach to prayer you need only understand Assyrian Orthodox practice.

However, the apple has fallen far from the tree in some ways. Surveying modern politics, few would characterize Christianity and Islam as brothers in faith. Today the relationship would be more accurately described as apprehensive. A quick scan of the The Economist will reveal how distrustful and strained this relationship has become. Hans Küng, the famous German theologian, once observed "There will be no peace among the nations until there is peace among the religions."[16] World peace is elusive without peace between its two largest religions. Well over half of humanity is either Christian or Muslim, and this will remain the case for as far as we can project.

The study of geography is the study of land. No land has been more contested than the Middle East, in particular its nerve center: Jerusalem, the homeland of two world religions. For centuries before Christ, Jerusalem was home to the Jewish temple. Jerusalem then became the holiest city in Christianity with the death and resurrection of Jesus occurring there. Jesus also held the city dear to his heart, saying:

> I must keep going today and tomorrow and the next day—for surely no prophet can die outside Jerusalem! O Jerusalem, Jerusalem, you who kill the prophets and stone those sent to you, how often I have longed to gather your children together, as a hen gathers her chicks under her wings, but you were not willing! Look, your house is left to you desolate. I tell you, you will not see me again until you say, "Blessed is he who comes in the name of the Lord."[17]

Possibly more blood has been shed over the city of Jerusalem than any other geographical location in human history.

What makes Jerusalem so volatile? Each day we hear about conflict in the Middle East: Palestinian refugees, the question of nationhood for both Israel and Palestine, the legitimacy of governments. Why has Jerusalem become the vortex of global conflict? The answer to that question centers on the all-important issue of homeland, an idea critical to the study of geography. Why would Islam care about this "homeland" if the Islamic homeland is obviously Mecca and Medina? For Muslims, Jerusalem is the location of Muhammad's sole miracle. Unlike Jesus, who is routinely credited with miracles in both Christianity and Islam, Muhammad's life is devoid of them, with one exception.

In the year 621, Muslims believe Muhammad took his famous "night journey." In Surah 17, *Al-Isra*, Muhammad travels to "the farthest mosque" and prays with the prophets. He then leaps up into heaven and speaks to God himself. God commands him to lead the *Ummah* (the early Islamic community) in prayer five times per day. The five daily prayers, known as *salat* in Islam, constitute the second of five pillars of the Muslim faith. In commemoration of that event, Muslims built two important structures on Jerusalem's famous hilltop: the al-Aqsa Mosque and the Dome of the Rock. The problem with the location of these two buildings is that they are precisely where Solomon's Temple once stood. In fact some believe the Dome of the Rock is located on the Holy of Holies—the axis mundi—the center of the world, the nexus point between heaven and earth.

While the Temple Mount is by far the holiest site in Judaism, it is the third holiest site in Islam, and was under Islamic control from the seventh to twelfth centuries. During the crusades (1095-1204), Christians reclaimed control of Jerusalem for nearly a century, but Saladin defeated the crusaders and enslaved most Christians in 1187. This event, the Siege of Jerusalem, was the decisive turning point in the crusades. Saladin wiped out a century of crusader gains within a few short months. My students are always surprised when they learn the crusades were an abysmal failure. It was Christendom's final grasp at the Holy Land, but came to nothing.

So why is the state of Israel so contested today? Is it not the Jewish homeland? Yes and no. It *was* the Jewish homeland for centuries prior to AD 70 when Rome conquered it and seized control. It became Christian territory under Emperor Constantine in the 300s. Muslims gained control in the 600s. The crusaders reigned for eighty-eight years only to let it slip away. In perhaps the irony of all ironies, Jerusalem came under Jewish control once again in 1948. It was a catastrophic development for Muslims who had fought valiantly for centuries to consolidate the Holy Land. Currently the issue is a stalemate, and the truce is fragile. It is unlikely Israel will remain in this heightened state of tension forever. Something will have to give. Only God knows what, or who, will give. As for now, three religious civilizations regard this geographical epicenter as their own.

While Jerusalem attracts a disproportionate amount of attention when it comes to the Middle East, the fact remains that it constitutes only a small part of the region's population. There are around twelve million people in Israel and the Occupied Territories, but approximately 300 million people in the Middle East. Israel, however, is the only nation in the Middle East that does not have a Muslim majority, making it quite unique. This fact is also a source of deep resentment by many Muslims in the region.

Nevertheless, while the Middle East is over 93% Islamic, it is not monolithic. Islam is not a monolithic religion; it has several variations that emphasize certain leaders or different approaches to being Islamic. Generally speaking, there are three sects in Islam: Sunni (by far the largest), Shia (majority in Iraq, Iran, Bahrain, Lebanon, and Azerbaijan), and Sufi (mystical forms of Islam). There are many other factions and sub-sects as well, primarily within Shia Islam, such as the Zaydis, Ismailis, and Ithna Ashari ("Twelvers").

The Middle East also features quite a diverse array of ethnicities: Arabic, Turkish, Kurdish, and Persian may be the largest people-groups, but there are many others such as Jewish and Uyghur peoples, and many sub-groups. Languages also vary, depending on the country. Various Arabic and Persian dialects are prominent, but English, French, Syriac, Hebrew, and Urdu are also spoken.

Today, there remains a small Christian witness in the Middle East, but virtually all these churches are in decline. Christians produce fewer children than Muslims generally, and accelerating emigration has impoverished the Middle East of many of its greatest Christian talents. Why live an unequal or persecuted existence in Iraq, Turkey, or Iran when great opportunities exist in the West? Nevertheless, in pockets across the Middle East, one encounters Roman Catholic, Armenian, Greek, Syriac, Chaldean, Maronite, Assyrian, and other ancient churches pressing on, almost in defiance. There are a few scattered Protestant movements across the land. The hand-writing is on the wall, however. Barring divine intervention, Christian presence will continue to slip.

To illustrate my point, esteemed historian of Christianity, Philip Jenkins, published an important book in 2008 with the ominous title, *The Lost History of Christianity: The Thousand-Year Golden Age of the Church in the Middle East, Africa, and Asia—and How It Died*. During his lecture tour Jenkins visited my institution, Pepperdine University. I had invited members of the Los Angeles Assyrian Orthodox community to attend. While they appreciated Jenkins's knowledge, some of them stood in protest after the lecture. They exclaimed that Christianity had not died in the Middle East. They have relatives who live at risk each day in order to preserve their ancient and prestigious Christian history. However, their protests really only strengthened Jenkins's thesis. Each of them had immigrated to the United States for safety and security, far removed from the seemingly inevitable demise of Christianity in their homeland.

Eastern European Christianity

Eastern Europe is the heartland of Orthodox Christianity. However, Orthodoxy comes in several different forms. While the Roman Catholic Church is
relatively homogenous, Orthodoxy tends to be organized along nationalistic
lines, which accounts for many of the differences. Russian Orthodoxy will have
a slightly different ethos from Greek Orthodoxy. While the national churches

of Romania and Bulgaria share much, they have developed differently according to their national histories and cultural distinctions. The Orthodox tradition has developed a word for this phenomenon: autocephaly. Each national church has its own autonomous, clerical hierarchy. The head of each national church reports to no one individual authority. The head of the Catholic Church is the Bishop of Rome. Orthodoxy does have an inspirational figurehead in the patriarch of Constantinople. However, the Ecumenical Patriarch—as he is known in the Orthodox world—is under the authority of the historic Christian councils.

Roman Catholics and Eastern Orthodox Christians share a tremendous amount in theology, practice, worship, and history. The primary issue that divides them is authority. This debate takes us back to a long-standing, complex debate in the history of Christianity. Who gets to dictate the rules? Who has the right to determine theology? Historically, the Western church argued final authority rests with the pope in Rome. The Eastern churches concluded that no authority is greater than that of the seven Ecumenical Councils: Nicea I in 325, Constantinople I in 381, Ephesus in 431, Chalcedon in 451, Constantinople II in 553, Constantinople III in 680, and Nicea II in 787.

Early in Christianity, a special significance developed for the role of the bishop. Bishops became, essentially, protectors of church doctrine and praxis. Normally a bishop had jurisdiction over a diocese—a Greek word meaning administration. The bishop was in charge of a geographical area consisting of numerous churches, priests, monasteries, convents, and other church institutions. While Rome developed a top-down system, the Orthodox churches considered bishops more or less equal. Special prominence, however, has always been accorded to the five great patriarchs of early Christianity: Jerusalem, Antioch, Alexandria, Rome, and Constantinople. While the bishops of these five cities are uniquely esteemed in Orthodoxy, major theological decisions require the participation of the bishops worldwide.

This disagreement reached a head in the year 1054 in a cataclysmic incident known as the Great Schism. No longer was Christianity united; it was rent into two. This incident explains the core differences between what we now call the Roman Catholic Church and the Eastern Orthodox Churches. It is very unfortunate that two major splits characterize the history of Christianity: the split between East and West in 1054 and the additional split in the West between Protestants and Catholics in 1517. It is striking that the Protestant Reformation—so crucial for understanding Western civilization—carries little meaning or significance in the Eastern churches. Orthodox Christians understand it this way: Catholics broke away in 1054 and simply broke again in 1517. Christendom will be reunited when Rome and all of its Protestant creations return to the Orthodox fold one day. God willing,

Christianity will unite in the future. We are getting ahead of ourselves, however. Let us step back and look at the bigger picture of Christianity in Eastern Europe.

Eastern Europe consists of twenty-five countries. Most of these countries touch the Baltic Sea in the north or the Adriatic Sea in the south. Geographically and demographically, Eastern Europe is dominated by Russia, by far the largest country in the world. Its population of 140 million is easily the largest in Eastern Europe. Russia remains dominant in Eastern Europe in many ways: politically, economically, and for our purposes, theologically. The Russian church is by far the largest Orthodox body on earth.

There are countries in this cultural block that Westerners, Americans in particular, know very little about. Few conferences are held in Latvia, Lithuania, or Montenegro. Rarely do my world traveling students even think to traverse Estonia or Bosnia-Herzegovina. There are reasons for this lack of experience with Eastern Europe. The Cold War damaged East-West relations to the point that the two sides of the Iron Curtain continue to have lingering suspicions. Additionally, the Great Schism of 1054 caused a deep and long-standing fracture. Politically, Eastern Europe is only now emerging from many of the factors that made it something of a reclusive society throughout the twentieth century.

It would be a mistake to protract the status quo of ignorance about Eastern Europe. Western church historians in particular need to know about Eastern Christianity. The Orthodox churches have preserved the most ancient forms of Christianity on earth. The Armenian Orthodox Church dates back to 301. Georgia's national church was founded in 326. Eastern Orthodoxy presents rich treasures to strengthen a Christian's faith. In 2009 I went on pilgrimage to Armenia with an Orthodox priest and was deeply impacted.

The Armenian Apostolic Orthodox Church is a poster child for Christian perseverance in the face of persecution. When Christians study the biblical book of First Peter—about faithfulness during trials—they should first examine the history of Armenian Orthodoxy. Despite centuries of Persian and later Islamic encroachment, their national faith stands firm. While the Armenian genocides of the late nineteenth and early twentieth centuries in the Ottoman Empire were catastrophic, Marxist atheism came along soon after and shoved its ideology down Armenian throats for nearly another century. Despite Soviet pressure for atheization, the Armenian faith stood firm.

Some of the holiest, most sacred events of my life took place in Armenia. I was accompanied by a group of college-aged pilgrims and a priest, Ter (Father) Avedis. I was given a rare opportunity, to see, firsthand, the oldest Christian country in the world. I will be able to share so many learning experiences with my students for years to come. My understanding of Orthodox Christianity in Eastern Europe was profoundly shaped by:

- worshipping God in a church built in the year 430;
- hearing angelic, haunting *a cappella* liturgies, which harken back to the first centuries of Christian faith;
- discussing the Armenian genocide with people whose lives have been indelibly impacted by the twentieth century's first holocaust;
- crawling down into the cave where St. Gregory the Illuminator was imprisoned for over a decade and emerged to become the founder of Christianity in Armenia;
- drinking from a spring inside the sanctuary of Geghard—a spectacular and labyrinthine monastic compound built into rock-cliff walls in the twelfth and thirteenth centuries; and
- eating *lavash* (Armenian flatbread) fresh out of the tandoor oven, wrapped around fresh goat meat and herbs, along with the Armenian national fruit—apricots—known affectionately in Armenia as *tsrian* (the scientific name for the apricot is "prunus armeniaca"—as they grow everywhere in Armenia).

The most important learning experience I had in Armenia was meeting the Armenian Catholicos—Armenia's pope—in a private audience at the Mother See of Holy Etchmiadzin, Armenia's spiritual capital. His Holiness, Karekin II, talked with us about his church. In a dramatic moment during our meeting, he decried Western Protestant and Catholic missionaries who flooded Eastern Europe when the Iron Curtain fell. This opportunism caused deep resentment for the Orthodox leaders who had given their lives preserving their precious faith for nearly a century of totalitarian, atheist rule. Karekin argued that the evangelization of this post-Soviet society was a task for Armenians, not foreigners. The moment was awkward because I distinctly remember my church and many other American churches sending scores of missionaries to Eastern Europe when the opportunity presented itself. Deep resentment persists from that chapter in history, but it seems the Orthodox churches are beginning to make real progress. Of the twenty-five countries in the Eastern European block, Orthodoxy is the largest religious group in fourteen of them. The Roman Catholic Church dominates in six: Croatia, the Czech Republic, Hungary, Lithuania, Poland, and Slovakia. Four Eastern European nations are Islamic majority: Albania, Azerbaijan, Bosnia-Herzegovina, and Kosovo. Estonia is unique in the region as it is Protestant.

What is the future of Orthodoxy in Eastern Europe? Based on current trends, it is not good. Vladimir Putin has repeatedly referred to low fertility as "Russia's gravest problem."[18] Eastern Europe has, by far, the lowest fertility rates in the world. Each woman has only 1.38 children on average in her life. Some social scientists have referred to this unprecedented phenomenon as auto-genocide. In addition, Eastern Europeans flock out of this cultural block annually for greener pastures in the West.

We cannot have a discussion of Eastern Europe without acknowledging the elephant in the room: communism. On the surface, communism actually has parallels to the teachings of Jesus: longing for a just society, economic equality, and a deep concern for the lowest classes. However, historically it tends to morph into totalitarianism, nepotism, unchallenged political aristocracy, and a trenchant hostility towards religion.

Communism swept across Russia from 1917 to 1991. The Soviet Union was a political leviathan that controlled Eastern Europe for nearly seventy years. Lenin, Stalin, and Khrushchev wantonly persecuted the Church. Stalin's orgy of death pummeled this once vibrant Christian culture to ruin. Khrushchev famously spoke of his dream to humiliate the last Russian Orthodox priest on national television for all to see. Hundreds of thousands of Christians were martyred during the Soviet period. Between 1917 and 1943, forty-five thousand priests were slaughtered.[19] This number corresponds almost exactly to the number of Roman Catholic priests serving in the United States today. It would be equivalent to lining up every single priest in America's largest denomination—the Roman Catholic Church—for execution.

We end this section by highlighting the more illustrious events in this region's Christian history. That brings us to Cyril and Methodius, two of the greatest missionaries in all of Christian history. Saints Cyril and Methodius were Byzantine Greeks from Thessaloniki. They had it on their hearts to evangelize the Slavs. They had remarkable success. Known today as the "apostles to the Slavs," they are deeply venerated in Eastern Orthodoxy almost on par with the Apostles themselves. Using Greek letters, they created a Slavic alphabet for this illiterate people group. Today that alphabet is called Cyrillic. The Russian Orthodox liturgy is still conducted in this language, affectionately referred to as Old Church Slavonic. An irony of history is while Cyril and Methodius worked to make the Bible available in the vernacular of the people, it calcified and is today a difficult language, known only to the clergy.

The work of Cyril and Methodius set the stage for that great event recounted in chapter one of this book: the Christianization of the Rus peoples in 988. Between 988 and 1015, Vladimir systematically converted the people of his empire to Christianity, to such a point that Moscow was designated "the third Rome." The evangelization of Ukraine and Russia occurred through the efforts of monks. Monasteries proliferated throughout the land. Whereas once isolated monasteries had initially endeavored to separate themselves from society, the masses would inevitably follow. Frontier Russia was a world of churches and monasteries, with small towns built around them. Vestiges of this system remain to the present.

The most important figure in this era is the Russian Saint Sergius of Radonezh (1314–1392). Sergius tapped into the Russian zeitgeist with his saintliness, care for the poor, and very humble lifestyle. On the one hand, he was considered the most important monk in Russia's sprawling monastic system; on the other, he never abandoned the daily routine of manual labor and living an ascetic life.

One of the reasons Sergius is so revered in Russia is because he lived a long, saintly life in the midst of the "Mongol Tatar Yoke." Between 1240 and 1480 Mongolian Muslims pillaged the capital city of Kiev and gained control of the Russian land mass. Russia, however, is not unique in this regard: "all Orthodox countries have been, at one time or another, under the domination of Islam."[20] Thus there is great tension between Muslim and Orthodox communities in Eastern Europe, most of all in the Balkans, where wars and even genocides have taken a heavy toll. Three distinct civilizations fought tooth and nail to win this strategic swath of land. While the dust of war continues to settle, what remains is a tenuous situation. Islam dominates in Albania and Kosovo. Roman Catholicism can claim Croatia. Orthodoxy holds sway in Bulgaria, Greece, Macedonia, Montenegro, Serbia, and Romania. Bosnia-Herzegovina is a mixture of Islam and Christianity.

We cannot talk about Eastern Orthodox Christianity without mentioning the Greek Orthodox Church. Koine Greek was the language of the New Testament and continues to be the liturgical language of the Greek church. The Greek language, because of its importance in the spread of early Christianity, has enmeshed itself into many different cultures and churches in Eastern Europe and beyond. Thus, people often refer to Eastern Orthodoxy as Greek Orthodoxy. Due to the Orthodox principle of autocephaly however, each Orthodox country may not interfere with other national churches. Regardless, the Greek Orthodox Church has been unusually influential due to the Greek language as well as numerous Greek theologians, mystics, and monks whose impact has been felt well beyond the confines of Greece.

Greece contains an illustrious monastic tradition. Perhaps the most important monastic center in the world is on a peninsula in Macedonia, northern Greece. It is known to the Orthodox as Mount Athos and is today a World Heritage Site. This extremely pious and isolated corner of the world is reserved exclusively for ascetic Christian monks who have given their life completely to prayer, worship, and labor. These twenty lonely, self-sufficient monastic communities scattered about the holy mountain inspire Christian monks worldwide. Women are not allowed for obvious reasons. Legend has it that even female animals have been eradicated from this entire peninsula so as not to distract monks from their prayers during the mating seasons.

Western European Christianity

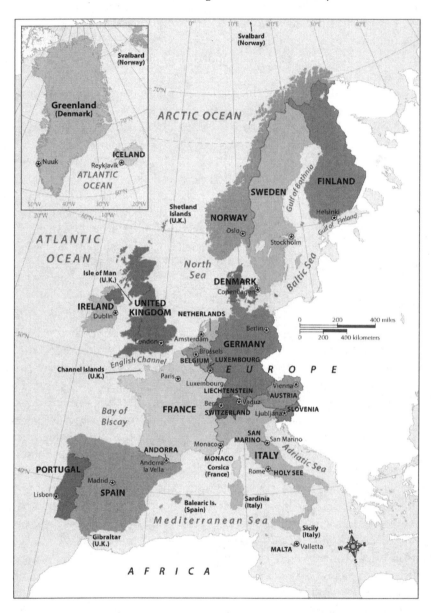

Rarely in history has an entire cultural block changed as radically as has Western Europe in the last century. This cultural block used to be referred to as "Christendom." Led by the Roman Catholic pope and the Holy Roman Emperor, Western Europe was, undeniably, the heart and soul of the Christian world. In recent decades this situation has completely changed.

When I travel to Western Europe, I stand in awe of the ornate basilicas, splendid monasteries, and breathtaking cathedrals. Western Europe was a thriving, bustling, vibrant Christian world where monks chanted, church bells rang, choirs sang, and an air of holiness penetrated all strata of society. Today, however, the Christian infrastructure looks more like a ghost town. Sure, we see tourists huddled around a guide, teenagers skateboarding on the sidewalks in front of the churches, and quaint cafés surrounding these lonely structures. However, these priceless, cavernous monuments of a Christian past are empty.

The link between Christianity and Western culture was suddenly broken in the twentieth century. Scholars debate why and how this could have happened. Some blame widespread resentment against the coupling of Christianity and politics. Others blame corruption in the churches. Still others believe the two World Wars may have rocked this part of the world to such an extent that they are dazed and confused. How could God let Western Europe, the Christian world, erupt into such barbaric violence on a scale humanity had never seen before or since? How could the Christian world fall into such blatantly immoral sins such as rampant pedophilia and hideous cover-ups? How could Nazi ideology have captivated the minds of Germany, perhaps the most brilliant people on earth? Whatever the case, Christian faith spiraled downward rapidly to the point that many churches now serve as pubs, warehouses, carpet stores, apartments, and mosques. The lucky ones get restored as museums. The era of Western Europe's Christian culture is finished. At least for now.

There are signs Christianity might be making a comeback in Western Europe, but it is not the Western Europeans who are responsible for this phenomenon. Rather it is immigrants. Caribs, Poles, and Africans of all stripes are setting up shop in store fronts, house churches, and in the back rooms of gigantic basilicas. While there is hope Christianity is making a comeback, it will take a lot longer to recover than it took for the region to secularize.

The secularization of Western Europe was breathtakingly rapid. In 1906, Western Europe was ablaze with Christian revivals, a massive and worldwide missionary enterprise, and an unbridled ambition to "evangelize the world in this generation." This catch-phrase was Nobel Peace Laureate John Mott's rally cry that resounded throughout the entire Western world. Ironically, a century later in 2006, Pope Benedict traveled to his native Germany and said basically the opposite, "We are no longer able to hear God ...God strikes us as pre-scientific, no longer suited for our age." The Bishop of Rome came to terms with the reality of the situation: God had seemingly left the building.

Led by Germany, France, United Kingdom, Italy and Spain, Western Europe consists of thirty countries and territories, and all of them, nominally, are Christian majority. By human standards, Western Europe is a healthy and prosperous society. Western Europe has the highest life expectancy in the world at 79.6 years. Like Eastern Europe, however, Western Europe has a low fertility rate (1.56). As more people retire, the high standard of living enjoyed in recent years is becoming difficult to sustain. Europe's economic crisis, punctuated by failed economies in several countries, has made this region of the world revisit its values and priorities. Western Europe's median age is easily the highest in the world, at 41. A reliance on immigration is necessary to pay the bills; it may be the only way Christianity can recover its lost ground. That being said, there is a new religion in town: Islam.

Muslims have been moving to Western Europe *en masse* since the end of colonial rule in the mid-twentieth century. As some scholars like to point out, the empire is striking back. Former French, Dutch, and British colonies have flooded to Western Europe for a better life, and they bring their religion with them. In some cases they would rather not assimilate. They prefer to mold and shape their society more along the lines of what they were used to back home. In London, for example, one easily finds Islamic neighborhoods. Some cultural enclaves in Western Europe have even gone so far as to set up their own civil courts separated from European society. They have prolific supporters. In 2008, the Archbishop of Canterbury, Dr. Rowan Williams, argued that Islamic Sharia law "seems unavoidable."[21] Many Muslim communities practice Sharia law anyway because of their background and great esteem for their clergy. This idea is not as radical as it might seem at first; Orthodox Jews have had separate civil courts in Western Europe for years.

Western Europe is today around 80% Christian, at least nominally. Out of these three-hundred million Christians, two-thirds of them are Roman Catholic and one-third is Protestant. Of the Western European countries, eighteen are Roman Catholic and twelve are Protestant. Geographically, we can think of it this way: the North is Protestant, and the South is Roman Catholic. Generally, in Western Europe, a country will be *either* Protestant or Catholic. There are a few exceptions to this such as Germany and the Netherlands, which are about half and half, but in general the countries are decidedly one or the other. Just to illustrate, Denmark's, Greenland's and Norway's Christians are 99% Protestant. Spain's, Italy's and France's Christians are over 90% Roman Catholic. The notable exception to this North-Protestant, South-Catholic typology is Ireland, which is decidedly Catholic.

Why is Western Europe divided like this? There are two significant dates that explain the story rather well: 1517 and 1648. In 1517, Martin Luther birthed the Protestant movement with his declaration that the Word of God, the Bible, was the key to understanding God's will in our lives. Luther's ideas were in utter opposition to the Roman Catholic Church, which argued that salvation was available exclusively through the church. Almost immediately after Luther's movement began, Western Europe erupted into a series of religiously motivated wars. In 1648 the Treaty of Westphalia stopped the bleeding. Essentially, the treaty declared that if your king or ruler was Roman Catholic, you need to be Roman Catholic. If he had become Protestant, then follow Protestantism. The Protestant-Catholic wars make clear just how religious Western Europe was during that period. Generations of fighting men gave their lives for either the pope or the protestant principle that each man should have the right to interpret the Bible for himself.

Let us not forget, however, that Western Europe had many centuries of a united Christian empire under the jurisdiction of the Roman bishop, the pope. How did Western Europe become so thoroughly Christianized? We know from the Bible that Christianity has deep roots in Western Europe. Paul was martyred in Rome. Church tradition tells us Peter spent time in Rome. Generations of faithful Christian evangelists made their way around the Mediterranean, over the mountains, up the plentiful rivers, and through the dense forests, all to bring the good news to a people who had no idea about this Jewish rabbi from Palestine.

Emperor Constantine (reigned 306–337) stands head and shoulders above the rest when it comes to the question of who is responsible for the evangelization of Western Europe. Prior to Constantine's Edict of Milan in 313, Christianity was illegal in the Roman Empire. However, Constantine became increasingly enamored with Christianity throughout his long reign. Christianity became not just protected under Constantine, but extremely privileged, due partly to his mother Helena's influence. Constantine began to pay the clergy from state coffers, erect churches all over his empire, and even sponsor major theological conferences. The Council of Nicea in 325 represents perhaps the clearest example in Christian history of a secular ruler explicitly cooperating with the church. Constantine's successors continued this strongly pro-Christian agenda to such an extent that by the end of that century, it was illegal *not* to be a Christian.

Western European Christianity developed in a way slightly different from Eastern Europe. In the East, the base language was Greek, yet there was a strong emphasis on the vernacular of the people being evangelized. In the West, Latin was the language of the church. The church father Jerome (347–420) translated the Bible into Latin and ultimately paved the way for what became a distinctly Western form of Christian faith. Ironically, Jerome's *Vulgate* was intended to put the Bible into the language of the people. In time, however, Latin evolved into a *lingua sacra* used only by the church and the uppermost segments of society. Jerome would turn over in his grave if he knew that his translation was definitive until the 1960s—long after anyone knew how to speak Latin. At the Second Vatican Council in the 1960s, the Roman Catholic Church finally conceded to worldwide pressure that church services incorporate languages intelligible to the masses.

Christianity became legal in Western Europe in the 300s and began spreading upward to the farthest reaches of the continent. It would be impossible to catalogue the thousands of men and women who gave their lives traversing land and water to offer good news. Let us however highlight a few of the more notable figures:

- St. Patrick (387–460) was the famous Scottish slave who evangelized Ireland.
- St. Benedict of Nursia (480–543) was the father of the illustrious Western monastic movement. His *Benedictine Rule* for monks was one of the most important medieval writings.
- St. Columba (521–597) based himself at Iona and evangelized the Picts of Scotland. His name is associated with Celtic Christianity, and he often receives credit for establishing a highly sophisticated culture of literacy in the region.
- St. Boniface (672–754) was "the apostle to the Germans." With great courage, Boniface challenged paganism and spread the gospel. Dramatic stories depict him taking up his axe and felling the sacred trees of pagan tribes.
- St. Ansgar (801–865) is the apostle to the North. He missionized the Nordic lands, and eventually became the first bishop of Denmark and Sweden.

The year 1000 is significant. That is the year Iceland, the last Scandinavian outpost, formally adopted Christianity. It took a millennium to fully evangelize Western Europe. Of course pockets of paganism remained. Evangelizing a geographical culture block is never *complete*, but at least the gospel had been proclaimed across all of the major thoroughfares, touched all the major islands, and in some cases, had penetrated to the very depths of certain people groups of the Western European landmass. This was Christendom—the kingdom of Christ on earth. The pope, the bishop of Rome, was its vicar.

In the first millennium of Western European Christianity, no year was more critical than 800. On Christmas day of that year, the greatest Frankish medieval emperor, "Charles the Great," officially allied himself to Christianity when Pope Leo III crowned him Emperor of the Romans. Western Europe no longer needed to look east to Byzantium for protection. Thus began a reciprocal rule that strengthened and expanded the Western Roman Empire in profound ways. "Charlemagne's" rule is associated with the Carolingian Renaissance—an era of intellectual, cultural, and spiritual revival. The Carolingian advances brought stability, allowed a large class of scholars to emerge, and made this geographical region home to one of the more sophisticated civilizations at the time.

Western Europe's second millennium was one of continued expansion, influence, and development. The Roman Catholic Church grew to unprecedented, towering influence, seen in the massive church buildings dominating the landscape. From the southern tip of Italy to the northern outposts of Scandinavia, the church was vibrant, pious and very, very powerful. Western Europe birthed the concept of the university in the twelfth century. Leading the way were the universities of Bologna (1088), Paris (1150), Oxford (1167), Cambridge (1209), and Salamanca (1218). Based on the ideal of academic freedom, the university brought together scholars and teachers for a common purpose: intellectual progress. Rooted in the monasteries and convents of early medieval Christianity, the university has become one of the chief contributions of Western Europe to the wider world. Medieval Western Europe is unimaginable apart from the church; modern Western Europe is unimaginable apart from the university.

Allowing scholars, artists, and other intellectuals to have free reign in developing their ideas had many upsides and downsides. The upsides were obvious: new ideas in the arts and sciences, dramatic improvements in technology, and critical thinking in unprecedented ways. Scholars struggle to articulate what was happening during the fourteenth and fifteenth centuries, but it has become known popularly as "the Renaissance."

The downside to these remarkable advances in human capability was divergence of opinion, which lies at the heart of the intellectual pursuit. Copernicus and Galileo, for example, demonstrated that we live in a heliocentric universe. To Rome, this idea was heretical. Philosophers such as Pico Mirandola (1463-1494) began to argue for the dignity of the human person. This cultural rebirth had a religious dimension to it that would culminate in the life and work of a German Augustinian monk: Martin Luther.

Martin Luther's (1483-1546) significance touches all areas of the humanities in an unparalleled way. Before Luther, people relied on the conclusions of the church to tell them what was true and right. Luther challenged that idea by teaching one should first go to the source itself rather than rely on secondhand knowledge, especially when it comes to one's salvation. God has given us his will in the Bible, and each person will stand before God alone on Judgment Day. Luther advocated a variety of methods for discerning truth:

- Ad fontis ("to the fountains")—a concept meaning we should return to the most ancient sources of knowledge possible;
- Sola scriptura ("Scripture alone")—in matters of faith, we should look solely to God's will as revealed in the Bible, not the traditions of man;
- Sola fide ("by faith alone")—salvation is based on one's faith, not on works, so that no one can boast; and

- The Priesthood of All Believers—the biblically rooted idea that each person is fully qualified to understand God's will and serve as a minister in his kingdom.

Luther was not the first to make these statements. What made him unique was that he did not burn at the stake for these heretical and inflammatory teachings. Rather he succeeded through the power of his prolific pen, combined with the power of the printing press.

To half of Western Europe, Luther was a criminal and a blasphemer who escaped death because of the political protection offered to him by his ruler, Frederick the Wise. To the other half, Luther was a spiritual giant who triggered much needed reform in the church, liberated a laity held captive, and sparked a new era in Western civilization that we characterize, simply, "modern." Scholars debate Luther's influence on the modern mind. Even if there is no consensus, it is clear: after Luther, everything changed. Everything.

Intellectual freedom soared to heights unknown in the wake of Luther's challenges. Literacy rates soared. People wanted to read for themselves, whether Luther was right or not. To satisfy this hunger for knowledge, Luther translated the Bible into the vernacular of his people: German. Luther's Bible is still revered in Protestant Germany, and it impacted the German language in a way comparable to how the King James Version affected English.

It is difficult to exaggerate Martin Luther's contribution to the great flowering of ideas and innovation in Western Europe. He put into motion an intellectual posture, a spirit of questioning, and a quest for truth that propelled Western Europe to unrivaled superpower status in the centuries to come. Western Europe and its offspring civilizations circled the globe, annexed nearly the entire world, and pooled knowledge on a scale never seen before.

Luther's chief idea has been described as dangerous. If each person in society is free to think independently, then might chaos break out? It certainly did for a time. However, the idea proved irrepressible and deeply satisfying. Luther's drive to think independently is an idea taken for granted in Western societies. Democracy is based on the notion of free thinking and the ability to choose. The individual pursuit of truth is considered one of the most sacred, most cherished values a human being can possess.

We are left with a quizzical situation in Western Europe today. Did Luther's breakthrough sink religiosity in Western Europe altogether? Is Luther the reason Western Europe turned away from religion? Certainly the argument can be made, although Luther would hardly have considered his ideas to be the seedbed of secularization.

Latin American and Caribbean Christianity

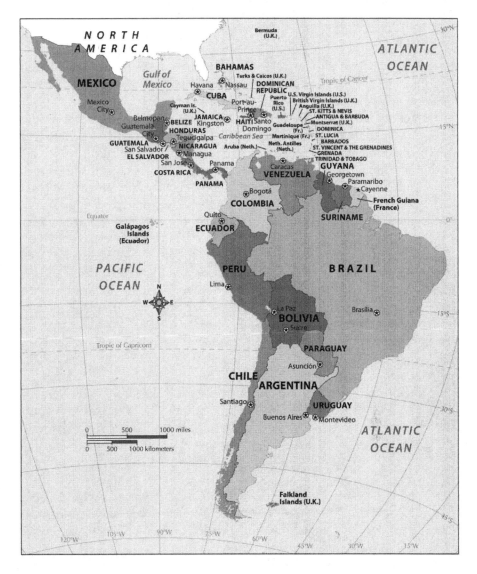

I write this portion of the chapter from an office in Buenos Aires, Argentina. This country is almost completely Roman Catholic. I have heard it said the very air you breathe in Latin American is Roman Catholic. In the case of Buenos Aires, this must be a positive attribute since Buenos Aires means "good air."

No continent in the world is more Catholic than Latin America. Protestants are somewhat rare here. Statistically, Latin America and the

Caribbean are about 80% Catholic, and the entire cultural block is unimaginable apart from the Roman Catholic Church. This region of the world is not only the most Catholic; it is the most *Christian* place on earth. Around 93% of the people claim to be Christian. That is over half a billion people. Latin America is rightly called one of the heartlands of world Christianity today.

We can say, with some reservation, that the population within Latin America and the Caribbean shares a cultural history of colonization, (mainly) Roman Catholic Christianity, and an ethos defined largely by three major people-groups: Iberian settlers from Spain and Portugal, indigenous peoples whose presence in the region pre-date the European-stock by thousands of years, and black Africans who were imported to provide labor for the massively expanding commercial enterprises that dominated the sixteenth through the twentieth century. There are other groups that a survey like this has to overlook such as the many Indians (from India) who went to Guyana, Suriname, and Trinidad and Tobago to work the farms in the aftermath of the abolition of slavery.

This region is highly populated, with nearly 600 million people and a robust fertility rate. In terms of economic development, Latin America is a mixed bag. Millions of people are without basic resources, yet some cities appear as developed as Western Europe. Visitors to Latin America are often struck by the economic disparity—there may be a large barrio or slum-neighborhood located right next to a high-rise American hotel used for international business and conferences. The economic situation reflects this polarization, and is today one of the great problems in the region. The wealth is concentrated into the hands of a few; however, the poor are really poor and to a large extent neglected. Millions of people in Latin America and the Caribbean (notably Haiti) lack access to clean water and decent sanitation technology. Latin America is just now beginning to make inroads into these complicated issues with long and painful histories.

The history of Christianity in Latin America is well documented. Christopher Columbus (1451–1506) arrived to the New World on October 12, 1492. He landed at an island they called Hispaniola, modern-day Dominican Republic and Haiti. Columbus was convinced to the end of his life that he had reached islands near India, thus the misnomer "Indians."

Few episodes in history can be considered truly revolutionary on a global scale. In the case of Columbus, however, a magnificent revelation occurred. Before him, world maps simply had water in the location of North and South America. It made perfect sense for Columbus to sail west and get to India. The only question was how much water separated Spain from India. Within a few decades, it became clear: Columbus had sailed into a gargantuan land mass. World maps would never be the same after him. This chapter deals with geography. Few moments in world history have been as significant, geographically, as Columbus's serendipitous discovery.

When Columbus arrived, there were over fifty million people living in the Americas, around one-eighth of the world's population. Upon discovering that the indigenous inhabitants had no iron, Columbus realized the fruits of this civilization were his for the taking. Within a very short period of time, the region we know as Latin America and the Caribbean had been conquered by Spain and Portugal and its people subjected to foreign powers.

There are forty-seven countries and territories in Latin America and the Caribbean. The majority of these are tiny Caribbean islands that give us a glimpse of what the era of European colonialism looked like—a hodge-podge of European languages and customs. Many Caribbean islands still connect themselves to Europe politically. There are over seven thousand islands in the Caribbean containing a plethora of cultures and subcultures. West of the Caribbean Sea is the Central American isthmus consisting of several countries stretching from Mexico in the north to Panama in the south. South America is easier to define. It consists of twelve countries and one territory, ranging from Columbia and Venezuela in the north to Chile and Argentina in the south. Brazil dominates South America and is easily the largest and most populated nation in the entire cultural block.

It did not take long for Spain and Portugal to cash in on their discovery. The Latin American and Caribbean lands offered copious resources that profited European economies for centuries. The first tribe Columbus encountered was the Tainos, who spoke Arawak. Next were the Caribs, Guanajatabeyes and Ciboneys. As the conquistadors—the professional conquerors—moved inland, they met many more. However, nothing prepared them for the magnificent Aztec Empire, based at Tenochtitlan, and later, the Inca Empire, based at Cuzco, Peru. Europeans were in awe of these two sophisticated civilizations. The Spanish explorers were amazed by the great towers, extensive waterways, cotton clothes, organized orchards and gardens, and sophisticated art. Everything was swiftly destroyed, however, in one of the most complete destructions of civilization on record.

While the conquistadors admired some of the cultures they encountered, they were not hired to stand in awe. Their paychecks came from Spain and they were paid to conquer, and they did, at will. They took indigenous women as their concubines, leading to a highly complicated racial system based on blood purity. Those who topped the scale had the highest percentage of Spanish blood, but in time, the entire system became complicated, especially when African slaves were brought in. Europeans developed categories for this mixed—*mestizo*—cornucopia of racial classification. The purest blood was considered that of the *peninsulares*—people actually born in Spain. Next were *criollos*—Spaniards born in the New World. Non-European blood was considered impure. Europeans thought of themselves atop a racial purity scale with everyone else below them in dizzying classifications.

The indigenous and mestizo people living under colonial domination were the lucky ones. The vast majority of Indians were killed either by European diseases or by the sword in very one-sided battles. UCLA professor Jared Diamond estimates that smallpox killed half the Aztecs, including their emperor.[22] The natives had no immunity against these diseases. There are many theories about this phenomenon. Some claim various plagues devastating Europe's population in the preceding centuries had strengthened the European immune system to disproportionate levels compared to New World inhabitants. To the indigenous, it was as if God was on the side of the Spaniards. Cortes and Pizarro overcame unbelievable odds in their complete domination of the Aztec and Inca civilizations. Pizarro's army of two hundred Spanish soldiers defeated roughly eighty thousand Incas to consolidate the western side of Latin America in 1532. Church historian Adrian Hastings wrote "Seldom has genocide, actually in no way intended, been so rapid or so complete."[23] Spaniards needed Indians to work the fields, but few were left to do the job after these brutal campaigns. The shortage of labor spawned the era of slavery in the New World beginning in the year 1517, ironically just as the Protestant Reformation was unleashed in Europe. Millions of African slaves were imported through the centuries, leading to a tripartite society of Whites, Blacks, and Indians, with all manner of mixed combinations as well.

The European "discovery" of the New World triggered a violent and unsavory era in human history. The life of an Indian or African slave was a life of subjugation and injustice. There were critics however. The most famous was Bartolomé de Las Casas (1484–1566). Las Casas was a Spanish priest involved in the conquering of Cuba. He reaped a bountiful harvest of land and serfs. His conscience was pricked, however, when he was overcome by the shocking events happening all around him: arbitrary murders, regular beatings, serial rape, and enslavement on a breathtaking scale. After rising to the position of bishop of Guatemala, he became an activist, fighting for the rights of the indigenous and the African. Late in his career, he denied the forgiveness of sins to slave owners in his diocese.

Justo Gonzalez, a historian of Latin American Christianity, describes Christianity in the region as Janus-faced. One face was hell-bent on converting these people, no matter the cost. This face reflected a Christianity wedded to empire. Behind the veneer of saving souls was an institution that legitimated centuries of violent rule in collusion with the dominant Spanish and Portuguese governments. The other face was one of protest and outrage. It considered this deplorable Constantinian Christianity dangerous if not illegitimate. This second face condemned the insane inhumanity. To this day, the soil cries out. It is unfortunate that the most Christianized cultural block in the world has a catalogue of crimes and injustices of such a scale. The conversion of Latin America is a profound lesson for those who would wish to bring the world to Christ without regard for basic human rights, human freedom, or equality for all—no matter ones' religion.

Why did so many atrocities occur under the banner of a conquering Christ? Much of the story can be explained with one word: gold. In the Sermon on the Mount, Jesus warned the people with this teaching:

> No one can serve two masters. Either he will hate one and love the other, or he will be devoted to one and despise the other. You cannot serve both God and money.

For Spain and Portugal, gold was money, and Europeans were merciless towards anything that came between themselves and the yellow stone. If there ever was a gold rush, this was it.

Another important issue that helps to explain the European massacres has to do, perhaps surprisingly, with Islam. The year 1492 is, famously, the year Columbus set sail. It is also the year that Ferdinand and Isabella finally conquered Granada with the unconditional surrender of Muhammad XII. Columbus was present when Spain was finally a united Christian empire once again. The Iberian Peninsula had been conquered by Muslims in the year 711 as part of the rapid expansion of Islam. The context of a post-Muslim Spain was one of Christian euphoria. For over seven hundred years, Spain had been ruled by Moors. With Ferdinand and Isabella's surprising triumph, it was clear that southwest Europe was a power on the rise. The event marks a major transition of power in the entire Mediterranean region. Islamic hegemony was in retreat. Europe's gradual ascent would culminate in the twentieth century with European colonialism blanketing the world. Europe's time had come.

Thus, the conquistadors were part of a much larger metanarrative. They had just reclaimed their homeland for Christianity—an event they called the *Reconquista*—and were forging ahead to expand their empire. They subjugated others in the process, much like they had learned from the Moors. It is ironic that those who had lived under foreign rule for so long now aspired to rule over others in foreign parts.

One of the more deplorable chapters of this era had to do with basic human dignity. Many Spaniards and Portuguese, in order to justify their crimes, argued that the Indians were not fully human. While there were detractors, the prevailing view was that natives were naturally inferior to Europeans. In 1550, under Holy Roman Emperor Charles V, a council was held at Valladolid, Spain, to determine whether it was lawful to wage war on Indians before evangelizing them. While Las Casas championed the defense of the Indian, his opponent, Juan Ginés de Sepulveda (1489-1573) argued that Amerindians were "natural slaves." While Las Casas was a prophet ahead of his time,

Sepulveda's argument—rooted in the writings of Aristotle—proved victorious. Las Casas ultimately prevailed, however. His writings are required reading in universities today; Sepulveda's arguments are dismissed as racist and destructive.

While Roman Catholicism is normative in Latin America today, we would be remiss if we did not acknowledge the obvious hybridity that has developed. While Christianity was superimposed on a subjected people, indigenous traditions were often kept alive underneath the surface. No figure illustrates this phenomenon as aptly as Juan Diego—the embodiment of religious hybridity in Latin American Christianity.

Juan Diego (1474-1548) was canonized in 2002 by the Roman Catholic Church as the first indigenous American saint. He witnessed the conquering of Mexico by "Cortes the Killer" in 1521. He and his wife were baptized by Franciscan missionaries three years later. In 1531, while walking on Tepeyac Hill, Juan Diego had a vision of the Virgin Mary. She asked for a chapel to be built for her at that very site. Interestingly, that site was where indigenous people worshipped the mother of all gods, the goddess Tonantzin. Diego went to his bishop, Zumarraga, to relay the Virgin Mary's request, but was denied.

Juan Diego continued to petition without success until one day he performed a miracle. He wrapped flowers in his cape and presented them to Zumarraga. The bishop was impressed for two reasons. First, it was winter time, and flowers had not made their appearance yet. Second, when Juan Diego opened his cape and the flowers fell, an amazing portrait of the Virgin was revealed. That cape is on display in Mexico City today and is the most important pilgrimage site for Latin American Catholics. The Virgin of Guadalupe is especially revered by Mexicans. No symbol captures the imagination or stirs the piety as does the shining Virgin, the Mother of God. In Latin American Christianity, Juan Diego represents the pristine faith of an Indian in a climate of powerlessness, but he also represents an underlying voice of protest in his refusal to capitulate to Zumarraga's refusals.

Many changes are taking place in Latin American Christianity that scholars do not fully understand yet. In the 1980s most Latin American nations began decoupling the church-state relationship that had survived for nearly 500 years. This unsettling change could potentially trigger secularization as it did in Western Europe. Only time will tell if the political marginalization of the Roman Catholic Church will have the same dramatic consequences as in the motherland—Spain and Portugal. Both of those countries are today highly secular.

Another major trend is the rise of Protestantism, primarily Pentecostalism, in this cultural block. In the 1990s, some scholars surmised that Latin America might turn Protestant. That judgment has been dramatically tempered, however. It is clear that Protestantism is rising, and in some cases, its growth has been impressive. For example, Latin America's largest country in both size and population is Brazil. Today, Brazil is around 30% Protestant—a statistic that would have been unthinkable just a century ago. Chile and Guatemala are also around 30% Protestant. There are significant Protestant minorities in several Latin American nations such as Bolivia, Mexico, Peru, and Venezuela. Nevertheless, at present, it is far too early to speak of Latin America's mass defection to Protestant forms of the Christian faith.

A final concept in our discussion of Latin American and Caribbean Christianity is Liberation Theology. In the 1970s, a Peruvian priest named Gustavo Gutierrez published a now famous book: *The Theology of Liberation*. Gutierrez's central argument was that God has a "preferential option for the poor." It proved to be a turning point in the history of Latin American Christianity. Many priests and professors lined up behind Gutierrez in his condemnation of neocolonialism and the exploitation of the poor. Couched in the critique was a fundamental re-imagination of the entire socio-economic paradigm of Latin America and the Caribbean. Liberation Theology has been critiqued as unnecessarily radical and overtly Marxist. Undoubtedly, however, it struck a chord and inspired similar movements all over the world.

The basic conviction of Liberation Theology is that Jesus routinely confronts the elites of society, chastising them for their hoarding of wealth and scandalous victimizing of the poor. Most clearly expressed in the Beatitudes, Jesus' message to the poor is that they are not forgotten. Rather, they are blessed. In the Kingdom of God, they are first, and the rich shall be last—if indeed the rich are even allowed entrance into the Kingdom. In the words of Jesus: "Again I say to you, it is easier for a camel to go through the eye of a needle than for a rich man to enter the kingdom of God."[24]

This new teaching provoked violent resistance from the power holders in Latin American society during the 1970s and 1980s. Many martyrs died for this message during a volatile era. The most significant figure of this period was Archbishop Oscar Romero, who changed course during his career from a status quo protector of the elite to a staunch defender of the poorest of the poor in El Salvador. Romero's defense of the weak cost him his life when he received a bullet into his heart on March 24, 1980, while administering Mass. He knew his death was imminent, but he had counted the cost. His blood spilled onto the altar, mixing with the blood of Christ. Romero's struggle has become the cry of many in this polarized society where the rights of the poor are routinely compromised and the elites only continue to "gain the whole world."

North American Christianity

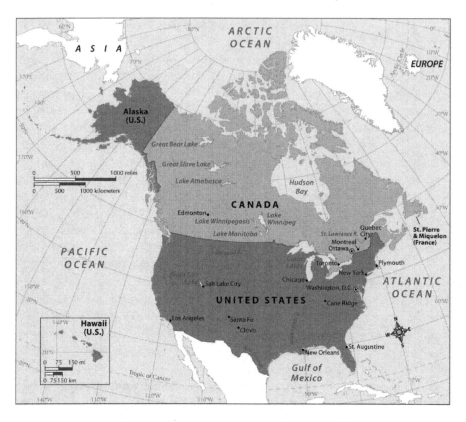

Perhaps no other cultural block has been as profoundly impacted by the geography of Christianity as this one. After European contact, North America was for many years a patchwork quilt of Christian denominations. While today it may be the cultural block easiest to define, it is also one of the most religiously complex. Consisting of the USA and Canada, this entire cultural block is over 80% Christian. However, these two countries have significant differences when it comes to Christianity. American Christianity is 66% Protestant and 33% Catholic. Canadian Christianity is essentially the opposite of that: 68% Catholic and 28% Protestant. North America is vital in understanding world Christianity today. For example, the USA has more Christians than any other nation on earth, and due to globalization, the United States has been a powerful exporter of religion and culture. North America's impact on global Christianity can scarcely be overstated. With the 1906 Azusa Street Revival in Los Angeles and the rise of global Pentecostalism, North American Christianity's influence is reverberating now more than ever before.

While North America is mainly English speaking, it was the Spanish who began founding colonies there in the late 1500s. Saint Augustine, Florida, one of the oldest cities in North America, is evidence of Spanish colonization. However, Florida was ceded to the USA in the early 1800s at a time when the concept of "manifest destiny" was pushing Americans to expand their newly established country as far and wide as they possibly could. America expanded vastly throughout the nineteenth century, rising in prestige and eventually matching their counterparts in Spain, France, and, most importantly, England. What began as a declaration of independence by thirteen fledgling colonies was transforming into an empire.

The geography of North America boomed in 1803 with the Louisiana Purchase. Fourteen American states between Louisiana and Montana were bought from Napoleon for a pittance, adding a million square miles of pristine land to be settled and civilized. It was inevitable that these adventurous Americans would set their sights on California, establishing a nation from sea to shining sea. The American southwest, once part of Mexico, was ceded to the United States in 1848. California was the great prize because of its vast natural resources—including gold—its access to the Pacific, and its developing infrastructure that had been spearheaded by Franciscan missionaries and the Spanish government since 1769. The Oregon Territory, including Idaho and Washington, was ceded by the British in 1846. Russia granted Alaska to the Americans in 1867, and Hawaii was annexed by the USA in 1898.

Canada has a different history altogether. Norseman Leif Ericson from Iceland established a settlement in Newfoundland around the year 1000 that did not last. In all likelihood, Ericson was the first Christian to walk the soil of North America. The French began exploring the St. Lawrence River in 1534. Explorer Jacques Cartier thought he had sailed into China. The Europeans struggled to understand how vast the New World was, and it took decades for them to realize they were not in Asia. Cartier gave the name "Canada" to what was known as New France based on his understanding of an Iroquois word.

Some French Protestants made their way to the New World in the 1560s and established a settlement at Fort Caroline, at modern day Jacksonville, Florida. Spanish Catholics discovered these Protestants and promptly slaughtered them. This episode illustrates how deep the resentments ran during the Protestant-Catholic wars of religion.

It was not until 1603 that the French were able to establish a continuous settlement in the New World. That is the year Samuel de Champlain arrived. In 1608, he founded Quebec City, French Canada's capital and one of the oldest cities in North America. Led by Jacques Marquette (1637–1675), the Jesuits established missions around the Great Lakes. Catholic mission work expanded southward on the Mississippi all the way to the Gulf of Mexico. One can still hear whispers of this venture when visiting New Orleans, a city founded by the French in 1718.

American Christianity could be described as a mosaic; it is a fascinating history with many different colors and shapes:

- While the French flag was raised over Quebec City in 1608, the British beat them to the trigger in 1607 with the Anglican establishment of Jamestown; this region came to be known as Virginia, named after the "Virgin Queen," Elizabeth I.
- Santa Fe, New Mexico, was founded in 1608 by Spanish settlers and became a Catholic stronghold.
- In 1620, the Puritans—English Calvinists—arrived in Massachusetts on the Mayflower. These "pilgrims" came to the New World to establish their own network of autonomous, Congregationalist churches. This fiercely independent form of Christianity is still present in the American consciousness today, evinced by manifold "Bible churches" and "community churches."
- New Amsterdam was established in the 1620s as a Dutch Reformed settlement; today we know it as New York, North America's largest city.
- Maryland was established by Lord Baltimore in 1632 as a refuge for English Catholics.
- Germans began their mass migration to the New World in the 1680s, bringing with them a variety of Christian movements: Mennonites, Moravians, Pietists, Lutherans, and Catholics.
- The Society of Friends had a major role in early American Christianity. William Penn, the most notable "Quaker," founded Pennsylvania in 1661 as an experiment in religious tolerance. Penn and Roger Williams of Rhode Island were the architects of the religious pluralism that is a fundamental part of American Christianity today. Williams was prolific as a theologian, scholar of Native American languages, and founder of the first Baptist church in America. Penn and Williams were ahead of their time; they paved the way for the separation of church and state in the United States.
- Between 1768 and 1784 Franciscan missionary Junipero Serra established several Roman Catholic missions along the coast of California. His legacy is still alive in the religious demographics of the state: the Roman Catholic Church is by far the largest denomination in the state.
- In 1791, Upper Canada—modern-day southern Ontario—was founded as a British colony, establishing an important Anglican presence on the north side of the Great Lakes.

- Saint Herman and his fellow Russian Orthodox priests began their missions to Alaska in the 1790s. Based on Kodiak Island, they had remarkable success working among the Aleutian people.
- Large numbers of Italians and Irish arrived on North America's shores in the late eighteenth and early nineteenth centuries, bolstering the Roman Catholic presence significantly. Another wave of Irish settlers went to North America in the mid-nineteenth century as a result of the catastrophic potato famines.

What was once a sparsely populated wilderness consisting of Native Americans—and no Christianity—became a mosaic of cultures: E pluribus unum, "Out of many, one." North America had become a bustling Christian context and it remains so today.

While North America was "civilized and Christianized" by Europeans, two people groups were marginalized in the process, the indigenous and the slaves. In the New World, Europeans encountered many different indigenous cultures. In a few cases, friendships were made and a level of interdependence developed. Overall, however, the story is a tragic one. One wonders why so many Native Americans are Christian today. Perhaps there was no real option: their world was collapsing all around them. The "white people" were colonizing even the remotest parts. Some natives fought to preserve their society, some fought back out of fear, but most kept their distance and interacted with the foreigners as little as possible. It was the missionaries, however, who found their way into indigenous life. It was the missionaries who established schools and churches with the intention of bridging two very different civilizations. In most cases, Native peoples accepted the white man's God, but rarely did they sever ties with their ancestral traditions. To this day, many Native Americans retain their ancient rituals and beliefs, but they have fused them with the core teachings of the gospel. The Indians who survived this difficult and at times violent confrontation of culture were pushed to the margins of North American society, where, unfortunately, they remain. Today, Amerindians comprise only around 1% of the North American population.

African-imported slavery was introduced by the Virginia colonists in the year 1619—twelve years after Jamestown was established and one year before the Mayflower arrived. Thus began a brutal, and very unchristian, chapter in North American history. African slavery began in Latin America in the early 1500s. In 1619 this deplorable practice was implemented in North America when two British ships—the *Treasurer* and the *White Lion*—arrived from Angola and the Congo. Recent discoveries have produced fascinating information about these people. There were three hundred and fifty of them, and it is very likely they were Christians. They spoke dialects of the Bantu language and their homeland, the kingdom of Ndongo, was conquered by the Portuguese in the 1500s. Roman Catholic missionaries had converted their king in the year 1490, and most of his people were baptized Catholics as a result. This painful era in North American history reached a climax in the Civil War (1861–1865) when slavery was finally abolished in the recalcitrant southern states. In 1860, about 13% of the American population was slaves; around 8% of American families were slave holders.[25] However, the issue of slavery touched virtually every aspect of life, particularly in the South.

With few exceptions, Africans who came to America's shores followed the religion of their owners. Christianity was thrust upon them. As we saw in the case of the indigenous peoples, however, hybridity was the norm. It would be irresponsible to say that Africans had no power in the adoption of Christianity as their own. Many Africans were repulsed by the whip-wielding God, but strongly attracted to the core biblical themes such as the Exodus story, the liberating message of Jesus, and the promise of a better life in the hereafter. Slaves took seriously Jesus' vocation "to proclaim good news to the poor, to proclaim freedom for the prisoners, to set the captive free, and to proclaim the year of the Lord's favor."[26] Africans began to cultivate a Christianity all their own, reinventing the faith in bold, creative, and subversive ways.

As Blacks became literate, a crop of talented and courageous leaders emerged to turn the tables in such a way that many Whites began fighting for their cause. The first Black denomination was founded in 1816 by Reverend Richard Allen. The African Methodist Episcopal Church was hugely successful in meeting the unique needs of the African American population. It galvanized Blacks, motivating them to do something about their plight in the American South. In the Northern states, slavery was abolished in 1807—the same year as Britain—but it took until 1865 for it to become abolished in the South. The transition was not easy, however. Over six-hundred thousand lives were lost in the Civil War, a war fought primarily over slavery.

American Christianity is very different from European Christianity. In Europe, religion was always closely linked to the state. American Christianity went through a brief period of church-state interdependence in colonial times, but it quickly became a context of diversity and competition, which precipitated the age of revivalism. As Americans expanded westward, different forms of Christianity spread across the frontier, leading to a remarkably diverse Christian culture. Preachers, pastors, and priests could no longer rely on the government to support their churches. Clergymen had to roll up their sleeves and build congregations from scratch.

Some have referred to American Christianity as consumerist in nature. Welcome to the obvious. Churches that meet the needs of the people will succeed, and churches that become stale and irrelevant will shrivel and vanish. Churches are compelled to offer better sermons, childcare, youth programs, or a better worship experience. American Christianity is today almost indistinguishable from the business world; churches must meet the needs of the consumer in a way unlike European or Orthodox Christianity.

The roots of the American revivalist movement are deep. The Great Awakenings of the eighteenth and nineteenth centuries featured some of the most prominent preachers in American history: Jonathan Edwards, George Whitefield, and Charles Grandison Finney. Thousands upon thousands of Americans flocked to hear powerful and convicting sermons. Frontier life was a difficult life, but the Christian gospel was a constant source of comfort as well as motivation. Unsurprisingly, the denominational tapestry in the USA became highly complicated. New religious movements mushroomed everywhere.

Four of these movements have become globally successful, each with around 15 million members worldwide:

- Emphasizing a "back to the Bible" message, Barton Stone and Alexander Campbell started the Restoration Movement in the early 1800s. Today they are known as Disciples of Christ, Churches of Christ, and Christian Churches.
- The Seventh Day Adventists began in the 1830s with William Miller and Ellen White. This group is known for healing, prophecy, missions, and a weekly gathering on Saturday—the Jewish Sabbath.
- The Church of Jesus Christ of Latter Day Saints, or Mormons, was begun by Joseph Smith in the 1820s. This movement attracted attention in the 2012 U.S. presidential bids of Mitt Romney and Jon Huntsman.
- The Jehovah's Witnesses movement was founded by Charles Taze Russell in the 1870s, focusing on the end of the world, the last days, and features a refusal to participate in patriotic events.

The proliferation continues. Americans are very entrepreneurial when it comes to religion. They are "free agents," to borrow a phrase from professional sports. If a church is not meeting their needs, they simply find another one, or start one themselves.

Perhaps the most important movement spawned in the history of North American Christianity is Pentecostalism. Rooted in John Wesley's revivalist approach, the Pentecostal movement began to go worldwide after the Azusa Street Revival of 1906 in Los Angeles. That event in southern California has impacted the Christian world significantly. Perhaps not since Martin Luther's Reformation in 1517 has the Christian world been so dramatically altered. Approximately one out of five Christians in the world could be described as Pentecostal or charismatic. Pentecostalism has been deemed the fasted growing religious movement in the world today.

Asian Christianity

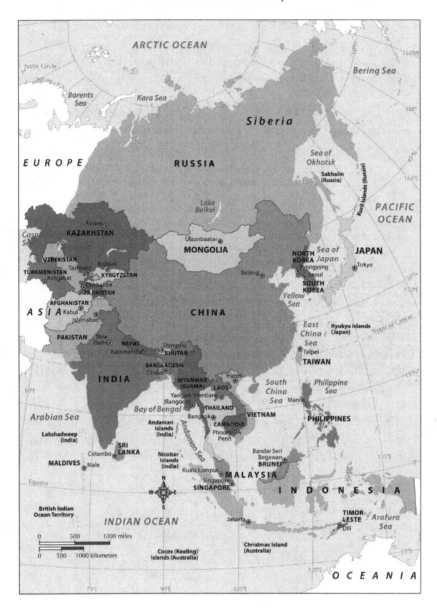

Over half the world's population lives in Asia, so we are dealing with a unique cultural block in this section—more variety, more ethnicities, more religions, and a lot more people. If we combine the populations of China and India, we are already over one-third of the earth's population.

Christianity is only beginning to grow in Asia. Christians account for only about 10% of the population. Of the world's eight cultural blocks, Christianity is the largest religion in six of them. The two exceptions are the Middle East and Asia. While Christians only represent around 2% of the Middle Eastern population, at one time the region was almost entirely Christian. The rise of Islam spelled disaster for Christianity there. Asia is a different story. While Christianity has had a presence in Asia since the first century, it is only in the beginning stages of its growth, and early signs are promising. In many corners of Asia, the power of the Christian message is being realized.

Asia is around 23% Hindu, 20% Muslim, 10% Buddhist, and 10% Christian. Of Asia's 33 countries and territories, thirteen are Islamic majority, eight are mainly Buddhist, two are overwhelmingly Hindu (India and Nepal), and Christianity is the most practiced religion in four: the Philippines, South Korea, Timor-Leste, and the British Indian Ocean Territory. The atheist era of Mao Tse Tung is coming to an end; only 3% of Asians are atheists.

While at first glance Christianity might appear marginal in Asia, a closer look reveals interesting trends. Around 350 million Christians live in Asia, meaning Asia has more Christians than Western Europe, Eastern Europe, or North America. Christianity is growing in Asia. In 1900, Asia was less than 1% Christian. A century later, that number had increased to 10%. Few scholars would doubt that we are only beginning to see the rise of Christianity in this densely populated cultural block.

Geographically, the northern border consists of Kazakhstan, China, and Mongolia. The western border includes Turkmenistan, Afghanistan, and Pakistan. The eastern border is Japan, Taiwan, and the Philippines, which are archipelagos, but the mainland's eastern border is North and South Korea, China, and Vietnam. The term South Asia is generally applied to the nations of Bangladesh, Bhutan, Nepal, Pakistan, Sri Lanka, and of course India.

Christianity entered Asia in four phases. The first phase consisted of early, relatively undocumented missions that occurred in the first centuries of the faith. Many of these Christians were Jews who made their way east on popular, well established trading routes of the eastern frontier of the Roman Empire. There is some evidence suggesting Syriac missionaries made their way to India as early as the first century. In Christian history we tend to emphasize the Western expansion of Christianity from Jerusalem to Rome. Many other missionaries went east, however. Those Christians tended to be Semitic: Arabic, Aramaic, Syriac, Hebrew, and Amharic.

The second phase of Christianity is known as the Nestorian period. Nestorians are not well known to Westerners since they were anathematized at the Council of Ephesus in 431. That council condemned the teachings of Nestorius, the patriarch of Constantinople. Nestorius was uncomfortable with the word *theotokos*—the idea that Mary is the mother of God. Nestorius had a large following in the Persian Empire and his influence expanded east for several hundred years. The Nestorian church became huge in modern-day Iraq, Iran, Turkmenistan, China, and south India. The famous "Nestorian Stele" commemorates missionaries who arrived at the Chinese capital, Xian, in the early 600s. Known today as the Assyrian Church of the East, the Nestorian church was crushed during the fourteenth century when the Mongolian superpowers began embracing Islam.

The third phase was the Roman Catholic missions during the age of exploration. Southern Europeans took the lead here due to their magnificent accomplishments in naval and ship building technologies. Vasco de Gama reached India in 1498 and was surprised to encounter Syrian Orthodox Christians. Francis Xavier—one of the founders of the Jesuit order—arrived to India in 1542. He also had great success in Japan. The Jesuits had successful missions to China in the late 1500s. They excelled at assimilating into Chinese aristocratic society in attire, customs, and language. By the late 1700s, however, Chinese emperors had become opposed to this religion of the West.

While the successes of Roman Catholic missions were very limited in Asia, there is one highly significant exception: the Philippines. Using the model they had employed in Central and South America, the Spanish were able to convert most of the important chiefs in Filipino society. Today the Philippines are 90% Christian, and three-fourths of them are Roman Catholic.

The fourth phase is the Protestant phase, linked mainly with Europe and North America. Protestant missions to Asia began in earnest in 1706 when German Bartholomaeus Ziegenbalg established several Lutheran churches in south-east India. He was followed by Dutch, British, and more German missionaries. William Carey arrived to north-east India in 1793 and focused his work on translating the Bible into Indian languages. Scotsman Robert Morrison worked in China from 1807 until 1834, becoming the first Protestant missionary there. The Opium Wars of the 1830s and 1850s, combined with the Taiping Rebellion (1850-1864) poisoned the cause of Christianity in China, making it appear as an imperialistic enterprise to subjugate the Chinese mind. Hudson Taylor (1832-1905) served in China for 51 years and founded the China Inland Mission—known today as the Overseas Missionary Fellowship (OMF). His movement restored some hope for Christian growth. However, the Boxer Rebellion (1899-1901) dashed most of the Christian gains that had been made. The anti-Western ethos of the Boxer Rebellion had a devastating effect on Christianity in China. With thousands of Chinese Christians slaughtered, Western missionaries who escaped with their lives were lucky. Several Western powers united to stop the rebellion, but the country spiraled into a series of civil wars that lasted until 1950—the year Mao Tse Tung (1893-1976) consolidated power, forced out all missionaries, and declared religion illegal.

Several notable Chinese leaders rose up in the twentieth century, keeping the faith alive during an extremely hostile period. These courageous pastors preached the gospel under severe threat. John Sung (Song Shangjie, 1901–1944) was the brilliant son of a Methodist pastor who dazzled his professors at Ohio State University. After earning his doctorate, he began studying for the ministry at Union Theological Seminary in New York. One night in 1927, he stopped into a Baptist church in Harlem and was utterly transformed by the sermon of a black woman preacher. The seminary authorities thought he had lost his mind and put him into an insane asylum for 193 days. During his confinement, Sung studied the Bible tirelessly and began to assume a highly Pentecostal form of Christianity that would transform his future. Upon his release, he returned to China and became the "Billy Graham of Asia." He died at the young age of 42, one of the most influential Asian evangelists in history.

A second major Chinese leader during the difficult years of the twentieth century was Watchman Nee (1903–1972), known to the Chinese as Ni Tuosheng. Although self-educated, Watchman Nee wrote many books that were read widely in many languages in the second half of the twentieth century. His following, known as Little Flock, has become highly international. His movement is based primarily in Taipei and Anaheim. It is an underground church, therefore not officially legal in China. Although imprisoned for the last two decades of his life, Nee was able to conduct a surreptitious ministry through his writings and colleagues who continued his ministry.

The twentieth century proved difficult for Asian Christians. While Mao Tse Tung crippled Christianity in China, this time was also a postcolonial period where many Asian nations were declaring their independence from Western empires. European nations had control of large swaths of Asia for decades, even centuries:

- Portugal held parts of India (Goa), China (Macau), Japan (Nagasaki), Malaysia (Malacca) and much of Indonesia;
- France held portions of eastern India, southeastern China (including Shanghai), Cambodia, Laos, Vietnam and part of Thailand;
- Denmark controlled the strategic Indian port Tranquebar;
- Spain controlled the Philippines and parts of Taiwan;
- Holland had much of Indonesia, Sri Lanka, Malaysia, and various ports of India;
- England controlled most of India, several Chinese ports (including Hong Kong), Singapore, parts of Malaysia and others;
- Although not European, the United States took over part of the Philippines from 1899 to 1946.

This long season of foreign rule was a double edged sword for Christianity in Asia. On one hand, it provided opportunity for Christian missionaries to travel and work under the protection of Western governments. On the other hand, Christianity became associated with foreign domination, robbing the gospel of one of its most central tenets: freedom.

Few would have predicted the best thing for Christianity in Asia would have been for Westerners to leave. Even so, that is what happened. When they left, Christianity began to indigenize into the local context. It assimilated better into the local language and the fibers of Asian customs. Christianity has become much healthier as a result of the great Western exodus. It is shocking to realize that nearly 20% of the world's Christians today live in Asia.

Asian Christianity is difficult to describe because of its vast heterogeneity. In the seven other cultural blocks of the world, there are more distinguishable patterns. For example, Western Europe has gone secular. Eastern Europe is highly Orthodox. Latin America shares a Catholic heritage. The Middle East has witnessed Christianity's steep decline. Asia is different. Considering a majority of the world's people live there, it is challenging to even find meaning in the word "Asia." South Indians have little in common with Kazakhs. Singapore is a very different country from Myanmar. The Philippines are almost entirely Christian while Afghanistan is almost entirely Muslim. Scholars have great difficulty trying to make sense of Asian Christianity.

A few observations are rather clear, however. Christianity in Asia is emerging from decades of oppression, and the opportunities are immense. Revivals are occurring on an unprecedented scale in countries like Vietnam, South Korea, Indonesia, Singapore, and China. People who scarcely knew the name of Jesus are proclaiming him as their Lord and Savior every day. House churches are booming to capacity. Church planting movements flourish.

Asian Christians are already making their mark on the world Christian scene. The largest church in the world is the Yoido Full Gospel Church in Seoul, South Korea. With around a million members, this massive Pentecostal church is showing us what may be in store should Asia's billions start turning to Christ. If so, it will be the largest mass movement in Christianity's history.

In the twentieth century, due to civil wars, anti-Western movements, and brutally intolerant Marxist regimes, Christianity was reduced to ashes. Christians were killed en masse, missionaries were sent home, and church buildings reduced to dust. Like the phoenix, however, Christianity has a way of rising. Could it be that the twenty-first century will be the age when Christianity finally blossoms in Asia? There are signs this could happen, particularly in China and south-east Asia. The Islamic strongholds of western Asia (the "-stans"), Malaysia, and Indonesia are unlikely to welcome Christianity's rising influence. Overall, however, the Light of the World is today burning brighter in Asia than ever before.

African Christianity

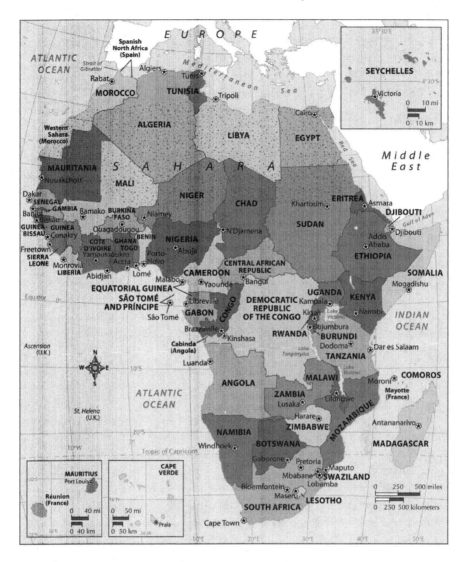

Rarely do entire people groups change religion. Normally people believe what their parents believe. In Africa, something remarkable happened in the twentieth century. It is one of those rare times in the history of humankind when entire families, tribes, and even nations began practicing a different religion. The statistics are breathtaking.

In 1900, Africa had 10 million Christians. By mid-century, the numbers of Christians were on pace with fertility rates; in 1945 there were about 30 million Christians in Africa. In the second half of the twentieth century, however, Africans began to convert to Christianity extraordinarily fast. Today, Africa has nearly 500 million Christians; that's around 47% of the entire continent's population.[27]

Put another way, in 1900, 2% of the world's Christians lived in Africa. In 2005, nearly 20% of the world's Christians lived there.[28]

What triggered this rapid conversion rate? Some predicted that once the European powers left Africa, Christianity would wither away. The reverse happened: "Africa's most dramatic Christian growth ...occurred *after* decolonization."[29] In the case of Protestant/Independent Christianity, growth rates have been exponential.

Christianity has deep roots in North Africa, due to the connection between Judaism and the Nile Valley. The Bible teaches that Christ was in Africa during his youth. The greatest theologians of early Christianity were Africans, and many Christian movements and ideas that Christians take for granted were in fact born on African soil.

The continent of Africa is vast; the number of people-groups vaster still. There are approximately one billion people in Africa today speaking around 2,000 languages.[30]

While only one African nation is today in the top ten of the world's most populated countries—Nigeria, with nearly 170 million people—it contains several highly populated countries. Both Ethiopia and Egypt are nearing the 100 million mark.

Additionally, Africa's fertility rate is higher than anywhere else in the world. The world's average fertility rate is 2.61 children born per woman. However, in Africa, the *average* woman will have five children during her lifetime.

Two other important trends in Africa are median age and life expectancy. Africa may have the highest fertility rate in the world, but it also has the lowest life expectancy. Africans, on average, barely reach the age of 50. This fact is glaring and unfortunate. In Eastern Europe, the cultural block with the second lowest life expectancy in the world, people live 20 years longer than Africans. Similarly, the low life expectancy brings down the median age in Africa to less than 20 years—easily the lowest in the world.

Economically, Africa is in crisis. Of the world's top 20 GDP countries, no African countries are represented, in spite of its being a continent teeming with valuable goods and natural gifts.[31] Many African economies seem hopelessly dependent on foreign aid, causing some to ask, "Is there life after debt?"[32] Ghanaian theologian Mercy Oduyoye outlines a slew of problems, both historical and contemporary, that have contributed to the difficulties:[33]

- Low literacy rates;[34]
- A pervasive fear of witchcraft;[35]

- A colonial legacy with many residual effects of dependency, corruption, and powerlessness;
- Systemic racism towards Africans has taken a dehumanizing toll on the consciousness of a continent, and the trauma does not abate quickly.

African scholars have also pointed to frailties within. Lamin Sanneh writes, "Corruption and despotic rule despoiled countries, divided society, and failed the national cause."[36]

Perhaps some Africans would express gratefulness to the Western missionaries who attempted to bring good news, although missionaries are implicated in postcolonial critiques. The Mau Mau fighters of Kenyan independence in the 1950s may have been the first to utter that now famous invective on imperial missions:

> When the white man came, he had the Bible and we had the land. He told us to close our eyes and pray, and when we opened our eyes he had the land and we had the Bible.[37]

This condemnation is not altogether justified, although it is not easily dismissed.

Missionaries came in all shades and sizes. Some were heralded as civilizing the Dark Continent; most however lived meagerly, founding small churches and passing leadership to Africans within a short time. Many gave their truncated lives to an adopted African home, witnessing for Christ in an isolated corner of the world, dying young because of malaria. They counted the cost and chose to obey the Great Commission, no matter where that led them. Today however, in a context of Western secularization, missionaries become the objects of scorn—pompous brainwashers from a bygone era.

For better or for worse, Africa would not be half Christian today without that massive era of European missions. It was inconceivable in 1900 to predict that Africa would be the heartland of Christianity in a century.

African Christianity has roots in Ethiopian Judaism, or at least in significant Ethiopian-Jewish contact before Jesus. Africa plays a role in several New Testament passages as well:

- Jesus may have spent his first few years of life living as a refugee in Egypt;
- Simon of Cyrene—modern-day Libya—was forced to carry Jesus' cross for him when he became too weak to do it himself. Thus, it was an African who first took up a cross and followed Jesus, up the hill to Golgotha.

- In Acts chapter two, on Pentecost Sunday, we read of Libyans and Egyptians at the birth of Christianity.
- In Acts 8, an Ethiopian eunuch, "...an important official in charge of all the treasury of Candace, queen of the Ethiopians" had gone to Jerusalem to worship.
- Africans were among the first to preach the gospel to non-Jews. Acts 11:19 discusses evangelists from Cyrene preaching to Greeks in Antioch, and "the Lord's hand was with them."
- Paul was probably ordained for ministry by a group that included Africans (Acts 13:1–4).
- One of the great evangelists of the New Testament was Apollos, a native of Alexandria (Acts 18:24).
- Church tradition states that Mark evangelized Egypt in the 40s and became the first pope of the Coptic Orthodox Church.

Africa's Christian pedigree outside the biblical text is revered as well:

- Saint Anthony the Great, the father of monasticism, was Egyptian;
- Several African church fathers defined the Christian faith for us today: Athanasius, Clement of Alexandria, Origen, Cyprian, and Tertullian.
- Alexandria was well known as "the leading academic center of the ancient world." Indeed Alexandria and Carthage (Tunisia) were pivotal in shaping the earliest medieval Western Universities. [38]
- Perhaps the single most important theologian in Western Christian history, Augustine (354 to 430), was an African Berber from Algeria.
- Axum in Ethiopia was one of the earliest Christian states.[39] Ethiopia is a proudly Christian country that remained isolated from Christendom for centuries. When contact with Ethiopia was restored in the 1400s, Portuguese Jesuit missionaries were appalled at their arrogance, saying, "They are possessed with a strange notion that they are the only true Christians in the world; as for us, they shunned us as heretics."[40]

The Christianization of Africa was complex. European missionaries are often associated with this era, but for every missionary there were dozens of African leaders. Many of these Africans inspired and initiated mass movements towards Christianity that culminated in the twentieth century:

- Samuel Ajayi Crowther (1806–1891) from Nigeria, the first African bishop in the Anglican Church;
- William Wade Harris (c. 1865–1929) from Liberia, considered to be "...the most successful missionary in West Africa."[41]

- Garrick Braide (c. 1880-1918), a well-known healer in Nigeria—people flocked to him as the second Elijah.
- John Chilembwe (1871-1915) preached armed resistance to the British in Malawi (Nyasaland)—in the name of Christ!
- Simon Kimbangu (1887-1951) invoked ancestors in his preaching, claiming that "God was changing the baton from whites to blacks."[42] His church numbers in the millions.
- Zulu prophet Isaiah Shembe's (1869-1935) Nazarite movement hailed him as a messianic figure. He purportedly resurrected from the dead and appeared to his followers.[43]
- Engenas Barnabas Lekganyane (1885-1948) established the Zion Christian Church in 1910. It boasts the largest annual gathering of Christians on earth. The ZCC's Easter gathering in Moria, South Africa is attended by over a million people and in 1992 featured Nelson Mandela as a speaker.[44]

The African Independent Church tradition continues to proliferate. John Mbiti once described the AIC movements as being,

> ...[A]n African opportunity to mess up Christianity in our own way. For the past two thousand years, other continents, countries, nations and generations have had their chances to do with Christianity as they wished. And we know that they have not been idle! Now Africa has got its chance at last.[45]

Mbiti is part of a growing body of African scholars who claim Christianity as their own and resent colonial charges which imply African Christianity may be less authentic.

So convinced of this message, many Africans now missionize the West, former Christendom. In 2009 an intriguing, lengthy article in the *New York Times* proclaimed:

> Pastor Daniel Ajayi-Adeniran is coming for your soul. ...He is on a mission to save you from eternal damnation. He realizes you may be skeptical, put off by his exotic name—he's from Nigeria ...but he's not deterred. He believes the Holy Spirit is working through him.[46]

The article goes on to discuss how the Lagos-based Redeemed Christian Church of God already has millions of members and is growing exponentially. It is a far cry from the declining memberships in mainline Protestant denominations in North America or stale, empty churches in Europe.

Today, Africa has 58 countries and territories. In 31 of them, Christianity is the largest religion. In 21 of them, Islam ranks first. In five of them, indigenous religions form the largest group. Mauritius is unique in that Hinduism ranks first there.

The majority of Africa's Christians are Protestant/Independent. The Catholic Church, however, claims almost exactly a third of the continent's Christian population. The ancient Orthodox Christians of Africa—based mainly in the Nile Valley—account for one-tenth of the Christian population on the continent.

Africa is today a major player in world Christianity:

- Two of seven General Secretaries of the World Council of Churches were African: Kenyan Samuel Kobia (from 2004 to 2009), and Philip Potter (from 1972 to 1984), of African descent but from the West Indies.
- Two of the ten General Assemblies of the World Council of Churches were held in Africa: in Kenya (1975) and Zimbabwe (1998).
- Africa has half a billion Christians and, within a generation or two, it will have more Christians than any other block, surpassing Latin America and the Caribbean, due to fertility rates.
- The African diaspora is huge and is changing world Christian demographics. The Archbishop of York—John Sentamu—is from Uganda. Sunday Adelaja, pastor of Kiev's megachurch Embassy of God, is Nigerian. The church holds 40 services weekly and claims to have planted congregations in 45 countries.[47]
- International denominations are being altered by African churches. The Anglican Communion, for example, has witnessed a shift in leverage as Africa takes the reins of leadership in that denomination.

Perhaps the most important aspect of African Christianity is that it represents the turning over of a new leaf in world Christianity. While Christianity in the West declines, Christianity in Africa grows in numbers, strength, and energy. While Western societies deepen the divide between Christianity and culture, sub-Saharan Africa seems poised to become the new Christendom. Western youth walked away from the faith of their ancestors in the twentieth century; however, African youth embraced Christianity with gusto.

So what does this mean? I believe our children and grandchildren will look back upon these days as a turning point. Christianity is still the largest religion in the world, yet it will not be a Western religion, as it has tended to be conceived for centuries. Christianity will become more identified with Africa than with any other place in the world. The reverberations can already be felt. The Christian narrative has for centuries been told mainly from a European perspective. An African narrator is now settling in.

The story of Christianity as told by an African narrator will have important implications. Let me provide a few illustrative anecdotes:

- Recently, I worshiped at a church in Dundee, Scotland. While the congregants were mainly white, the music was led by young men from Africa. They danced, held up their hands, and appeared very comfortable in their unrestrained approach to worship. That is very different from the Christianity from my youth.
- Gone are the days when Westerners "take the gospel" to Africa. It is already there. My students go to Africa to get revived. Africans now evangelize the West.
- Africans will deeply impact the way Christians read the Bible. In Western seminaries, we have taught F. C. Bauer, Bultmann, Altizer, and Tillich. The future of biblical interpretation may not necessarily include those names. Africans offer a different set of biblical interpreters who come to very different conclusions than those reached in the West.
- African Christians bring confidence. Their context is radically different. Christ represents victory and success in Africa. In the West many churches struggle to survive. There is a reticence in preaching the gospel in Europe. Africans are unashamed; their sermons are bold and confident.
- Africans bring momentum to Christianity. Western Europeans can hardly speak of momentum and Christianity in the same sentence. Christianity is in recession, even crisis in many places in the West.

The age of the African Christian narrator will bring opportunities. As an American citizen, I think it is a bit like having a new president. We do not know how he will go about his task. We do not really know if he will be able to achieve what he sets out to do. We do not know exactly what his priorities will be. What we do know is that we have elected a new president, and most of us cheer him on, hoping he can improve the condition of our country with his approach, policies, and decisions.

Similarly, an African-infused Christianity holds many possibilities. World Christianity waits in expectation for new revelations. None of us knows precisely how African Christianity will affect our faith, but we do know that changes are coming. We hope the changes will be good and will ultimately improve the condition of our faith. We remain excited and eager that the new leadership will prove to be a blessing, both to the individual and to the international state of world Christianity.

Oceanic Christianity

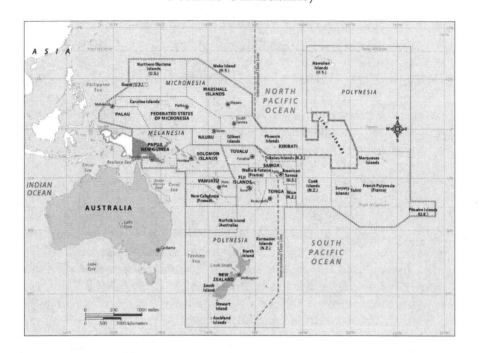

Oceania is defined as much by the Pacific Ocean as it is by its ten thousand islands located on both sides of the equator. The northern border of Oceania is the Northern Mariana Islands—a commonwealth of the United States—and the Marshall Islands, an independent republic that touches the International Date Line. The eastern edge of Oceania consists of the Pitcairn Islands and French Polynesia, including Tahiti. The southern edge of Oceania is New Zealand. The western side is dominated by Australia, Papua New Guinea, Palau, and the U.S. territory of Guam.

There are twenty-five countries and territories in Oceania, and they are divided into three geographic divisions: Melanesia, Micronesia, and Polynesia. Melanesia—meaning "Black Islands" because of the skin color of the people—is the largest and most diverse of these three regions. It encompasses six nations/territories: Papua New Guinea, the Solomon Islands, New Caledonia, Fiji, Norfolk Island, and Vanuatu.

Micronesia—meaning "small islands"—is in the north and generally includes seven nations/territories: Guam, Kiribati, Marshall Islands, the Federated States of Micronesia, Nauru, Northern Mariana Islands, and Palau.

Polynesia—meaning "many islands"—is the largest of the three regions and includes over one thousand islands, organized into eleven countries and territories: American Samoa, Cook Islands, French Polynesia, New Zealand, Niue, Pitcairn Islands, Samoa, Tokelau Islands, Tonga, Tuvalu, and Wallis and

Futuna Islands. Although inside Polynesia, Hawaii belongs to the U.S., and Easter Island belongs to Chile.

The Oceanic cultural block has a population of about 35 million people, which is almost exactly the population of Canada. Over half of the region's population lives in Australia. The other two major nations are Papua New Guinea and New Zealand which combine for another eleven million people. The remaining five million people are scattered across numerous islands with relatively low populations.

Oceania's human history goes back 60,000 years. By the year AD 1000, virtually all of the inhabitable islands had human settlements. By no means were they monolithic. Indigenous Australians remained hunters and gatherers until European contact. The people of New Guinea, however, turned to agriculture around five thousand years ago. Due to watery borders, many of the island societies developed in rather perplexing and unique ways. Oceania attracts anthropologists because of this diversifying phenomenon.

The region is highly Christianized today. This development is recent, however. In a way similar to Africa, the watery world of islands and atolls rapidly changed from animism to Christianity. Outside of the highly Europeanized islands of Australia and New Zealand, the region is today like a new Christendom. One scholar put it this way: "The religion of Christ ...appears to have been more universally accepted and integrated here than in any other comparable region in modern times."[48]

In 1521, the great circumnavigator Ferdinand Magellan became the first European to cross the Pacific Ocean. He had just passed through southern Chile's Tierra del Fuego, making him the first to find a southern passage from the Atlantic to the Pacific. Magellan believed the lucrative Spice Islands of Indonesia were not far from the South American coast. His prediction proved terribly wrong as he and his crew sailed for four months, many of them dying along the way, until they happened upon Guam. His Spanish crewmen were the first Europeans in Oceania, but they stayed only three turbulent days, marred with mutual fear, surprise, and violence.

While various other Europeans, such as the Portuguese and Dutch, had sporadic encounters with the region, it was the arrival of British Captain James Cook in 1770 that brought it into the Western worldview. It is unfortunate that early encounters between Oceanic peoples and Europeans ended violently, but it proved to be the norm. Europeans had far more advanced weaponry, and were able to subdue native inhabitants. Oceanic peoples had to respond creatively. For example, Tahitians offered their women to British crewmembers, triggering frenzy among European sailors. Tahitian women seemed sexually carefree and peculiarly open to conjugal relations. In reality, it was a maneuver for survival. Sexually transmitted diseases moved both ways: Captain Cook's men complained frequently of venereal complications, but more devastation was on the Tahitian side. This pattern occurred repeatedly as British sailors made their rounds in the South Pacific. Hawaii's population, for example, was depleted by as much as 80% in the decades following Cook's arrival.[49] It was not without a fight, however; Captain Cook and several of his crewmen were clubbed to death in 1779 as a result of a misunderstanding.

While the European presence sparked a new Christian era in Oceania, it was plagued with problems from the beginning. Oceania's aboriginal population was decimated by European diseases such as smallpox and measles. As the island cultures struggled to survive, Europeans began their settlement of the region in very inauspicious ways. In 1788, a penal colony consisting of 800 convicts and 200 settlers arrived in Sydney and sustained themselves through sheep herding. In 1800, Australia had only a few thousand Europeans; by 1900 there were nearly four million.

In the 1800s, European powers scrambled to stake their claims in the region, beginning in 1841 with France's snatching up of, perhaps predictably, Tahiti. French Polynesia is a legacy of the imperial era. The British dominated the South Pacific with their annexation of Australia, New Zealand, Fiji, and many others. Germany claimed the Marshall Islands in the 1880s. The USA claimed Hawaii in 1875 and took possession of Guam in 1898 after winning the Spanish-American War. By 1900, only Tonga remained officially independent although in reality it was a British protectorate.

Shortly after European contact, Oceania developed a reputation for barbarism, cannibalism, and sexual laxity. Missionaries flocked to this region to bring their civilizing message of Christ. Roman Catholic priests accompanied Spanish explorers in the 1500s, but their presence was sporadic and their influence limited. It was not until the closing years of the eighteenth century that Anglican missionary societies began a concerted effort at mass evangelization. French Catholic missionaries got to work around this same time. In those days missionaries often moved to a particular location for life, earning the deep admiration of the local people. They devoted their life work to planting the gospel, and their converts revered them. To this day Christian leaders in the Pacific islands are deeply respected by their flocks.

In Oceania, religious competition was kept to a minimum. There were so many different cultures that needed evangelization it would have been counterproductive to recruit from the already Christianized. When one denomination decided to work among a particular tribe, other denominations tended not to interfere. British Congregationalists worked in eastern Polynesia, English Methodists in Tonga and Fiji, American Congregationalists in Hawaii and Micronesia, Anglicans in Melanesia, and Catholics in French parts. Christian clergy came to know their flocks intimately, taking detailed notes of their manners and customs, laying the groundwork for what would eventually become the field of social anthropology. Unlike anthropologists, however, who do field research in a particular society for perhaps a few years in total, missionaries weaved their lives into the fabric of the culture in ways uncommon today. A reciprocal relationship developed between missionary and native. The missionary relied on local people for survival while indigenous societies came to rely on missionary leadership in the highly chaotic, disruptive age of European imperialism.

An unfortunate phenomenon known as cargo cults developed in various islands due to the impressive cargo that foreigners brought. Some islanders perceived Westerners as almost magically producing highly valuable manufactured goods. While it would be a mistake to assume the islanders adopted Christianity in order to attain precious cargo, it was definitely part of the picture. Missionaries introduced all manner of Western ways by founding schools, churches, hospitals, and missionary compounds. Large, thatched, palm-leaf church buildings sprouted up all across the South Pacific. These societies were being transformed, and it was unavoidable to associate the foreigners with these impressive developments.

While cooperating with indigenous leaders to evangelize these unfamiliar cultures, European missionaries became heroes of their time, inspiring a wealth of literature. Englishman John Williams is perhaps the most famous. In 1839, he was killed and eaten by cannibals in modern day Vanuatu while evangelizing. George Selwyn (1809-1878), the first Anglican bishop of New Zealand, took a leading role in the Christianization of the Maoris. Scotsman James Chalmers worked in the Cook Islands and New Guinea from 1866 to 1901. He, too, met a violent death when he fell into the hands of cannibals.

Native missionaries played a pivotal role in the evangelization of their own cultures, and they are rather unheralded in the Western world. They are held in deepest esteem, however, in their own societies. Maheanui was a Tahitian who ministered for over thirty years in French Polynesia. Jose Palomo, a Chamorro from Guam, was the first indigenous Catholic priest in the Pacific islands, ordained in 1859. Gucheng and his wife are deeply revered in Papua New Guinea and the Tories Strait Islands for training scores of evangelists in the late nineteenth century. In the 1830s and 1840s, the islands of Fiji were evangelized by three indigenous Christians from French Polynesia: Taharaa, Fuatai, and Faaruea. George Sarawia became the first Melanesian clergyman in 1868 when he was ordained deacon at the age of 26. He and his wife worked among his people, the Vanuatuans, for 35 years.

In general terms, the Roman Catholic Church remained heavily dependent upon Western leadership well into the second half of the twentieth century while Protestant churches indigenized fairly rapidly in the early 1900s. Both approaches have proven effective, however.

Oceania is about 80% Christian today. This number would be higher if it were not for the strong secularization occurring in Australia and New Zealand.

These two countries, like Western Europe, have secularized. However, all 25 territories that make up Oceania have a Christian majority. Some of these nations are profoundly Christian. For example, Samoa's motto is "Samoa is founded on God." The first Prime Minister of Vanuatu, Walter Lini, was an Anglican priest.

An indigenous form of Christianity has emerged in Oceania that fuses Pacific culture with Christian teaching. One example of this fusion is the Tongan theologian Sione 'Amanaki Havea, considered the architect of a "coconut theology" emphasizing the indigenous character of Oceanic Christianity. Havea has played a powerful role in challenging a Western bias in Polynesian theology. For example, he has opted to use the coconut as a more fitting metaphor for understanding Jesus Christ. Bread and wine are foreign objects in Polynesia, but the coconut is local and meaningful. Undoubtedly, in the years to come, Oceanic Christianity will continue to move in this indigenizing direction.

A hundred years ago white people worked feverishly to Christianize the people of this watery world in the Pacific. However, that time has passed. Now is the time for the inhabitants of Oceania's islanders to launch mission campaigns into the secular white populations of Australia and New Zealand. I have little doubt the task has already begun. Certainly the baton of evangelism has been passed. The question now is which direction the recipients of that baton will run? It would be ironic indeed if they made their way back to Europe!

Conclusion: Disciples of All Nations

Scholars and media alike took great interest in a recent research report by Pew Forum, an important research center based in Washington, D.C. Entitled "Global Christianity," the report confirmed what scholars of Christianity have known for years.[50] It has been fascinating, however, to watch people outside religious studies express such surprise by the statistics generated. One of the findings that caused a stir was the following:

> Although Christians comprise just under a third of the world's people, they form a majority of the population in 158 countries and territories, about two-thirds of all the countries and territories in the world.[51]

Further, there are today far more Christians in the Global South (61%) than in the Global North (39%). Again, common knowledge for church historians, but amusing to see the numbers shock non-specialists in the same way it shocked academics two decades ago.

Historian Lamin Sanneh has written extensively about Christianity's unique "translatability."[52] He argues that from early times Christianity has excelled in translating itself linguistically and theologically. Missionaries throughout history often used the local name for the High God to describe the Christian God they were representing. This technique could open the door for peoples to understand their traditional God in a new way. In addition, it preserved what was best from their ancestral traditions. This pattern has proved extremely effective. Jesus, an Aramaic-speaking Jew, was quickly embraced by Greeks, Romans, Armenians, Egyptians, Celts, Slavs, and on and on to the present. Today, however, the people embracing the teachings of this Galilean Jew are Africans and Asians, and they are speaking in tongues most of us have never heard.

Sanneh was born Muslim but converted to Christianity as a young man, and he has devoted considerable time to comparing the two religions. He argues that while Islam is heavily dependent on the superiority of the Arabic language, Christianity does not uphold a linguistic hierarchy. Rather, the opposite is the case. Sure, Greek is important in the study of the New Testament, but it is not somehow mandated for the gospel to maintain its effectiveness. When Muslims emphasize Arabic as the divine language, Christians opt for the vernacular. Even today, when Christians read the Bible, they do so in a language they understand. The Bible is every bit as authoritative in one language as in any other.

Indeed, Christianity privileges the local language—the host language. The roots of this phenomenon are in Judaism. The Hebrew Bible, by the time of Jesus, was more popular in Greek—the Septuagint—than in Hebrew. Scholars claim that by the time of Jesus, only a small minority of Jews even used Hebrew. As a people they had embraced their holy texts in the language that nearly everybody around them was speaking—Koine ("common") Greek.

The message is critical, the medium of that message peripheral. We are again reminded of Christianity's "borderlessness," that very geographical concept.

Christianity's diffusion has profoundly affected our world. In many ways it has brought people together. One out of three people has accepted this message as somehow central in his or her life. Globally, two out of three nations and territories have Christian majorities. There is an unprecedented level of unity in the world because of this faith. As these Christians interact, intermarry, communicate, and cooperate, we see globalization unfolding before our very eyes.

Borders lose their potency in the Christian worldview. Taboos become broken. No longer is any people group considered greater than any other. The borderlessness of Christianity permeates all institutions of power. As the gospel translates into local dialects, people claim it as their own. They now have the power. They now have the Son of God in their own cultures. They are now "the children of God" since God shows no impartiality. As the apostle Paul so eloquently put it in his Epistle to the Romans: "Now if we are children, then we are heirs—heirs of God and co-heirs with Christ."

The Christian doctrine of the incarnation is perhaps the most borderless idea that has ever come to humankind: God, the creator of the world, sends his son in the form of a human. Humans are empowered to understand God best when they put their faith in this nearly unbelievable miracle. Without the testimony of the New Testament witnesses the idea would be consigned to a rubbish heap because of its preposterousness. It remains extant, however. It is celebrated across the world when Christians light their candles and sing "Silent Night, Holy Night." It resounds anew when Christians the world over exclaim "Christ Is Risen Indeed" during Eastertide. This idea brings people together on an unprecedented scale.

We conclude this chapter on a geographical approach to church history by remembering a story in the Gospel of Mark, chapter three. Jesus had just attended a synagogue service where he was accused of a grievous sin: he had unlawfully violated the Sabbath by healing a man with a shriveled hand. He had broken one of the Ten Commandments: thou shalt not do any work on the Sabbath. Mark tells us that crowds of people were following him, pushing forward to touch him, clamoring to catch a glimpse. The gospel writer provides the fascinating detail that the crowds prevented Jesus and his apostles from eating.

Jesus' family arrived on the scene to check things out but the crowds prevented even them from getting close to Jesus. Someone said "Your mother and brothers are outside looking for you." Jesus responded with a question and a very revealing, even scandalous statement. First he asked, "Who are my mother and my brothers?" Then he asserted: "Here are my mother and brothers! Whoever does God's will is my brother and sister and mother."

The geographical approach to church history forces Christians to realize they have brothers, sisters, and, yes, even mothers on the other side of the world. Christians believe this world is not our permanent home; it is only a preparation for the life to come. What may appear to be family here is only a mirage. Our real, eternal family is the church, and it is a very large family these days.

My grandfather was a preacher. He never referred to people by their given name. He always referred to them as "Sister Earwood" or "Brother Foster." My grandfather's world was a small one. Small-town New Mexico does, in many ways, present a familial atmosphere, especially in the community church setting. I am curious as to whether or not my grandfather realized he had family in a place as far away and exotic as Ethiopia. I doubt he knew much about Ethiopia, but he did know his Bible. For some reason I suspect that if he heard that he had brothers and sisters in Africa, Asia, Latin America, and beyond, he probably would have responded in biblical language, as he often did. I cannot help but to think he would have recalled what many consider to be the earliest hymn of Christianity:

> ...At the name of Jesus every knee should bow, in heaven and on earth and under the earth, and every tongue confess that Jesus Christ is Lord, to the glory of God the Father.[53]

The title of this chapter, "Go and Make Disciples of All Nations," causes us to reflect on that very geographical command Jesus gave to his apostles at the close of the Gospel of Matthew. Looking back 2000 years later, it is breathtaking to consider how effective they were in their response.

Questions for Analysis

1. Consider the concept of foreignness. What causes a person to view another person as a foreigner? How is the concept of "foreignness" created and sustained in culture?

2. Historically, Christians have transcended borders in order to bring the gospel to new people. What do you deem to be the key ideas that have motivated Christians to take on such a task?

3. Weigh in on Christianity's adaptability. Why do you think Christianity has experienced so much success in this regard?

4. The geographical approach to church history takes us deep into political spheres. Many kings and other political leaders "baptized" their people through the years. Does "baptizing a people" constitute a mass violation of human rights?

5. The title of this chapter contains two commands: "Go" and "make disciples." Is it possible to emphasize one of these commands to the detriment of the other? If so, what happens in those cases?

WHO DO PEOPLE SAY I AM?

A Biographical Approach to Church History

"Jesus and his disciples went on to the villages ...On the way he asked them, 'Who do people say I am?' They replied, 'Some say John the Baptist; others say Elijah; and still others, one of the prophets.' 'But what about you? Who do you say I am?' Peter answered, 'You are the Messiah.'"
Mark 8:27–29

Introduction

Over the years, various students have asked why I decided to become a church historian. My decision had as much to do with biography as with religion. My studies were enjoyable to me, even entertaining, because of the people I encountered in the books I read. My wonderful professors lectured on these people and pulled me into endless and fascinating life stories. I could hardly tear myself away from the books assigned in my courses.

Outside of the Bible, no book impacted me more than the *Confessions* of Saint Augustine. I found it uncanny how this late fourth-century writer could have possibly dealt with the exact same issues I was dealing with as a university student. Never had the phrase rang so true: "the more things change, the more they stay the same."

- Bad influences: Like Augustine I had a hard time shaking companions and habits that pulled me down.
- Profound regret: I felt I had mistreated many people and made destructive choices during my adolescence.
- Concupiscence: Like most adolescents, I could relate to Augustine's wrestling with cupid, the Roman god of desire.

- Religious questioning: While I never embraced a non-Christian religion as Augustine did (Manichaeism), I strongly related to his persistent quest for truth.
- Loss: About the time I was reading *Confessions*, I was dealing with two recent, painful forms of loss. A friend of mine committed suicide, and my girlfriend broke off our engagement.
- Christian conversion: Christianity was a major part of my childhood, but I too wandered as a youth. I found Augustine's famous "take and read" passage haunting and strangely familiar.
- Deep love for his mother: In my university studies I began to realize just how much my mother loved me. I was terrorized with dread and moved to tears when I read of Augustine's devastation following his mother's death. I knew I would probably have to walk that painful path one day.
- "Born again" experience: As an evangelical Protestant, I cannot help but to use this language, which Augustine likely would not have used. Nevertheless, this biblical metaphor is precisely what happened to Augustine, and he was never the same. I resonated deeply with his experience. During my sophomore year of college, I became born again and renewed my commitment to Christian living.

Augustine's influence on me was significant and lasting.

During my student days, many notable figures from church history entered my imagination, indelibly shaping my understanding of life and strengthening my commitment to faith. The early monastic fathers such as Anthony, John Cassian, and Benedict dared me to ponder the more challenging teachings of Jesus, like abandoning one's possessions in order to serve the poor. I am still inspired by the examples of Francis and Clare in the High Middle Ages. My wife and I named our eldest daughter Clare out of respect for this godly woman who surrendered her life of privilege for the habit of a nun. It was a joy for us to visit Assisi in 2008 and walk the same grounds that Clare and Francis did.

I was deeply moved by the holiness of Thomas a' Kempis's *The Imitation of Christ* and to this day consider it the single most important devotional text ever written. I have sent copies of this classic to young men and women upon their high school or college graduation.

Like most Protestant school boys, I was impressed by the Reformers, from John Wycliffe to the Anabaptists. Perhaps no other story has penetrated the Protestant collective imagination as has Martin Luther's courageous, nay, valiant decision to publicly denounce corruption within his church. We tend to forget that Luther was a Roman Catholic monk. He longed for a church more relevant, and he risked his life to introduce changes he thought beneficial. Embellished or not, his "Here I stand" speech ranks among the most courageous moments in Western civilization. In those days people were routinely put to death for speaking out publicly and so brazenly. Luther made me question whether or not I had the audacity to stand up for what I considered right.

It was biography that introduced me to my own theological tradition, the Restoration Movement. This Scottish-American "back to the Bible" style of primitive Christianity caused scales to fall from my eyes. The leaders of my ecclesial fellowship, Alexander Campbell and Barton W. Stone, made me realize I have a history. While reading about them, I was able to recall my grandfather—a preacher—studying the theological tracts, commentaries, and published debates of these Christian stalwarts. I remember sitting in class one day, realizing I have a place in the Christian tradition. I am connected to Augustine, Hildegard, Huss, Menno Simons, and Dorothy Day. I belong to this mighty narrative that connects me with modern, medieval, and ancient saints who gave their lives for this faith I too hold dear.

I have a distinct memory of reading how Alexander Campbell preferred to study in a detached office, in hexagonal shape, with a windowed ceiling so that his light came "from above."[1] For some odd reason I imagined myself sitting in that study, reading the Greek New Testament, just as my religious forebears had. I realized I belong. I have a purpose. I am part of the story. Like the author of Hebrews, I too am "surrounded by a great cloud of witnesses." My life changed after that realization. I had found my niche.

The Biographical Approach

Christianity is a biographical religion. It is organized around the life of Jesus Christ. Considering Christianity is the largest religion in the world, it would be safe to say that Matthew, Mark, Luke, and John were among the most successful biographers of all time.

Biography is an ancient style of writing. By the time the gospel writers set to work in the first century AD, they had many examples that would have shaped their approaches to life-writing. The genre was well-established both in the Jewish and Greco-Roman world. Much of the Old Testament is biographical in nature with its long discussions of patriarchs, prophets, priests, and kings. Perhaps surprisingly, the Old Testament also discusses people we might consider rather normal: Miriam—the girl who hid her baby brother Moses in the bulrushes and famously led the women in dancing and singing after crossing the Red Sea; Ruth—a Moabite woman praised for her steadfast loyalty to her Jewish mother in law; and Naaman, a Syrian army chief healed of leprosy by the Israelite prophet Elisha.

The Greco-Roman world was full of biography as well. Perhaps the greatest biographers of the ancient Greco-Roman world were Plutarch (45-120 AD), Tacitus (56-117 AD), and Suetonius (70-130 AD). Plutarch famously wrote about the lives of the Roman Emperors as well as many other important Greeks and Romans such as Alexander the Great and the Greek general Pyrrhus. Tacitus, a Roman senator, is considered one of our most important primary sources for the Roman Empire. His *Annals* and *Histories* are heavily biographical. Suetonius penned *The Twelve Caesars*—biographies of the first twelve emperors—according to a set pattern: their physical appearance, omens, family history, quotations, and an account of their reign. These writers' primary motive was to exalt their subjects, but they frequently described more mundane matters such as personal habits, food preferences, health, and close friends.

The authors of the Christian gospels—as well as most church historians up to modern times—were not preoccupied with historical facts in the way we are today. They wanted to inspire others with the stories they told. This is not to say they lied. Rather they wrote to exalt Jesus Christ. Precise chronology was not a major goal of the gospel writers. Their goals were more profound in nature: they wanted people to understand the "good news"—that the long-awaited Jewish Messiah had entered the world.

There is a persuasive element to the gospels. They were written to foster belief in Jesus as Messiah. While there is little written about the physical appearance of Jesus, there is great detail about his character. It is unfair when critics compare the gospels to the field of scientific biography today, with all of its concern for footnotes, documentation, and corroboration with credible sources. The gospels are religious literature. In genre, they stand closer to modern-day sermons than historical biographies. Additionally, they only deal with a limited portion of Jesus' life: his birth, his short public ministry, and the events surrounding his death and resurrection. Thus, if Jesus lived to be around 35 years, we have limited insight since his public ministry lasted only three years or so.

Early in Christian history, a new genre emerged that continues to inspire Christians worldwide: hagiography. In Greek, the word "hagios" means "holy" or "saint," and the word "graphein" means "to write." Hagiography emerged as the chief form of encouragement for early Christians who were being perse-cuted. It intended to inspire Christians by pointing out the saintliness of those who had gone before. Many saints had died brutal deaths at the hands of the creatively destructive Romans—they amused their people through torture and public deaths such as crucifixion, gladiator contests, and wild animals being unleashed on violators. Christians needed strength to sustain them during these times. Christian faith was illegal in Roman lands from the time of Emperor Nero (reigned AD 54-68) until Constantine's Edict of Milan in 313.

Hagiography served dual purposes: it memorialized the dead while inspiring the living.

Personally, I have devoted a fair bit of my academic career to biographical research, making me particularly enthusiastic about this approach to church history. In 2008 I published a book on Anglican bishop Stephen Neill.[2] I have also written several scholarly articles that are biographical in nature. Biography is one of the great historical approaches because it is so fascinating; it seems we are intrinsically interested in other people's personal lives. We can hardly think about movements and institutions without appealing, at some level, to the individual. Indeed the study of church history—or history for that matter—is nearly impossible without incorporating biography. I cannot imagine a study of the Revolutionary War without delving into the personal. Why did so many Americans want independence from England? Did George III sympathize with them at all? How did a ragtag military gain the wherewithal to overcome something as powerful and iconic as the British military?

Historical biography is not free from struggles and tensions however. We have a tendency to relate to our subjects, making us prone to the extremes of exaltation or defamation. Immersing ourselves into biography takes us deep into a political web of human interaction, subtle cultural minutia, and power plays. Why do we exalt one person and defame another? Why would a democracy sympathizer publish his views while a citizen of North Korea? The problem is that he probably would not. There is everything to lose. What good is it for an American to write a treatise about the grand mistake it was to break free from England? The political powers would work against her, effectively causing her to become a pariah in her immediate social context.

While rare and difficult, it is possible to write about a person in a sophisticated and nuanced way that steers the middle course. It can be done, and it has been done. While no person can claim complete objectivity, a trained historian is likely more objective than a person without training. The more critical historiographical questions have to do with *how* objective we can become in our biography, not whether we can.

Brief Overview

This chapter's methodology is straightforward. I have chosen one or two subjects from each century of Christian faith, using them as a touchstone for exploring larger issues going on during their lives.

The chapter will unfold chronologically from Jesus' century to our own. I have tried to think broadly rather than bringing up the same people discussed in all the old church history books. I have included lesser known figures. I have worked for balance: Orthodox/Protestant/Catholic, men and women, east and west, wealthy and poor, famous and relatively obscure. Hopefully this hodgepodge of Christian faith will cast some light on the diversity of this global religion. While my primary aim is to inform, I will not be disappointed if readers walk away a little inspired. What is life without inspiration? What good is religious biography if it fails to inspire the religious?

After all, Christian history is a log of billions of people who have attempted to answer Jesus' question over the course of 2000 years, "But what about you? Who do you say I am?" Although some of their answers have been suspect, bizarre, or demented, more than a few have been magnificently inspiring, evincing the human spirit at its best.

21 Centuries of Christian Life

1st Century: Barnabas

This biographical narrative of church history begins with Barnabas, a Hellenized Jew from Cyprus, and one of the many unheralded figures of early Christianity. Originally named Joseph, he acquired the name Barnabas ("son of encouragement") when the apostles witnessed his extraordinary surrender to the cause of Christ. He sold some property and put the proceeds at the feet of the apostles. The fledgling movement of "Disciples"—since they were not yet known as Christians—was strengthened and inspired by his act.

I like Barnabas's style. He was a quiet leader. He labored alongside the apostle Paul for some time, eventually attaining the elite status of an apostle.[3] For years he and Paul labored shoulder to shoulder in sharing the gospel. He attended the important Council of Jerusalem in the year AD 50. For all his accomplishments, he is not well known among Christians today. He has been overshadowed by Paul. Things might have been different if Tertullian—an early church father—had his way. Tertullian believed Barnabas was the author of the New Testament book of Hebrews. This notion makes sense. Barnabas was sensitive towards Hebraic Christians; they were poor. Barnabas gathered offerings from other Christians to help those in the holy city of Jerusalem.

Barnabas is described in Acts 11 as "a good man, full of the Holy Spirit and faith." He is known to have introduced Paul to the apostles.[4] Like Paul he was a fearless rhetorician and apologist for the Christian faith. He and Paul were the dream team, thought to be gods on one occasion in the city of Lystra.[5] In a somewhat humorous scene, the Lycaonians believed Barnabas to be Zeus—king of the gods. It is revealing that they considered Paul to be Hermes—the messenger of the gods. A priest from the Zeus temple actually presented some bulls to be sacrificed to the two celebrities. Barnabas and Paul only upset them by insisting they were mere men. Paul actually ended up getting stoned by the people, but they left Barnabas alone.

Barnabas was known for his encouragement, but he was no pushover. In Acts 15 we see him debating with conservative Jews that circumcision was not essential for newly converted Gentiles. He and Paul hushed the audience when they told of their amazing and successful missionary journeys to Gentiles. He courageously stood up to Paul on one occasion when they disagreed over whether to take Mark with them on their journeys. Mark deserted them on a previous trip and Paul refused to allow Mark a second chance. Barnabas, in his gracious way, forgave Mark and even parted ways with Paul over the matter. The author Luke described the incident as a "sharp disagreement." At that point Barnabas drops out of the book of Acts since Luke began travelling with Paul around that time according to the various "we" passages.

Paul's status increased from that point while Barnabas's whereabouts after the fracture are known only through scattered sources. Paul complained in 1 Corinthians 9 that he and Barnabas had to hold down jobs in addition to their ministries, whereas the other apostles and Christ's brothers appear to have received their livelihood from their ministries. Paul also seems annoyed that the other leaders, namely Peter, were allowed to take their wives with them on their travels.

Barnabas's final years remain a mystery. We are left with extra-canonical sources that tell of his martyrdom, by stoning, at the hands of Jews in Salamis, Cyprus, around the year AD 61. Supposedly Mark, after witnessing the events, interred his body in a cave where it was discovered in the fifth century. The hagiography claims his relics had a Hebrew version of the gospel of Matthew on his chest. Barnabas is revered by the autocephalous Orthodox Church of Cyprus and is considered its founder and first bishop.

2nd Century: Blandina, Perpetua, and Felicity

In the first few centuries of Christianity, many were persecuted. At times these intense periods became brutal and savage. The future of Christianity was hanging in the balance for some time. Certain Roman leaders wanted the Christians annihilated. Slowly and steadily, however, Christians evangelized, put their lives on the line, and withstood hellish experiences due to their belief that Jesus was the Messiah, the Son of God, the reason for human existence. Their faith was repulsive yet curiously attractive. What was it about these people who were willing to die for this man Jesus? In the year AD 197, church father Tertullian wrote "The blood of the martyrs is the seed of the church."

The three figures highlighted in this section lived around the time of Tertullian's famous observation: Blandina (162–177), Perpetua (181–203), and Felicity (died 203). These women were victims of the persecutions of Roman emperors Marcus Aurelius (reigned 161–180) and Septimius Severus (reigned 193–211).

Church history books celebrate the church fathers of this period: Justin Martyr, Tertullian, Irenaeus, and Origen. However, while this period represents a high watermark in the development of Christian theology, it was also a treacherous period, when one could be forced to choose either human life or Christian faith. Many Christians chose human life, many chose eternal life. Many chose to keep their lives by making sacrifices to the Roman gods and emperors, only to later try regaining admission into the church. These Christians who abandoned Christ out of self-preservation, but wished to return to the church, were the subject of much controversy. They were called "the lapsed," or, "Lapsi," and good theologians took different positions on what to do with these people. The case of the lapsed Christians brought many issues to the fore: the nature of forgiveness, apostasy, predestination, a cheapening of the Christian commitment, and resentment. After all, it would be difficult to accept a person back into a church where several others had surrendered their lives. How does one commune with an apostate who desires acceptance into the community after the refining fires of persecution have cooled? Does that amount to cheap grace?

The case of the lapsed was a thorny issue, especially in northern Africa, in the regions of modern-day Tunisia and Algeria. Two groups, known as Novatianists and Donatists, rose up in North Africa. Both of them were reactions to the lax approach of the mainline bishops on accepting the lapsed Christians back into the Christian assembly. Novatius and Donatus were bishops who held to a rigorous, Puritan form of Christianity. They took inspiration from the Christian martyrs who had publicly surrendered their lives for the truth of Jesus Christ. To them, it was not fair that these wishy-washies simply return to the Christian fold, hat in hand. The persecutions were purifying fires, and to cave into Roman pressure meant to abandon everything taught by Christ and his apostles. Jesus said finding your life might mean losing it. In the words of the apostle Paul, another martyr: "For to me, to live is Christ and to die is gain."[6]

It is one of the great ironies of Christian history that Augustine—perhaps the most influential person in the history of the Roman Catholic Church—argued vehemently against the Donatists. Augustine believed the answers to these problems were found in the central concepts of grace, forgiveness, and mercy. His views won the day. Did he cause the church to have less conviction? It is difficult to assess. What we do know is when Islam came to town in the seventh century, they had little problem converting the people. Today, Christians are very few and far between in the land of Augustine. North Africa is nearly devoid of Christians. It is Islamic land now.

The word "martyr" is actually a Greek word that is translated into English as "witness." Blandina, Perpetua, and Felicity were eager to be "witnesses" for

Jesus Christ, their sole reason for existence. Their stories are difficult to read, but inspirational for followers of Christ.

Blandina was a teenage slave in Lyons, France. Her death became legendary because of the overwhelming suffering she endured before the end.[7] According to the church historian Eusebius (263–339), Blandina was one of many victims killed during a festival for the Roman Emperor each year around August 1. Gladiators were expensive, but Christians and other prisoners were cheap. Blandina, just 15 years old at the time, was part of a group to be publicly executed for entertainment purposes. She was taken to the amphitheater and suspended on a stake for wild beasts, but they did not attack her. While hanging there, other Christians in the ring took great inspiration from her courage, comparing her to Jesus on the cross. The soldiers took her down and kept her in prison a few more days.

On the last day of the festival, Blandina and another 15-year-old—a boy named Ponticus—were again brought into the ring. They were forced to watch other Christians die for several days prior and were given the opportunity to renounce their Christian faith and pay respect to Roman idols. They refused, and paid dearly. After Ponticus died, Blandina was whipped and placed in the "roasting seat." She endured, and the public was amazed by her stamina. Finally, petite Blandina was "enclosed in a net, and thrown before a bull." She was tossed into the air until nearly dead. Finally a soldier sliced her throat. Her body was exposed for six days, burned, and the ashes were placed into the Rhone River. Blandina is today considered a saint and her feast day is June 2.

More famous is the story of Perpetua and Felicity. In Carthage, Tunisia, they got entangled in the Roman dragnet intended to bring unpatriotic dissenters to judgment. They were both young mothers. Felicity was the eight-months pregnant slave to the noblewoman Perpetua, who was nursing a child. Their story, written by Perpetua and edited by Tertullian, has inspired Christians for centuries.

Perpetua was bright, literate, and observant. Her autobiographical record is considered by some to be the earliest Christian text authored by a woman. Her martyrdom is attached to her text in an appendix that has also survived.

In prison, Perpetua had visions that the end was near. She was at peace, but she worried about her young son. Her mother successfully bribed the jailers to allow Perpetua to nurse her baby while incarcerated. Perpetua's father was not a Christian and begged her to renounce her faith. She refused and was condemned to wild beasts in the arena. She came to believe that facing the animals would in reality be her duel with Satan. God convinced her she would prevail, however. In her visions she was rescued by a heavenly ladder.

Two days before the public execution, the slave Felicity gave birth to a daughter. The Christian community took the child into its care. On the day of the arena games, these two Christian women, along with four Christian men, were scourged with whips before the animals were unleashed: a boar, bear, leopard, and wild cow. After being wounded by the animals, the Christians all gave each other the kiss of peace, and then the soldiers finished the deed. The hagiography has Perpetua putting the sword to her own neck because the soldier was only a novice. Their feast day is March 7. Taken together, the names of these two saints means "eternal happiness," and they have inspired many over the centuries to seek the everlasting treasures of heaven rather than the fleeting gains of the physical world.

3rd Century: Chrysanthus and Daria

Here we have a beautiful love story. The early centuries of Christianity are dominated by those who abstained from romance. In Chrysanthus and Daria, however, we have marriage being exalted. Clearly, the rendition of the story that was passed down was meant to be a teaching tool because it contains a bizarre detail: this married couple never had sex. It is also tied to the deep veneration for martyrs killed in the brutal persecutions prior to Constantine's Edict of Milan in 313.

The story begins with a young nobleman, Chrysanthus, receiving a top-notch education in Rome. During his studies he became disenchanted with the excesses of Roman privilege. He encountered Christianity through reading Christian scriptures, especially the book of Acts, and received baptism from a hermetic monk named Carpophorus. Chrysanthus's father, an Egyptian nobleman, was livid and resolved to bring his son back to traditional Roman understandings. The father had no success, so at the advice of friends he came up with one last rescue attempt: he would arrange a marriage with a beautiful Roman Vestal Virgin. The Vestal Virgins were a group of priestesses linked to the good fortunes of Rome. They protected a sacred fire dedicated to Vesta, goddess of home and family.

Daria, one of the priestly virgins, agreed to the plot. She was an intelligent and beautiful young woman. The plan was that she would marry Chrysanthus and bring him back to Roman patriotism. They did marry, but the outcome surprised everybody. Through a series of intellectual arguments, Daria became convinced by her new husband that the gods of Rome were false; only Jesus Christ should be worshiped. The couple began to evangelize the community and eventually brought an important Roman official, along with his family and soldiers, to Christian faith. This man's name was Claudius the Tribune and according to the hagiography he and his family were martyred.

Converting a respected Roman official brought the young couple un-wanted attention from the authorities. Led to a sandpit off the Via Salaria—an important road that connected Rome to the Adriatic Sea—they were buried alive around the year 283. Christians began to visit a cave near the execution site in order to pay respects to the young, martyred couple.

Chrysanthus and Daria created a posthumous stir in 2011 when they were featured on National Geographic television.[8] Scientists and scholars were surprised when they found two skeletons in an Italian cathedral that were purported to be the remains of the couple. Professors from the Universities of Genoa and Turin concluded this might well be the famous martyrs. According to carbon dating, DNA tests, and other analyses, the bones were from the period AD 80-340, and were of a young couple in their late teens or early twenties.

The courageous couple is honored with feast days in both the Western and Eastern traditions. Their story is a good example of hagiography. No doubt there is some truth to the story, but we will never have proof of the details. The couple's decision to get married yet remain celibate is suspect at best. It shows just how highly celibacy was praised in the church—even among the married! The story is also helpful for understanding the dynamics of a changing Roman empire. People were converting to Christianity by the thousands, and the government had a difficult time coping. What should be done with all of these people who would not pay the traditional respects to Roman power, religious norms, and culture?

Perhaps most fundamentally, the Chrysanthus and Daria story is about married love and true teamwork within the institution of marriage. We see an intelligent couple, working shoulder to shoulder as equals, falling in love with each other, and sharing a deep devotion to Christ as Lord. It would have served as an apt example of how Christian marriages were different from most Greco-Roman marriages in the sense that women were considered equals according to the Bible. For all of the talk of patriarchy in the writings of the apostle Paul, we also find the following:

> Husbands love your wives, just as Christ loved the church and gave himself up for her. ...He who loves his wife loves himself....After all, no one ever hated their own body, but they feed and care for their body, just as Christ does the church.[9]

In another place, Paul reminds his readers that for those who have been baptized, hierarchy disappears: "There is neither Jew nor Gentile, neither slave nor free, nor is there male and female, for you are all one in Christ Jesus."[10]

4th Century: Empress Helena

In 313 co-emperors Constantine the Great (lived 272–337) and Licinius (lived 263–325) issued the Edict of Milan while celebrating Licinius's wedding to Constantine's younger half-sister. This edict was crucial for Christian history and was preserved by two of the foremost Roman historians of the time, Eusebius (263–339) and Lactantius (240–320), both of whom were Christians. The Edict of Milan was a full-frontal refutation of anti-Christian policies. It has been celebrated for 1,700 years as the moment when Christianity moved from illegal status to legal status in the Greco-Roman world. However, in reality it was an edict of religious freedom for all.

Just a decade prior, in 303, the Emperor Diocletian along with the other three emperors of the tetrarchy initiated the "Edict against the Christians," the document that triggered the Diocletian Persecution. It was a brutal campaign of horror against Christians. It ratcheted up policies that had been in place for some time but were only sporadically and regionally implemented. Although relatively brief (two years), many historians consider it the most severe persecution of Christians in Roman history.

Surprisingly, one of the emperors who initiated the series of atrocities was Constantius (250–306), the husband of Empress Helena, and the father of Constantine. Today, Constantine is synonymous with the legalization and eventual dominance of Christianity in the Roman Empire. While striking that a son could disagree with his emperor father, in truth Constantius only reluctantly implemented a few token acts of persecution to satisfy his colleagues in the tetrarchy. Historians of the period observe that the Christian persecution was minimal in Constantius's domain, which was in the West: Gaul (France, Luxembourg, Belgium, Switzerland, Northern Italy, and parts of the Netherlands and Germany), Britannia (England and Wales), and Hispania (Spain and Portugal). In fact, many agree with the historian Eusebius that Constantius may have been a closet Christian, converted by his first wife Helena.

Helena may have been lost to history were it not for her famous son and only child, Constantine. After all, her husband Constantius divorced her in order to move up the political ladder, and she began living as an exile. Almost immediately Constantius married Theodora, had six children with her, and remained with her until death. End of story for Helena, right? Not so fast.

Helena's boy Constantine grew up in the court of Diocletian. It was obvious that he was capable and talented. In his twenties he began an immensely successful military career, fighting on the Danube, in Syria, in Mesopotamia, and in Britain. He moved through the ranks swiftly, leading battles alongside his father. Constantius died in Britain in 306 after declaring his son should succeed him as Augustus. The troops loyal to Constantius agreed, but the other Augustus of the time—Galerius—refused to allow the title "Augustus" for Constantine, but rather the slightly less significant title of "Caesar." Nevertheless, Constantine was now one of the emperors of the Roman Empire. Like his father he took charge of Britain, Gaul, and Spain.

Constantine consolidated his authority by defeating the other emperors, Maxentius and Licinius, in civil wars. Maxentius was defeated at the famous Battle at the Milvian Bridge near Rome in 312. Before fighting, Constantine had a vision of a Chi and a Rho—the first two letters for Christ in Greek—and had this "heavenly sign" emblazoned onto his soldiers' shields.

Emperor Licinius proved to be a thorn in Constantine's side for several years. While they were civil to each other in 313 at the wedding of Licinius to Constantine's half-sister Constantia, deep distrust was always present. They battled each other several times in the following years. In 320 Licinius began a new round of persecution against Christians and thus their rivalry became partially a religious one: Constantine represented Christianity and Licinius represented old Roman beliefs. A final clash occurred in 324 with Constantine's victory. The following year—the year of the famed Nicene Council—Constantine accused Licinius of plotting an assassination and ordered him hanged. Constantine was now without rivals, and the massive Roman Empire was once again ruled by one man.

Why was Constantine partial to Christianity? There is a good chance it was because of deep loyalty to his mother. It has been said, "The hand that rocks the cradle rules the world." Indeed Helena acquired a reputation for being "the power behind the throne" and is revered in the Christian tradition. The Orthodox churches bequeath an exceedingly rare title on this woman and her son: "Holy Great Sovereigns, Equal to the Apostles." Much of this praise is obviously for political purposes. However, there is more to the story. While Constantine's Christian commitments have been questioned for centuries, Helena was a devout Christian, truly pious. She was one of the architects of what would become "Christendom." Her vision was that the Roman Empire would become profoundly Christian, and she spent her extremely influential life in pursuit of this goal. What has been coined the "Constantinianization" of the Roman Empire might in actual fact have been an act of "Helenazation" (not to be confused with Hellenization—the spread of Greek culture under Alexander the Great).

Little is known about Helena's (250-328) early life other than she was not born into privilege. Her parents were innkeepers. Many British legends claim her as one of their own, but this is conjecture. She enters the historical record when Constantine acquired power. In 325 he elevated Helena to the status of Augusta, "mother of the sovereign." Coins were struck in her effigy. As empress she was allowed to wear the imperial regalia. By all accounts her son remained deeply loyal to her throughout his life.

Even so, for all the adoration heaped upon his mother, her saintliness was a reputation she earned herself. She became a champion of the masses. She was a Christian empress at the right place and at the right time. Christianity was rising and she was at the vanguard of the advance. Eusebius recorded her many acts of charity. With unfettered access to the treasury, she built churches and monasteries, disbursed funds to the poor, and financed the Christianization of her lands in creative and popular ways.

Some consider Helena to be the first Christian archaeologist because of a pilgrimage she made to the Holy Land at the end of her life, from 326 to 328. During her Palestine trip she ordered churches built at many of her stops: Bethlehem, Calvary, Mount of Olives, Bethany, and other sites associated with the life of Christ. On the site of an Aphrodite temple she authorized construction of the Church of the Holy Sepulcher, one of the holiest sites in Christendom.

The most important discoveries Helena made on her Holy Land pilgrimage were the purported "True Cross of Christ," the nails used to crucify him, and the holy tunic. None of this information can be verified, but her deeds inspired the masses. The incredible and at times outrageous period of relic searching owes much to Helena. Her pilgrimage to the Holy Land and veneration of relics became a crucial part of medieval Christianity. The scramble for relics hijacked Christianity to the point of absurdity; at one point there were seven heads of John the Baptist scattered about. Theologians explained it away as God's ability to perform a miracle, as when the loaves and fish were multiplied by Christ. Of course these events were well before the emergence of the modern mind. Christian devotion was the rule and remained so for centuries to come.

5th Century: Mesrob Mashtots

Constantine legalized Christianity in Roman lands in 313. However, Armenia had been Christian since 301, the first officially Christian nation on earth. Perhaps no other nation is as proud of its Christian history, for it came at a very high cost. For many centuries, Armenian Christianity withstood constant sieges from Persian Zoroastrians, Roman pagans, Roman Christians, a slew of Islamic empires, Soviet atheists, and others. Of all the nations in the world that are Christian today, Armenia is perhaps the most unlikely.

Why has Armenia remained solidly Christian against such odds? One way to answer that question is through the life and work of Mesrob Mashtots (361–440), the father of the Armenian alphabet. Revered nationally as a monk, theologian, linguist, and saint, it is to him we owe Armenia's written language. However, we owe him so much more: a treasury of Armenian-Christian writing, an ancient Christian civilization, and Armenia's culture of literacy.

At an early age Mesrob was identified as uniquely gifted in linguistics. His talents landed him in the secretariat of the king, where he translated royal communication into Greek, Persian, and Syriac since no Armenian alphabet existed yet. In time Mesrob became a monk and left his life of civil service for the monastery. Later he emerged as an evangelist among his people although the lack of a vernacular Bible proved to be an obstacle. His solution was to create a 36-letter written language for his people, and get a vernacular Bible into their hands. Can the scriptures genuinely speak to the masses in a foreign tongue? Mesrob's idea worked and many books preserved in other languages were carefully translated. Knowledge of Armenian is extremely useful in the study of biblical and church history manuscripts. As in the case of Syriac, Coptic, and Ethiopic writings, the Armenian corpus presents an independent resource for historical comparison. Some documents are preserved only in the Armenian language, such as Eusebius's *Chronicle*, which is lost in Greek but survives intact in Armenian.

Mesrob launched his newly written language with a fitting verse from Proverbs, "To know wisdom and instruction; to perceive the words of understanding." Thus, Armenian literature in its written form had begun. The impact on Armenian pride and identity was immediate. Schools began to pop up all over Armenia. Mesrob traveled to Constantinople to obtain permission that he might spread the new language in Armenian lands administered by the Byzantines, and he was successful. One of his great accomplishments was sending pupils to the great centers of early Christian learning—Edessa, Constantinople, Athens, Antioch, and Alexandria—to learn the Greek language and translate critical texts into Armenian. Again he had great success.

In 434, near the end of Mesrob's life, the entire Bible had been translated into the Armenian language. This translation remains the authorized version used in Armenian Apostolic Divine Liturgy.

It is a sad story how the ancient Armenian Church became marginalized by the larger Orthodox world. Scholars and Orthodox leaders today recognize the split had less to do with theology than with politics, culture, linguistics, and geographical distance. The Armenian Church is part of the Oriental Orthodox family of Christians which includes the following six autocephalous (independent) churches: Coptic (Egypt), Ethiopian, Eritrean, Syriac, Malankara Syrian (India), and Armenian. Church historians refer to these six churches as the "Non-Chalcedonian" churches. While they were fully part of wider Orthodoxy at the Councils of Nicea (325) and Ephesus (431), by the time of the third Ecumenical Council in Chalcedon, there were problems.

The Council of Chalcedon in 451 was one of the great misfortunes in the history of Christianity. A great debate arose concerning whether Jesus had two natures (divine and human) or just one. The Oriental Orthodox churches argued Christ only had one nature, and they were labeled "monophysites" ("single nature") as a result. It should be pointed out that these Christians generally reject the term monophysite in favor of "miaphysitism" ("one nature") which they claim emphasizes their actual belief—that Christ has only one nature, but that nature retains a united divine and human character.

Today, important ecumenical work is being done to repair the damage caused by Christians excommunicating each other. The Eastern Orthodox and Oriental Orthodox have held important ecumenical discussions in recent years. Christian unity is today a priority for many denominations. In the twentieth century, the World Council of Churches emerged as a Protestant-Orthodox forum for ecumenical conversation. Since the 1960s the Roman Catholic Church has been involved. It is vital to the health of Christianity that reconciliation occurs among all branches. Important and inspiring figures like Mesrob Mashtots—virtually unknown in the West—deserve to be recovered as the world's Christians learn to accept one another's cultural distinctions.

6th Century: Benedict of Nursia

Any history of Christianity would be remiss to omit the story of Christian monasticism. The person generally credited as the founder of monasticism was Anthony the Great (251–356). Known as a "Desert Father," his movement began in Egypt and expanded all over the world, wherever Christians settled. Anthony was a hermit who inspired Christians to move to the wilderness in pursuit of holiness and isolation from "the world." Disciples flocked to him and feasted on his words of wisdom.

In the fifth century, the monastic movement became systematized and organized by the writings of Benedict of Nursia (480–547). The medieval church, with its vast systems of monasteries and convents, is incomprehensible without a thorough discussion of monasticism, and it is impossible to understand medieval monasticism in the Western church apart from Saint Benedict. I once heard *Benedict's Rule* was quite possibly the most widely read book during medieval times, even more than the scriptures. The literate tended to be monks and the *Rule* was the central text regulating communal life.

Benedict had his precursors. His most important influence was John Cassian (360–435), a monk who established the Abbey of St. Victor near Marseille, France in the year 415. Cassian's work was archetypal, from its architecture to its austere and extremely regulated practice. For understanding how *Benedict's Rule* developed historically, the most significant figure is Basil the Great (330–379), who compiled a set of rules to be used in monasteries. The rules for monks are extremely ascetic to modern sensibilities, but they were written down for the cultivation of a pure and virtuous life that would hasten "theosis."

John Cassian took great inspiration from Saint Anthony and other Egyptian Desert Fathers who followed three steps to union with God: Purgation, Illumination, and Unity. These levels could take years, but they were essentially a slow movement from relying on the flesh to complete dependence on God. Various ascetic practices were incorporated to purge the monk of selfishness and lust. Taught to rely on the power of the Holy Spirit, they overcame all of their temptations, just as Jesus did in the wilderness. Eventually the monk began to serve the people around him, offering advice or helping the sick and poor. The final stage, often not reached, was "theosis," when distinctions between the monk and his God faded. All that was left was God. The man had become crucified, or, in the words of the Eastern theologians, deified. He surrendered himself so completely that only divinity remained. The concept was summarized well by Gregory of Nazianzus: "Let us become gods for his sake, since he became human for ours."[11]

Benedict and Cassian were the spiritual offspring of the Cappadocian Fathers: Basil the Great, his brother Gregory of Nyssa (335-384), and Gregory Nazianzus (329-391, known as "the Theologian"). These three monks became famous bishops and served in the Cappadocian region of modern-day Turkey. Their writings survive, and they are credited with laying the pattern for how Christians still understand the mystery of the Holy Trinity. Basil the Great, Gregory the Theologian, and John Chrysostom (347-407) are given the highest honor in the Eastern Orthodox Church and are respectfully named The Three Holy Hierarchs. Chrysostom, known in his day as "Golden Mouth" because of his eloquence, served as the Archbishop of Constantinople at the end of his life.

Benedict's name is known all over the Roman Catholic world because of his unsurpassable contribution to Western monasticism in the writing of his *Rule*. He is considered the patron saint of Europe. Sixteen popes have taken his name as their official title, including Joseph Ratzinger, Pope Benedict XVI. He is the namesake for the Benedictine Orders, both men and women, which were founded after his death. He is known as the Father of Western Monasticism due to his *Rule* becoming the dominant approach to monastic life.

Generally, when people think of monasticism, they have in mind Franciscans and Dominicans, who sprang up in the thirteenth century, or the Jesuits who were founded in the sixteenth. The Benedictine movement, however, goes back to the sixth century!

Benedict worked tirelessly to establish a dozen monasteries. The abbot or abbess has full control of the community and the monks or nuns are to live out the "Benedictine vow," remaining in full submission to their superior. The daily schedule is organized, so no time is wasted. Activities include prayer, worship, work, meals, spiritual reading, and sleep. Silence is emphasized and unnecessary chatter is forbidden.

Benedict's Rule was intended to be a balanced approach to monastic life.[12] He tried to avoid the extremes of radical asceticism and high formalism. It was written to monks of all kinds: cenobites living in community, hermits who lived alone, and wanderers who went from one place to another. The role of the abbot or abbess was critical, and there was to be no partiality towards any individual. There was to be an aura of unhesitating obedience that would lead to profound humility. In fact, much of the *Rule* is devoted to fostering humility. The scriptures were to be read and recited in strictly organized fashion. Prayer was to be short and heartfelt. Each monk got his own bed and was to rise early. No private possessions were allowed; everything was distributed. Monks took turns in the kitchen. Spiritual reading occurred during the two daily meals. Meat was prohibited unless one was sick or weak. Each monk was allowed a pound of bread and a pint of wine daily. Tardiness, laxity, pride, and misconduct were punished in a graduated manner: first private admonition, then public reprimand, then separation at meals, and finally excommunication.

7th Century: Bede

English Church history owes much to the man known as "The Venerable Bede." He lived from 673 to 735. He was a monk in the north of England and is known today for his *Ecclesiastical History of the English People*. Bede is considered a "Doctor of the Church" in the Roman Catholic tradition. Historians consider his work vital for understanding the development of Christianity in Britain. Bede lived during a crucial period of church history. He witnessed a power struggle between Celtic and Roman Catholic Christianity. Paganism and Druidism were on the decline as Christianity, like leaven, was making its way through the British Isles.

Scholars debate the degree to which Celtic Christianity differed from the larger context of Roman Catholic Christianity. We know there were some differences; however, the nostalgic idea that the Celtic tradition represents an early, distinct form of faith is problematic. In all likelihood, there was significant interplay between the two forms, and differences were mainly cultural. The most significant difference was how they were organized: Celtic Christianity centered on the monasteries, whereas the Roman Catholic Church focused on the office of the bishop. Another significant point of contention was how to date Easter. In 664 the matter was settled at the Synod of Whitby—considered a turning point in the history of the British church—when the Roman system prevailed. Another recognizable difference is the Celtic cross, distinctive because of a ring at the intersection.

By the time of Bede in the seventh century, Britain already had a rather illustrious Christian heritage. Born in Ireland, but later based at the Scottish island of Iona, the Gaelic missionary Columba (521–597) had remarkable success evangelizing the Picts of Scotland. He introduced a *Rule* and founded many monasteries. For reasons we do not fully understand, the monastic tradition mushroomed during this period, leading to a surprisingly literate, thriving monastic system. Founded in 563, Iona became the nerve center for monasticism throughout the region and has become synonymous with Celtic Christianity. Columba himself was a man of incredible energy. Not only did he manage his priestly duties, but he also transcribed hundreds of books, wrote hymns, served as a diplomat in the region, and taught Latin and theology to the monks in his charge. Columba is immortalized in the hearts of the Irish as one of the "Twelve Apostles of Erin (Ireland)." His famous abbey at Iona stands to this day.

A great product of the Iona monastery was Saint Aidan (died 651). Like Columba, Aidan was an Irishman. Also like Columba, Aidan established an island monastery: Lindisfarne. Founded in the 630s, Lindisfarne was home base for mission work in northern England. Today, people know of the amazing "Lindisfarne Gospels," an illuminated, complete Latin manuscript. Created around the year 700, it represents the finest achievement of Anglo-Saxon and Celtic art. In the tenth century, a scholar named Aldred translated the Lindisfarne gospels into Old English in between the lines of the Latin text; this is our earliest surviving copy of the gospels in English. It represents a remarkable achievement, and it also serves to demonstrate just how zealous these Celtic monks were to get the scriptures into the language of the people. Generally we think of William Tyndale and Martin Luther as the great proponents of vernacular Bibles; these men were doing it 800 years before!

The Venerable Bede is our primary source for many of these stories. He wrote a biography of Aidan and is probably the earliest source for Columba. He is our most reliable source for the life of Augustine of Canterbury (died 604), the first Archbishop of the English church. It is also from Bede we receive the precious story of Caedmon, an eighth-century monk who wrote many Christian poems and songs based on scripture. In his history, Bede tells us that Caedmon cared for the animals at the Whitby Abbey and wrote religious poetry in the English vernacular to encourage people in their faith. Caedmon is significant in the history of the English language because he is one of our earliest examples of Old English poetry.

Bede is a shining example of Christian scholarship in the Early Medieval period. He had access to many books, he understood the importance of primary sources (he used both Christian and non-Christian historians), and he realized literacy was the key to a healthy and lasting church. One notable inheritance we have received from Bede is the Anno Domini (AD) system of dating. While not invented by Bede—it was invented by Dionysius Exiguus in 525—it was Bede who popularized it by using it in his *Ecclesiastical History*.

8th Century: Nestorian Patriarch Timothy and John of Damascus

The prophet of Islam, Muhammad, died in the year 632. In a very short time Islam had spread all across the Middle East, North Africa, Spain, and made its way northward until meeting Charles Martel at the Battle of Tours in 732. In only 100 years, the Christian West was severely fractured and in some places lay in tatters, never to recover. For example, Christians now constitute only 2% of the Middle Eastern population. The Middle East is, firmly, a Muslim land. The same is true of North Africa. What did Christians make of these events? How did they respond to Islamic expansion? Islam is now the second largest religion in the world, but what were Christians thinking in those early days? We can engage these questions by looking at the careers of two important Christians who dealt with Islam personally: Nestorian Patriarch Timothy and John of Damascus.

The Nestorian church was named after Nestorius (386–451), Archbishop of Constantinople from 428 to 431. He became famous for his view that Mary should not be called "Theotokos," or, God-bearer (or, Mother of God). Thus, historically, he was considered a heretic. Few Protestants refer to Mary as the "Mother of God," thus the heretical nature of his views are highly contested, unless we are willing to declare Protestants heretics. For Nestorius's day and age, however, to claim that Mary was not God's mother was a mortal sin. Nestorius preferred to call Mary "Christotokos," or, "Christ's Mother." His view was condemned at the Third Ecumenical Council at Ephesus in 431, and he was forced to abdicate. Many Christians in the East, however, felt he had done nothing wrong. These "Churches of the East" in Persia and beyond were extraordinary missionaries and thus acquired a "heretical" reputation in the West. Westerners simply dismissed these churches as "Nestorian." It was a tragic time in Christian history; people were excommunicated over theological minutiae that are still rather opaque.

One of the great Nestorian leaders was the Patriarch Timothy (in office 780–823), based in the city of Seleucia, in modern-day Iraq. Historian Philip Jenkins referred to Timothy as,

> ...arguably the most significant Christian spiritual leader of his day, much more influential than the Western pope, in Rome, and on a par with the Orthodox patriarch in Constantinople. Perhaps a quarter of the world's Christians looked to Timothy as both spiritual and political head. At least as much as the Western pope, he could claim to head the successor of the ancient apostolic church.[13]

Jenkins describes Timothy's 19 metropolitans and 85 bishops, scattered across the vast area known as "the East": Persia, Syria, Turkestan, Armenia, Arabia, Afghanistan, India, India, China, and Tibet. Timothy oversaw churches that had no idea about the existence of the Roman church. Latin was utterly foreign to these communities that functioned in Syriac, Persian, Turkish, Sogdian, and Chinese.

Timothy's was a world where Islam was in control politically, and he was gaining adherents quickly. He worked closely with the Muslim caliph, the leader of the Islamic world who was based in Baghdad. In many letters that are preserved, and in recorded debates, Timothy is clearly competent in Islam. Publicly in 781 he debated the caliph al-Mahdi, and he did not hold back. However, he was respectful of Islam, and spoke of Muhammad as a prophet. Given the context, however, he had little choice.

Timothy witnessed the high point of Nestorian Christianity, known today as the Assyrian Church of the East. The expansion of Islam meant the slow-choking of the once-dynamic Eastern families of Christian faith. Tamerlane (a.k.a. Timur), the fourteenth-century Mongol-Muslim ruler, dealt a series of death blows to Eastern Christianity as his powerful military hammered Christian communities all across Asia. The Nestorian Church never recovered from these catastrophes. Today they number less than a half million members.

John of Damascus (676-749) was another important Christian leader in the heyday of Islamic expansion. Known as the "last of the church fathers," he is equally respected in the East and West. He became famous for his defense of icons (images) during the period of iconoclasm (image smashing) in the Greek East. He argued that if Jesus is the icon of God, then it is legitimate to venerate icons of the saints.

Historians link iconoclasm to the successful military campaigns of Muslim Arabs, who had no tolerance for images. In Islam, an icon is an idol, as in the Hebrew Ten Commandments. Byzantine Emperor Leo III wished to rid his lands of constant Muslim raids and began opposing icons. John of Damascus attacked the Emperor through his writings, rousing the masses. He was also at a safe distance from the Byzantine administration. Out of reach of elites in Constantinople, he lived in very close proximity to an increasingly Muslim populace. It is insightful to note that John "...saw Islam not as a new religion but as a Christian heresy."[14] He was familiar with the Quran and argued publicly against it, sometimes openly mocking it. It is curious how he managed to stay out of trouble. One possible explanation is that whoever was against the Byzantine Emperor must be a friend of Islam. Another possibility is that John was held in such high regard by his contemporaries that it would have been unthinkable to put him to death.

9th Century: Cyril and Methodius

Slavic languages are based on Cyrillic—a Greek-based alphabet inspired by the Bible translation work of Cyril and Methodius, the "apostles to the Slavs." Cyril (827-869) and Methodius (815-885) famously evangelized the Slavic peoples in the ninth century and created an alphabet to help them in the task. These brothers are deeply venerated in all of the Eastern Orthodox Churches, considered on a par with the apostles themselves.

The conversion of the Slavs in the ninth century is a remarkable story. Cyril and Methodius were Byzantine Greeks from Thessaloniki. They realized that to the north and northwest of the Byzantine Empire lay several people-groups who had up to that time not received the gospel in a meaningful way: Moravians (modern-day Czech Republic and Slovakia), Bulgarians, Serbs, Ukrainians and Russians. Saint Photius the Great (810–893) was the Patriarch of Constantinople who commissioned the brothers to take the gospel to the Slavs. The language they created for the Bible and liturgy is known as "Old Church Slavonic" and is still used by the Russian Orthodox and other Slavic churches. Their translation work proved to be supremely important, for the people came to understand the Bible in their own languages.

Throughout history, the Roman Catholic Church generally insisted that the liturgy be in Latin if at all possible. However, the tendency of the Orthodox was to favor local vernaculars. The German Latin Catholics of the ninth century were as eager as the Byzantine-Greek churches to expand their mission projects, and they undermined Cyril and Methodius in Moravia. They put Methodius in prison and expelled Greek missionaries from the land. Their efforts succeeded. Still today the Czech Republic and Slovakia are strongly Catholic, with only a tiny Orthodox representation, around 1%. Such was the inauspicious beginning to Cyril and Methodius's work. However, their disciples were persistent, particularly in the work of Bible translation. They completed Slavonic translations of the scriptures, liturgy, and many other religious texts.

Driven from Moravia, the disciples of Cyril and Methodius turned to the region of Bulgaria in the late 800s, where they again competed for souls with the German Latin Catholics. Orthodoxy won this battle; the Bulgarian Church was awarded its own independent archbishopric, and the people were able to use their own Slavonic language thanks to Cyril and Methodius and their followers. Serbia watched all of this play out and they knew they could go either Catholic or Orthodox. They chose to go Orthodox, mainly due to the language factor.

The entire region that is on the border of Eastern-Western Europe is a fascinating study of Latin Catholic-Byzantine Greek relations. Some regions went Orthodox and some went Catholic. Some, however, were split. The region of Albania and Bosnia-Herzegovina is an example of people-groups that divided over religion. Even today the demographics of those two countries reflect centuries old trends. Albania is 64% Muslim and 30% Christian; however, the Christians are divided about half and half between Catholic and Orthodox. Bosnia-Herzegovina is perhaps even more complicated. It is about 55% Islamic and nearly 40% Christian. The Christians, though, are divided between Orthodoxy (70%) and Catholic (30%). Other regions came together, uniting under the banner of one religion, as in Greece (Orthodox) and Poland (Catholic).

Russia's Christianization is the most crucial event in the history of Slavic Christianity because it is home to the largest Orthodox Church in the world. During the 860s, Photius tried to convert the Slavs of Russia. He had some success, but no Byzantine could have predicted how wonderfully their endeavors would pay off in 988 when King Vladimir converted to Christianity and required the same of his subjects. Moscow, the "Third Rome" of Christianity, likely would not have become Christian without the herculean spade work of the famous Thessalonian brothers.

10th Century: Pope John XII

Christianity has its dark periods. One of the darkest in the history of the Roman papacy is known as the *saeculum obscurum*, Latin for "the dark age." This period of church history has been called the "pornocracy" because of the profligate character of the Roman Catholic hierarchy. Historian Will Durant was not off the mark when he referred to it as the "nadir of the papacy."[15] While there are several options from which to choose, one would be hard pressed to find a pope more despicable than Pope John XII, who reigned from 955 to 964.

This low point in the Roman papacy was characterized by simony (paying money for church offices), sexual immorality, political maneuvering, and grave corruption. Octavianus, the man later known as John XII, was born around 937 to Alberic II, the absolute ruler of Rome at the time. Near the end of his life, Alberic petitioned the governing nobles to allow his son to fill the see of St. Peter after the current pope died. This move would unite the spiritual and temporal powers under one man if successful. Indeed, Octavianus, his son, became pope at the ripe age of eighteen. He adopted the regnal name John XII. He was one of the first popes to name himself, a practice that is now customary. History has not been kind to this young man; he is generally described as vile and guilty of all manner of unprincipled behavior.

John XII struck a deal with German king Otto I that would be mutually beneficial: John would crown Otto the Holy Roman Emperor, and Otto would recognize John as pope, substantiating the legitimacy of both across Europe. Indeed it happened, but no sooner had Otto left Rome when John regretted what had been done: he had, in effect, accidentally elevated the authority of Otto above his own. Immediately he began working with other European leaders to undermine Otto's authority, but he failed. Otto, incensed by the betrayal, marched his troops right back to Rome. Pope John fled.

Upon arriving in Rome, Otto gathered the leaders of the church and held a council with fifty bishops in attendance. John XII was called onto the carpet to defend himself of the sins of simony, adultery, incest, murder, and sacrilege. He refused to attend. Instead, he simply wrote a letter explaining that whoever tried to strip him of the papacy would be excommunicated. Unmoved, Otto pushed forward with the proceedings and John was unseated. In December 963 a new pope was elected, Leo VIII, a mere layman.

Disgraced John XII, not to be outdone, played the waiting game. Months later, when Emperor Otto left town, John came back to Rome with his troops and authorized severe punishment on those complicit in his dethronement. Predictably, he excommunicated Leo VIII. Everything shuffled again, however, when John XII died suddenly. The cardinals quickly elected another pope, Benedict V. (Benedict's papacy lasted exactly one month and one day, from May 22 to June 23, 964.) The question remained: what to do with Leo? Was he pope or not? Leo and Otto teamed up to denounce the new Pope Benedict V. The confusion did not really calm down until Leo's death in 965. A new pope was elected, John XIII, but he was promptly banished from the city by the people. Indeed these were chaotic times in the papacy.

While painful to read, these "dark ages," or, *saeculum obscurum*, live on in Western civilization as among the lowest periods in its history. The papacy was debilitated for some time after that. For example, in the tenth century we see the rise of Benedict IX (lived 1012–1056), the only man to serve as pope on three separate occasions. The *Catholic Encyclopedia* describes him tersely: "He was a disgrace to the Chair of Peter."[16] At the age of 19 or 20, Benedict was appointed pope by his powerful father Alberic III. He knew what the job entailed because two of his uncles had already held the papacy. Benedict was also known for his reprobate life, and was harshly condemned by contemporaries such as St. Peter Damian. Later he sold the papacy to his godfather (Gregory VI) but quickly experienced seller's remorse and snatched it back. He was finally excommunicated after making a mockery of the papal office.

11th Century: Cathedrals

In the history of Christianity, the eleventh century is synonymous with the Great Schism of 1054, when the church split into two halves, East and West. That year stands as a testament to how intensely political humans can become, even at the cost of destroying Christian unity. Pope Leo IX and Patriarch Michael Cerularius inflicted serious, long-lasting damage to the church when they split the Christian world into two. The damage has yet to be repaired.

However, while the Great Schism dominates most eleventh-century discussions, it is appropriate to take an entirely different approach to this period. Perhaps the single most important figure of this century is not a person at all, but a people, and their collective accomplishment: the cathedral. What caused Christians to build spectacular, magnificent, gargantuan churches all across

Christendom? They became the most definitive and lasting feature of the High Middle Ages, from 1000 to 1300. The work put into these titanic edifices must have been breathtaking. Countless hours were spent on erecting these behemoths that transcend the power of one man, or even one generation. The scale of construction offers us several insights: these people were intensely committed to the church; communities selflessly worked together to create a house of worship for which they could be proud; the vast majority of community resources must have been devoted to the task of raising them up. Taking decades or even more than a century to complete, most people who worked on them never saw their completion.

Around 1000, hundreds of staggering, tastefully designed churches began to ascend from the earth. It was a creative time in church architecture as the traditional Romanesque style was being challenged by the "Gothic" style, an initially pejorative term more associated with paganism than with Christendom. However, the label stuck.

Romanesque architecture was rooted in the basilica—the meeting hall concept of ancient Greece and Rome. The basilica was a public building in the city center. When the Roman Empire became Christianized these basilicas morphed into important church buildings.

The ground plan of the basilica was simple: it was cruciform (cross-shaped); it contained three naves ("nave" means "ship") or columns leading to the high altar; and it presented an apse ("arch" or "vault"). The apse is the semi-dome at the front of the church, faced by the congregants. Generally people would enter the nave, located on the west side of the building, and face the east as they walked in. Once inside they would be inspired by the apse with its intricate depictions of Jesus, Mary, and the holy apostles.

However, around 1000, this standard Romanesque style that had survived a millennium began to become challenged by Gothic, a style very different, yet refreshing to many. While Romanesque churches were intentionally solemn and meditative, the Gothic style was intentionally bright, beckoning parishioners to look and think outwardly. It is a subtle difference with profound effects. From the inside, Gothic style bathed congregants in light; from the outside, the needle point spires caused them to raise their heads upward and cast their thoughts to the heavens. Whereas Romanesque is earthy, round, and practical, Gothic is airy, vertical, and tall. It was the invention of the "flying buttress"—a strong masonry arch that transferred the weight of the roof outward—that allowed this development to take place.

In an age of illiteracy, towering churches also served as the forum for religious education for the masses through art. Stained-glass windows told the stories of the Bible, the history of the church, and the life to come. All persons in the community would have been intimately connected to their church through the rhythms of life: baptisms, weddings, frequent masses and holy days, and funerals. It was a place of refuge and could be seen from afar. The church was a source of pride. It took the entire community working in sacrificial service for several decades to create one. A cathedral, the most important church in the diocese, often took over a century to complete. Once when I visited the truly amazing Cologne Cathedral in Germany I asked for the date of construction. My host delighted in telling me that, while it was officially constructed between 1248 and 1880, it has been under renovation for several hundred years.

Churches were places of business. Pilgrims went there to rest during their journeys. Entertainment took place outside on the steps. The church was shelter from the elements or asylum during war. A professional clergy was on call to hear confessions, offer prayers and blessings, or listen to the anxiety of a troubled soul and offer healing. It is impressive that these architectural wonders have been preserved. It is sad, however, that in Europe most of these churches are frequented more by tourists catching a glimpse of the past than by worshipers exalting the inspiration for creating these masterpieces in the first place.

12th Century: Saladin

A Muslim warrior is a key figure in church history? Absolutely. The Christian crusades dominated twelfth-century church history, and Muslim sultan Saladin (1138-1193) ensured their failure when he defeated the crusaders at the Battle of Hattin in 1187.

One of the most polarizing episodes in church history, and certainly among the most complex, is the period historians call the crusades, from 1095 to 1291. Fundamentally, they were a series of attacks launched by the Christian West, first of all to wrest the Holy Land from Islam, and, second, to neutralize an ever-present Islamic military threat that had been growing for centuries. The crusades failed on both counts.

The crusades were part of a large, centuries-long struggle between Christians and Muslims with antecedents going back to the earliest jihads in the seventh century—when Arabs conquered vast amounts of territory that had previously been Christian. Many complex issues were involved, notably the importance of land. Whoever controlled the ports and passageways gained revenue through taxation. The Middle East, North Africa, and Spain were all lands that had suddenly shifted to Muslim control.

In 1095 the Byzantine Emperor Alexius I Komnenos issued a call for help to the Latin West. The powerful Seljuk Turks—a Persian empire lasting from the eleventh to the fourteenth century—had cut off access to Jerusalem. This separation was problematic. Jerusalem was Christianity's holiest city, where Jesus had died and resurrected. It was the city where Christianity began. It was the home of the Holy Sepulcher, where Jesus was buried. The city had been under Muslim control since 637 when the Byzantines were defeated following a six-month battle. For almost four hundred years, Islamic rulers allowed Christians and Jews to live there in peace as long as they paid their taxes. Pilgrims were also allowed unfettered access. Matters changed markedly in 1009 when the Muslim caliph authorized a campaign against Christian holy sites. Most shocking was his order that the Church of the Holy Sepulcher be destroyed, the very act that precipitated the crusades decades later.

In 1095 Byzantine Emperor Alexius made a formal request to Pope Urban II. He asked that the pope might offer military protection against the Seljuks, and he also hinted that the Great Schism of 1054 might become healed. Urban gathered support in his homeland of France and eventually called the Council of Clermont. He called upon Christians under his charge to come to the aid of the Greeks. He pressed for an armed pilgrimage, and offered eternal life to those who might die on the journey. Thousands of peasants and knights rose up for the cause, and the crusades began.

The First Crusade was actually quite successful if measured by what it set out to do. The Byzantine Empire was indeed helped and Jerusalem was in Roman hands by the summer of 1099. Crusader states were established at several crucial areas that held great sentimental and strategic value: the Kingdom of Jerusalem, Principality of Antioch, County of Tripoli (in modern-day Syria and Lebanon), and County of Edessa. The crusader states region became known as "Outremer," a French word meaning "overseas." For the first time in nearly 500 years, the holy city was in Christian hands, protected by these Christian principalities to the north, including Armenian Cilicia. However, to the south and all around, Muslim forces recovered and prepared for a clash of civilizations.

Cracks in the crusader states began to show in 1144 when the County of Edessa fell to Muslim forces. This defeat motivated the Second Crusade. Crusaders focused their efforts on the Iberian Peninsula, however, and won the city of Lisbon back from Islam. Thus began the Reconquista which reached fruition in 1492 when Christian armies finally consolidated control of what we now call Spain and Portugal.

The Third Crusade (1187–1192) was a major turning point. Under the leadership of Saladin, Islamic factions that had hitherto argued among themselves came together to form a united front. Saladin was not invincible. He had won and lost battles against his crusader foes: Guy of Lusignan—king of Jerusalem, Raynald of Chatillon—prince of Antioch, and others. However, with true grit and courage, Saladin and his men clawed back many times. Their resilience and tenacity paid great dividends when Saladin's forces decisively defeated the crusaders at the Battle of Hattin (in present-day Israel) on July 4, 1187. It was the turning point in the crusades and in the battle for the Holy Land. King Guy and Raynald were both captured. Saladin famously offered Guy iced water and then personally beheaded Raynald—a man known for his brutality. Europe was shocked and disheartened by Christianity's changing fortunes.

Saladin's work was not complete, however. Richard Lionheart (1157–1199), the King of England, rose up as an able defender of the faith. He embarked on a long journey to the Holy Land, vowing to win back land for Christ. In 1191 he came to the aid of King Guy to win back the strategically important city of Acre. In a real-life game of chess, Richard Lionheart and Saladin battled and negotiated for over a year. They agreed to terms in 1192, but the writing was on the wall: the crusader states had no chance of long-term survival in a sea of Islam. All over Europe, Saladin was respected as a fair warrior. While firmly in control of the Holy Land, notably Jerusalem, Saladin personally guaranteed safe passage for pilgrims travelling to Jerusalem.

The crusades whimpered off and on unsuccessfully for another century. Saladin's victories had turned the tide. The holy city remained in Islamic hands until the twentieth century when the state of Israel emerged. While the crusades are popularly condemned for their wanton brutality, the truth is that they were part of a larger war involving atrocities on all sides. For all the condemnation of the crusades, the fact remains that overall they were a colossal failure. Outside of the Iberian Peninsula, all lands conquered by the crusaders were eventually lost.

Historians observe that the crusades opened up relations between the West and Asia in significant ways. Trade, academic learning, and scientific inventions began to travel back and forth more fluidly after the crusades. Nonetheless, the toll paid on the Byzantine East was hefty. The crusades spelled the beginning of the end for Christianity in the Middle East. One wonders if Emperor Alexius's call to Rome for help may have been a tragic mistake.

13ᵗʰ Century: Clare of Assisi and Rabban Bar Sauma

While the thirteenth century is known for its atrocities—chiefly the 1204 crusader massacre at Constantinople and the infamous Inquisition led by Dominicans—it also contains a cast of Christian all-stars: Francis of Assisi, Anthony of Padua, Thomas Aquinas, Elizabeth of Hungary, Peter Waldo, William of Ockham, Saint Bonaventure, Pope Celestine V, Dante Alighieri, and many others. I want to focus on two individuals who tend to receive short shrift in the mainstream history books: Clare of Assisi and Rabban Bar Sauma. I have chosen them because they represent two important developments in thirteenth-century Christianity: women's leadership in the church and the growing connection between the churches of Europe and Asia.

Clare of Assisi (1194-1253) is usually associated with her male counter-part, Francis, one of the most pious lives in the annals of Christian history. Clare, however, stands shoulder to shoulder with Francis and deserves her own discussion. Truly, she is one of the shining lights in the Christian heritage.

Clare was born in Assisi to a wealthy, landowning family. She had become strangely fascinated by the courage of a young preacher named Francis. Clare was deeply religious from her youth; however, she was also very beautiful and would have made a great catch for a wealthy nobleman. Her parents found her a suitor when she was 15, but she persuaded them to wait until she was older. By the time she was 18 she had become enamored with the example and teachings of Francis, a once-wealthy young man who publicly stripped himself naked, gave away all his possessions, preached in the streets, and begged for his daily bread.

Francis's significance on Christian history is difficult to describe. He is known for bearing the stigmata—the wounds of Christ, arranging the first Christmas manger scene, tending to the sick and dying, evangelizing Muslims in Egypt, and caring for animals. One crucial aspect of Francis's work is it was formally endorsed by Pope Innocent III in the year 1210. Francis received papal affirmation and was soon honored by his contemporaries. He was pronounced a saint within two years of his death in 1226.

Knowing her parents would disapprove, Clare ran away and hid in order to follow Francis's approach to a life of poverty, service, and prayer. Her sister Agnes followed shortly thereafter, and they took up residence in San Damiano church, which Francis had rebuilt. Eventually, even Clare's mother joined them. The "Poor Clares" became known for their extreme austerity based on Clare's *Rule*—likely the first monastic rule authored by a woman. Clare's charitable works became legendary. She was admired by popes as well as the masses. She nursed Francis to his death and is revered for her deep piety, incessant prayer, and rigorous daily schedule of manual labor. Like Francis, she inspired thousands during her own lifetime and was declared a saint only two years after death. A basilica was built in her honor just a few years later. Her legacy is huge. Today there are more than 20,000 sisters in over 70 nations.[17]

Rabban Bar Sauma (1220-1294) is one of the more adventurous biog-raphies in Christian history. Sometimes called "the reverse Marco Polo," he traversed the Eurasian continent, from Beijing to Rome, a breathtaking accomplishment for the 1200s. His Western contemporary Marco Polo (1254-1324) is famous, but Rabban Bar Sauma—a deeply committed Christian monk—is little known. His name deserves to be shortlisted as one of the great Christian adventurers. His life highlights the remarkable missionary accom-plishments achieved by the Nestorians. His life can also serve as an ecumenical tool for repairing the unfortunate fracture between Christians East and West.

Commissioned by the Great Khan Arghun (ruled Mongol Empire from 1284 to 1291), Bar Sauma and his student Markos left Beijing around the year 1275 in order to establish connections with the kings of the West. As Christian monks, they also wanted to visit the holy city of Jerusalem and, in their minds, receive full and complete absolution for their sins.[18] They traveled all the way to Baghdad, a Nestorian stronghold, and Markos was, somewhat surprisingly, elevated to the top job in the church: the Patriarch of the East. Similarly Bar Sauma was appointed to a very high office, that of Visitor-General.

While Markos was now obligated to stay in Baghdad, Bar Sauma was commissioned to continue his journey to Byzantium, Italy, France, and of course the Holy Land. Bar Sauma's main responsibilities were to meet the Western kings and the pope, deliver gifts, and propose a plan to reclaim Jerusalem from Muslim control.[19]

Setting out from Baghdad around the year 1284 with a caravan including priests, deacons, 30 good horses, and much gold, Bar Sauma made his way to Constantinople. The Byzantine Emperor Andronicus II housed him and treated him honorably. Bar Sauma next made his way to Rome to greet the pope, Honorius IV, who had incidentally just died. The cardinals were fascinated to hear about the close relationship that existed between the Nestorian Church and the Mongol kings. They were enthused by Bar Sauma's offer that the powerful Khans were willing to help regain Jerusalem.

From Rome Bar Sauma traveled to Paris and met with King Philippe IV. The French king agreed to help Khan Arghun capture Jerusalem for Christ. Bar Sauma was impressed by the 30,000 pupils studying in the university, entirely supported by the king.

Setting out from Paris, Bar Sauma went back to Rome to meet with the newly elected Pope Nicholas IV. It was a splendid meeting, full of fanfare, exchanging of gifts, and very cordial relations. They celebrated the Eucharist together in both rites, Latin and Nestorian. The relationship became so warm that the pope begged Bar Sauma to stay in Rome under special protection. Bar Sauma felt he was needed in the East, however, and made his way back successfully to Khan Arghun, full of extravagant gifts from Pope Nicholas. He retired to the city of Maragheh, in modern Iran, fully endowed by the Khan to build a large church. It was completed in 1293 and he died the following year.

Bar Sauma's amazing voyage was successful in many ways and continued to open relations between both sides of the Eurasian continent. Jerusalem, however, remained elusive. As the great plan for a coordinated attack on the Muslim Mamluks was coming together, Arghun died. The year was 1291, the same year the Mamluks decimated the crusader states in the Siege of Acre. That siege is significant. No longer did the crusaders have a stronghold in the Holy Land. While the era of the crusades limped on pathetically for centuries, the Holy Land was now firmly and completely controlled by Muslim forces. Furthermore, in 1295, the Mongol Empire—the largest contiguous empire in world history—began embracing Islam as a state religion.[20]

14th Century: William of Ockham, Avignon Crisis, and John Wycliffe

Our three figureheads for the fourteenth century are interrelated, and all had profound and lasting effects on the church. We begin with the Avignon crisis in the papacy, known to many Catholics as the "Babylonian Captivity of the Church."

During the fourteenth century, the Roman Catholic Church was beginning its long decline in political influence. Most historians consider Innocent III (pope 1198-1216) to represent the pinnacle of papal power. Innocent proudly declared the church as greater than the state. Using the illustration of the sun (church) and moon (state), he famously argued that the state is powerless unless the church grants it power. The state has no inherent authority. True authority comes only from God. God grants authority to the pope, who in turn allows the state a portion of authority for earthly governance.

Those days were over, however. National identities were being forged. There began a great power struggle between the French and Italians over control of the papacy and the College of Cardinals. For about seven decades in the fourteenth century, the French won. This period is known as the Avignon papacy. Seven popes, all French, based themselves in this city in southern France, living in the splendid papal palace still standing there. The Avignon papacy lasted from 1309 to 1377. Here Ockham enters the record.

William of Ockham (1288-1348) was one of the major pivots in the history of Western philosophy. He is famous for his philosophical method: "Ockham's razor," also known as ontological parsimony. The simplest explanation is usually the best. Assume the least in order to keep one's thinking clear. In general, the best philosophical arguments are dependent upon the fewest hypothetical variables.

This idea was rather simple, making it stand out as challenging, even heretical during its day. Whether he knew it or not, he was setting the foundation for Western logic. He was cutting away centuries of tradition that had developed around philosophical ideas. If an idea is overly complex, cut away the fluff. If one argument gets conflated with another, slice it apart and deal with one at a time. Then build your argument. Be concise. Like a razor, Ockham cut ideas into individual components, forcing philosophers to think systematically, rationally, logically. It is hard work to assume nothing when laying out an argument. It constantly forces one towards coherence and clarity.

Ockham was an English Franciscan. He studied and taught at Oxford before getting into trouble with the pope. In 1324 he was summoned to Avignon to defend himself, but the deck was stacked against him. He was declared a heretic and spent four years under house arrest. In 1328 he escaped to the protection of the Holy Roman Emperor Louis IV, "the Bavarian." Fortunately for Ockham, Louis sympathized with his cause; he too had issues with the pope, John XXII. Louis used Ockham to argue, theologically, that the office of the Holy Roman Emperor had ultimate authority over all things, including the church. Pope John XXII responded by excommunicating Ockham.

Ockham's arguments, as well as his general approach to philosophy, gained in stature while the influence of the papacy declined. A low point occurred in 1378 when the papacy was moved back to Rome. Many in Avignon protested, however, and elected another pope in Avignon. The problem? There were now two popes. Thus was the inglorious beginning of the "Western schism." A council was convened at Pisa in 1409 to resolve the issue by removing both popes and electing a new one. However, when the new one was elected the other two refused to resign, resulting in three popes! The issue was not resolved until the Council of Constance in 1414. Tremendous damage, however, had been inflicted on the authority of the church.

John Wycliffe (1328–1384), an English theologian, is usually called "the Morning Star of the Reformation." Indeed most of Martin Luther's ideas were originally Wycliffe's. Wycliffe made his case 150 years before Luther. Virtually all of Luther's major ideas were embedded in Wycliffe's teachings. The church had become too powerful and corrupt. It was in dire need of reform. The pope cannot say he is head of the church, as only Christ is head. The church should not be a wealthy, temporal power. It should be poor. The Bible should be translated into the languages of the people, so they can read and understand. Lay preachers ("Lollards") should be dispatched to take the message of the Bible to the common folk.

Wycliffe's ideas grew as his poor preachers branched out. Word spread quickly. Jan Hus (1369–1415) disseminated Wycliffe's ideas all over Bohemia and was eventually burned at the stake for it, triggering the "Hussite Wars" between the papacy and followers of Hus in the 1420s. The cat was out of the bag. The large swath of territory between Wycliffe's Oxford and Hus's Prague had been exposed to the dangerous ideas of reform.

Wycliffe and Hus would not have gained such traction without a weakened, and weakening, papacy. The Roman church was losing its grip on Christendom as common people began to read the Bible, question the secular power of the church, and develop national identities. One issue important to Wycliffe would raise its head in the sixteenth century and trigger events unimaginable: the sale of indulgences for a person's salvation. Wycliffe concluded salvation could not be bought with money. This seemingly small issue would eventually transform Europe.

15th Century: Ars Moriendi

One of the key figures in fifteenth century church history was a text, and it was not the Bible. The mass production of the Bible in the languages of the people flowered in the sixteenth century, even though Johannes Gutenberg (1398-1468) unveiled his moveable type printing press as early as the 1440s. Bibles were very expensive in those days. The cost of a Gutenberg Bible would have been much more than a good house, affordable only for churches, monasteries, and monarchs. Nevertheless, while the "Gutenberg Revolution" took root in the 1400s, the full impact became palpable in the 1500s. The revolution accelerated in theological realms due to the work of two distinguished scholars, Luther and Erasmus, both born in the 1400s. In the sixteenth century, Martin Luther instigated a revolution of his own, but he was dependent upon Gutenberg's technology to accomplish it. He also relied heavily on the outstanding scholarship of Desiderius Erasmus (1466-1536), the first to publish a New Testament in Greek—the famed *Novum Instrumentum omne*—in 1516.[21] It was published one year before Luther's *95 Theses* and spawned a new academic discipline, textual criticism.

That is propelling us forward too quickly, however. Let us settle down in the 1400s. A good grasp of the fifteenth century is necessary for understanding the critical sixteenth century, so let us take a look at the *Ars Moriendi*, a fifteenth-century text.

At its most basic level, the *Ars Moriendi*, or "The Art of Dying," was a Latin instruction manual that offered spiritual comfort for the dying, and correct procedures on how to have a good death. There were two versions of the book. A long version was produced in 1415 by an anonymous Dominican monk. The text became crucial for Christians, and it was translated into nearly all of the languages of Western Europe. A shorter version appeared in 1450 and became the basis for the "block books," which were printed with eleven woodcut illustrations. The illustrations show a dying man in bed surrounded by angels, demons, goblins, saints, friends, kings, priests, Jesus, and other figures. Satan is besieging the dying man with five temptations: doubt, despair, impatience, pride, and greed (traditionally called avarice). Most people were illiterate, so the woodcuts made an indelible impression on a culture under attack by a mysterious power.

Martin Luther was one of many who lived in fear of the "Black Plague" and was distraught by guilt. Why did God save some and not others? Today we understand the bacteria was dispersed by infected rodents and fleas. However at the time it was inexplicable. Estimates are that half the European population succumbed during the fourteenth and fifteenth centuries, leaving a work shortage and perhaps triggering higher wages and economic advance. For the average person though, there was no upside. If one became sick on Monday, she had a 50/50 chance of being dead by week's end. It was catastrophic and terrifying, and nobody knew what to do. Indeed, from the 1300s to the mid-1900s, plague was an ever-present enemy lying in wait all over the world.

The *Ars Moriendi* was commonly used during the grimmest years of Europe's Bubonic plague, and it remained popular for centuries. Some scholars think it may have been disseminated so widely because the plague claimed substantial numbers of clergy, leaving people without a priest at death. It has also been argued that priests feared contamination. Thus, the book may have served as a virtual priest, present in a text, so that people could face death with confidence in the absence of a church official. This manual for dying was probably conceived at the Council of Constance (1414–1418) and was thus sanctioned by the church.

The *Ars Moriendi* was one of the first books printed with moveable type and went through hundreds of editions and renditions, all over Western Europe. Some editions were over 400 pages long. Generally it consisted of six chapters:

1. Death is inevitable and should not be feared, especially for the Christian;
2. The five temptations can be overcome with Christian virtue;
3. Seven questions are posed to the dying person, geared to lead the person to repentance and Christian conviction;
4. The dying person is encouraged to emulate Christ's approach to death on the cross;
5. The fifth chapter is directed to the friends and relatives present, prescribing how they are to behave and what they are to do while assisting the dying;
6. When death is near, friends and family are to gather and pray so the person can achieve release with peace and confidence.

In my estimation, the *Ars Moriendi* has been understudied. There needs to be more scholarship on this vital topic that played such a major role during the Black Death and beyond. It was a text widely used among all social classes. On a more practical note, it seems that at a time when death has become so specialized and professionalized, the *Ars Moriendi* could serve as a helpful resource for Christians. Professionalism has overtaken the realm of the dying, a problem that the hospice movement recognized and addressed. Perhaps instead of isolating a dying person we could, as in the *Ars Moriendi*, place the dying at the center of our communities so that he or she can experience love, support, and communal solidarity during the final hours of life.

16th Century: Katharina von Bora

Martin Luther's future wife was a teenager when he posted his 95 *Theses* and set in motion a social and religious revolution. Born in 1499, Katharina von Bora (1499–1552) was placed in a Benedictine cloister when her mother died.[22] She was only five years old. At the age of sixteen she took her vows to live as a nun and began her education, which included Latin.

Katharina became interested in the Reformation during her studies and decided she was not called to a life of cloistered celibacy. Somehow she was able to make her case to Luther that she and several others longed to escape, but they did not know how to go about it without breaking the laws of both church and state. According to Protestant legend, Luther talked with a merchant who delivered fish to the convent and hatched a plan to get the young ladies into fish barrels so that they could flee safely to Wittenberg, where Luther's Reformation was based. The local students in Wittenberg were abuzz with the emancipated maidens.

Luther struggled to find husbands, employment, or places to live for the young women. Eventually they were all settled except Katharina. Several men considered Katharina for a wife, but for various reasons they never panned out. Finally, Luther himself proposed marriage to her after talking with his parents about it.

In 1525 Luther and Katharina were married without much forewarning. She was 26 years compared to his 41. His colleagues were surprised since he seemed rather content in his singleness, and he considered Katharina somewhat arrogant. They lived in the Augustinian monastery in Wittenberg, where Luther had previously resided between 1507 and 1521. The Elector of Saxony gave it to Luther as a wedding gift. Katharina took charge of the home and proved to be a highly capable manager. She raised cattle and farmed, ran a brewery, took in a constant stream of student boarders and visitors, ministered to the sick, managed the finances, and bore six children between 1526 and 1534: Hans, Elizabeth, Magdalena, Martin, Paul, and Margaret. Elizabeth died in infancy and Magdalena died at age thirteen. The Luthers also raised four orphans and suffered a miscarriage in 1539.

Significantly, Luther's marriage to Katharina officially legitimized clerical marriage for Protestants, although many other prominent Protestant pastors had already married such as Ulrich Zwingli, Philipp Melancthon, Andreas Karlstadt, and Thomas Muntzer. It was common for Protestant pastors to marry emancipated nuns, although occasionally they married widows (as with

John Calvin) or much younger women (as with Karlstadt). Unsurprisingly, the Protestant proclivity for marriage proved an easy target for Catholic critiques.

For twenty years the Luther-Katharina union was a happy one, and set a standard for Protestant marriages in the years to come.[23] Luther praised Katharina in his writings and delighted in the married life:

> Katy is kind, submissive in all things, and pleasing, more so (thank God) than I could hope, so that I would not exchange my poverty for the riches of Croesus. ...Even if I were a young man, I would sooner die than marry a second time, knowing what I do of the world, though a queen should be offered me after my Katy. ...A more obedient wife I could not find, unless I were to chisel one out of marble. ...I prize her above the kingdom of France, or the state of Venice; she is a pious, good wife, given me of God.[24]

Luther's death in 1546 spelt disaster for Katharina. She lost her husband, and his salary ceased. War and plague broke out that year, forcing her to move her family several times until resettling in Wittenberg in 1547. Her properties and land were in ruin, however, and she was dependent upon the Elector of Saxony for modest support. In 1552 the Black Death reached Wittenberg again and she fled. While traveling, her wagon overturned and she was injured severely. She died three months later at the age of 53. The hagiography purports that her dying words were "I shall cling to Christ as a burr clings to a coat."

17th Century: Kimpa Vita

In the late fifteenth century, Christianity began a period of massive global expansion that lasted 500 years. We are familiar with Christopher Columbus reaching the New World in 1492, or Vasco da Gama landing in India in 1498. Less familiar is the remarkable, and earlier, story of the Portuguese arriving to the Kingdom of Kongo in 1483.

The early years of Kongolese-Portuguese contact was sporadic and at times hostile, as both powers took hostages from one another. In time, however, the Kongolese leaders became attracted to Christianity for complex reasons. We know that the Kongolese needed military aid and received it from the Portuguese to defend their borders and expand their influence. There is no doubt this was part of the equation. However, conversion is rarely a simple matter, as much is involved: political power, emotions, conviction of truth, socioeconomic benefits and/or pressures. Whatever the case, in 1491, the Kongolese King João I (originally called Nzinga a Nkuwu, ruled 1470–1509) was baptized, triggering a mass movement towards Roman Catholic Christianity.

While we know little of King João I, much more is known of his powerful successor and son, Afonso I of Kongo (aka Nzinga Mvemba, ruled 1509–

1543). Afonso lived a long life—nearly 90 years—and ruled the Kingdom of Kongo for nearly 35 of those years. It is likely he became a Christian in his thirties and proved to be an enthusiastic student of Christianity. He kept in constant contact with the Portuguese kings and worked tirelessly to convert his empire to Christ. He declared idolatry illegal, provoking the ire of many traditional Kongolese. He was not afraid to challenge the Portuguese, either. He vigorously critiqued their unrestrained approach to slavery. However, overall, he proved to be a friend to Portugal.

The Christianity that Afonso supported began to indigenize early on, to the dismay of European missionaries. It included a theology that merged Kongolese ancestor veneration with Roman Catholic saints. This combination was important because the Kongolese holy ancestors were not dismissed as heathens in the changeover. Neither were Kongolese holy places desecrated; rather, they were blended into the syncretic Christianity taking root.

Portuguese efforts continued with the arrival of Jesuits in the mid-sixteenth century and later Carmelites, Dominicans, and Capuchins—a branch of the Franciscans. It was the Capuchin monks who had great success in the Kingdom of Kongo. This was ironic because they were the most intolerant of local traditions and practices. As a part of the counter-reformation going on at the time, they wanted pure, Roman Christianity. The Capuchins kept detailed records of their missions. Theirs are the best primary sources for understanding this turbulent era until their departure in the early 1800s.[25]

Beatriz Kimpa Vita (1682–1706) was born into a context of crisis in the Kingdom of Kongo. There was a civil war going on in addition to acute social upheaval, increased slavery, food shortages, cultural disintegration, and religious tension. Baptized very young, as the Kingdom had been Catholic for around two centuries, she married twice in her youth but both marriages failed. She immersed herself into religion, both Catholic and traditional Kongolese.

Around 1704, Beatriz began to have visions of St. Anthony of Padua, a beloved thirteenth-century Portuguese monk. She began to preach that she had actually died and St. Anthony had reincarnated in her flesh. Many people believed her and argued she spoke as a prophet of God. Her teachings were politically charged and highly unorthodox. She argued that Jesus wanted the civil wars in the kingdom to end. She assailed the use of idols, charms, and amulets. Some of her teachings were very strange. For example, she claimed Jesus, the Virgin Mary, and St. Anthony were actually Kongolese in origin. Dismissed by the political elite, she amassed a considerable following of common folk who were hostile to European missionaries but, oddly, loyal to the pope. The movement became known as Antonianism and proved to be a considerable force in the kingdom. In 1705 her followers reoccupied the abandoned capital of São Salvador and gained the support of certain nobility.

She began sending out missionaries to other regions of the Kingdom, with some success.

In 1706, Beatriz was arrested and accused of conspiring against King Pedro IV. She was also convicted of heresy by the Capuchin friars and condemned as a witch. She was burned at the stake on July 2, 1706, along with her infant son.[26] Her movement continued, however, as many doubted she had been killed.

Historians believe Simon Kimbangu (1890–1951) may have patterned his "African Independent" model of prophethood on Kimpa Vita. The connection is significant because Kimbangu is one of the more important figures in the explosive growth of African Christianity in the twentieth century. With over five million followers, Kimbangu's blending of African ways with Christianity has proven to be highly effective in the conversion of sub-Sahara to Christ.

While the scale of African Indigenous Christianity is today staggering, the Roman Catholic heritage still holds a major presence in the former Kingdom of Kongo territories. Angola and the Republic of the Congo are today mainly Roman Catholic. The D.R. Congo is half Catholic. Other countries in the region have strongly Catholic populations such as Burundi, Gabon, and Rwanda. There is no doubt that the Portuguese missions to the Kingdom of Kongo contributed to the situation we see today: Africa is now half Christian. The story of Kimpa Vita reminds us not to neglect the indigenous movements and African kings that pushed to create a Christian sub-Sahara.

18th Century: Robert Raikes

Christianity in modern times is almost unimaginable without Sunday School. It may come as a surprise to know that the entire concept of Sunday School is fairly recent. While there were many antecedents, the modern movement as we know it can be dated to July of 1780. It was the brainchild of Robert Raikes (1736–1811), a printer in Gloucester, England. Several people bought into his ideas and the Sunday School Movement mushroomed all across England, proliferating to become a global phenomenon. Millions of children came to understand the basic principles of the Bible and Christian living through the institution of Sunday School. They still do.

The late 1700s were miserable times for the poor of England. It was the beginning of the industrial revolution, and children were by no means immune from the drive to progress. Cities became crowded, but jobs were plentiful, so people migrated to the urban centers. Conditions could become horrible. Poor children and orphans were routinely put to work in the factories and mills rather than required to attend school. Education was a luxury for upper classes. Workers labored six days per week and had Sunday as their day of rest. It became a day of trouble, however, as these working-class kids blew their steam and were often uncontrollable. It was a self-perpetuating problem. There was no accountability. In the countryside everybody knew each other. However, the urban environment was an anonymous existence where most people simply tried to make enough to survive. Kids became ruffians and church was the last thing on their minds.

Robert Raikes's father owned a printing business that published the successful *Gloucester Journal*, a city newspaper. When Raikes inherited the business upon his father's death, he was able to publicize his belief that the working children needed to receive basic education, and the only time to do it was on Sunday. Raikes considered it a win-win situation: the neighborhoods would benefit by not having delinquents running loose, and children would benefit by receiving secular and Christian education.

In 1780, Raikes and his friend Rev. Thomas Stock (1749–1803) established their first Sunday School program in Sooty Alley, Gloucester, just opposite the city prison. There were many unsung heroes who stepped up by contributing, teaching, writing curricula, and holding Sunday School gatherings in their homes and yards. As a printer, Raikes was strategically positioned to publicize the charitable work, and the progressive evangelical community rallied around him immediately. Notably, the popular writer and activist Hannah More (1745–1833) got on board, as did William Wilberforce (1759–1833), Britain's famous opponent of slavery. John Wesley's (1703–1791) endorsement opened the floodgates. With the support of figures such as these, the movement's future was secure. Even adults started attending Sunday School to receive basic training in reading and writing. Offshoot programs expanded at breakneck speed.

The Sunday Schools began by ministering to boys aged five to fifteen. Programs quickly expanded to girls. Classes usually ran from 8:00 a.m. to 10:00 a.m. and paused for church and lunch. Afternoon classes went from 2:00 p.m. to as late as 6:00 p.m. Most programs were incentive-based as children received prizes for learning, such as shoes, clothes, books, and candy.

In Britain alone, the legacy of the Sunday School Movement is massive. Until Britain's Elementary Education Act of 1870, it was the only source of formal education for most children. One institution—the Stockport Sunday School in London—accommodated 5,000 students. Estimates are that by the 1830s around a fourth of Britain's kids, or 1.2 million, were attending each week. Sunday Schools became a key part of British missions, exporting the concept to churches worldwide. In 1889 a Sunday School world convention was held in London and sowed the seeds for the World Council of Christian Education. The WCCE joined the World Council of Churches in 1971.[27] Millions of children all over the world attend Sunday School. It has become a necessary, almost assumed, ministry of churches today.

19th Century: Barton W. Stone

The only American to headline in this chapter is Barton W. Stone (1772–1844), little known outside the United States. Even in America Stone's memory pales in the shadow of his iconic counterpart, Alexander Campbell (1788–1866). Stone represents the cutting edge of Christianity in the nineteenth century. Many of his ideas still resonate among Christians around the world: ecumenism, charismatic worship, non-denominationalism, and a willingness to completely re-think the form of Christianity we have inherited.

Born in Maryland, Stone grew up in the Church of England but was influenced by several branches of Christianity including Baptist, Methodist, and Presbyterian. He reached the height of his powers during the Second Great Awakening, a revivalist movement that swept across Britain and North America in the 1800s, sparking a great wave of Christian fervor that in many ways is still palpable in the United States.

In 1801 Stone rose to prominence at the Cane Ridge Revival, in Kentucky, "...the largest and most famous camp meeting revival in American history."[28] Perhaps 30,000 people attended, but what was extraordinary was the religious energy. We have reports of people howling, barking, falling down, jerking, running around in circles praising Jesus, laughing in the Holy Spirit, dancing in God's presence, and sobbing over their sins. Stone believed these manifestations were evidence that the Holy Spirit was upon them. What was even more conspicuous was that the people experiencing these "exercises" as he called them were from different ecclesial backgrounds. This religious diversity led Stone to conclude that divisions within Christianity are scandalous, and a unifying movement should take place since all believers are washed in the same blood—that of Jesus Christ.

When historians discuss the origins of the modern Pentecostal movement, they point to the Azusa Street Revival in Los Angeles, which began in 1906. However, the Cane Ridge Revival a century earlier was a major tributary. People were simply not used to this, especially in 1801. Church was a place of stillness and respect.

Moreover, church was a place where you gathered with like-minded people. Stone wanted to throw open the doors to any Tom, Dick, or Harry who claimed to trust Christ. His most famous motto was "Let Christian unity be our polar star." Gone were creeds. Stone's followers argued "We have no creed but the Bible." Gone were lengthy examinations to inspect whether or not someone's faith measured up. Stone himself was criticized for expressing misgivings about the Trinity. After all, it is a word not found in the Bible. He opposed predestination, which brought him into conflict with his Presbyterian friends. Stone was opposed to hierarchical thinking altogether. He fiercely opposed slavery and advocated an egalitarian structure in the local church. Churches were to be autonomous, submissive only to one authority: God as revealed in the Holy Scriptures. In his words, it makes no sense to rely on the authority of others because the Bible is "the only sure guide to heaven."[29]

Stone's somewhat stringent biblicism was uncharacteristically balanced with his high view of the Holy Spirit, the "forgotten God," a neglect that has plagued the church since the short-shrifting of the Holy Ghost in the Apostles Creed.[30] This embrace of the Holy Spirit was a challenge during Stone's day—a philosophical context dominated by John Locke's emphasis on reason. Stone's famous colleague, Alexander Campbell, seemed slightly embarrassed by Stone's emphasis on "the Holy Ghost sent down from heaven, without any mixture of philosophy, vain deceit, traditions of men, or rudiments of the world."[31] Eventually, though, they joined forces and made a formidable partnership. They rejected manmade names for their fellowship, preferring only biblical appellations such as the Church of Christ, Disciples of Christ, and the Christian Church. They thought of themselves as spawning a Restoration Movement—a restoring of the New Testament pattern. Ironically, today this stream of Christianity is labeled "the Stone Campbell Movement."

Stone's formula was perfect for the American frontier. It was simple. A group of Christians get together, pull out their Bibles, and put into practice what it says. If they want a pastor, they can take up free will offerings to support him. No Ph.D., M.A., or M.Div. was required. No bureaucracy, no red tape, no quarreling with administrators who might reside hundreds of miles away. This new form of Christianity was organic, fluid, lean, and most importantly, biblical. Like the apostle Paul modeled, you recruit a group of believers and gather regularly for prayer and communion. We humans make it so complicated.

It is fascinating to see the world Christian movement spread all over the Global South. Many of the rapidly expanding forms of Christianity are very similar in organization to Stone's plea for autonomy and unity. Churches are mushrooming all over the world—most of all in Africa—that set up shop with a Bible as the sole guide, and a charismatic pastor who relies on the Holy Spirit. African indigenous churches, "emerging" churches, storefront churches, "underground" churches and the like are sweeping across world Christianity, blissfully unaware that much blood, sweat, and tears were spilt to make this capitalistic, laissez-faire form of Christian entrepreneurialism possible. Stone's model seems to have won out as the notion of a state-church becomes increasingly untenable in a globalizing world.

20th Century: Richard Wurmbrand

Who epitomizes the twentieth century? Peruvian Gustavo Gutierrez with his watershed teaching on Liberation Theology? Dietrich Bonhoeffer's conspiracy against Hitler? Billy Graham's global crusades? C.S. Lewis's writings that shaped a generation? Desmond Tutu's fight against apartheid in South Africa? Korea's David Yonggi Cho, pastor of the world's largest church? Reinhard Bonnke's tireless global missionary travels? Given the violence and unspeakable horrors of the twentieth century, it is appropriate to discuss a man who spent much of his life a prisoner, tortured for Christ's sake. Perhaps this story best represents the happenings of the twentieth century.

Richard Wurmbrand (1909–2001) was born in Bucharest, Romania. His family was Jewish. At the age of nine he lost his father. As a youth he avidly supported Communism. In 1936 he married Sabina Oster. Two years later they became Christians after being evangelized by an elderly carpenter in their Romanian village.[32] They became Anglicans but later joined the Lutheran church.

In 1941 Romania joined Nazi Germany to fight the Soviet Union. The Wurmbrands evangelized soldiers but mourned the loss of Sabina's family who were Jewish and placed into concentration camps. Russia's decisive victory over the Nazis at the Battle of Stalingrad in 1943 changed the fortunes of Romania. In 1944, a *coup d'etat* ensued inside Romania and led to them being a close Soviet ally. Once flooded with Nazis, Romania became a Soviet satellite. It was in this context that Richard and his wife conducted an underground ministry to Soviet soldiers. Richard spoke out publicly against Soviet control of the churches and against atheism. It took courage, and there were consequences.

In 1948 Wurmbrand was kidnapped on his way to church. He was placed in completely dark solitary confinement and was nicknamed "Prisoner number one" due to his growing influence among Christians. He experienced Soviet brainwashing and physical torture which he wrote about many years later in his book *Tortured for Christ*. He was cut and burned and endured bones broken including four vertebrae. He later wrote about his prison ministry using Morse code on the walls to communicate with others. Many Christians under torture during those years did not live to tell their stories.

In 1950 Sabina was arrested and sent to forced labor. Their 11-year-old son Michael was orphaned. Sabina, however, was released in 1953 and became active again in the underground church. Richard was released from prison in 1956 after serving eight and a half years. He was forbidden to participate in Christian propagation. Upon release, he defied authorities and resumed his ministry.

In 1959 one of Wurmbrand's close friends informed against him and he was again incarcerated, sentenced to 25 years. Sabina was told that he had been killed, but she did not believe it. After serving six brutal years of regular torture Richard was again released in 1964 due to a special amnesty. He was surprised to find that he had become a hero for Western churches. Missionaries came to visit this defiant fool for Christ. In 1965, a Norwegian ministry negotiated with the government to get the Wurmbrands out of Romania. They secretly believed they could become a voice for underground Christians around the world. The ransom was set at $10,000, and the family was warned that they must never speak about their experiences. No one could have foreseen how enthusiastically the Wurmbrands would embrace their new ministry.

Shortly after release, Richard was invited to testify before a committee of the United States Senate in Washington, D.C. In May of 1966 he gave his televised testimony and removed his shirt to show grotesque scars from his years of torture. The following year he formed the ministry that would become his life's work, *Voice of the Martyrs*, an interdenominational effort to raise awareness of the thousands of Christians harassed, tortured, and killed for their faith all around the world.[33]

In 1967 Pastor Wurmbrand published *Tortured for Christ*. It became a worldwide bestseller, appearing in nearly 100 languages. Wurmbrand publicly denounced and secretly undermined the Communist world, illegally smuggling Bibles and Christian literature into their borders. He confronted pro-Communist movements in the West, shaming them for supporting such a demented cause from the luxury of the free world. Some of his methods were unusual. He launched balloons into China and North Korea filled with local translations of the gospels. A huge loudspeaker was placed in South Korea on the border so that Communists in the north could hear the gospel in their own tongue. Now in Africa, Latin America, Eastern Europe, China, India, Southeast Asia, and the Middle East—Wurmbrand's ministry is ubiquitous.

The couple worked indefatigably to the end. Sabina died in 2000 just as their medical ministry to Pakistan was launched. Richard died months later, as his "Christmas Care Project for Egypt" began.

Pastor Richard Wurmbrand is a beloved and revered saint in his homeland of Romania. His many books continue to be read, and his message continues to resonate: hate evil systems but redeem your persecutors through love. The Wurmbrands believed in the goodness of humanity although they witnessed the dark side firsthand. Their message was that eventually, with enough love and concern, people's hearts can change. The power of Christ can transform people.

21st Century: The World

According to the gospels, the last statement Jesus made before ascending to heaven was that his disciples should go out into all *the world*. It took twenty centuries, but today the good news of Jesus Christ has indeed been preached nearly everywhere. The Christian story has become a global narrative, from "Jerusalem ...to the ends of the earth."[34]

There is little reason to think Christianity has ceased its expansion. Indeed Western Europe has secularized, but it seems premature to predict Christianity is gone from the region forever. Separation of church and state is a new reality for many nations, and the shocks will reverberate for years to come. However, there is as much ground for arguing for the return of Christianity to Western Europe as there is for arguing Christianity's demise there.

Christianity in Eastern European is resurging. Christianity in China is, by most accounts, exploding. Asia is being rocked by Asian missionaries reminiscent of the selfless, dedicated Western missionaries of old times. Christianity in the United States continues to revive and reinvent itself, although one prominent scholar has recently declared that "Caucasian people groups in the United States (and, indeed, wherever these groups are found) represent the fastest growing mission field in the world."[35] Latin America and the Caribbean, while strongly Christian in name, are adjusting to the separation of church and state; it remains to be seen whether revival or regression will follow. Africa is on fire for Christianity, but so far the results have not penetrated the political and social institutions deeply. By all accounts African governments are mired in corruption. Christianization will certainly address that problem, but it will take time.

The Muslim world is the great exception here. Christianity is not making significant inroads into Islam. However, Muslims and Christians are first cousins in faith. They share so much. It is crucial that Christians understand the basics of Islam so they can witness in an intelligent way. Muslims share many of the same beliefs as Christians, even some regarding Jesus Christ: he was the Messiah, born of a virgin, lived a life without sin, is coming back one day.

The problem is this: why would Muslims listen to Western Christians after years of war? They are reluctant to listen to the same people who have been bombing them, especially when we describe Jesus as the Prince of Peace and all that. The West blew its opportunity to minister effectively to Muslims. Asian, African, and Eastern European missionaries will need to take up that challenge.

In the New Testament writings, "the world" generally refers to non-Christians. There is a fairly clear distinction between followers of Christ and the rest. What a difference a couple of millennia make! Today one out of three of us in "the world" is Christian. Christians are everywhere. At times it is very difficult to figure out who is Christian and who is not. There are today millions of Muslims, Hindus, and Buddhists who claim to worship Jesus. How do we categorize those people? Are they Christians? Half-Christian? Is that even possible?

While the future of Christianity appears secure, there is no doubt that globalization will usher in a new era. Ideas are bounced back and forth like never before through easy international travel, Facebook, blogs, exchange programs, immigration, study abroad, and the like. "The world" is no longer a foggy, foreign concept of "otherness." Today we know the Ethiopian—that symbol of foreignness in the New Testament. Perhaps we have been to Ethiopia, the end of the world in New Testament times. We have welcomed the Ethiopian into our lands and watched him thrive in the West. We now eat in Ethiopian restaurants in our Western cities. What represented the outermost edge of "the world" is a place we can access tomorrow by plane—or today through the Web. Most perplexing of all, that Ethiopian is likely a Christian, and his people have been Christian far longer than our tribes have.

Twenty-first-century Christianity will be dominated by names I cannot even pronounce. What we are seeing are these people with different languages, ethnicities, and cultures working together with the same purpose in mind. Together, they are answering the question, "Who do people say I am?" Their answers are strikingly similar to Peter's.

Conclusion: Who Do People Say I Am?

This chapter began with Mark 8:27-29.

> Jesus and his disciples went on to the villages ...On the way he asked them, "Who do people say I am?" They replied, "Some say John the Baptist; others say Elijah; and still others, one of the prophets." "But what about you? Who do you say I am?" Peter answered, "You are the Messiah."

It was biography that drew me into the study of church history. However, there was one biography that surpassed them all: Jesus. Much ink has been spilt through the years over "the historical Jesus." What did he really say and do? Who was he? In this text, Jesus asked "Who do people say I am?"

Christian history poses many, many answers to this question. From the earliest days, some thought Jesus was, gulp, a reincarnated John the Baptist? Others thought him to be one of the great prophets who had returned to earth, perhaps the likes of Elijah, who ordered the 450 prophets of Baal slaughtered in order to demonstrate the reality of his God. Throughout the Middle Ages, Jesus was often portrayed by Roman Catholics as the suffering, crucified Christ, gaunt and victimized. The Eastern Orthodox Christians have tended to present him as the "Pantocrator"—the all-powerful one, reigning supreme, looking down on them from the inner sanctum of richly decorated domes. It is perplexing to me why Rome emphasizes the suffering servant while the Orthodox Christians prefer Christ's kingly attributes. It is often said that the Catholics and the Orthodox represent the two "lungs" of the Church. The only problem with this analogy is that it leaves out the Protestants, who broke away from the Catholics, and today constitute 40% of the world's Christians!

Whatever we think of Jesus, or the church, we cannot sidestep that existential question posed by the Lord himself: "Who do you say I am?"

Peter's answer was rather simple. "You are the Messiah."

As much as I admire the Apostles Creed and the Nicene Creed, I think Peter's answer surpasses them all. Peter knew Jesus in a way we never will. He knew him as a man. Flesh and blood. Eating and sleeping. Hair, fingernails, skin, eyes, breath, and voice. Today we know Jesus as a symbol, a figure of history, a theological formulation, or even a sacred presence. We know Jesus through the memories of his faithful disciples who passed long before. We know Jesus only through the memories of those who passed long before. However, if those witnesses who passed down the gospel to us over 2,000 years were correct, then Jesus poses this question to us as well: "But you ...who do you say I am?" Peter gave a rather Jewish answer. It is simple. You are the Messiah. The apostle did not try to unpack the interrelationships of God the father, God the son, and God the spirit. He described Jesus as the fulfillment of the Jewish hope: Messiah. The Anointed One from God. The one who was promised in the scriptures.

The apostle Thomas, on the other hand, was given the chance to describe Jesus *after* the resurrection. Remember this is the Thomas who was more famous for his doubt than for his belief. After rising from the dead, Jesus walked to Thomas and faced him. "Peace be with you" he said. "Stop doubting, and believe." Thomas replied with gusto, "My Lord and my God."[36]

This chapter deals with biography: life writing. Bio and graph. However, the Christian faith has never been primarily about human lives or ink and paper. Christian faith is first and foremost about answering the question. "But what about you? Who do you say I am?" How we answer that question will determine the direction our lives take.

Questions for Analysis

1. What do you believe to be the most important quality of biography? Accuracy? Ability to inspire? Relatability? Teaching value?

2. Why have women been rather neglected in church history? What should be done about that? Is it a problem that can be fixed?

3. Why do humans seem to have an insatiable appetite for heroes? Do you think we have the same need for villains? What do heroes and villains do for us?

4. Who in this chapter strikes you as particularly important? Why are you drawn to this person?

5. Imagine the year 2100. Take a guess as to what the distribution of the world's Christians will look like. Where will Christianity be weakest or strongest? What do you think Christians will accomplish in the 21st century?

APPENDICES

Methodology

This section details the methodology and sources used to compile statistics used throughout this book. The first section is titled "Geography" and includes a brief summary of the location and comparative land area. All of the data given for the location is taken directly from the *CIA World Factbook*. For the comparative land area, some of the data is taken directly from the *CIA World Factbook*, while other parts have been modified to include a comparative analysis that integrates European countries/cities, as well as cities within the United States. The second section is titled "People" and includes specific data on the total population, total median age, life expectancy, and fertility rate. All of this data is taken directly from the *CIA World Factbook*. The third section is titled "Religion" and includes specific data on the top religion percentages, number of Christians, and the major Christian groupings for each country or territory. The data given for the top religion percentages is taken directly from the *World Christian Database*. The data given for the number of Christians was figured by multiplying the total population by the percentage of the country or territory that is Christian. Finally, the data given for the major Christian groupings was figured out by using the denomination statistics on the *World Christian Database*. For this current study, the different denominations have been divided into three possible groups: Catholic, Orthodox, and Protestant/Independent.

EXAMPLE:

Name of Country/Territory:

GEOGRAPHY:
- Location: Taken directly from the CIA World Factbook, 2008.

- Comparative Land Area: Some of the data is taken directly from the CIA World Factbook, while other parts have been modified to include a comparative analysis that integrates European countries/cities, as well as cities and states within the United States.
- CIA World Factbook and various other sources for comparison. 2008–2009.

PEOPLE:
- Total Population: Taken directly from the CIA World Factbook. 2008
- Total Median Age: Taken directly from the CIA World Factbook. 2008
- Life Expectancy: Taken directly from the CIA World Factbook. 2008
- Fertility Rate: Taken directly from the CIA World Factbook. 2008

RELIGION:
- Top Religion Percentages: Taken directly from the World Christian Database, 2008.
- Number of Christians: This number is figured by multiplying the total population by the percentage of the country or territory that is Christian.
- Major Christian Groupings: There are three possible groups of Christians that are used: Catholic, Orthodox, and Protestant/Independent. These percentages are figured by using data from the World Christian Database.

THE WORLD

PEOPLE

Total Population:	6,709,393,092
Total Median Age:	28.1 years
Life Expectancy:	66.26 years
Fertility Rate:	2.61 children born/woman

RELIGION

Top Religion Percentages:	Christian (33.33%)
	Muslim (20.87%)
	Hinduism (13.41%)
	Nonreligious (11.71%)
	Buddhist (5.78%)
	Chinese Universalist (5.83%)
	Indigenous Religions (4.21%)
	Atheist (2.27%)
	Neoreligionist (1.61%)
	Sikh (0.35%)
	Jewish (0.226%)
	Baha'i (0.114%)
	Confucianism (0.097%)
	Jainism (0.082%)
	Shinto (0.055%)
	Taoist (0.05%)
	Other Religionist (0.003%)
	Zoroastrianism (0.003%)
Number of Christians:	2,236,255,415
Major Christian Groupings:	Catholic (49%)
	Protestant/Independent (40%)
	Orthodox (11%)

WORLD RANKINGS

Population	Median Age
1. Asia (3,767,141,703)	1. Western Europe (41.1)
2. Africa (973,699,893)	2. Eastern Europe (38.1)
3. Latin America/Caribbean (580,413,248)	3. North America (37)
4. Western Europe (389,846,133)	4. Oceania (33.1)
5. Eastern Europe (356,470,738)	5. Asia (28.9)
6. North America (337,044,380)	6. Latin America/Caribbean (26.9)
7. Middle East (270,398,623)	7. Middle East (24.7)
8. Oceania (34,373,095)	8. Africa (19.4)

Life Expectancy	Fertility Rate
1. Western Europe (79.6)	1. Africa (4.72)
2. North America (78.44)	2. Middle East (2.88)
3. Oceania (77.77)	3. Latin America/Caribbean (2.42)
4. Latin America/Caribbean (73.14)	4. Asia (2.35)
5. Middle East (71.9)	5. Oceania (2.26)
6. Asia (70.67)	6. North America (2.05)
7. Eastern Europe (70.15)	7. Western Europe (1.56)
8. Africa (50.05)	8. Eastern Europe (1.38)

Number of Christians	Percent of Christians
1. Latin America/Caribbean (537,579,955)	1. Latin America/Caribbean (92.62%)
2. Africa (453,085,307)	2. North America (81.44%)
3. Asia (348,299,020)	3. Eastern Europe (79.76%)
4. Western Europe (304,430,845)	4. Oceania (79.74%)
5. Eastern Europe (284,328,648)	5. Western Europe (78.09%)
6. North America (274,505,073)	6. Africa (46.53%)
7. Oceania (27,410,997)	7. Asia (9.25%)
8. Middle East (6,611,769)	8. Middle East (2.45%)

AFRICA

PEOPLE

Total Population: 973,699,893
Total Median Age: 19.4 years
Life Expectancy: 50.05 years
Fertility Rate: 4.72 children born/woman

RELIGION

Top Religion Percentages: Christian (46.53%)
Muslim (40.46%)
Indigenous Religions (11.80%)
Nonreligious (0.59%)
Hindu (0.27%)
Baha'i (0.17%)
Atheist (0.06%)
Buddhist (0.013%)
Other (0.107%)
Number of Christians: 3,801
Major Christian Groupings: Protestant/Independent (60%)
Catholic (40%)

ALGERIA

Geography:
Location: Northern Africa, bordering the Mediterranean Sea, between Morocco and Tunisia
Comparative Land Area: About 1/3 the size of Australia
Capital City: Algiers
People:
Total Population: 33,769,668
Total Median Age: 26 years
Life Expectancy: 73.77 years
Fertility Rate: 1.82 children born/woman
Religion:
Top Religion Percentages: Muslim (98.01%), Nonreligious (1.80%), Christian (0.18%), Baha'i (0.01%), Atheist (0.01%)
Number of Christians: 60,785
Major Christian Groupings: Protestant/Independent (92%), Catholic (8%)

ANGOLA

Geography:
Location: Northern Africa, bordering the South Atlantic Ocean, between Namibia and Democratic Republic of the Congo
Comparative Land Area: About twice the size of France
Capital City: Luanda
People:
Total Population: 12,531,357
Total Median Age: 18 years
Life Expectancy: 37.92 years
Fertility Rate: 6.2 children born/woman
Religion:
Top Religion Percentages: Christian (94.07%), Indigenous Religions (4.74%), Nonreligious (0.96%), Atheist (0.21%), Baha'i (0.01%)
Number of Christians: 11,788,247
Major Christian Groupings: Catholic (65%), Protestant/Independent (35%)

BENIN

Geography:
Location: Western Africa, between Nigeria and Togo
Comparative Land Area: Slightly smaller than Pennsylvania
Capital City: Porto-Novo
People:
Total Population: 8,532,547
Total Median Age: 17.1 years
Life Expectancy: 58.56 years
Fertility Rate: 5.58 children born/woman
Religion:
Top Religion Percentages: Indigenous Religions (50.05%), Christian (31.50%), Muslim (18.09%), Nonreligious (0.18%), Baha'i (0.12%)
Number of Christians: 2,687,752
Major Christian Groupings: Catholic (62%), Protestant/Independent (38%)

BOTSWANA

Geography:
Location: Southern Africa, north of South Africa
Comparative Land Area: Slightly smaller than France
Capital City: Gaborone
People:
Total Population: 1,842,323
Total Median Age: 21.2 years
Life Expectancy: 50.16 years
Fertility Rate: 2.66 children born/woman
Religion:
Top Religion Percentages: Christian (63.53%), Indigenous Religions (34.98%), Baha'i (0.84%), Muslim (0.28%), Hindu (0.14%)
Number of Christians: 1,207,274
Major Christian Groupings: Protestant/Independent (92%) Catholic (8%)

BURKINA FASO

Geography:
Location: Western Africa, north of Ghana
Comparative Land Area: Slightly larger than Colorado
Capital City: Ouagadougou
People:
Total Population: 15,264,735
Total Median Age: 16.7 years
Life Expectancy: 52.55 years
Fertility Rate: 6.34 children born/woman
Religion:
Top Religion Percentages: Muslim (48.33%), Indigenous Religions (30.82%), Christian (20.17%), Nonreligious (0.65%), Baha'i (0.02%)
Number of Christians: 3,078,897
Major Christian Groupings: Catholic (56%), Protestant/Independent (44%)

BURUNDI

Geography:
Location: Central Africa, east of Democratic Republic of the Congo
Comparative Land Area: Slightly smaller than Maryland
Capital City: Bujumbura
People:
Total Population: 8,691,005
Total Median Age: 16.7 years
Life Expectancy: 51.71 years
Fertility Rate: 6.4 children born/woman
Religion:
Top Religion Percentages: Christian (91.27%), Indigenous Religions (7.13%), Muslim (1.38%), Hindu (0.08%)   ,
Baha'i (0.08%)
Number of Christians: 7,932,280
Major Christian Groupings: Catholic (67%), Protestant/Independent (33%)

CAMEROON

Geography:
Location: Western Africa, between Equilateral Guinea and Nigeria
Comparative Land Area: Slightly larger than California
Capital City: Yaounde
People:
Total Population: 18,467,692
Total Median Age: 19 years
Life Expectancy: 53.3 years
Fertility Rate: 4.41 children born/woman
Religion:
Top Religion Percentages: Christian (56.23%), Indigenous Religions (22.59%), Muslim (20.04%), Nonreligious (0.51%), Baha'i (0.45%)
Number of Christians: 10,384,383
Major Christian Groupings: Protestant/Independent (57%), Catholic (43%)

CAPE VERDE

Geography:
Location: Western Africa, group of islands in the North Atlantic Ocean, west of Senegal
Comparative Land Area: Slightly larger than Rhode Island
Capital City: Praia
People:
Total Population: 426,998
Total Median Age: 20.6 years
Life Expectancy: 71.33 years
Fertility Rate: 3.17 children born/woman
Religion:
Top Religion Percentages: Christian (95.05%), Muslim (2.77%), Indigenous Religions (1.13%), Nonreligious (0.89%), Baha'i (0.15%)
Number of Christians: 405,861
Major Christian Groupings: Catholic (92%), Protestant/Independent (8%)

CENTRAL AFRICAN REPUBLIC

Geography:
Location: Central Africa, north of Democratic Republic of the Congo
Comparative Land Area: Slightly smaller than France
Capital City: Bangui
People:
Total Population: 4,444,330
Total Median Age: 18.7 years
Life Expectancy: 44.22 years
Fertility Rate: 4.23 children born/woman
Religion:
Top Religion Percentages: Christian (65.64%), Indigenous Religions (18.80%), Muslim (14.62%), Nonreligious (0.68%), Baha'i (0.25%)
Number of Christians: 2,917,258
Major Christian Groupings: Protestant/Independent (70%), Catholic (30%)

CHAD

Geography:
Location: Central Africa, south of Libya
Comparative Land Area: About three times the size of California
Capital City: N'Djamena
People:
Total Population: 10,111,337
Total Median Age: 16.4 years
Life Expectancy: 47.43 years
Fertility Rate: 5.43 children born/woman
Religion:
Top Religion Percentages: Muslim (57.25%), Christian (25.21%), Indigenous Religions (16.64%), Baha'i (0.83%), Nonreligious (0.05%)
Number of Christians: 2,549,068
Major Christian Groupings: Protestant/Independent (70%), Catholic (30%)

COMOROS

Geography:
Location: Southern Africa, group of islands about two-thirds of the way between northern Madagascar and northern Mozambique
Comparative Land Area: Slightly smaller than Luxembourg
Capital City: Moroni
People:
Total Population: 731,775
Total Median Age: 18.7 years
Life Expectancy: 63.1 years
Fertility Rate: 4.9 children born/woman
Religion:
Top Religion Percentages: Muslim (98.29%), Indigenous Religions (0.97%), Christian (0.52%), Nonreligious (0.12%), Baha'i (0.09%)
Number of Christians: 3,805
Major Christian Groupings: Protestant/Independent (54%), Catholic (46%)

DEMOCRATIC REPUBLIC OF THE CONGO

Geography:
Location: Central Africa, northeast of Angola
Comparative Land Area: About ¼ the size of the United States
Capital City: Kinshasa
People:
Total Population: 66,514,504
Total Median Age: 16.3 years
Life Expectancy: 53.98 years
Fertility Rate: 6.29 children born/woman
Religion:
Top Religion Percentages: Christian (95.37%), Indigenous Religions (2.54%), Muslim (1.08%), Baha'i (0.43%), Nonreligious (0.40%)
Number of Christians: 63,434,882
Major Christian Groupings: Catholic (52%), Protestant/Independent (48%)

DJIBOUTI

Geography:
  Location: Eastern Africa, bordering the Gulf of Aden and the Red Sea, between Eritrea and Somalia
  Comparative Land Area: Slightly smaller than Massachusetts
  Capital City: Djibouti City
People:
  Total Population: 506,221
  Total Median Age: 18.2 years
  Life Expectancy: 43.31 years
  Fertility Rate: 5.14 children born/woman
Religion:
  Top Religion Percentages: Muslim (96.93%), Christian (2.68%), Nonreligious (1.15%), Baha'i (0.09%),   Atheist (0.05%)
  Number of Christians: 13,566
  Major Christian Groupings: Catholic (55%), Orthodox (40%), Protestant/Independent (5%)

EQUATORIAL GUINEA

Geography:
  Location: Western Africa, between Cameroon and Gabon
  Comparative Land Area: Slightly smaller than Maryland
  Capital City: Malabo
People:
  Total Population: 616,459
  Total Median Age: 18.9 years
  Life Expectancy: 61.23 years
  Fertility Rate: 5.16 children born/woman
Religion:
  Top Religion Percentages: Christian (88.68%), Muslim (4.05%), Nonreligious (3.17%), Atheist (1.82%), Indigenous Religions (1.72%)
  Number of Christians: 546,676
  Major Christian Groupings: Catholic (90%), Protestant/Independent (10%)

ETHIOPIA

Geography:
  Location: Eastern Africa, west of Somalia
  Comparative Land Area: About twice the size of France
  Capital City: Addis Ababa
People:
  Total Population: 82,544,840
  Total Median Age: 16.9 years
  Life Expectancy: 54.99 years
  Fertility Rate: 6.17 children born/woman
Religion:
  Top Religion Percentages: Christian (55.47%), Muslim (33.84), Indigenous Religions (10.43%), Nonreligious (0.18%), Baha'i (0.03%)
  Number of Christians: 45,787,623
  Major Christian Groupings: Orthodox (62%), Protestant/Independent (37%), Catholic (1%)

GAMBIA

Geography:
  Location: Western Africa, bordering the North Atlantic Ocean and Senegal
  Comparative Land Area: About twice the size of Delaware
  Capital City: Banjul
People:
  Total Population: 1,735,464
  Total Median Age: 17.9 years
  Life Expectancy: 54.95 years
  Fertility Rate: 5.13 children born/woman
Religion:
  Top Religion Percentages: Muslim (86.26%), Indigenous Religions (7.91%), Christian (4.36%), Baha'i (0.86%), Nonreligious (0.60%)
  Number of Christians: 75,666
  Major Christian Groupings: Catholic (60%), Protestant/Independent (40%)

EGYPT

Geography:
  Location: Northern Africa, bordering the Mediterranean Sea, between Libya and the Gaza Strip
  Comparative Land Area: About twice the size of Spain
  Capital City: Cairo
People:
  Total Population: 81,713,520
  Total Median Age: 24.5 years
  Life Expectancy: 71.85 years
  Fertility Rate: 2.72 children born/woman
Religion:
  Top Religion Percentages: Muslim (84.79%), Christian (14.66%), Nonreligious (0.44%), Atheist (0.10%),   Baha'i (0.01%)
  Number of Christians: 11,979,202
  Major Christian Groupings: Orthodox (91%), Protestant/Independent (7%), Catholic (2%)

ERITREA

Geography:
  Location: Eastern Africa, bordering the Red Sea, between Djibouti and Sudan
  Comparative Land Area: Slightly larger than Pennsylvania
  Capital City: Asmara
People:
  Total Population: 5,502,026
  Total Median Age: 18.3 years
  Life Expectancy: 61.38 years
  Fertility Rate: 4.84 years
Religion:
  Top Religion Percentages: Muslim (49.22%), Christian (47.26%), Nonreligious (2.86%), Indigenous Religions (0.62%), Baha'i (0.03%)
  Number of Christians: 2,600,257
  Major Christian Groupings: Orthodox (90%), Catholic (7%), Protestant/Independent (3%)

GABON

Geography:
  Location: Western Africa, bordering the Atlantic Ocean at the Equator, between Republic of the Congo and Equatorial Guinea
  Comparative Land Area: Slightly smaller than Colorado
  Capital City: Libreville
People:
  Total Population: 1,485,832
  Total Median Age: 18.6 years
  Life Expectancy: 53.52 years
  Fertility Rate: 4.68 children born/woman
Religion:
  Top Religion Percentages: Christian (90.53%), Muslim (4.62%), Indigenous Religions (3.18%), Nonreligious (0.87%), Neoreligionist (0.72%)
  Number of Christians: 1,345,124
  Major Christian Groupings: Catholic (64%), Protestant/Independent (36%)

GHANA

Geography:
  Location: Western Africa, bordering the Gulf of Guinea, between Cote d'Iviore and Togo
  Comparative Land Area: Slightly smaller than Oregon
  Capital City: Accra
People:
  Total Population: 23,382,848
  Total Median Age: 20.4 years
  Life Expectancy: 59.49 years
  Fertility Rate: 3.78 children born/woman
Religion:
  Top Religion Percentages: Christian (57.26%), Indigenous Religions (22.12%), Muslim (20.11%), Nonreligious (0.30%), Neoreligionist (0.11%)
  Number of Christians: 13,389,019
  Major Christian Groupings: Protestant/Independent (79%), Catholic (21%)

GUINEA

Geography:
  Location: Western Africa, bordering the North Atlantic Ocean, between Guinea-Bissau and Sierra Leone
  Comparative Land Area: Slightly smaller than Oregon
  Capital City: Conakry
People:
  Total Population: 9,806,509
  Total Median Age: 18.4 years
  Life Expectancy: 56.58 years
  Fertility Rate: 5.25 children born/woman
Religion:
  Top Religion Percentages: Muslim (68.76%), Indigenous Religions (27.55%), Christian (3.48%), Nonreligious (0.17%), Atheist (0.05%)
  Number of Christians: 341,267
  Major Christian Groupings: Catholic (67%), Protestant/Independent (33%)

GUINEA-BISSAU

Geography:
  Location: Western Africa, bordering the North Atlantic Ocean, between Guinea and Senegal
  Comparative Land Area: Slightly smaller than The Netherlands
  Capital City: Bissau
People:
  Total Population: 1,503,182
  Total Median Age: 19.2 years
  Life Expectancy: 47.52 years
  Fertility Rate: 4.72 children born/woman
Religion:
  Top Religion Percentages: Indigenous Religions (44.86%), Muslim (42.20%), Christian (11.61%), Nonreligious (1.22%), Atheist (0.09%)
  Number of Christians: 174,519
  Major Christian Groupings: Catholic (71%), Protestant/Independent (29%)

IVORY COAST

Geography:
  Location: Western Africa, bordering the North Atlantic Ocean, between Ghana and Liberia
  Comparative Land Area: Slightly larger than New Mexico
  Capital City: Yamoussoukro
People:
  Total Population: 20,179,602
  Total Median Age: 19 years
  Life Expectancy: 54.64 years
  Fertility Rate: 4.23 children born/woman
Religion:
  Top Religion Percentages: Indigenous Religions (36.69%), Christian (34.37%), Muslim (28.33%), Nonreligious (0.37%), Baha'i (0.15%)
  Number of Christians: 6,935,729
  Major Christian Groupings: Catholic (53%), Protestant/Independent (47%)

KENYA

Geography:
  Location: Eastern Africa, bordering the Indian Ocean, between Somalia and Tanzania
  Comparative Land Area: Slightly smaller than France
  Capital City: Nairobi
People:
  Total Population: 37,953,840
  Total Median Age: 18.6 years
  Life Expectancy: 56.64 years
  Fertility Rate: 4.7 children born/woman
Religion:
  Top Religion Percentages: Christian (79.95%), Indigenous Religions (11.11%), Muslim (7.03%), Baha'i (1.03%), Hindu (0.48%)
  Number of Christians: 30,344,095
  Major Christian Groupings: Protestant/Independent (70%), Catholic (28%), Orthodox (2%)

LESOTHO

Geography:
  Location: Southern Africa, an enclave of South Africa
  Comparative Land Area: Slightly smaller than Maryland
  Capital City: Maseru
People:
  Total Population: 2,128,180
  Total Median Age: 21.2 years
  Life Expectancy: 40.17 years
  Fertility Rate: 3.13 children born/woman
Religion:
  Top Religion Percentages: Christian (91.75%, Indigenous Religions (7.04%), Baha'i (0.89%), Nonreligious (0.19%), Hindu (0.06%)
  Number of Christians: 1,952,605
  Major Christian Groupings: Catholic (58%), Protestant/Independent (42%)

LIBERIA

Geography:
  Location: Western Africa, bordering the North Atlantic Ocean, between Cost d'Ivoire and Sierra Leone
  Comparative Land Area: Slightly larger than Tennessee
  Capital City: Monrovia
People:
  Total Population: 3,334,587
  Total Median Age: 18 years
  Life Expectancy: 41.13 years
  Fertility Rate: 5.87 children born/woman
Religion:
  Top Religion Percentages: Indigenous Religions (42.30%), Christian (39.85%), Muslim (16.04%), Nonreligious (1.51%), Baha'i (0.28%)
  Number of Christians: 1,328,833
  Major Christian Groupings: Protestant/Independent (85%), Catholic (15%)

LIBYA

Geography:
  Location: Northern Africa, bordering the Mediterranean Sea, between Egypt and Tunisia
  Comparative Land Area: Slightly larger than Alaska
  Capital City: Tripoli
People:
  Total Population: 6,173,579
  Total Median Age: 23.6 years
  Life Expectancy: 77.07 years
  Fertility Rate: 3.15 children born/woman
Religion:
  Top Religion Percentages: Muslim (96.63%), Christian (2.70%), Buddhist (0.32%), Nonreligious (0.17%), Hindu (0.09%)
  Number of Christians: 166,687
  Major Christian Groupings: Catholic (54%), Orthodox (41%), Protestant/Independent (5%)

MADAGASCAR

Geography:
  Location: Southern Africa, island in the Indian Ocean, east of Mozambique
  Comparative Land Area: About twice the size of Arizona
  Capital City: Antananarivo
People:
  Total Population: 20,042,552
  Total Median Age: 17.9 years
  Life Expectancy: 65.52 years
  Fertility Rate: 5.19 children born/woman
Religion:
  Top Religion Percentages: Christian (50.84%), Indigenous Religions (46.63%), Muslim (1.95%), Nonreligious (0.28%), Baha'i (0.10%)
  Number of Christians: 10,189,633
  Major Christian Groupings: Protestant/Independent (61%), Catholic (39%)

MALAWI

Geography:
Location: Southern Africa, east of Zambia
Comparative Land Area: Slightly smaller than Pennsylvania
Capital City: Lilongwe
People:
Total Population: 13,931,831
Total Median Age: 16.8 years
Life Expectancy: 43.45 years
Fertility Rate: 5.67 children born/woman
Religion:
Top Religion Percentages: Christian (79.71%), Muslim (13.21%), Indigenous Religions (6.36%), Nonreligious (0.26%), Baha'i (0.23%)
Number of Christians: 11,105,062
Major Christian Groupings: Protestant/Independent (63%), Catholic (37%)

MALI

Geography:
Location: Western Africa, southwest of Algeria
Comparative Land Area: About twice the size of France
Capital City: Bamako
People:
Total Population: 12,324,029
Total Median Age: 15.8 years
Life Expectancy: 49.94 years
Fertility Rate: 7.34 children born/woman
Religion:
Top Religion Percentages: Muslim (80.82%), Indigenous Religions (16.22%), Christian (2.84%), Nonreligious (0.10%), Baha'i (0.01%),
Number of Christians: 350,002
Major Christian Groupings: Catholic (71%), Protestant/Independent (29%)

MAURITANIA

Geography:
Location: Northern Africa, bordering the North Atlantic Ocean, between Senegal and Western Sahara
Comparative Land Area: About twice the size of Spain
Capital City: Nouakchott
People:
Total Population: 3,364,940
Total Median Age: 17.2 years
Life Expectancy: 53.91 years
Fertility Rate: 5.69 children born/woman
Religion:
Top Religion Percentages: Muslim (99.09%), Indigenous Religions (0.52%), Christian (0.27%), Nonreligious (0.10%), Baha'i (0.01%)
Number of Christians: 9,085
Major Christian Groupings: Catholic (58%), Protestant/Independent (42%)

MAURITIUS

Geography:
Location: Southern Africa, island in the Indian Ocean, east of Madagascar
Comparative Land Area: About ½ the size of Rhode Island
Capital City: Port Louis
People:
Total Population: 1,274,189
Total Median Age: 31.5 years
Life Expectancy: 73.75 years
Fertility Rate: 1.83 children born/woman
Religion:
Top Religion Percentages: Hindu (43.93%), Christian (32.63%), Muslim (16.85%), Nonreligious (2.53%), Baha'i (1.89%),
Number of Christians: 415,768
Major Christian Groupings: Catholic (73%), Protestant/Independent (27%)

MAYOTTE

Geography:
Location: Southern Indian Ocean, island in the Mozambique Channel, about half way between northern Madagascar and northern Mozambique
Comparative Land Area: About ½ the size of New York City
Capital City: Mamoudzou
People:
Total Population: 216,306
Total Median Age: 17.2 years
Life Expectancy: 62.54 years
Fertility Rate: 5.6 children born/woman
Religion:
Top Religion Percentages: Muslim (98.43%), Christian (0.81%), Indigenous Religions (0.46%), Nonreligious (0.27%), Atheist (0.04%)
Number of Christians: 1,752
Major Christian Groupings: Catholic (55%), Protestant/Independent (45%)

MOROCCO

Geography:
Location: Northern Africa, bordering the North Atlantic Ocean and the Mediterranean Sea, between Algeria and Western Sahara
Comparative Land Area: Slightly larger than California
Capital City: Rabat
People:
Total Population: 34,343,220
Total Median Age: 24.7 years
Life Expectancy: 71.52 years
Fertility Rate: 2.57 children born/woman
Religion:
Top Religion Percentages: Muslim (98.78%), Nonreligious (0.93%), Christian (0.18%), Baha'i (0.10%), Jewish (0.01%),
Number of Christians: 61,818
Major Christian Groupings: Protestant/Independent (58%), Catholic (42%)

MOZAMBIQUE

Geography:
Location: Southeastern Africa, bordering the Mozambique Channel, between South Africa and Tanzania
Comparative Land Area: About twice the size of California
Capital City: Maputo
People:
Total Population: 21,284,700
Total Median Age: 17.4 years
Life Expectancy: 41.04 years
Fertility Rate: 5.24 children born/woman
Religion:
Top Religion Percentages: Indigenous Religions (49.83%), Christian (39.15%), Muslim (10.24%), Nonreligious (0.49%), Hindu (0.16%)
Number of Christians: 8,332,960
Major Christian Groupings: Catholic (58%), Protestant/Independent (42%)

NAMIBIA

Geography:
Location: Southern Africa, bordering the South Atlantic Ocean, between Angola and South Africa
Comparative Land Area: Over twice the size of Spain
Capital City: Windhoek
People:
Total Population: 2,088,669
Total Median Age: 20.7 years
Life Expectancy: 49.89 years
Fertility Rate: 2.81 children born/woman
Religion:
Top Religion Percentages: Christian (90.93%), Indigenous Religions (6.33%), Nonreligious (1.73%), Baha'i (0.48%), Muslim (0.39%)
Number of Christians: 1,899,227
Major Christian Groupings: Protestant/Independent (80%), Catholic (20%)

NIGER

Geography:
Location: Western Africa, southeast of Algeria
Comparative Land Area: About twice the size of Texas
Capital City: Niamey
People:
Total Population: 13,272,679
Total Median Age: 16.4 years
Life Expectancy: 44.28 years
Fertility Rate: 7.29 children born/woman
Religion:
Top Religion Percentages: Muslim (92.30%), Indigenous Religions (7.21%), Christian (0.40%), Nonreligious (0.06%), Baha'i (0.04%)
Number of Christians: 53,091
Major Christian Groupings: Protestant/Independent (68%), Catholic (32%)

NIGERIA

Geography:
Location: Western Africa, bordering the Gulf of Guinea, between Benin and Cameroon
Comparative Land Area: About twice the size of Sweden
Capital City: Abuja
People:
Total Population: 146,255,312
Total Median Age: 18.9 years
Life Expectancy: 46.53 years
Fertility Rate: 5.01 children born/woman
Religion:
Top Religion Percentages: Christian (46.07%), Muslim (44.15%), Indigenous Religions (9.43%), Nonreligious (0.27%), Atheist (0.03%)
Number of Christians: 67,379,822
Major Christian Groupings: Protestant/Independent (78%), Catholic (22%)

REPUBLIC OF THE CONGO

Geography:
Location: Western Africa, bordering the South Atlantic Ocean, between Angola and Gabon
Comparative Land Area: Slightly smaller than Montana
Capital City: Brazzaville
People:
Total Population: 3,903,318
Total Median Age: 16.7 years
Life Expectancy: 53.74 years
Fertility Rate: 5.92 children born/woman
Religion:
Top Religion Percentages: Christian (89.76%), Indigenous Religions (4.76%), Nonreligious (2.97%), Muslim (1.39%), Baha'i (0.64%)
Number of Christians: 3,503,618
Major Christian Groupings: Catholic (71%), Protestant/Independent (29%)

REUNION

Geography:
Location: Southern Africa, island in the Indian Ocean, east of Madagascar
Comparative Land Area: Slightly smaller than Rhode Island
Capital City: Saint-Denis
People:
Total Population: 802,000
Total Median Age: 26.7 years
Life Expectancy: 73.95 years
Fertility Rate: 2.47 children born/woman
Religion:
Top Religion Percentages: Christian (87.58%), Hindu (4.51%), Muslim (4.17%), Nonreligious (1.90%), Baha'i (0.86%)
Number of Christians: 702,392
Major Christian Groupings: Catholic (92%), Protestant/Independent (8%)

RWANDA

Geography:
Location: Central Africa, east of Democratic Republic of the Congo
Comparative Land Area: Slightly smaller than Maryland
Capital City: Kigali
People:
Total Population: 10,186,063
Total Median Age: 18.7 years
Life Expectancy: 49.76 years
Fertility Rate: 5.31 children born/woman
Religion:
Top Religion Percentages: Christian (78.12%), Muslim (12.72%), Indigenous Religions (8.77%), Nonreligious (0.20%), Baha'i (0.18%)
Number of Christians: 7,957,352
Major Christian Groupings: Catholic (57%), Protestant/Independent (43%)

SAINT HELENA

Geography:
Location: Islands in the South Atlantic Ocean, about midway between South America and Africa
Comparative Land Area: About twice the size of Washington D.C.
Capital City: Jamestown
People:
Total Population: 7,601
Total Median Age: 37.1 years
Life Expectancy: 78.27 years
Fertility Rate: 1.56 children born/woman
Religion:
Top Religion Percentages: Christian (95.81%), Nonreligious (3.30%), Baha'i (0.80%), Atheist (0.09%)
Number of Christians: 7,283
Major Christian Groupings: Protestant/Independent (98%), Catholic (2%)

SAO TOME & PRINCIPE

Geography:
Location: Western Africa, islands in the Gulf of Guinea, straddling the Equator, west of Gabon
Comparative Land Area: Slightly larger than Berlin, Germany
Capital City: Sao Tome
People:
Total Population: 206,178
Total Median Age: 16.3 years
Life Expectancy: 68 years
Fertility Rate: 5.43 children born/woman
Religion:
Top Religion Percentages: Christian (96.10%), Baha'i (2.38%), Nonreligious (1.24%), Indigenous Religions (0.24%), Muslim (0.04%)
Number of Christians: 198,137
Major Christian Groupings: Catholic (88%), Protestant/Independent (12%)

SENEGAL

Geography:
Location: Western Africa, bordering the North Atlantic Ocean, between Guinea-Bissau and Mauritania
Comparative Land Area: A little smaller than South Dakota
Capital City: Dakar
People:
Total Population: 12,853,259
Total Median Age: 18.8 years
Life Expectancy: 57.08 years
Fertility Rate: 4.86 children born/woman
Religion:
Top Religion Percentages: Muslim (88.20%), Indigenous Religions (6.16%), Christian (5.05%), Nonreligious (0.33%), Baha'i (0.19%), Atheist (0.07%)
Number of Christians: 649,090
Major Christian Groupings: Catholic (94%), Protestant/Independent (6%)

SEYCHELLES

Geography:
Location: Archipelago in the Indian Ocean, northeast of Madagascar
Comparative Land Area: About the size of New Orleans
Capital City: Victoria
People:
Total Population: 82,247
Total Median Age: 28.7 years
Life Expectancy: 72.6 years
Fertility Rate: 1.73 children born/woman
Religion:
Top Religion Percentages: Christian (96.50%), Nonreligious (2.08%), Hindu (0.54%), Baha'i (0.41%), Muslim (0.21%)
Number of Christians: 79,368
Major Christian Groupings: Catholic (88%), Protestant/Independent (12%)

SIERRA LEONE

Geography:
Location: Western Africa, bordering the North Atlantic Ocean, between Guinea and Liberia
Comparative Land Area: Slightly smaller than South Carolina
Capital City: Freetown
People:
Total Population: 6,294,774
Total Median Age: 17.5 years
Life Expectancy: 40.93 years
Fertility Rate: 5.95 children born/woman
Religion:
Top Religion Percentages: Muslim (46.41%), Indigenous Religions (39.46%), Christian (12.38%), Nonreligious (1.44%), Baha'i (0.23%),
Number of Christians: 779,293
Major Christian Groupings: Protestant/Independent (71%), Catholic (29%)

SOMALIA

Geography:
Location: Eastern Africa, bordering the Gulf of Aden and the Indian Ocean, east of Ethiopia
Comparative Land Area: Slightly smaller than Texas
Capital City: Mogadishu
People:
Total Population: 9,558,666
Total Median Age: 17.5 years
Life Expectancy: 49.25 years
Fertility Rate: 6.6 children born/woman
Religion:
Top Religion Percentages: Muslim (98.49%), Christian (1.26%), Indigenous Religions (0.13%), Nonreligious (0.04%), Hindu (0.04%)
Number of Christians: 120,439
Major Christian Groupings: Orthodox (93%), Protestant/Independent (7%)

SOUTH AFRICA

Geography:
Location: Southern Africa, at the southern tip of the continent of Africa
Comparative Land Area: About twice the size of France
Capital City: Pretoria
People:
Total Population: 48,782,756
Total Median Age: 24.2 years
Life Expectancy: 48.89 years
Fertility Rate: 2.43 children born/woman
Religion:
Top Religion Percentages: Christian (81.80%), Indigenous Religions (8.99%), Nonreligious (2.99%), Muslim (2.49%), Hindus (2.38%)
Number of Christians: 39,904,294
Major Christian Groupings: Protestant/Independent (91%), Catholic (9%)

SPANISH NORTH AFRICA

Geography:
Location: North Africa, bordering Morocco
Comparative Land Area: About ½ the size of Manhattan Island in New York City, USA
Capital City: Ceuta
People:
Total Population: 145,336
Total Median Age: NA
Life Expectancy: 69 years
Fertility Rate: NA
Religion:
Top Religion Percentages: Christian (68.33%), Muslim (25.79%), Nonreligious (4.20%), Jewish (0.97%), Baha'i (0.71%)
Number of Christians: 99,308
Major Christian Groupings: Catholic (85%), Protestant/Independent (15%)

SUDAN

Geography:
Location: Northern Africa, bordering the Red Sea, between Egypt and Eritrea
Comparative Land Area: About ¼ the size of the United States
Capital City: Khartoum
People:
Total Population: 40,218,456
Total Median Age: 18.9 years
Life Expectancy: 50.28 years
Fertility Rate: 4.58 children born/woman
Religion:
Top Religion Percentages: Muslim (71.25%), Christian (16.30%), Indigenous Religious (11.26%), Nonreligious (1.01%), Atheist (0.17%)
Number of Christians: 6,555,608
Major Christian Groupings: Protestant/Independent (50%), Catholic (50%)

SWAZILAND

Geography:
Location: Southern Africa, between Mozambique and South Africa
Comparative Land Area: Slightly smaller than New Jersey
Capital City: Mbabane
People:
Total Population: 1,128,814
Total Median Age: 18.7 years
Life Expectancy: 31.99 years
Fertility Rate: 3.34 children born/woman
Religion:
Top Religion Percentages: Christian (87.64%), Indigenous Religions (9.92%), Nonreligious (1.16%), Muslim (0.65%), Baha'i (0.45%)
Number of Christians: 989,293
Major Christian Groupings: Protestant/Independent (92%), Catholic (8%)

TANZANIA

Geography:
Location: Eastern Africa, bordering the Indian Ocean, between Kenya and Mozambique
Comparative Land Area: About twice the size of Sweden
Capital City: Dodoma
People:
Total Population: 40,213,160
Total Median Age: 17.8 years
Life Expectancy: 51.45 years
Fertility Rate: 4.62 years
Religion:
Top Religion Percentages: Christian (52.97%), Muslim (30.41%), Indigenous Religions (14.80%), Hindu (0.86%), Baha'i (0.46%)
Number of Christians: 21,300,911
Major Christian Groupings: Protestant/Independent (51%), Catholic (49%)

TOGO

Geography:
  Location: Western Africa, bordering the Bight of Benin, between Benin and Ghana
  Comparative Land Area: Slightly smaller than West Virginia
  Capital City: Lome
People:
  Total Population: 5,858,673
  Total Median Age: 18.6 years
  Life Expectancy: 58.28 years
  Fertility Rate: 4.85 children born/woman
Religion:
  Top Religion Percentages: Christian (44.87%), Indigenous Religions (34.98%), Muslim (19.36%), Baha'i (0.50%), Nonreligious (0.22%)
  Number of Christians: 2,628,787
  Major Christian Groupings: Catholic (61%), Protestant/Independent (39%)

TUNISIA

Geography:
  Location: Northern Africa, bordering the Mediterranean Sea, between Algeria and Libya
  Comparative Land Area: Slightly larger than Georgia
  Capital City: Tunis
People:
  Total Population: 10,383,577
  Total Median Age: 28.8 years
  Life Expectancy: 75.56 years
  Fertility Rate: 1.73 children born/woman
Religion:
  Top Religion Percentages: Muslim (99.26%), Christian (0.44%), Nonreligious (0.23%), Atheist (0.03%), Jewish (0.02%)
  Number of Christians: 45,688
  Major Christian Groupings: Protestant/Independent (54%), Catholic (46%)

UGANDA

Geography:
  Location: Eastern Africa, west of Kenya
  Comparative Land Area: Slightly smaller than Oregon
  Capital City: Kampala
People:
  Total Population: 31,367,972
  Total Median Age: 15 years
  Life Expectancy: 52.34 years
  Fertility Rate: 6.81 children born/woman
Religion:
  Top Religion Percentages: Christian (85.47%), Muslim (9.80%), Indigenous Religious (3.21%), Hindu (0.80%), Nonreligious (0.38%)
  Number of Christians: 26,810,206
  Major Christian Groupings: Protestant/Independent (52%), Catholic (48%)

WESTERN SAHARA

Geography:
  Location: Northern Africa, bordering the North Atlantic Ocean, between Mauritania and Morocco
  Comparative Land Area: About the size of Colorado
  Capital City: None
People:
  Total Population: 393,831
  Total Median Age: NA
  Life Expectancy: 53.92 years
  Fertility Rate: 5.69 children born/woman
Religion:
  Top Religion Percentages: Muslim (99.40%), Nonreligious (0.31%), Christian (0.16%), Atheist (0.09%), Baha'i (0.04%)
  Number of Christians: 6,301
  Major Christian Groupings: Protestant/Independent (80%), Catholic (20%)

ZAMBIA

Geography:
  Location: Southern Africa, east of Angola
  Comparative Land Area: Slightly larger than Texas
  Capital City: Lusaka
People:
  Total Population: 11,669,534
  Total Median Age: 16.9 years
  Life Expectancy: 38.59 years
  Fertility Rate: 5.23 children born/woman
Religion:
  Top Religion Percentages: Christian (83.69%), Indigenous Religions (12.86%), Baha'i (1.96%), Muslim (1.07%), Nonreligious (0.17%)
  Number of Christians: 9,766,233
  Major Christian Groupings: Protestant/Independent (63%), Catholic (37%)

ZIMBABWE

Geography:
  Location: Southern Africa, between South Africa and Zambia
  Comparative Land Area: About size of Montana
  Capital City: Harare
People:
  Total Population: 11,350,111
  Total Median Age: 17.6 years
  Life Expectancy: 44.28 years
  Fertility Rate: 3.72 children born/woman
Religion:
  Top Religion Percentages: Christian (68.30%), Indigenous Religions (29.22%), Nonreligious (1.01%), Muslim (0.73%), Baha'i (0.32%)
  Number of Christians: 7,752,126
  Major Christian Groupings: Protestant/Independent (86%), Catholic (14%)

ANTARCTICA

PEOPLE

Total Population: 5,279
Total Median Age: N/A
Life Expectancy: N/A
Fertility Rate: N/A

RELIGION

Top Religion Percentages: Christian (72.00%)
Nonreligious (23.60%)
Muslim (2.71%)
Hinduism (1.00%)
Buddhist (0.0%)

Number of Christians: 3,801
Major Christian Groupings: Protestant/Independent (60%)
Catholic (40%)

ANTARCTICA
Geography:
Location: Continent mostly south of the Antarctic Circle
Comparative Land Area: About 1 ½ times the size of the United States
Capital City: None
People:
Total Population: No indigenous inhabitants, but approximately 5,279 permanent and summer-only staffed researchers
Total Median Age: NA
Life Expectancy: NA
Fertility Rate: NA
Religion:
Top Religion Percentages: Christian (72.00%), Nonreligious (23.60%), Muslim (2.71%), Hindu (1.00%), Buddhist (0.70%)
Number of Christians: 3,801
Major Christian Groupings: Protestant/Independent (60%), Catholic (40%)

ASIA

PEOPLE

Total Population: 3,767,141,703
Total Median Age: 28.9 years
Life Expectancy: 70.67 years
Fertility Rate: 2.35 children born/woman

RELIGION

Top Religion Percentages: Hindu (23.35%)
Muslim (19.34%)
Nonreligious (16.05%)
Chinese Universalist (10.16%)
Buddhism (10.06%)
Christian (9.25%)
Atheist (3.20%)
Neoreligionist (2.76%)
Indigenous Religions (2.38%)
Sikh (0.58%)
Other (2.87%)

Number of Christians: 348,299,020
Major Christian Groupings: Protestant/Independent (65%)
Catholic (33%)
Orthodox (2%)

AFGHANISTAN:	BANGLADESH
Geography:	**Geography:**
Location: Southern Asia, north and west of Pakistan, east of Iran	**Location:** Southern Asia, bordering the Bay of Bengal, between Burma and India
Comparative Land Area: Slightly smaller than Texas	**Comparative Land Area:** Slightly smaller than Iowa
Capital City: Kabul	**Capital City:** Dhaka
People:	**People:**
Total Population: 32,738,376	**Total Population:** 153,546,896
Total Median Age: 17.6 years	**Total Median Age:** 22.8 years
Life Expectancy: 44.21 years	**Life Expectancy:** 63.21 years
Fertility Rate: 6.58 children born/woman	**Fertility Rate:** 3.08 children born/woman
Religion:	**Religion:**
Top Religion Percentages: Muslim (99.74%), Christian (0.10%), Baha'i (0.05%), Hindu (0.04%), Nonreligious (0.02%)	**Top Religion Percentages:** Muslim (88.52%), Hindu (9.62%), Buddhist (0.64%), Christian (0.59%), Indigenous Religions (0.52%)
Number of Christians: 32,738	**Number of Christians:** 905,927
Major Christian Groupings: Protestant/Independents (80%), Catholic (20%)	**Major Christian Groupings:** Protestant/Independent (67%), Catholic (33%)

BHUTAN

Geography:
   Location: Southern Asia, between China and India
   Comparative Land Area: Slightly larger than Denmark
   Capital City: Thimphu
People:
   Total Population: 682,321
   Total Median Age: 23.5 years
   Life Expectancy: 65.53 years
   Fertility Rate: 2.48 children born/woman
Religion:
   Top Religion Percentages: Buddhist (65.90%), Hindu
   (27.10%), Indigenous Religions (4.52%), Christian (1.29%),
   Muslim (1.03%)
   Number of Christians: 7,028
   Major Christian Groupings: Protestant/Independent (88%),
   Catholic (12%)

BRITISH INDIAN OCEAN TERRITORY

Geography:
   Location: Archipelago in the Indian Ocean, south of India,
   about halfway between Africa and Indonesia
   Comparative Land Area: About the size of Manhattan Island
   in New York City, USA
   Capital City: Diego Garcia
People:
   Total Population: 2000. However, the only inhabitants are
   temporary military personal and civilian contractors
   Total Median Age: NA
   Life Expectancy: NA
   Fertility Rate: NA
Religion:
   Top Religion Percentages: Christian (85.40%), Nonreligious
   (10.70%), Hindu (2.30%), Atheist (0.85%), Muslim (0.70%)
   Number of Christians: 1,708
   Major Christian Groupings: Catholic (53%),
   Protestant/Independent (47%)

BRUNEI

Geography:
   Location: Southeastern Asia, bordering the South China Sea
   and Malaysia
   Comparative Land Area: Slightly smaller than Delaware
   Capital City: Bandar Seri Begawan
People:
   Total Population: 381,371
   Total Median Age: 27.5 years
   Life Expectancy: 75.52 years
   Fertility Rate: 1.94 children born/woman
Religion:
   Top Religion Percentages: Muslim (55.17%), Christian
   (14.99%), Indigenous Religions (10.72%), Buddhist (9.66%),
   Chinese Universalist (5.25%)
   Number of Christians: 57,168
   Major Christian Groupings: Protestant/Independent (52%),
   Catholic (48%)

CAMBODIA

Geography:
   Location: Southeastern Asia, bordering the Gulf of Thailand,
   between Thailand, Vietnam, and Laos
   Comparative Land Area: Slightly smaller than Oklahoma
   Capital City: Phnom Penh
People:
   Total Population: 14,241,640
   Total Median Age: 21.7 years
   Life Expectancy: 61.69 years
   Fertility Rate: 3.08 children born/woman
Religion:
   Top Religion Percentages: Buddhist (85.28%), Indigenous
   Religions (4.66%), Chinese Universalist (2.95%), Nonreligious
   (2.27%), Muslim (2.20%), Christian (1.72%)
   Number of Christians: 245,423
   Major Christian Groupings: Protestant/Independent (90%),
   Catholic (10%)

CHINA

Geography:
   Location: Eastern Asia, bordering the East China Sea, Korea
   Bay, Yellow Sea, and South China Sea, between North Korea
   and Vietnam
   Comparative Land Area: Slightly smaller than the United
   States
   Capital City: Beijing
People:
   Total Population: 1,337,608,854
   Total Median Age: 33.6 years
   Life Expectancy: 73.18 years
   Fertility Rate: 1.77 children born/woman
Religion:
   Top Religion Percentages: Nonreligious (41.47%), Chinese
   Universalist (27.47%), Buddhist (8.53%), Christian (8.44%),
   Atheist (8.23%), Muslim (1.52%), Hindu (0.01%)
   Number of Christians: 112,894,187
   Major Christian Groupings: Protestant/Independent (93%),
   Catholic (7%)

CHRISTMAS ISLAND

Geography:
   Location: Southeastern Asia, island in the Indian Ocean, south
   of Indonesia
   Comparative Land Area: About twice the size of Manhattan
   Island in New York City, USA
   Capital City: The Settlement
People:
   Total Population: 1,402
   Total Median Age: 38 years
   Life Expectancy: 79 years
   Fertility Rate: NA
Religion:
   Top Religion Percentages: Chinese Universalist (26.20%),
   Christian (25.13%), Muslim (17.87%), Nonreligious (15.60%),
   Buddhist (12.27%)
   Number of Christians: 352
   Major Christian Groupings: Catholic (50%),
   Protestant/Independent (50%)

COCOS (KEELING) ISLANDS

Geography:
   Location: Southeastern Asia, group of islands in the Indian
   Ocean, southwest of Indonesia, about halfway from Australia to
   Sri Lanka
   Comparative Land Area: About 5 square miles
   Capital City: West Island
People:
   Total Population: 596
   Total Median Age: 37 years
   Life Expectancy: 79 years
   Fertility Rate: N/A
Religion:
   Top Religion Percentages: Muslim (66.56%), Christian
   (27.19%), Nonreligious (5.31%), Chinese Universalist (0.94%)
   Number of Christians: 162
   Major Christian Groupings: Protestant/Independent (77%),
   Catholic (23%)

INDIA

Geography:
   Location: Southern Asia, bordering the Arabian Sea and the
   Bay of Bengal, between Burma and Pakistan
   Comparative Land Area: About 1/3 the size of the United
   States
   Capital City: New Delhi
People:
   Total Population: 1,147,995,904
   Total Median Age: 25.1 years
   Life Expectancy: 69.25 years
   Fertility Rate: 2.76 children born/woman
Religion:
   Top Religion Percentages: Hindu (72.03%), Muslim
   (13.67%), Christian (5.81%), Indigenous Religions (3.88%),
   Sikh (1.88%), Buddhism (0.80%)
   Number of Christians: 66,698,562
   Major Christian Groupings: Protestant/Independent (65%),
   Catholic (30%), Orthodox (5%)

INDONESIA

Geography:
Location: Southwestern Asia, archipelago between the Indian Ocean and the Pacific Ocean
Comparative Land Area: Slightly larger than Alaska
Capital City: Jakarta
People:
Total Population: 237,512,352
Total Median Age: 27.2 years
Life Expectancy: 70.46 years
Fertility Rate: 2.34 children born/woman
Religion:
Top Religion Percentages: Muslim (56.22%), Neoreligionist (20.76%), Christian (13.16%), Hindu (3.19%), Indigenous Religions (2.57%)
Number of Christians: 31,256,626
Major Christian Groupings: Protestant/Independent (78%), Catholic (22%)

JAPAN

Geography:
Location: Eastern Asia, island chain between the North Pacific Ocean and the Sea of Japan, east of the Korean Peninsula
Comparative Land Area: Slightly smaller than California
Capital City: Tokyo
People:
Total Population: 127,288,416
Total Median Age: 43.8 years
Life Expectancy: 82.07 years
Fertility Rate: 1.22 children born/woman
Religion:
Top Religion Percentages: Buddhist (56.14%), Neoreligionist (25.93%), Nonreligious (10.18%), Atheist (2.87%), Christian (2.28%), Shinto (2.10%)
Number of Christians: 2,902,176
Major Christian Groupings: Protestant/Independent (79%), Catholic (21%)

KAZAKHSTAN

Geography:
Location: Central Asia, northwest of China; a small portion west of the Ural River in eastern-most Europe
Comparative Land Area: About 1/3 the size of Australia
Capital City: Astana
People:
Total Population: 15,340,533
Total Median Age: 29.3 years
Life Expectancy: 67.55 years
Fertility Rate: 1.88 children born/woman
Religion:
Top Religion Percentages: Muslim (49.85%), Nonreligious (26.34%), Christian (14.06%), Atheist (9.38%); Indigenous Religions (0.16%)
Number of Christians: 2,156,879
Major Christian Groupings: Orthodox (69%), Protestant/Independent (23%), Catholic (8%)

KYRGYZSTAN

Geography:
Location: Central Asia, west of China
Comparative Land Area: Slightly smaller than South Dakota
Capital City: Bishkek
People:
Total Population: 5,356,869
Total Median Age: 24.2 years
Life Expectancy: 69.12 years
Fertility Rate: 2.67 children born/woman
Religion:
Top Religion Percentages: Muslim (65.33%), Nonreligious (21.51%), Christian (6.26%), Atheist (5.93%), Buddhist (0.46%)
Number of Christians: 335,340
Major Christian Groupings: Orthodox (76%), Protestant/Independent: (24%)

LAOS

Geography:
Location: Southeastern Asia, northeast of Thailand, west of Vietnam
Comparative Land Area: Slightly larger than Utah
Capital City: Vientiane
People:
Total Population: 6,677,534
Total Median Age: 19.2 years
Life Expectancy: 56.29 years
Fertility Rate: 4.5 children born/woman
Religion:
Top Religion Percentages: Buddhist (53.00%), Indigenous Religions (38.89%), Nonreligious (3.70%), Christian (2.63%), Atheist (1.01%)
Number of Christians: 175,619
Major Christian Groupings: Protestant/Independent (72%), Catholic (28%)

MALAYSIA

Geography:
Location: Southeastern Asia, peninsula bordering Thailand and northern one-third of the island of Borneo, bordering Indonesia, Brunei, and the South China Sea, south of Vietnam
Comparative Land Area: Slightly larger than New Mexico
Capital City: Kuala Lumpur
People:
Total Population: 25,274,132
Total Median Age: 24.6 years
Life Expectancy: 73.03 years
Fertility Rate: 2.98 children born/woman
Religion:
Top Religion Percentages: Muslim (55.33%), Chinese Universalist (18.38%), Christians (9.03%), Hindu (6.27%), Buddhist (5.12%)
Number of Christians: 2,282,254
Major Christian Groupings: Catholic (51%), Protestant/Independent (49%)

MALDIVES

Geography:
Location: Southern Asia, group of atolls in the Indian Ocean, south-southwest of India
Comparative Land Area: About the size of Las Vegas, USA
Capital City: Male`
People:
Total Population: 385,925
Total Median Age: 25.1 years
Life Expectancy: 73.72 years
Fertility Rate: 1.97 children born/woman
Religion:
Top Religion Percentages: Muslim (98.44%), Buddhist (0.65%), Christian (0.45%), Hindu (0.33%), Nonreligious (0.09%)
Number of Christians: 1,737
Major Christian Groupings: Catholic (67%), Protestant/Independent (33%)

MONGOLIA

Geography:
Location: Northern Asia, between China and Russia
Comparative Land Area: Slightly smaller than Alaska
Capital City: Ulaanbaatar
People:
Total Population: 2,996,081
Total Median Age: 24.9 years
Life Expectancy: 67.32 years
Fertility Rate: 2.24 children born/woman
Religion:
Top Religion Percentages: Indigenous Religions (31.72%), Nonreligious (30.10%), Buddhist (22.50%), Atheist (8.84%), Muslim (4.75%), Christianity (1.49%)
Number of Christians: 44,642
Major Christian Groupings: Protestant/Independent (99%), Catholic & Orthodox (1%)

MYANMAR (BURMA)

Geography:
Location: Southeastern Asia, bordering the Andaman Sea and the Bay of Bengal, between Bangladesh and Thailand
Comparative Land Area: Slightly smaller than Texas
Capital City: Naypyidaw

People:
Total Population: 47,758,180
Total Median Age: 27.8 years
Life Expectancy: 62.94 years
Fertility Rate: 1.92 children born/woman

Religion:
Top Religion Percentages: Buddhist (73.96%), Indigenous Religions (11.02%), Christian (7.12%), Muslim (3.79%), Hindu (1.71%)
Number of Christians: 3,400,382
Major Christian Groupings: Protestant/Independent (83%), Catholic (17%)

NEPAL

Geography:
Location: Southern Asia, between China and India
Comparative Land Area: Slightly larger than Arkansas
Capital City: Kathmandu

People:
Total Population: 29,519,114
Total Median Age: 20.7 years
Life Expectancy: 60.94 years
Fertility Rate: 3.91 children born/woman

Religion:
Top Religion Percentages: Hindu (69.11%), Indigenous Religions (12.48%), Buddhist (10.76%), Muslim (4.36%), Christian (2.81%)
Number of Christians: 829,487
Major Christian Groupings: Protestant/Independent (99%), Catholic (1%)

NORTH KOREA

Geography:
Location: Eastern Asia, half of the Korean Peninsula bordering the Korean Bay and the Sea of Japan, between China and South Korea
Comparative Land Area: Slightly smaller than Mississippi
Capital City: Pyongyang

People:
Total Population: 23,479,088
Total Median Age: 32.7 years
Life Expectancy: 72.2 years
Fertility Rate: 2 children born/woman

Religions:
Top Religion Percentages: Nonreligious (55.69%), Atheist (15.58%), Neoreligionist (12.88%), Indigenous Religions (12.28%), Christian (1.98%)
Number of Christians: 464,886
Major Christian Groupings: Protestant/Independent (92%), Catholic (8%)

PAKISTAN

Geography:
Location: Southern Asia, bordering the Arabian Sea, between India on the East and Iran and Afghanistan on the west and China in the North
Comparative Land Area: About twice the size of California
Capital City: Islamabad

People:
Total Population: 172,800,048
Total Median Age: 20.5 years
Life Expectancy: 64.13 years
Fertility Rate: 3.73 children born/woman

Religion:
Top Religion Percentages: Muslim (96.03%), Christian (2.33%), Hindu (1.30%), Indigenous Religions (0.11%), Buddhist (0.06%)
Number of Christians: 4,026,241
Major Christian Groupings: Protestant/Independent (71%), Catholic (29%)

PHILIPPINES

Geography:
Location: Southeastern Asia, archipelago between the Philippine Sea and the South China Sea, east of Vietnam
Comparative Land Area: Slightly larger than Arizona
Capital City: Manila

People:
Total Population: 96,061,680
Total Median Age: 22.3 years
Life Expectancy: 70.8 years
Fertility Rate: 3.32 children born/woman

Religion:
Top Religion Percentages: Christian (89.30%), Muslim (6.44%), Indigenous Religions (2.83%), Nonreligious (0.73%), Baha'i (0.29%)
Number of Christians: 85,783,080
Major Christian Groupings: Catholic (74%), Protestant/Independent (26%)

SINGAPORE

Geography:
Location: Southeastern Asia, islands between Malaysia and Indonesia
Comparative Land Area: Slightly smaller than New York City, USA
Capital City: Singapore

People:
Total Population: 4,608,167
Total Median Age: 38.4 years
Life Expectancy: 81.89 years
Fertility Rate: 1.08 children born/woman

Religion:
Top Religion Percentages: Chinese Universalist (39.71%), Muslim (18.37%), Christian (15.75%), Buddhist (14.07%), Hindu (4.95%)
Number of Christians: 725,786
Major Christian Groupings: Protestant/Independent (66%), Catholic (34%)

SOUTH KOREA

Geography:
Location: Eastern Asia, southern half of the Korean Peninsula bordering the Sea of Japan and the Yellow Sea
Comparative Land Area: Slightly larger than Indiana
Capital City: Seoul

People:
Total Population: 48,379,392
Total Median Age: 36.7 years
Life Expectancy: 78.64 years
Fertility Rate: 1.2 children born/woman

Religion:
Top Religion Percentages: Christian (41.19%), Indigenous Religions (15.63%), Neoreligionist (15.19%), Buddhist (15.11%), Confucianist (10.94%), Muslim (1.47%)
Number of Christians: 19,927,472
Major Christian Groupings: Protestant/Independent (79%), Catholic (21%)

SRI LANKA

Geography:
Location: Southern Asia, island in the Indian Ocean, south of India
Comparative Land Area: Slightly larger than West Virginia
Capital City: Sri Jayewardenepura Kotte

People:
Total Population: 21,128,772
Total Median Age: 30.4 years
Life Expectancy: 74.97 years
Fertility Rate: 2.02 children born/woman

Religion:
Top Religion Percentages: Buddhist (67.98%), Hindu (13.16%), Muslim (9.55%), Christian (8.67%), Nonreligious (0.46%)
Number of Christians: 1,831,865
Major Christian Groupings: Catholic (76%), Protestant/Independent (24%)

TAIWAN

Geography:
  Location: Eastern Asia, islands north of the Philippines, off the southeastern coast of China
  Comparative Land Area: Slightly smaller than Switzerland
  Capital City: Taipei
People:
  Total Population: 22,920,946
  Total Median Age: 36 years
  Life Expectancy: 77.76 years
  Fertility Rate: 1.13 children born/woman
Religion:
  Top Religion Percentages: Chinese Universalist (42.65%), Buddhist (26.49%), Taoist (12.63%), Neoreligionist (6.75%), Christian (6.40%)
  Number of Christians: 1,466,941
  Major Christian Groupings: Protestant/Independent (75%), Catholic (25%)

TAJIKISTAN

Geography:
  Location: Central Asia, west of China
  Comparative Land Area: Slightly smaller than Wisconsin
  Capital City: Dushanbe
People:
  Total Population: 7,211,884
  Total Median Age: 21.6 years
  Life Expectancy: 64.97 years
  Fertility Rate: 3.04 children born/woman
Religion:
  Top Religion Percentages: Muslim (84.00%), Nonreligious (12.19%), Atheist (1.91%), Christian (1.52%), Jewish (0.14%)
  Number of Christians: 109,621
  Major Christian Groupings: Orthodox (75%), Protestant/Independent (25%)

THAILAND

Geography:
  Location: Southeastern Asia, bordering the Andaman Sea and the Gulf of Thailand, southeast of Burma
  Comparative Land Area: About the size of Spain
  Capital City: Bangkok
People:
  Total Population: 65,493,296
  Total Median Age: 32.8 years
  Life Expectancy: 72.83 years
  Fertility Rate: 1.64 children born/woman
Religion:
  Top Religion Percentages: Buddhist (85.96%), Muslim (7.06%), Indigenous Religions (2.32%), Nonreligious (1.76%), Christian (1.27%)
  Number of Christians: 831,765
  Major Christian Groupings: Protestant/Independent (67%), Catholic (33%)

TIMOR-LESTE

Geography:
  Location: Southeastern Asia, northwest of Australia in the Lesser Sunda Islands at the eastern end of the Indonesian archipelago
  Comparative Land Area: Slightly larger than Connecticut
  Capital City: Dili
People:
  Total Population: 1,108,777
  Total Median Age: 21.5 years
  Life Expectancy: 66.94 years
  Fertility Rate: 3.36 children born/woman
Religion:
  Top Religion Percentages: Christian (84.17%), Indigenous Religions (11.15%), Muslim (3.16%), Neoreligionist (0.57%), Nonreligious (0.39%)
  Number of Christians: 933,258
  Major Christian Groupings: Catholic (95%), Protestant/Independent (5%)

TURKMENISTAN

Geography:
  Location: Central Asia, bordering the Caspian Sea, between Iran and Kazakhstan
  Comparative Land Area: Slightly larger than California
  Capital City: Ashgabat
People:
  Total Population: 5,179,571
  Total Median Age: 22.6 years
  Life Expectancy: 68.6 years
  Fertility Rate: 3.07 children born/woman
Religion:
  Top Religion Percentages: Muslim (99.24%), Nonreligious (8.69%), Christian (1.61%), Atheist (1.34%), Jewish (0.06%)
  Number of Christians: 83,391
  Major Christian Groupings: Orthodox (74%), Protestant/Independent (26%)

UZBEKISTAN

Geography:
  Location: Central Asia, north of Afghanistan
  Comparative Land Area: Slightly larger than California
  Capital City: Tashkent
People:
  Total Population: 27,345,026
  Total Median Age: 24.3 years
  Life Expectancy: 71.69 years
  Fertility Rate: 2.01 children born/woman
Religion:
  Top Religion Percentages: Muslim (76.55%), Nonreligious (18.03%), Atheist (3.45%), Christian (1.41%), Indigenous Religions (0.20%)
  Number of Christians: 385,565
  Major Christian Groupings: Orthodox (63%), Protestant/Independent (37%)

VIETNAM

Geography:
  Location: Southeastern Asia, bordering the Gulf of Thailand, Gulf of Tonkin, and South China Sea, alongside China, Laos, and Cambodia
  Comparative Land Area: Slightly larger than New Mexico
  Capital City: Hanoi
People:
  Total Population: 86,116,560
  Total Median Age: 26.9 years
  Life Expectancy: 71.33 years
  Fertility Rate: 1.86 children born/woman
Religion:
  Top Religion Percentages: Buddhist (48.69%), Nonreligious (12.65%), Neoreligionist (11.05%), Indigenous Religions (10.36%), Christian (8.71%), Muslim (7.43%)
  Number of Christians: 7,500,752
  Major Christian Groupings: Catholic (78%), Protestant/Independent (22%)

EASTERN EUROPE

PEOPLE
Total Population: 356,470,738
Total Median Age: 38.1 years
Life Expectancy: 70.15 years
Fertility Rate: 1.38 children born/woman

RELIGION
Top Religion Percentages: Christian (79.76%)
Muslim (9.33%)
Nonreligious (8.46%)
Atheist (1.81%)
Indigenous Religions (0.27%)
Jewish (0.12%)
Other (0.25%)
Number of Christians: 284,328,648
Major Christian Groupings: Orthodox (67%)
Catholic (23%)
Protestant/Independent (10%)

ALBANIA:
Geography:
Location: Southeastern Europe, bordering the Adriatic Sea and Ionian Sea, between Greece in the south and Montenegro and Kosovo to the north
Comparative Land Area: Slightly smaller than Maryland
Capital City: Tirana
People:
Total Population: 3,619,778
Total Median Age: 29.5 years
Life Expectancy: 77.78 years
Fertility Rate: 2.02 children born/woman
Religion:
Top Religion Percentages: Muslim (64.01%), Christian (29.79%), Nonreligious (5.28%), Atheist (0.67%), Baha'i (0.23%),
Number of Christians: 1,078,331
Major Christian Groupings: Catholic (50%), Orthodox (45%), Protestant/Independent (5%)

ARMENIA
Geography:
Location: Southwestern Asia, east of Turkey
Comparative Land Area: Slightly smaller than Maryland
Capital City: Yerevan
People:
Total Population: 2,968,586
Total Median Age: 31.1 years
Life Expectancy: 72.4 years
Fertility Rate: 1.35 children born/woman
Religion:
Top Religion Percentages: Christian (83.42%), Nonreligious (9.75%), Atheist (4.36%), Muslim (2.35%), Baha'i (0.04%)
Number of Christians: 2,476,394
Major Christian Groupings: Orthodox (90%), Catholic (10%)

AZERBAIJAN
Geography:
Location: Southwestern Asia, bordering the Caspian Sea, between Iran and Russia, with a small European portion north of the Caucasus Range
Comparative Land Area: Slightly smaller than Maine
Capital City: Baku
People:
Total Population: 8,177,717
Total Median Age: 27.9 years
Life Expectancy: 66.31 years
Fertility Rate: 2.05 children born/woman
Religion:
Top Religion Percentages: Muslim (87.86%), Nonreligious (9.08%), Christian (2.45%), Jewish (0.32%), Atheist (0.25%)
Number of Christians: 200,354
Major Christian Groupings: Orthodox (92%), Protestant/Independent (8%)

BELARUS
Geography:
Location: Eastern Europe, east of Poland
Comparative Land Area: Slightly smaller than Kansas
Capital City: Minsk
People:
Total Population: 9,685,768
Total Median Age: 38.4 years
Life Expectancy: 70.34 years
Fertility Rate: 1.23 children born/woman
Religion:
Top Religion Percentages: Christian (71.06%), Nonreligious (24.15%), Atheist (4.35%), Jewish (0.27%), Muslim (0.26%)
Number of Christians: 6,882,707
Major Christian Groupings: Orthodox (73%), Catholic (17%), Protestant/Independent (10%)

BOSNIA-HERZEGOVINA

Geography:
Location: Southeastern Europe, bordering the Adriatic Sea and Croatia
Comparative Land Area: Slightly smaller than West Virginia
Capital City: Sarajevo
People:
Total Population: 4,590,310
Total Median Age: 39.4 years
Life Expectancy: 78.33 years
Fertility Rate: 1.24 children born/woman
Religion:
Top Religion Percentages: Muslim (55.42%), Christian (39.14%), Nonreligious (3.66%), Atheist (1.77%), Jewish (0.01%)
Number of Christians: 1,796,647
Major Christian Groupings: Orthodox (70%), Catholic (30%)

BULGARIA

Geography:
Location: Southeastern Europe, bordering the Black Sea, between Romania and Turkey
Comparative Land Area: Slightly larger than Tennessee
Capital City: Sofia
People:
Total Population: 7,262,675
Total Median Age: 41.1 years
Life Expectancy: 72.83 years
Fertility Rate: 1.4 children born/woman
Religion:
Top Religion Percentages: Christian (83.76%), Muslim (12.10%), Nonreligious (3.08%), Atheist (1.00%), Jewish (0.05%)
Number of Christians: 6,083,217
Major Christian Groupings: Orthodox (89%), Protestant/Independent (10%), Catholic (1%)

CROATIA

Geography:
Location: Southeastern Europe, bordering the Adriatic Sea, between Bosnia and Herzegovina and Slovenia
Comparative Land Area: Slightly smaller than West Virginia
Capital City: Zagreb
People:
Total Population: 4,491,543
Total Median Age: 40.8 years
Life Expectancy: 75.13 years
Fertility Rate: 1.41 children born/woman
Religion:
Top Religion Percentages: Christian (91.37%), Nonreligious (4.86%), Muslim (2.29%), Atheist (1.47%), Jewish (0.02%)
Number of Christians: 4,103,923
Major Christian Groupings: Catholic (87%), Orthodox (7%), Protestant/Independent (6%)

CYPRUS

Geography:
Location: Island in the Mediterranean Sea, south of Turkey
Comparative Land Area: Slightly more than ½ the size of Connecticut
Capital City: Nicosia
People:
Total Population: 801,600
Total Median Age: 35.3 years
Life Expectancy: 78.15 years
Fertility Rate: 1.79 children born/woman
Religion:
Top Religion Percentages: Christian (80.83%), Muslim (11.00%), Nonreligious (4.50%), Sikh (1.14%), Atheist (0.94%), Buddhist (0.75%)
Number of Christians: 736,109
Major Christian Groupings: Orthodox (93%), Protestant/Independent (4%), Catholic (3%)

CZECH REPUBLIC

Geography:
Location: Central Europe, southeast of Germany
Comparative Land Area: A little smaller than South Carolina
Capital City: Prague
People:
Total Population: 10,220,911
Total Median Age: 39.8 years
Life Expectancy: 76.62 years
Fertility Rate: 1.23 children born/woman
Religion:
Top Religion Percentages: Christian (57.16%), Nonreligious (37.62%), Atheist (5.05%), Jewish (0.07%), Buddhist (0.05%)
Number of Christians: 5,842,273
Major Christian Groupings: Catholic (65%), Protestant/Independent (34%), Orthodox (1%)

ESTONIA

Geography:
Location: Eastern Europe, bordering the Baltic Sea and Gulf of Finland, between Latvia and Russia
Comparative Land Area: About twice the size of New Jersey
Capital City: Tallinn
People:
Total Population: 1,307,605
Total Median Age: 39.6 years
Life Expectancy: 72.56 years
Fertility Rate: 1.42 children born/woman
Religion:
Top Religion Percentages: Christian (64.88%), Nonreligious (24.50%), Atheist (10.09%), Muslim (0.28%), Jewish (0.11%)
Number of Christians: 848,374
Major Christian Groupings: Protestant/Independent (71%), Orthodox (29%)

GEORGIA

Geography:
Location: Southwestern Asia, bordering the Black Sea, between Turkey and Russia
Comparative Land Area: A little smaller than South Carolina
Capital City: Tbilisi
People:
Total Population: 4,630,841
Total Median Age: 38.3 years
Life Expectancy: 76.51 years
Fertility Rate: 1.43 children born/woman
Religion:
Top Religion Percentages: Christian (83.90%), Muslim (9.98%), Nonreligious (5.02%), Atheist (0.61%), Jewish (0.44%)
Number of Christians: 3,885,276
Major Christian Groupings: Orthodox (97%), Protestant/Independent (2%), Catholic (1%)

GREECE

Geography:
Location: Southern Europe, bordering the Aegean Sea, Ionian Sea, and the Mediterranean Sea, between Albania and Turkey
Comparative Land Area: Slightly smaller than Alabama
Capital City: Athens
People:
Total Population: 10,722,816
Total Median Age: 41.5 years
Life Expectancy: 79.52 years
Fertility Rate: 1.36 children born/woman
Religion:
Top Religion Percentages: Christian (92.21%), Muslim (4.83%), Nonreligious (2.38%), Atheist (0.34%), Hindu (0.13%)
Number of Christians: 9,887,509
Major Christian Groupings: Orthodox (95%), Protestant/Independent (4%), Catholic (1%)

HUNGARY

Geography:
  Location: Central Europe, northwest of Romania
  Comparative Land Area: Slightly smaller than Indiana
  Capital City: Budapest
People:
  Total Population: 9,930,915
  Total Median Age: 39.1 years
  Life Expectancy: 73.18 years
  Fertility Rate: 1.34 children born/woman
Religion:
  Top Religion Percentages: Christian (86.76%), Nonreligious (7.67%), Atheist (4.27%), Jewish (0.97%), Muslim (0.24%)
  Number of Christians: 8,616,062
  Major Christian Groupings: Catholic (68%), Protestant/Independent (30%), Orthodox (2%)

KOSOVO

Geography:
  Location: Southeast Europe, between Serbia and Macedonia
  Comparative Land Area: Slightly larger than Delaware
  Capital City: Pristina
People:
  Total Population: 2,126,708
  Total Median Age: 40.4 years
  Life Expectancy: 74 years
  Fertility Rate: 2.7 children born/woman
Religion:
  Top Religion Percentages: Muslim (89.5%), Christian (8.87%), Nonreligious (1.21%), Atheist (0.33%),
  Number of Christians: 188,639
  Major Christian Groupings: Orthodox (59%), Catholic (38%), Protestant/Independent (3%)

LATVIA

Geography:
  Location: Eastern Europe, bordering the Baltic Sea, between Estonia and Lithuania
  Comparative Land Area: Slightly larger than West Virginia
  Capital City: Riga
People:
  Total Population: 2,245,423
  Total Median Age: 39.9 years
  Life Expectancy: 71.88 years
  Fertility Rate: 1.29 children born/woman
Religion:
  Top Religion Percentages: Christian (67.97%), Nonreligious (25.44%), Atheist (5.87%), Jewish (0.41%), Muslim (0.25%)
  Number of Christians: 1,526,214
  Major Christian Groupings: Orthodox (46%), Protestant/Independent (27%), Catholic (27%)

LITHUANIA

Geography:
  Location: Eastern Europe, bordering the Baltic Sea, between Latvia and Russia
  Comparative Land Area: Slightly larger than West Virginia
  Capital City: Vilnius
People:
  Total Population: 3,565,205
  Total Median Age: 39 years
  Life Expectancy: 74.67 years
  Fertility Rate: 1.22 children born/woman
Religion:
  Top Religion Percentages: Christian (87.97%), Nonreligious (10.91%), Atheist (0.73%), Muslim (0.19%), Jewish (0.14%),
  Number of Christians: 3,136,311
  Major Christian Groupings: Catholic (92%), Orthodox (5%), Protestant/Independent (3%)

MACEDONIA

Geography:
  Location: Southeastern Europe, north of Greece
  Comparative Land Area: Slightly larger than Vermont
  Capital City: Skopje
People:
  Total Population: 2,061,315
  Total Median Age: 34.8 years
  Life Expectancy: 74.45 years
  Fertility Rate: 1.58 children born/woman
Religion:
  Top Religion Percentages: Christian (64.00%), Muslim (28.97%), Nonreligious (5.67%), Atheist (1.32%), Jewish (0.05%)
  Number of Christians: 1,319,242
  Major Christian Groupings: Orthodox (94%), Protestant/Independent (5%), Catholic (1%)

MOLDOVA

Geography:
  Location: Eastern Europe, northeast of Romania
  Comparative Land Area: Slightly larger than Maryland
  Capital City: Chisinau
People:
  Total Population: 4,324,450
  Total Median Age: 34.3 years
  Life Expectancy: 70.5 years
  Fertility Rate: 1.26 children born/woman
Religion:
  Top Religion Percentages: Christian (89.75%), Nonreligious (7.77%), Jewish (0.85%), Muslim (0.78%), Atheist (0.84%)
  Number of Christians: 3,881,194
  Major Christian Groupings: Orthodox (77%), Protestant/Independent (23%)

MONTENEGRO

Geography:
  Location: Southeastern Europe, between the Adriatic Sea and Serbia
  Comparative Land Area: Slightly smaller than Connecticut
  Capital City: Podgorica
People:
  Total Population: 678,177
  Total Median Age: 40.4 years
  Life Expectancy: 77.1 years
  Fertility Rate: 1.69 children born/woman
Religion:
  Top Religion Percentages: Christian (76.57%), Muslim (16.45%), Nonreligious (5.81%), Atheist (1.17%)
  Number of Christians: 519,280
  Major Christian Groupings: Orthodox (89%), Protestant/Independent (7%), Catholic (4%)

POLAND

Geography:
  Location: Central Europe, east of Germany
  Comparative Land Area: Slightly smaller than New Mexico
  Capital City: Warsaw
People:
  Total Population: 38,500,696
  Total Median Age: 37.6 years
  Life Expectancy: 75.41 years
  Fertility Rate: 1.27 children born/woman
Religion:
  Top Religion Percentages: Christian (96.26%), Nonreligious (3.39), Atheist (0.26%), Jewish (0.03%), Muslim (0.02%), Neoreligionist (0.02%)
  Number of Christians: 37,060,770
  Major Christian Groupings: Catholic (96%), Orthodox (2%), Protestant/Independent (2%)

ROMANIA

Geography:
 Location: Southeastern Europe, bordering the Black Sea, between Bulgaria and Ukraine
 Comparative Land Area: Slightly smaller than Oregon
 Capital City: Bucharest

People:
 Total Population: 22,246,862
 Total Median Age: 37.3 years
 Life Expectancy: 72.18 years
 Fertility Rate: 1.38 children born/woman

Religion:
 Top Religion Percentages: Christian (98.54%), Nonreligious (0.88%), Muslim (0.37%), Atheist (0.15%), Jewish (0.03%)
 Number of Christians: 21,922,058
 Major Christian Groupings: Orthodox (82%), Protestant/Independent (10%), Catholic (8%)

RUSSIA

Geography:
 Location: Northern Asia (the area west of the Urals is considered part of Europe), bordering the Arctic Ocean, between Europe and the North Pacific Ocean
 Comparative Land Area: Slightly less than twice the size of the United States
 Capital City: Moscow

People:
 Total Population: 140,702,096
 Total Median Age: 38.3 years
 Life Expectancy: 65.94 years
 Fertility Rate: 1.4 children born/woman

Religion:
 Top Religion Percentages: Christian (79.55%), Muslim (10.39%), Nonreligious (7.28%) Atheist (1.53%), Indigenous Religions (0.70%)
 Number of Christians: 111,928,517
 Major Christian Groupings: Orthodox (94%), Protestant/Independent (5%), Catholic (1%)

SERBIA

Geography:
 Location: Southeastern Europe, between Macedonia and Hungary
 Comparative Land Area: Slightly smaller than South Carolina
 Capital City: Belgrade

People:
 Total Population: 10,159,046
 Total Median Age: 37.5 years
 Life Expectancy: 75.29 years
 Fertility Rate: 1.69 children born/woman

Religion:
 Top Religion Percentages: Christian (79.01%), Nonreligious (10.28%), Muslim (6.99%), Atheist (3.63%), Jewish (0.04%)
 Number of Christians: 8,026,662
 Major Christian Groupings: Orthodox (90%), Catholic (6%), Protestant/Independent (4%)

SLOVAKIA

Geography:
 Location: Central Europe, south of Poland
 Comparative Land Area: Slightly larger than Denmark
 Capital City: Bratislavia

People:
 Total Population: 5,455,407
 Total Median Age: 36.5 years
 Life Expectancy: 75.17 years
 Fertility Rate: 1.34 children born/woman

Religion:
 Top Religion Percentages: Christian (84.71%), Nonreligious (11.55%), Atheist (3.67%), Jewish (0.04%), Baha'i (0.01%),
 Number of Christians: 4,621,275
 Major Christian Groupings: Catholic (87%), Protestant/Independent (12%), Orthodox (1%)

UKRAINE

Geography:
 Location: Eastern Europe, bordering the Black Sea, between Poland, Romania, and Moldova in the west and Russia in the east
 Comparative Land Area: Slightly smaller than Texas
 Capital City: Kiev

People:
 Total Population: 45,994,288
 Total Median Age: 39.4 years
 Life Expectancy: 68.06 years
 Fertility Rate: 1.25 children born/woman

Religion:
 Top Religion Percentages: Christians (82.10%), Nonreligious (12.24%), Atheist (3.08%), Muslim (2.14%), Jewish (0.39%)
 Number of Christians: 37,761,310
 Major Christian Groupings: Orthodox (67%), Protestant/Independent (21%), Catholic (12%)

LATIN AMERICA & THE CARIBBEAN

PEOPLE

Total Population: 580,413,248
Total Median Age: 26.9 years
Life Expectancy: 73.14 years
Fertility Rate: 2.42 children born/woman

RELIGION

Top Religion Percentages: Christian (92.62%)
Indigenous Religions (2.91%)
Nonreligious (2.88%)
Atheist (1.00%)
Other (0.59%)
Number of Christians: 537,579,955
Major Christian Groupings: Catholic (82.60%)
Protestant/Independent (17.17%)
Orthodox (0.23%)

ANGUILLA

Geography:
Location: Caribbean, islands between the Caribbean Sea and North Atlantic Ocean, east of Puerto Rico
Comparative Land Area: About half the size of Washington D.C., USA
Capital City: The Valley
People:
Total Population: 14,108
Total Median Age: 32.3 years
Life Expectancy: 80.53 years
Fertility Rate: 1.75 children born/woman
Religion:
Top Religion Percentages: Christian (91.19%), Indigenous Religions (3.37%), Nonreligious (3.27%), Baja'i (1.04%), Muslim (0.57%)
Number of Christians: 12,865
Major Christian Groupings: Protestant/Independent (87%), Catholic (13%)

ANTIGUA & BARBUDA

Geography:
Location: Caribbean, islands between the Caribbean Sea and the North Atlantic Ocean, east-southeast of Puerto Rico
Comparative Land Area: About ½ the size of New York City
Capital City: Saint John's
People:
Total Population: 84,522
Total Median Age: 29.5 years
Life Expectancy: 74.25 years
Fertility Rate: 2.08 children born/woman
Religion:
Top Religion Percentages: Christian (93.00%), Indigenous Religions (3.62%), Nonreligious (1.58%), Baha'i (0.97%), Muslim (0.55%)
Number of Christians: 78,605
Major Christian Groupings: Protestant/Independent (79%), Catholic (21%)

ARGENTINA

Geography:
Location: Southern South America, bordering the South Atlantic Ocean, between Chile and Uruguay
Comparative Land Area: About twice the size of Alaska
Capital City: Buenos Aires
People:
Total Population: 40,482,000
Total Median Age: 29.7 years
Life Expectancy: 76.36 years
Fertility Rate: 2.37 children born/woman
Religion:
Top Religion Percentages: Christian (92.01%), Nonreligious (3.05%), Muslim (1.95%), Jewish (1.32%), Atheist (0.85%)
Number of Christians: 37,247,488
Major Christian Groupings: Catholic (98%), Protestant/Independent (2%)

ARUBA

Geography:
Location: Caribbean, island in the Caribbean Sea, north of Venezuela
Comparative Land Area: Slightly larger than Washington D.C., USA
Capital City: Oranjestad
People:
Total Population: 101,541
Total Median Age: 37.6 years
Life Expectancy: 75.06 years
Fertility Rate: 1.85 children born/woman
Religion:
Top Religion Percentages: Christian (96.41%), Nonreligious (1.64%), Indigenous Religions (1.10%), Muslim (0.21%), Chinese Universalist (0.16%)
Number of Christians: 97,895
Major Christian Groupings: Catholic (83%), Protestant/Independent (17%)

BAHAMAS

Geography:
  Location: Caribbean, chain of islands in the North Atlantic Ocean, southeast of Florida, northeast of Cuba
  Comparative Land Area: Slightly smaller than Connecticut
  Capital City: Nassau
People:
  Total Population: 307,451
  Total Median Age: 28.4 years
  Life Expectancy: 65.72 years
  Fertility Rate: 2.13 children born/woman
Religion:
  Top Religion Percentages: Christian (91.95%), Nonreligious (5.44%), Indigenous Religions (1.90%), Baha'i (0.40%), Atheist (0.15%)
  Number of Christians: 282,701
  Major Christian Groupings: Protestant/Independent (90%), Catholic (10%)

BARBADOS

Geography:
  Location: Caribbean, island in the North Atlantic Ocean, northwest of Venezuela
  Comparative Land Area: Over twice as large as Washington D.C., USA
  Capital City: Bridgetown
People:
  Total Population: 281,968
  Total Median Age: 35.4 years
  Life Expectancy: 73.21 years
  Fertility Rate: 1.65 children born/woman
Religion:
  Top Religion Percentages: Christian (95.50%), Nonreligious (1.73%), Baha'i (1.22%), Muslim (0.76%), Hindu (0.33%)
  Number of Christians: 269,279
  Major Christian Groupings: Protestant/Independent (96%), Catholic (4%)

BELIZE

Geography:
  Location: Central America, bordering the Caribbean Sea, between Guatemala and Mexico
  Comparative Land Area: Slightly smaller than Massachusetts
  Capital City: Belmopan
People:
  Total Population: 301,270
  Total Median Age: 20.1 years
  Life Expectancy: 68.19 years
  Fertility Rate: 3.44 children born/woman
Religion:
  Top Religion Percentages: Christian (91.14%), Baha'i (2.49%), Hindu (1.97%), Jewish (1.08%), Indigenous Religions (0.96%)
  Number of Christians: 274,577
  Major Christian Groupings: Catholic (68%), Protestant/Independent (32%)

BERMUDA

Geography:
  Location: North America, group of islands in the North Atlantic Ocean, east of South Carolina
  Comparative Land Area: About the size of Manhattan Island in New York City, USA
  Capital City: Hamilton
People:
  Total Population: 66,536
  Total Median Age: 41 years
  Life Expectancy: 78.3 years
  Fertility Rate: 1.88 children born/woman
Religion:
  Top Religion Percentages: Christian (90.42%), Nonreligious (5.04%), Indigenous Religions (2.74%), Baha'i (0.63%), Buddhist (0.50%)
  Number of Christians: 60,162
  Major Christian Groupings: Protestant/Independent (84%), Catholic (16%)

BOLIVIA

Geography:
  Location: Central South America, southwest of Brazil
  Comparative Land Area: About twice the size of Spain
  Capital City: La Paz
People:
  Total Population: 9,247,816
  Total Median Age: 22.6 years
  Life Expectancy: 66.53 years
  Fertility Rate: 2.67 children born/woman
Religion:
  Top Religion Percentages: Christian (92.02%), Indigenous Religions (3.79%), Baha'i (2.24%), Nonreligious (1.64%), Atheist (0.14%)
  Number of Christians: 8,509,840
  Major Christian Groupings: Catholic (85%), Protestant/Independent (15%)

BRAZIL

Geography:
  Location: Eastern South America, bordering the Atlantic Ocean
  Comparative Land Area: Slightly larger than Australia
  Capital City: Brasilia
People:
  Total Population: 196,342,592
  Total Median Age: 28.3 years
  Life Expectancy: 71.71 years
  Fertility Rate: 2.22 children born/woman
Religion:
  Top Religion Percentages: Christian (91.31%), Indigenous Religions (5.04%), Nonreligious (2.55%), Atheist (0.34%), Neoreligionist (0.26%)
  Number of Christians: 179,280,421
  Major Christian Groupings: Catholic (73%), Protestant/Independent (27%)

BRITISH VIRGIN ISLANDS

Geography:
  Location: Caribbean, between the Caribbean Sea and the North Atlantic Ocean, east of Puerto Rico
  Comparative Land Area: Slightly smaller than Washington D.C., USA
  Capital City: Road Town
People:
  Total Population: 24,041
  Total Median Age: 32 years
  Life Expectancy: 77.07 years
  Fertility Rate: 1.71 children born/woman
Religion:
  Top Religion Percentages: Christian (84.50%), Indigenous Religions (8.39%), Nonreligious (3.81%), Hindu (1.19%), Muslim (1.15%)
  Number of Christians: 20,314
  Major Christian Groupings: Protestant/Independent (96%), Catholic (4%)

CAYMAN ISLANDS

Geography:
  Location: Caribbean, amidst three-island group in Caribbean Sea
  Comparative Land Area: About the size of Sacramento, USA
  Capital City: George Town
People:
  Total Population: 47,862
  Total Median Age: 37.8 years
  Life Expectancy: 80.32 years
  Fertility Rate: 1.89 children born/woman
Religion:
  Top Religion Percentages: Christian (81.08%), Indigenous Religions (10.14%), Nonreligious (5.41%), Jewish (1.77%), Baha'i (0.77%)
  Number of Christians: 38,807
  Major Christian Groupings: Protestant/Independent (89%), Catholic (11%)

CHILE

Geography:
  Location: Southern South America, bordering the South
  Pacific Ocean, between Argentina and Peru
  Comparative Land Area: Slightly larger than Texas
  Capital City: Santiago
People:
  Total Population: 16,454,143
  Total Median Age: 31.1 years
  Life Expectancy: 77.15 years
  Fertility Rate: 1.95 children born/woman
Religion:
  Top Religion Percentages: Christian (87.81%), Nonreligious
  (7.39%), Atheist (2.39%), Indigenous Religions (1.59%),
  Muslim (0.43%)
  Number of Christians: 14,448,383
  Major Christian Groupings: Catholic (70%),
  Protestant/Independent (29%), Orthodox (1%)

COLOMBIA

Geography:
  Location: Northern South America, bordering the Caribbean
  Sea, between Panama and Venezuela, and bordering the North
  Pacific Ocean, between Ecuador and Panama
  Comparative Land Area: About twice the size of France
  Capital City: Bogota
People:
  Total Population: 45,013,672
  Total Median Age: 26.8 years
  Life Expectancy: 72.54 years
  Fertility Rate: 2.49 children born/woman
Religion:
  Top Religion Percentages: Christian (96.08%), Nonreligious
  (1.81%), Indigenous Religions (1.66%), Atheist (0.20%),
  Baha'i (0.15%)
  Number of Christians: 43,249,136
  Major Christian Groupings: Catholic (94%),
  Protestant/Independent (6%)

COSTA RICA

Geography:
  Location: Central America, bordering both the Caribbean Sea
  and the North Pacific Ocean, between Nicaragua and
  PanamaComparative Land Area: Slightly smaller than West
  Virginia
  Capital City: San Jose
People:
  Total Population: 4,195,914
  Total Median Age: 27.1 years
  Life Expectancy: 77.4 years
  Fertility Rate: 2.17 children born/woman
Religion:
  Top Religion Percentages: Christian (96.99%), Nonreligious
  (1.60%), Chinese Universalist (0.52%), Baha'i (0.29%),
  Atheist (0.24%)
  Number of Christians: 4,069,617
  Major Christian Groupings: Catholic (93%),
  Protestant/Independent (7%)

CUBA

Geography:
  Location: Caribbean, island between the Caribbean Sea and
  the North Atlantic Ocean, 150 km south of Key West, Florida
  Comparative Land Area: Slightly smaller than Pennsylvania
  Capital City: Havana
People:
  Total Population: 11,423,952
  Total Median Age: 36.8 years
  Life Expectancy: 77.27 years
  Fertility Rate: 1.6 children born/woman
Religion:
  Top Religion Percentages: Christian (57.79%), Nonreligious
  (18.69%), Indigenous Religions (17.18%), Atheist (5.78%),
  Hindu (0.21%)
  Number of Christians: 6,601,902
  Major Christian Groupings: Catholic (88%),
  Protestant/Independent (12%)

DOMINICA

Geography:
  Location: Caribbean, island between the Caribbean Sea and
  North Atlantic Ocean, about half way between Puerto Rico and
  Trinidad and Tobago
  Comparative Land Area: About the size of New York City,
  USA
  Capital City: Roseau
People:
  Total Population: 72,514
  Total Median Age: 29.4 years
  Life Expectancy: 75.33 years
  Fertility Rate: 2.1 children born/woman
Religion:
  Top Religion Percentages: Christian (94.42%), Indigenous
  Religions (2.90%), Baha'i (1.70%), Nonreligious (0.49%),
  Muslim (0.14%)
  Number of Christians: 68,467
  Major Christian Groupings: Catholic (65%),
  Protestant/Independent (35%)

DOMINICAN REPUBLIC

Geography:
  Location: Caribbean, eastern two-thirds of the island of
  Hispaniola, between the Caribbean Sea and the North Atlantic
  Ocean, east of Haiti
  Comparative Land Area: About twice the size of New
  Hampshire
  Capital City: Santo Domingo
People:
  Total Population: 9,507,133
  Total Median Age: 24.7 years
  Life Expectancy: 73.39 years
  Fertility Rate: 2.78 children born/woman
Religion:
  Top Religion Percentages: Christian (94.98%), Indigenous
  Religions (2.18%), Nonreligious (2.14%), Atheist (0.47%),
  Chinese Universalist (0.08%)
  Number of Christians: 9,029,875
  Major Christian Groupings: Catholic (89%),
  Protestant/Independent (11%)

ECUADOR

Geography:
  Location: Western South America, bordering the Pacific
  Ocean at the Equator, between Colombia and Peru
  Comparative Land Area: Slightly smaller than Nevada
  Capital City: Quito
People:
  Total Population: 13,927,650
  Total Median Age: 24.2 years
  Life Expectancy: 76.81 years
  Fertility Rate: 2.59 children born/woman
Religion:
  Top Religion Percentages: Christian (97.10%), Nonreligious
  (1.43%), Indigenous Religions (0.94%), Atheist (0.15%),
  Baha'i (0.12%)
  Number of Christians: 13,523,748
  Major Christian Groupings: Catholic (93%),
  Protestant/Independent (7%)

EL SALVADOR

Geography:
  Location: Central America, bordering the North Pacific
  Ocean, between Guatemala and Honduras
  Comparative Land Area: Slightly smaller than Massachusetts
  Capital City: San Salvador
People:
  Total Population: 7,066,403
  Total Median Age: 22.2 years
  Life Expectancy: 72.06 years
  Fertility Rate: 3.04 children born/woman
Religion:
  Top Religion Percentages: Christian (97.39%), Nonreligious
  (1.42%), Indigenous Religions (0.57%), Baha'i (0.44%),
  Atheist (0.09%)
  Number of Christians: 6,881,970
  Major Christian Groupings: Catholic (76%),
  Protestant/Independent (24%)

FALKLAND ISLANDS

Geography:
Location: Southern South America, islands in the South Atlantic Ocean, east of southern Argentina
Comparative Land Area: Slightly smaller than Connecticut
Capital City: Stanley
People:
Total Population: 3,140
Total Median Age: 27.8 years
Life Expectancy: 78.30 years
Fertility Rate: 2.98 children born/woman
Religion:
Top Religion Percentages: Christian (82.96%), Nonreligious (11.09%), Baha'i (2.96%), Neoreligionist (1.82%), Atheist (0.97%)
Number of Christians: 2,605
Major Christian Groupings: Protestant/Independent (75%), Catholic (25%)

FRENCH GUIANA

Geography:
Location: Northern South America, bordering the North Atlantic Ocean, between Brazil and Suriname
Comparative Land Area: Slightly smaller than Indiana
Capital City: Cayenne
People:
Total Population: 209,000
Total Median Age: 28.3 years
Life Expectancy: 76.89 years
Fertility Rate: 2.98 children born/woman
Religion:
Top Religion Percentages: Christian (84.41%), Indigenous Religions (5.53%), Chinese Universalist (3.57%), Nonreligious (2.93%), Hindu (1.6%)
Number of Christians: 176,417
Major Christian Groupings: Catholic (92%), Protestant/Independent (8%)

GRENADA

Geography:
Location: Caribbean, island between the Caribbean Sea and Atlantic Ocean, north of Trinidad and Tobago
Comparative Land Area: About twice the size of Washington D.C., USA
Capital City: Saint George's
People:
Total Population: 90,343
Total Median Age: 22.4 years
Life Expectancy: 65.60 years
Fertility Rate: 2.27 children born/woman
Religion:
Top Religion Percentages: Christian (96.58%), Indigenous Religions (1.27%), Nonreligious (0.94%), Hindu (0.68%), Muslim (0.33%)
Number of Christians: 87,253
Major Christian Groupings: Catholic (55%), Protestant/Independent (45%)

GUADELOUPE

Geography:
Location: Caribbean, islands between the Caribbean Sea and the North Atlantic Ocean, southeast of Puerto Rico
Comparative Land Area: About the size of London, U.K.
Capital City: Basse-Terre
People:
Total Population: 452,776
Total Median Age: 32.2 years
Life Expectancy: 78.06 years
Fertility Rate: 1.9 children born/woman
Religion:
Top Religion Percentages: Christian (95.86%), Nonreligious (1.86%), Atheist (0.62%), Hindu (0.50%), Indigenous Religions (0.39%)
Number of Christians: 434,031
Major Christian Groupings: Catholic (89%), Protestant/Independent (11%)

GUATEMALA

Geography:
Location: Central America, bordering the North Pacific Ocean, between El Salvador and Mexico
Comparative Land Area: Slightly smaller than Tennessee
Capital City: Guatemala City
People:
Total Population: 13,002,206
Total Median Age: 19.2 years
Life Expectancy: 69.99 years
Fertility Rate: 3.59 children born/woman
Religion:
Top Religion Percentages: Christian (97.36%), Indigenous Religions (1.06%), Nonreligious (0.93%), Atheist (0.43%), Baha'i (0.14%)
Number of Christians: 12,658,948
Major Christian Groupings: Catholic (74%), Protestant/Independent (26%)

GUYANA

Geography:
Location: Northern South America, bordering the North Atlantic Ocean, between Suriname and Venezuela
Comparative Land Area: Slightly smaller than Idaho
Capital City: Georgetown
People:
Total Population: 770,794
Total Median Age: 28.2 years
Life Expectancy: 66.43 years
Fertility Rate: 2.03 children born/woman
Religion:
Top Religion Percentages: Christian (50.96%), Hindu (32.89%), Muslim (8.24%), Indigenous Religions (2.38%), Baha'i (1.71%)
Number of Christians: 392,797
Major Christian Groupings: Protestant/Independent (77%), Catholic (21%), Orthodox (2%)

HAITI

Geography:
Location: Caribbean, western one-third of the island of Hispaniola, between the Caribbean Sea and the North Atlantic Ocean, west of the Dominican Republic
Comparative Land Area: Slightly smaller than Maryland
Capital City: Port-au-Prince
People:
Total Population: 8,924,553
Total Median Age: 18.5 years
Life Expectancy: 57.56 years
Fertility Rate: 4.79 children born/woman
Religion:
Top Religion Percentages: Christian (95.29%), Indigenous Religions (2.71%), Nonreligious (1.66%), Baha'i (0.23%), Atheist (0.05%)
Number of Christians: 8,504,207
Major Christian Groupings: Catholic (77%), Protestant/Independent (23%)

HONDORUS

Geography:
Location: Central America, bordering the Caribbean Sea, between Guatemala and Nicaragua and bordering the Gulf of Fonseca (North Pacific Ocean), between El Salvador and Nicaragua
Comparative Land Area: Slightly larger than Tennessee
Capital City: Tegucigalpa
People:
Total Population: 7,639,327
Total Median Age: 20 years
Life Expectancy: 69.37 years
Fertility Rate: 3.38 children born/woman
Religion:
Top Religion Percentages: Christian (96.67%), Indigenous Religions (1.45%), Nonreligious (0.93%), Baha'i (0.49%), Atheist (0.21%)
Number of Christians: 7,384,937
Major Christian Groupings: Catholic (81%), Protestant/Independent (19%)

JAMAICA

Geography:
Location: Caribbean, island in the Caribbean Sea, south of Cuba
Comparative Land Area: About the size of Connecticut
Capital City: Kingston

People:
Total Population: 2,804,332
Total Median Age: 23.4 years
Life Expectancy: 73.59 years
Fertility Rate: 2.3 children born/woman

Religion:
Top Religion Percentages: Christian (84.55%), Indigenous Religions (10.15%), Nonreligious (4.12%), Hindu (0.60%), Baha'i (0.19%)
Number of Christians: 2,371,063
Major Christian Groupings: Protestant/Independent (95%), Catholic (5%)

MARTINIQUE

Geography:
Location: Caribbean, island between the Caribbean Sea and the North Atlantic Ocean, north of Trinidad and Tobago
Comparative Land Area: Slightly smaller than Los Angeles, USA
Capital City: Fort-de-France

People:
Total Population: 436,000
Total Median Age: 32.7 years
Life Expectancy: 78.72 years
Fertility Rate: 1.79 children born/woman

Religion:
Top Religion Percentages: Christian (96.65%), Nonreligious (1.68%), Baha'i (0.52%), Atheist (0.44%), Hindu (0.24%)
Number of Christians: 421,394
Major Christian Groupings: Catholic (88%), Protestant/Independent (12%)

MEXICO

Geography:
Location: Middle America, bordering the Caribbean Sea and the Gulf of Mexico, between Belize and the US and bordering the North Pacific Ocean, between Guatemala and the US
Comparative Land Area: About three times the size of France
Capital City: Mexico City

People:
Total Population: 109,955,400
Total Median Age: 26 years
Life Expectancy: 75.84 years
Fertility Rate: 2.37 children born/woman

Religion:
Top Religion Percentages: Christian (95.86%), Nonreligious (2.49%), Indigenous Religions (1.13%), Muslim (0.20%), Atheist (0.11%)
Number of Christians: 105,403,246
Major Christian Groupings: Catholic (90%), Protestant/Independent (9%), Orthodox (1%)

MONTSERRAT

Geography:
Location: Caribbean, island in the Caribbean Sea, southeast of Puerto Rico
Comparative Land Area: About twice the size of Manhattan Island in New York City, USA
Capital City: Plymouth

People:
Total Population: 5,079
Total Median Age: 28.1 years
Life Expectancy: 72.6 years
Fertility Rate: 1.22 children born/woman

Religion:
Top Religion Percentages: Christian (95.40%), Nonreligious (2.90%), Baha'i (1.46%), Indigenous Religions (0.14%), Hindu (0.11%)
Number of Christians: 4,845
Major Christian Groupings: Protestant/Independent (93%), Catholic (7%)

NETHERLANDS ANTILLES

Geography:
Location: Caribbean, two island groups in the Caribbean Sea – group of five islands off the coast of Venezuela and east of the US Virgin Islands
Comparative Land Area: About the size of New York City, USA
Capital City: Willemstad

People:
Total Population: 225,369
Total Median Age: 33.4 years
Life Expectancy: 76.45 years
Fertility Rate: 1.98 children born/woman

Religion:
Top Religion Percentages: Christian (93.92%), Nonreligious (3.13%), Indigenous Religions (1.09%), Buddhist (0.50%), Jewish (0.32%)
Number of Christians: 211,667
Major Christian Groupings: Catholic (80%), Protestant/Independent (20%)

NICARAGUA

Geography:
Location: Central America, bordering both the Caribbean Sea and the North Pacific Ocean, between Costa Rica and Honduras
Comparative Land Area: Slightly smaller than the state of New York
Capital City: Managua

People:
Total Population: 5,785,846
Total Median Age: 21.7 years
Life Expectancy: 71.21 years
Fertility Rate: 2.63 children born/woman

Religion:
Top Religion Percentages: Christian (96.18%), Indigenous Religions (2.02%), Nonreligious (1.47%), Baha'i (0.19%), Buddhist (0.12%)
Number of Christians: 5,564,827
Major Christian Groupings: Catholic (77%), Protestant/Independent (23%)

PANAMA

Geography:
Location: Central America, bordering the Caribbean Sea and the North Pacific Ocean, between Colombia and Costa Rica
Comparative Land Area: A little smaller than South Carolina
Capital City: Panama City

People:
Total Population: 3,309,679
Total Median Age: 26.7 years
Life Expectancy: 76.88 years
Fertility Rate: 2.57 children born/woman

Religion:
Top Religion Percentages: Christian (87.17%), Muslim (4.42%), Nonreligious (3.08%), Indigenous Religions (1.60%), Baha'i (1.29%)
Number of Christians: 2,885,047
Major Christian Groupings: Catholic (78%), Protestant/Independent (22%)

PARAGUAY

Geography:
Location: Central South America, northeast of Argentina
Comparative Land Area: Slightly smaller than California
Capital City: Asuncion

People:
Total Population: 6,831,306
Total Median Age: 21.7 years
Life Expectancy: 75.56 years
Fertility Rate: 3.8 children born/woman

Religion:
Top Religion Percentages: Christian (95.51%), Indigenous Religions (1.98%), Nonreligious (1.79%), Buddhist (0.23%), Atheist (0.23%)
Number of Christians: 6,524,580
Major Christian Groupings: Catholic (90%), Protestant/Independent (10%)

PERU

Geography:
  Location: Western South America, bordering the South Pacific Ocean, between Chile and Equador
  Comparative Land Area: Slightly smaller than Alaska
  Capital City: Lima
People:
  Total Population: 29,180,900
  Total Median Age: 25.8 years
  Life Expectancy: 70.44 years
  Fertility Rate: 2.42 children born/woman
Religion:
  Top Religion Percentages: Christian (96.45%), Indigenous Religions (1.37%), Nonreligious (1.20%), Neoreligionist (0.32%), Buddhist (0.22%)
  Number of Christians: 28,144,978
  Major Christian Groupings: Catholic (87%), Protestant/Independent (13%)

PUERTO RICO

Geography:
  Location: Caribbean, island between the Caribbean Sea and the North Atlantic Ocean, east of the Dominican Republic
  Comparative Land Area: About three times the size of Rhode Island
  Capital City: San Juan
People:
  Total Population: 3,958,128
  Total Median Age: 35.6 years
  Life Expectancy: 78.58 years
  Fertility Rate: 1.76 children born/woman
Religion:
  Top Religion Percentages: Christian (96.66%), Nonreligious (1.92%), Indigenous Religions (0.71%), Atheist (0.39%), Hindu (0.09%)
  Number of Christians: 3,825,927
  Major Christian Groupings: Catholic (73%), Protestant/Independent (27%)

SAINT KITTS & NEVIS

Geography:
  Location: Caribbean, islands in the Caribbean Sea, about one-third of the way from Puerto Rico to Trinidad and Tobago-
  Comparative Land Area: About the size of Sacramento, USA
  Capital City: Basseterre
People:
  Total Population: 39,817
  Total Median Age: 28.4 years
  Life Expectancy: 72.94 years
  Fertility Rate: 2.28 children born/woman
Religion:
  Top Religion Percentages: Christian (94.62%), Nonreligious (1.59%), Hindu (1.50%), Indigenous Religions (1.27%), Baha'i (0.49%),
  Number of Christians: 37,675
  Major Christian Groupings: Protestant/Independent (90%), Catholic (10%)

SAINT LUCIA

Geography:
  Location: Caribbean, island between the Caribbean Sea and North Atlantic Ocean, north of Trinidad and Tobago
  Comparative Land Area: About the size of Chicago, USA
  Capital City: Castries
People:
  Total Population: 159,585
  Total Median Age: 29.2 years
  Life Expectancy: 76.25 years
  Fertility Rate: 1.86 children born/woman
Religion:
  Top Religion Percentages: Christian (95.93%), Indigenous Religions (1.68%), Hindu (0.91%), Muslim (0.46%), Neoreligionist (0.38%)
  Number of Christians: 153,090
  Major Christian Groupings: Catholic (70%), Protestant/Independent (30%)

SAINT VINCENT & THE GRENADINES

Geography:
  Location: Caribbean, islands between the Caribbean Sea and the North Atlantic Ocean, north of Trinidad and Tobago
  Comparative Land Area: About twice the size of Washington D.C., USA
  Capital City: Kingstown
People:
  Total Population: 118,432
  Total Median Age: 28 years
  Life Expectancy: 74.34 years
  Fertility Rate: 1.79 children born/woman
Religion:
  Top Religion Percentages: Christian (88.69%), Hindu (3.35%), Nonreligious (2.42%), Indigenous Religions (1.99%), Muslim (1.49%)
  Number of Christians: 105,037
  Major Christian Groupings: Protestant/Independent (93%), Catholic (7%)

SURINAME

Geography:
  Location: Northern South America, bordering the North Atlantic Ocean, between French Guiana and Guyana
  Comparative Land Area: Slightly larger than Georgia
  Capital City: Paramaribo
People:
  Total Population: 475,996
  Total Median Age: 27.5 years
  Life Expectancy: 73.48 years
  Fertility Rate: 2.01 children born/woman
Religion:
  Top Religion Percentages: Christian (51.21%), Hindu (17.21%), Muslim (13.65%), Indigenous Religions (5.64%), Neoreligionist (4.91%), Nonreligious (4.66%)
  Number of Christians: 243,758
  Major Christian Groupings: Catholic (60%), Protestant/Independent (40%)

TRINIDAD & TOBAGO

Geography:
  Location: Caribbean, islands between the Caribbean Sea and the North Atlantic Ocean, northeast of Venezuela
  Comparative Land Area: Slightly smaller than Delaware
  Capital City: Port-of-Spain
People:
  Total Population: 1,047,366
  Total Median Age: 32.3 years
  Life Expectancy: 67 years
  Fertility Rate: 1.73 children born/woman
Religion:
  Top Religion Percentages: Christian (62.69%), Hindu (24.33%), Muslim (7.18%), Nonreligious (2.24%), Indigenous Religions (1.44%)
  Number of Christians: 656,594
  Major Christian Groupings: Protestant/Independent (52%), Catholic (48%)

TURKS & CAICOS ISLANDS

Geography:
  Location: Caribbean, two island groups in the North Atlantic Ocean, southeast of the Bahamas, north of Haiti
  Comparative Land Area: Slightly smaller than New Orleans, USA
  Capital City: Cockburn Town
People:
  Total Population: 22,352
  Total Median Age: 27.8 years
  Life Expectancy: 75.19 years
  Fertility Rate: 2.98 children born/woman
Religion:
  Top Religion Percentages: Christians (92.09%), Nonreligious (4.60%), Indigenous Religions (2.66%), Baha'i (0.62%), Atheist (0.04%)
  Number of Christians: 20,584
  Major Christian Groupings: Protestant/Independent (100%)

URUGUAY

Geography:
 Location: Southern South America, bordering the South
 Atlantic Ocean, between Argentina and Brazil
 Comparative Land Area: Slightly smaller than the state of
 Washington
 Capital City: Montevideo
People:
 Total Population: 3,477,778
 Total Median Age: 33.2 years
 Life Expectancy: 76.14 years
 Fertility Rate: 1.94 children born/woman
Religion:
 Top Religion Percentages: Christians (64.68%), Nonreligious
 (27.38%), Atheist (6.29%), Jewish (1.22%), Baha'i (0.22%)
 Number of Christians: 2,249,427
 Major Christian Groupings: Catholic (88%),
 Protestant/Independent (12%)

U.S. VIRGIN ISLANDS

Geography:
 Location: Caribbean, islands between the Caribbean Sea and
 the North Atlantic Ocean, east of Puerto Rico
 Comparative Land Area: About twice the size of Washington
 D.C., USA
 Capital City: Charlotte Amalie
People:
 Total Population: 109,840
 Total Median Age: 38.5 years
 Life Expectancy: 78.92 years
 Fertility Rate: 1.88 children born/woman
Religion:
 Top Religion Percentages: Christian (94.98%), Nonreligious
 (3.37%), Baha'i (0.63%), Hindu (0.42%), Jewish (0.32%),
 Number of Christians: 104,326
 Major Christian Groupings: Protestant/Independent (70%),
 Catholic (30%)

VENEZUELA

Geography:
 Location: Northern South America, bordering the Caribbean
 Sea and the North Atlantic Ocean, between Colombia and
 Guyana
 Comparative Land Area: About twice the size of California
 Capital City: Caracas
People:
 Total Population: 26,414,816
 Total Median Age: 25.2 years
 Life Expectancy: 73.45 years
 Fertility Rate: 2.52 children born/woman
Religion:
 Top Religion Percentages: Christians (94.51%), Nonreligious
 (2.25%), Indigenous Religions (1.77%), Baha'i (0.58%),
 Muslim (0.33%)
 Number of Christians: 24,964,643
 Major Christian Groupings: Catholic (90%),
 Protestant/Independent (10%)

THE MIDDLE EAST

PEOPLE
Total Population: 270,398,623
Total Median Age: 24.7 years
Life Expectancy: 71.9 years
Fertility Rate: 2.88 children born/woman

RELIGION
Top Religion Percentages: Muslim (93.20%)
Christian (2.45%)
Jewish (2.08%)
Nonreligious (1.14%)
Hindu, Baha'i, Buddhist, Atheist, Zoroastrian, Sikh, Other Religionist (1.13%)
Number of Christians: 3,801
Major Christian Groupings: Catholic (58%), Orthodox (29%), Protestant/Independent (13%)

BAHRAIN
Geography:
Location: Middle East, archipelago in the Persian Gulf, east of Saudi Arabia
Comparative Land Area: Slightly larger than Chicago, USA
Capital City: Manama
People:
Total Population: 718,306
Total Median Age: 29.9 years
Life Expectancy: 74.92 years
Fertility Rate: 2.53 children born/woman
Religion:
Top Religion Percentages: Muslim (83.60%), Christian (8.93%), Hindu (6.47%), Nonreligious (0.40%), Baha'i (0.22%)
Number of Christians: 64,144
Major Christian Groupings: Catholic (59%), Protestant/Independent (37%), Orthodox (4%)

IRAN
Geography:
Location: Middle East, bordering the Gulf of Oman, the Persian Gulf, and the Caspian Sea, between Iraq and Pakistan
Comparative Land Area: Slightly larger than Alaska
Capital City: Tehran
People:
Total Population: 65,875,224
Total Median Age: 26.4 years
Life Expectancy: 70.86 years
Fertility Rate: 1.71 children born/woman
Religion:
Top Religion Percentages: Muslim (98.28%), Baha'i (0.59%), Christian (0.58%), Nonreligious (0.33%), Zoroastrian (0.09%)
Number of Christians: 382,076
Major Christian Groupings: Orthodox (71%), Protestant/Independent (22%), Catholic (7%)

IRAQ
Geography:
Location: Middle East, bordering the Persian Gulf, between Iran and Kuwait
Comparative Land Area: Slightly larger than California
Capital City: Baghdad
People:
Total Population: 28,221,180
Total Median Age: 20.2 years
Life Expectancy: 69.62 years
Fertility Rate: 3.97 children born/woman
Religion:
Top Religion Percentages: Muslim (97.11%), Christian (2.01%), Nonreligious (0.48%), Other Religionist (0.19%), Atheist (0.16%)
Number of Christians: 567,246
Major Christian Groupings: Catholic (47%), Protestant/Independent (30%), Orthodox (23%)

ISRAEL & THE OCCUPIED TERRITORIES
Geography:
Location: Middle East, bordering the Mediterranean Sea, between Egypt and Lebanon
Comparative Land Area: Slightly larger than New Jersey
Capital City: Jerusalem
People:
Total Population: 11,258,242
Total Median Age: 25.4 years
Life Expectancy: 78.21
Fertility Rate: 3.22 children born/woman
Religion:
Top Religion Percentages: Jewish (50.07%), Muslim (41.45%), Nonreligious (4.74%), Christian (2.75%), Atheist (0.36%)
Number of Christians: 310,205
Major Christian Groupings: Catholic (49%), Orthodox (28%), Protestant/Independent (23%)

JORDAN

Geography:
   Location: Middle East, northwest of Saudi Arabia
   Comparative Land Area: Slightly smaller than Indiana
   Capital City: Amman
People:
   Total Population: 6,198,677
   Total Median Age: 23.9 years
   Life Expectancy: 78.71 years
   Fertility Rate: 2.47 children born/woman
Religion:
   Top Religion Percentages: Muslim (93.45%), Christian (3.24%), Nonreligious (2.52%), Atheist (0.49%),   Baha'i (0.26%)
   Number of Christians: 200,837
   Major Christian Groupings: Orthodox (67%), Catholic (19%), Protestant/Independent (14%)

KUWAIT

Geography:
   Location: Middle East, bordering the Persian Gulf, between Iraq and Saudi Arabia
   Comparative Land Area: Slightly smaller than New Jersey
   Capital City: Kuwait City
People:
   Total Population: 2,596,799
   Total Median Age: 26.1 years
   Life Expectancy: 77.53 years
   Fertility Rate: 2.81 children born/woman
Religion:
   Top Religion Percentages: Muslim (86.07%), Christian (9.50%), Hindu (3.25%), Nonreligious (0.69%),   Baha'i (0.33%)
   Number of Christians: 246,696
   Major Christian Groupings: Catholic (77%), Protestant/Independent (15%), Orthodox (8%)

LEBANON

Geography:
   Location: Middle East, bordering the Mediterranean Sea, between Israel and Syria
   Comparative Land Area: Slightly smaller than Connecticut
   Capital City: Beirut
People:
   Total Population: 3,971,941
   Total Median Age: 28.8 years
   Life Expectancy: 73.41 years
   Fertility Rate: 1.87 children born/woman
Religion:
   Top Religion Percentages: Muslim (59.28%), Christian (34.36%), Nonreligious (3.37%), Buddhist (2.07%), Atheists (0.77%)
   Number of Christians: 1,364,759
   Major Christian Groupings: Catholic (75%), Orthodox (22%), Protestant/Independent (3%)

OMAN

Geography:
   Location: Middle East, bordering the Arabian Sea, Gulf of Oman, and Persian Gulf, between Yemen and UAE
   Comparative Land Area: Slightly smaller than Kansas
   Capital City: Muscat
People:
   Total Population: 3,311,640
   Total Median Age: 18.9 years
   Life Expectancy: 73.91 years
   Fertility Rate: 5.62 children born/woman
Religion:
   Top Religion Percentages: Muslim (87.89%), Hindu (5.51%), Christian (4.55%), Buddhist (0.78%), Sikh (0.66%)
   Number of Christians: 150,680
   Major Christian Groupings: Catholic (45%), Protestant/Independent (45%), Orthodox (10%)

QATAR

Geography:
   Location: Middle East, peninsula bordering the Persian Gulf and Saudi Arabia
   Comparative Land Area: Slightly smaller than Connecticut
   Capital City: Doha
People:
   Total Population: 824,789
   Total Median Age: 30.7 years
   Life Expectancy: 75.19 years
   Fertility Rate: 2.47 children born/woman
Religion:
   Top Religion Percentages: Muslim (83.19%), Christian (9.92%), Hindu (2.52%), Nonreligious (2.26%),   Buddhist (1.90%)
   Number of Christians: 81,819
   Major Christian Groupings: Catholic (76%), Protestant/Independent (20%), Orthodox (4%)

SAUDI ARABIA

Geography:
   Location: Middle East, bordering the Persian Gulf and the Red Sea, north of Yemen
   Comparative Land Area: Slightly larger than Mexico
   Capital City: Riyadh
People:
   Total Population: 28,146,656
   Total Median Age: 21.5 years
   Life Expectancy: 76.09 years
   Fertility Rate: 3.89 children born/woman
Religion:
   Top Religion Percentages: Muslim (92.83%), Christian (4.48%), Hindu (1.13%), Nonreligious (0.64%),   Buddhist (0.33%)
   Number of Christians: 1,260,970
   Major Christian Groupings: Catholic (85%), Protestant/Independent (10%), Orthodox (5%)

SYRIA

Geography:
   Location: Middle East, bordering the Mediterranean Sea, between Lebanon and Turkey
   Comparative Land Area: Slightly larger than North Dakota
   Capital City: Damascus
People:
   Total Population: 19,747,586
   Total Median Age: 21.4 years
   Life Expectancy: 70.9 years
   Fertility Rate: 3.21 children born/woman
Religion:
   Top Religion Percentages: Muslim (92.19%), Christian (5.77%), Nonreligious (1.92%), Atheist (0.12%)
   Number of Christians: 1,139,436
   Major Christian Groupings: Orthodox (55%), Catholic (38%), Protestant/Independent (7%)

TURKEY

Geography:
   Location: Southeastern Europe and Southwestern Asia (that portion of Turkey west of the Bosporus is geographically part of Europe), bordering the Black Sea, between Bulgaria and Georgia, and bordering the Aegean Sea and the Mediterranean Sea, between Greece and Syria
   Comparative Land Area: Slightly larger than Texas
   Capital City: Ankara
People:
   Total Population: 71,892,808
   Total Median Age: 29 years
   Life Expectancy: 73.14 years
   Fertility Rate: 1.87 children born/woman
Religion:
   Top Religion Percentages: Muslim (97.37%), Nonreligious (1.90%), Christian (0.31%), Other Religionist (0.18%), Atheist (0.09%)
   Number of Christians: 222,868
   Major Christian Groupings: Orthodox (56%), Protestant/Independent (30%), Catholic (14%)

UNITED ARAB EMIRATES	YEMEN
Geography:	**Geography:**
Location: Middle East, bordering the Gulf of Oman and the Persian Gulf, between Oman and Saudi Arabia	**Location:** Middle East, bordering the Arabian Sea, Gulf of Aden, and Red Sea, between Oman and Saudi Arabia
Comparative Land Area: Slightly smaller than Maine	**Comparative Land Area:** Slightly larger than Spain
Capital City: Abu Dhabi	**Capital City:** Sana'a
People:	**People:**
Total Population: 4,621,399	**Total Population:** 23,013,376
Total Median Age: 30.1 years	**Total Median Age:** 16.7 years
Life Expectancy: 75.89 years	**Life Expectancy:** 62.9 years
Fertility Rate: 2.43 children born/woman	**Fertility Rate:** 6.41 children born/woman
Religion:	**Religion:**
Top Religion Percentages: Muslim (75.20%), Christian (12.57%), Hindu (6.55%), Baha'i (2.26%), Buddhist (1.99%)	**Top Religion Percentages:** Muslim (99.08%), Hindu (0.63%), Christian (0.17%), Nonreligious (0.08%), Atheist (0.02%)
Number of Christians: 580,910	**Number of Christians:** 39,123
Major Christian Groupings: Catholic (79%), Orthodox (11%), Protestant/Independent (10%)	**Major Christian Groupings:** Protestant/Independent (57%), Orthodox (28%), Catholic (15%)

NORTH AMERICA

PEOPLE

Total Population: 337,044,380
Total Median Age: 37 years
Life Expectancy: 78.44 years
Fertility Rate: 2.05 children born/woman

RELIGION

Top Religion Percentages: Christian (81.44%)
Nonreligious (11.47%)
Jewish (1.73%)
Muslim (1.59%)
Buddhist (0.85%)
Number of Christians: 274,505,073
Major Christian Groupings: Protestant/Independent (63%)
Catholic (35%), Orthodox (2%)

CANADA
Geography:
  Location: Northern North America, bordering the North Atlantic Ocean on the east, North Pacific Ocean on the west, and the Arctic Ocean on the north, north of the US
  Comparative Land Area: Slightly larger than the United States
  Capital City: Ottawa
People:
  Total Population: 33,212,696
  Total Median Age: 40.1 years
  Life Expectancy: 81.16 years
  Fertility Rate: 1.57 children born/woman
Religion:
  Top Religion Percentages: Christian (76.18%), Nonreligious (12.92%), Chinese Universalist (1.98%), Atheist (1.90%), Muslim (1.68%), Hindu (1.02%)
  Number of Christians: 25,301,432
  Major Christian Groupings: Catholic (68%), Protestant/Independent (28%), Orthodox (4%)

SAINT-PIERRE & MIQUELON
Geography:
  Location: Northern North America, islands in the North Atlantic Ocean, south of Newfoundland (Canada)
  Comparative Land Area: About the size of Sacramento, USA
  Capital City: Saint-Pierre
People:
  Total Population: 7,044
  Total Median Age: 34.9 years
  Life Expectancy: 78.91 years
  Fertility Rate: 1.98 children born/woman
Religion:
  Top Religion Percentages: Christian (94.71%), Nonreligious (3.81%), Baha'i (1.34%), Muslim (0.16%)
  Number of Christians: 6,671
  Major Christian Groupings: Catholic (98%), Protestant/Independent (2%),

UNITED STATES OF AMERICA
Geography:
  Location: North America, bordering both the North Atlantic Ocean and the North Pacific Ocean, between Canada and Mexico
  Comparative Land Area: About ½ the size of Russia
  Capital City: Washington D.C.
People:
  Total Population: 303,824,640
  Total Median Age: 36.7 years
  Life Expectancy: 78.14 years
  Fertility Rate: 2.1 children born/woman
Religion:
  Top Religion Percentages: Christian (82.02%), Nonreligious (11.31%), Jewish (1.92%), Muslim (1.58%), Buddhist (0.94%)
  Number of Christians: 249,196,970
  Major Christian Groupings: Protestant/Independent (66%), Catholic (32%), Orthodox (2%)

OCEANIA

PEOPLE

Total Population: 34,373,095
Total Median Age: 33.1 years
Life Expectancy: 77.77 years
Fertility Rate: 2.26 children born/woman

RELIGION

Top Religion Percentages: Christian (79.74%)
Nonreligious (11.95%)
Buddhist (1.62%)
Hindu (1.58%)
Atheist (1.21%)
Muslim (1.20%)
Indigenous Religions (0.70%)
Baha'i (0.34%)
Other (1.66%)
Number of Christians: 27,410,997
Major Christian Groupings: Protestant/Independent (65%)
Catholic (32%), Orthodox (3%)

AMERICAN SAMOA	AUSTRALIA
Geography:	**Geography:**
Location: Oceania, group of islands in the South Pacific Ocean, about half way between Hawaii and New Zealand-	**Location:** Oceania, continent between the Indian Ocean and the South Pacific Ocean
Comparative Land Area: Slightly larger than Washington D.C., USA	**Comparative Land Area:** Slightly smaller than the Continental US
Capital City: Pago Pago	**Capital City:** Canberra
People:	**People:**
Total Population: 64,827	**Total Population:** 21,007,310
Total Median Age: 22.8 years	**Total Median Age:** 37.1 years
Life Expectancy: 73.47 years	**Life Expectancy:** 81.53 years
Fertility Rate: 3.35 children born/woman	**Fertility Rate:** 1.78 children born/woman
Religion:	**Religion:**
Top Religion Percentages: Christian (95.88%), Nonreligious (1.97%), Baha'i (1.49%), Chinese Universalist (0.36%), Buddhist (0.30%)	**Top Religion Percentages:** Christian (76.59%), Nonreligious (15.15%), Buddhist (2.11%), Atheist (1.73%), Muslim (1.66%). Hindu (0.73%)
Number of Christians: 62,156	**Number of Christians:** 16,089,498
Major Christian Groupings: Protestant/Independent (85%), Catholic (15%)	**Major Christian Groupings:** Protestant/Independent (60%), Catholic (35%), Orthodox (5%)

COOK ISLANDS

Geography:
Location: Oceania, group of islands in the South Pacific Ocean, about half way between Hawaii and New Zealand-
Comparative Land Area: Slightly larger than Seattle, USA
Capital City: Avarua

People:
Total Population: 12,271
Total Median Age: 29.8 years
Life Expectancy: 71.14 years
Fertility Rate: 3.1 children born/woman

Religion:
Top Religion Percentages: Christian (96.60%), Nonreligious (2.57%), Baha'i (0.78%), Atheist (0.04%)
Number of Christians: 11,854
Major Christian Groupings: Protestant/Independent (81%), Catholic (19%)

FIJI

Geography:
Location: Oceania, island group in the South Pacific Ocean, about two-thirds of the way from Hawaii to New Zealand
Comparative Land Area: Slightly smaller than New Jersey
Capital City: Suva

People:
Total Population: 931,741
Total Median Age: 25.2 years
Life Expectancy: 70.44 years
Fertility Rate: 2.68 children born/woman

Religion:
Top Religion Percentages: Christian (58.87%), Hindu (32.13%), Muslim (6.10%), Nonreligious (1.28%), Baha'i (0.85%)
Number of Christians: 548,515
Major Christian Groupings: Protestant/Independent (83%), Catholic (17%)

FRENCH POLYNESIA

Geography:
Location: Oceania, archipelagoes in the South Pacific Ocean about half way between South America and Australia
Comparative Land Area: About the size of Rhode Island
Capital City: Papeete

People:
Total Population: 283,019
Total Median Age: 28.7 years
Life Expectancy: 76.51 years
Fertility Rate: 1.95 children born/woman

Religion:
Top Religion Percentages: Christian (86.37%), Chinese Universalist (7.81%), Nonreligious (4.61%), Atheist (0.55%), Baha'i (0.30%)
Number of Christians: 244,444
Major Christian Groupings: Protestant/Independent (60%), Catholic (40%)

GUAM

Geography:
Location: Oceania, island in the North Pacific Ocean, about three-quarters of the way from Hawaii to the Philippines
Comparative Land Area: Slightly smaller than Chicago, USA
Capital City: Hagatna

People:
Total Population: 175,877
Total Median Age: 28.9 years
Life Expectancy: 78.93 years
Fertility Rate: 2.55 children born/woman

Religion:
Top Religion Percentages: Christian (94.16%), Nonreligious (1.62%), Baha'i (1.15%), Buddhist (1.05%), Chinese Universalist (1.05%)
Number of Christians: 165,606
Major Christian Groupings: Catholic (83%), Protestant/Independent (17%)

KIRIBATI

Geography:
Location: Oceania, group of 33 coral atolls in the Pacific Ocean, straddling the Equator; the capital Tarawa is about half way between Hawaii and Australia
Comparative Land Area: Slightly smaller than New York City, USA
Capital City: South Tarawa

People:
Total Population: 110,356
Total Median Age: 20.6 years
Life Expectancy: 62.85 years
Fertility Rate: 4.08 children born/woman

Religion:
Top Religion Percentages: Christian (96.52%), Baha'i (2.96%), Nonreligious (0.51%), Buddhist (0.01%)
Number of Christians: 106,516
Major Christian Groupings: Protestant/Independent (51%), Catholic (49%)

MARSHALL ISLANDS

Geography:
Location: Oceania, two archipelagic island chains of 29 atolls, each made up of many small islets, and five single islands in the North Pacific Ocean, about half way between Hawaii and Australia
Comparative Land Area: About the size of Washington D.C
Capital City: Majuro

People:
Total Population: 63,174
Total Median Age: 21 years
Life Expectancy: 70.9 years
Fertility Rate: 3.68 children born/woman

Religion:
Top Religion Percentages: Christian (96.00%), Baha'i (1.59%), Nonreligious (1.37%), Indigenous Religions (0.97%), Atheist (0.07%)
Number of Christians: 60,647
Major Christian Groupings: Protestant/Independent (94%), Catholic (6%)

MICRONESIA

Geography:
Location: Oceania, island group in the North Pacific Ocean, about three-quarters of the way from Hawaii to Indonesia
Comparative Land Area: Slightly smaller than New York City, USA
Capital City: Palikir

People:
Total Population: 107,665
Total Median Age: 21.6 years
Life Expectancy: 70.65 years
Fertility Rate: 2.98 children born/woman

Religion:
Top Religion Percentages: Christian (93.18%), Indigenous Religions (3.35%), Baha'i (1.62%), Nonreligious (0.72%), Buddhist (0.43%)
Number of Christians: 100,322
Major Christian Groupings: Catholic (54%), Protestant/Independent (46%)

NAURU

Geography:
Location: Oceania, island in the South Pacific Ocean, south of the Marshall Islands
Comparative Land Area: About 8 square miles
Capital City: None

People:
Total Population: 13,770
Total Median Age: 21.3 years
Life Expectancy: 63.81 years
Fertility Rate: 2.94 children born/woman

Religion:
Top Religion Percentages: Christian (75.02%), Chinese Universalist (10.47%), Baha'i (9.60%), Nonreligious (3.52%), Buddhist (1.37%)
Number of Christians: 10,330
Major Christian Groupings: Protestant/Independent (66%), Catholic (34%)

NEW CALEDONIA

Geography:
Location: Oceania, islands in the South Pacific Ocean, east of Australia
Comparative Land Area: Slightly smaller than New Jersey
Capital City: Nouméa

People:
Total Population: 224,824
Total Median Age: 28.4 years
Life Expectancy: 74.75 years
Fertility Rate: 2.21 children born/woman

Religion:
Top Religion Percentages: Christian (84.14%), Nonreligious (9.01%), Muslim (2.73%), Neoreligionist (1.69%), Atheist (1.05%)
Number of Christians: 189,167
Major Christian Groupings: Catholic (72%), Protestant/Independent (28%)

NEW ZEALAND

Geography:
Location: Oceania, islands in the South Pacific Ocean, southeast of Australia
Comparative Land Area: About the size of Colorado
Capital City: Wellington

People:
Total Population: 4,173,460
Total Median Age: 36.3 years
Life Expectancy: 80.24 years
Fertility Rate: 2.11 children born/woman

Religion:
Top Religion Percentages: Christian (71.99%), Nonreligious (19.91%), Buddhist (2.18%), Hindu (2.03%), Atheist (1.19%)
Number of Christians: 3,004,474
Major Christian Groupings: Protestant/Independent (80%), Catholic (20%)

NIUE

Geography:
Location: Oceania, island in the South Pacific Ocean, east of Tonga
Comparative Land Area: About the size of Sacramento, USA
Capital City: Alofi

People:
Total Population: 1,444
Total Median Age: 29 years
Life Expectancy: 70.5 years
Fertility Rate: 3.01 children born/woman

Religion:
Top Religion Percentages: Christian (96.69%), Nonreligious (1.59%), Baha'i (1.53%), Chinese Universalist (0.18%)
Number of Christians: 1,396
Major Christian Groupings: Protestant/Independent (91%), Catholic (9%)

NORFOLK ISLAND

Geography:
Location: Oceania, island in the South Pacific Ocean, east of Australia
Comparative Land Area: About ½ the size of Manhattan Island in New York City, USA
Capital City: Kingston

People:
Total Population: 2,128
Total Median Age: NA
Life Expectancy: 79 years
Fertility Rate: NA

Religion:
Top Religion Percentages: Christian (85.83%), Nonreligious (14.07%), Atheist (0.09%)
Number of Christians: 1,826
Major Christian Groupings: Protestant/Independent (84%), Catholic (16%)

NORTHERN MARIANA ISLANDS

Geography:
Location: Oceania, islands in the North Pacific Ocean, about three-quarters of the way from Hawaii to the Philippines
Comparative Land Area: About the size of Prague, Czech Republic
Capital City: Saipan

People:
Total Population: 86,616
Total Median Age: 29.9 years
Life Expectancy: 76.5 years
Fertility Rate: 1.18 children born/woman

Religion:
Top Religion Percentages: Christian (81.29%), Buddhist (10.56%), Chinese Universalist (4.86%), Nonreligious (0.99%), Muslim (0.68%)
Number of Christians: 70,410
Major Christian Groupings: Catholic (80%), Protestant/Independent (20%)

PALAU

Geography:
Location: Oceania, group of islands in the North Pacific Ocean, southeast of the Philippines
Comparative Land Area: About the size of New Orleans
Capital City: Melekeok

People:
Total Population: 21,093
Total Median Age: 32.3 years
Life Expectancy: 71 years
Fertility Rate: 2.45 children born/woman

Religion:
Top Religion Percentages: Christian (95.07%), Nonreligious (2.51%), Buddhist (0.85%), Baha'i (0.73%), Indigenous Religions (0.58%)
Number of Christians: 20,053
Major Christian Groupings: Protestant/Independent (55%), Catholic (45%)

PAPUA NEW GUINEA

Geography:
Location: Oceania, group of islands including the eastern half of the island of New Guinea between the Coral Sea and the South Pacific Ocean, east of Indonesia
Comparative Land Area: Slightly larger than California
Capital City: Port Moresby

People:
Total Population: 5,931,769
Total Median Age: 21.5 years
Life Expectancy: 66 years
Fertility Rate: 3.71 children born/woman

Religion:
Top Religion Percentages: Christian (94.81%), Indigenous Religions (3.41%), Baha'i (0.87%), Nonreligious (0.59%), Buddhist (0.16%)
Number of Christians: 5,623,910
Major Christian Groupings: Protestant/Independent (71%), Catholic (29%)

PITCAIRN ISLANDS

Geography:
Location: Oceania, islands in the South Pacific Ocean, about midway between Peru and New Zealand
Comparative Land Area: Slightly smaller than Manhattan Island in New York City, USA
Capital City: Adamstown

People:
Total Population: 48
Total Median Age: NA
Life Expectancy: 73 years
Fertility Rate: NA

Religion:
Top Religion Percentages: Christian (92.00%), Nonreligious (8.00%)
Number of Christians: 44
Major Christian Groupings: Protestant/Independent (100%)

SAMOA

Geography:
   Location: Oceania, group of islands in the South Pacific Ocean, about half way between Hawaii and New Zealand
   Comparative Land Area: Slightly smaller than Rhode Island
   Capital City: Apia
People:
   Total Population: 217,083
   Total Median Age: 20.6 years
   Life Expectancy: 71.58 years
   Fertility Rate: 4.18 children born/woman
Religion:
   Top Religion Percentages: Christian (96.41%), Baha'i (2.33%), Nonreligious (1.24%), Buddhist (0.01%), Chinese Universalist (0.01%)
   Number of Christians: 209,290
   Major Christian Groupings: Protestant/Independent (84%), Catholic (16%)

SOLOMON ISLANDS

Geography:
   Location: Oceania, group of islands in the South Pacific Ocean, east of Papua New Guinea
   Comparative Land Area: Slightly smaller than Maryland
   Capital City: Honiara
People:
   Total Population: 581,318
   Total Median Age: 19.4 years
   Life Expectancy: 73.44 years
   Fertility Rate: 3.65 children born/woman
Religion:
   Top Religion Percentages: Christian (95.18%), Indigenous Religions (3.19%), Baha'i (0.71%), Buddhist (0.32%), Muslim (0.32%)
   Number of Christians: 553,298
   Major Christian Groupings: Protestant/Independent (81%), Catholic (19%)

TOKELAU ISLANDS

Geography:
   Location: Oceania, group of three atolls in the South Pacific Ocean, about one-half of the way from Hawaii to New Zealand
   Comparative Land Area: About 5 square miles
   Capital City: None
People:
   Total Population: 1,433
   Total Median Age: NA
   Life Expectancy: NA
   Fertility Rate: NA
Religion:
   Top Religion Percentages: Christian (94.65%),   Baha'i (4.35%),Nonreligious (1.00%)
   Number of Christians: 1,356
   Major Christian Groupings: Protestant/Independent (67%), Catholic (33%)

TONGA

Geography:
   Location: Oceania, archipelago in the South Pacific Ocean, about two-thirds of the way from Hawaii to New Zealand
   Comparative Land Area: About the size of New York City
   Capital City: Nuku'alofa
People:
   Total Population: 119,009
   Total Median Age: 21.8 years
   Life Expectancy: 70.44 years
   Fertility Rate: 2.5 children born/woman
Religion:
   Top Religion Percentages: Christian (92.66%), Baha'i (6.68%), Nonreligious (0.43%), Buddhist (0.12%),   Hindu (0.10%)
   Number of Christians: 110,274
   Major Christian Groupings: Protestant/Independent (89%), Catholic (11%)

TUVALU

Geography:
   Location: Oceania, island group consisting of nine coral atolls in the South Pacific Ocean, about one-half of the way from Hawaii to Australia
   Comparative Land Area: About ½ the size the Manhattan Island in New York City, USA
   Capital City: Funafuti
People:
   Total Population: 12,177
   Total Median Age: 25.2 years
   Life Expectancy: 68.97 years
   Fertility Rate: 2.94 children born/woman
Religion:
   Top Religion Percentages: Christian (89.11%), Nonreligious (5.25%), Baha'i (4.95%), Atheist (0.57%), Buddhist (0.12%)
   Number of Christians: 10,851
   Major Christian Groupings: Protestant/Independent (100%)

VANUATU

Geography:
   Location: Oceania, group of islands in the South Pacific Ocean, about three-quarters of the way from Hawaii to Australia
   Comparative Land Area: Slightly larger than Connecticut
   Capital City: Port-Vila
People:
   Total Population: 215,446
   Total Median Age: 23.8 years
   Life Expectancy: 63.61 years
   Fertility Rate: 2.57 children born/woman
Religion:
   Top Religion Percentages: Christian (92.79%), Indigenous Religions (3.48%), Baha'i (2.85%), Nonreligious (0.58%)
   Number of Christians: 199,912
   Major Christian Groupings: Protestant/Independent (85%), Catholic (15%)

WALLIS & FUTUNA ISLANDS

Geography:
   Location: Oceania, islands in the South Pacific Ocean, about two-thirds of the way from Hawaii to New Zealand
   Comparative Land Area: About the size of Sacramento, USA
   Capital City: Mata-Utu
People:
   Total Population: 15,237
   Total Median Age: NA
   Life Expectancy: NA
   Fertility Rate: NA
Religion:
   Top Religion Percentages: Christian (97.45%), Indigenous Religions (1.17%), Baha'i (0.80%), Nonreligious (0.54%), Atheist (0.05%)
   Number of Christians: 14,848
   Major Christian Groupings: Catholic (100%)

WESTERN EUROPE

PEOPLE
Total Population: 389,846,133
Total Median Age: 41.1 years
Life Expectancy: 79.6 years
Fertility Rate: 1.56 children born/woman

RELIGION
Top Religion Percentages: Christian (78.09%)
Nonreligious (14.21%)
Muslim (3.86%)
Atheist (2.73%)
Jewish (0.31%)
Hindu (0.16%)
Other (0.64%)
Number of Christians: 27,410,997
Major Christian Groupings: Protestant/Independent (65%)
Catholic (32%), Orthodox (3%)

ANDORRA
Geography:
 Location: Southwestern Europe, between France and Spain
 Comparative Land Area: Slightly more than half the size of New York City, USA
 Capital City: Andorra la Vella
People:
 Total Population: 82,627
 Total Median Age: 38.9 years
 Life Expectancy: 82.67 years
 Fertility Rate: 1.32 children born/woman
Religion:
 Top Religion Percentages: Christian (92.42%), Nonreligious (5.43%), Muslim (0.83%), Hindu (0.50%), Atheist (0.36%)
 Number of Christians: 76,364
 Major Christian Groupings: Catholic (100%)

AUSTRIA
Geography:
 Location: Central Europe, North of Italy and Slovenia
 Comparative Land Area: Slightly smaller than Maine
 Capital City: Vienna
People:
 Total Population: 8,205,533
 Total Median Age: 41.7 years
 Life Expectancy: 79.36 years
 Fertility Rate: 1.38 children born/woman
Religion:
 Top Religion Percentages: Christian (81.08%), Nonreligious (12.84%), Muslim (4.27%), Atheist (1.34%), Buddhist (0.13%)
 Number of Christians: 6,653,046
 Major Christian Groupings: Catholic (85%), Protestant/Independent (13%), Orthodox (2%)

BELGIUM
Geography:
 Location: Western Europe, bordering the North Sea, between France and the Netherlands
 Comparative Land Area: About the size of Maryland
 Capital City: Brussels
People:
 Total Population: 10,403,951
 Total Median Age: 41.4 years
 Life Expectancy: 79.07 years
 Fertility Rate: 1.65 children born/woman
Religion:
 Top Religion Percentages: Christian (83.31%), Nonreligious (10.60%), Muslim (3.57%), Atheist (1.79%), Jewish (0.27%)
 Number of Christians: 8,667,531
 Major Christian Groupings: Catholic (90%), Protestant/Independent (10%)

CHANNEL ISLANDS
Geography:
 Location: A group of islands in the English Channel, off the French coast of Normandy.
 Comparative Land Area: Slightly larger than Washington D.C., USA
 Capital City: Saint Peter Port (Guernsey Island) and Saint Helier (Jersey)
People:
 Total Population: 200,000
 Total Median Age: 42 years
 Life Expectancy: 78 years
 Fertility Rate: 1.4 children born/woman
Religion:
 Top Religion Percentages: Christian (85.23%), Nonreligious (13.13%), Atheist (1.07%), Baha'i (0.34%), Hindu (0.08%)
 Number of Christians: 170,460
 Major Christian Groupings: Protestant/Independent (82%), Catholic (18%)

DENMARK

Geography:
  Location: Northern Europe, bordering the Baltic Sea and the
  North Sea, on a peninsula north of Germany (Jutland); also
  includes two major islands (Sjaelland and Fyn)
  Comparative Land Area: twice the size of Massachusetts
  Capital City: Copenhagen
People:
  Total Population: 5,484,723
  Total Median Age: 40.3 years
  Life Expectancy: 78.13 years
  Fertility Rate: 1.74 children born/woman
Religion:
  Top Religion Percentages: Christian (86.00%), Nonreligious
  (8.16%), Muslim (3.51%), Atheist (1.43%), Buddhist (0.38%)
  Number of Christians: 4,716,862
  Major Christian Groupings: Protestant/Independent (99%),
  Catholic (1%)

FAEROE ISLANDS

Geography:
  Location: Northern Europe, island group between the
  Norwegian Sea and the North Atlantic Ocean, about half way
  between Iceland and Norway
  Comparative Land Area: Slightly larger than Phoenix, USA
  Capital City: Torshavn
People:
  Total Population: 48,668
  Total Median Age: 37.6 years
  Life Expectancy: 79.29 years
  Fertility Rate: 2.45 children born/woman
Religion:
  Top Religion Percentages: Christian (98.04%), Nonreligious
  (1.67%), Baha'i (0.29%)
  Number of Christians: 47,714
  Major Christian Groupings: Protestant/Independent (99%),
  Catholic (1%)

FINLAND

Geography:
  Location: Northern Europe, bordering the Baltic Sea, Gulf of
  Bothnia, and Gulf of Finland, between Sweden and Russia
  Comparative Land Area: Slightly smaller than Montana
  Capital City: Helsinki
People:
  Total Population: 5,244,749
  Total Median Age: 41.8 years
  Life Expectancy: 78.82 years
  Fertility Rate: 1.73 children born/woman
Religion:
  Top Religion Percentages: Christian (90.15%), Nonreligious
  (7.16%), Atheist (1.96%), Muslim (0.45%), Buddhist (0.09%)
  Number of Christians: 4,728,141
  Major Christian Groupings: Protestant/Independent (99%),
  Orthodox (1%)

FRANCE

Geography:
  Location: Western Europe, bordering the Bay of Biscay and
  English Channel, between Belgium and Spain, southeast of the
  UK, bordering the Mediterranean Sea, between Italy and Spain.
  Comparative Land Area: About the size of Texas
  Capital City: Paris
People:
  Total Population: 62,158,016
  Total Median Age: 39.2 years
  Life Expectancy: 80.87 years
  Fertility Rate: 1.98 children born/woman
Religion:
  Top Religion Percentages: Christian (69.30%), Nonreligious
  (15.90%), Muslim (8.31%), Atheist (3.95%), Jewish (1.00%)
  Number of Christians: 43,075,505
  Major Christian Groupings: Catholic (92%),
  Protestant/Independent (7%), Orthodox (1%)

GERMANY

Geography:
  Location: Central Europe, bordering the Baltic Sea and the
  North Sea, between the Netherlands and Poland, south of
  Denmark
  Comparative Land Area: Slightly smaller than Montana
  Capital City: Berlin
People:
  Total Population: 82,369,552
  Total Median Age: 43.4 years
  Life Expectancy: 79.1 years
  Fertility Rate: 1.41 children born/woman
Religion:
  Top Religion Percentages: Christian (71.81%), Nonreligious
  (20.76%), Muslim (4.47%), Atheist (2.38%), Jewish (0.27%)
  Number of Christians: 59,149,575
  Major Christian Groupings: Protestant/Independent (54%),
  Catholic (44%), Orthodox (2%)

GIBRALTAR

Geography:
  Location: Southwestern Europe, bordering the Strait of
  Gibralter, which links the Mediterranean Sea and the North
  Atlantic Ocean, on the Southern Coast of Spain
  Comparative Land Area: About 3 square miles
  Capital City: Gibraltar
People:
  Total Population: 28,002
  Total Median Age: 40.3 years
  Life Expectancy: 80.6 years
  Fertility Rate: 1.65 children born/woman
Religion:
  Top Religion Percentages: Christian (88.26%), Muslim
  (4.88%), Nonreligious (2.47%), Jewish (2.00%),   Hindu
  (1.80%)
  Number of Christians: 24,715
  Major Christian Groupings: Catholic (88%),
  Protestant/Independent (12%)

GREENLAND

Geography:
  Location: Island between the Arctic Ocean and the North
  Atlantic Ocean, northeast of Canada
  Comparative Land Area: About three times the size of Texas
  Capital City: Nuuk
People:
  Total Population: 57,564
  Total Median Age: 33.5 years
  Life Expectancy: 69.46 years
  Fertility Rate: 2.22 children born/woman
Religion:
  Top Religion Percentages: Christian (96.08%), Nonreligious
  (2.28%), Indigenous Religions (0.79%), Baha'i (0.63%),
  Atheist (0.20%)
  Number of Christians: 55,307
  Major Christian Groupings: Protestant/Independent (99%),
  Catholic (1%)

HOLY SEE

Geography:
  Location: Southern Europe, an enclave of Rome (Italy)
  Comparative Land Area: Less than 1 square mile
  Capital City: Vatican City
People:
  Total Population: 824
  Total Median Age: NA
  Life Expectancy: 79 years
  Fertility Rate: NA
Religion:
  Top Religion Percentages: Christian (100.00%)
  Number of Christians: 824
  Major Christian Groupings: Catholic (100%)

ICELAND

Geography:
Location: Northern Europe, island between the Greenland Sea and the North Atlantic Ocean, northwest of the UK
Comparative Land Area: Slightly smaller than Kentucky
Capital City: Reykjavik
People:
Total Population: 304,367
Total Median Age: 34.8 years
Life Expectancy: 80.55 years
Fertility Rate: 1.91 children born/woman
Religion:
Top Religion Percentages: Christian (95.79%), Nonreligious (2.48%), Indigenous Religions (0.46%), Atheist (0.38%), Hindu (0.26%)
Number of Christians: 291,553
Major Christian Groupings: Protestant/Independent (98%), Catholic (2%)

IRELAND

Geography:
Location: Western Europe, occupying the five-sixths of the island of Ireland in the North Atlantic Ocean, west of Great Britain
Comparative Land Area: Slightly larger than West Virginia
Capital City: Dublin
People:
Total Population: 4,156,119
Total Median Age: 34.6 years
Life Expectancy: 78.07 years
Fertility Rate: 1.85 children born/woman
Religion:
Top Religion Percentages: Christian (95.44%), Nonreligious (3.30%), Muslim (0.67%), Atheist (0.25%), Chinese Universalism (0.10%)
Number of Christians: 3,966,600
Major Christian Groupings: Catholic (95%), Protestant/Independent (5%)

ISLE OF MAN

Geography:
Location: Western Europe, island in the Irish Sea, between Great Britain and Ireland
Comparative Land Area: Slightly smaller than Chicago, USA
Capital City: Douglas
People:
Total Population: 76,220
Total Median Age: 40 years
Life Expectancy: 78.8 years
Fertility Rate: 1.65 children born/woman
Religion:
Top Religion Percentages: Christian (84.10%), Nonreligious (13.22%), Atheist (2.19%), Hindu (0.21%), Muslim (0.21%)
Number of Christians: 64,101
Major Christian Groupings: Protestant/Independent (86%), Catholic (14%)

ITALY

Geography:
Location: Southern Europe, a peninsula extending into the central Mediterranean Sea, northeast of Tunisia
Comparative Land Area: Slightly larger than Arizona
Capital City: Rome
People:
Total Population: 58,145,320
Total Median Age: 42.9 years
Life Expectancy: 80.07 years
Fertility Rate: 1.3 children born/woman
Religion:
Top Religion Percentages: Christian (80.93%), Nonreligious (12.91%), Atheist (3.62%), Muslim (2.28%), Chinese Universalist (0.08%)
Number of Christians: 47,057,007
Major Christian Groupings: Catholic (97%), Protestant/Independent (2%), Orthodox (1%)

LIECHTENSTEIN

Geography:
Location: Central Europe, between Austria and Switzerland
Comparative Land Area: Slightly smaller than Washington D.C., USA
Capital City: Vaduz
People:
Total Population: 34,498
Total Median Age: 40.5 years
Life Expectancy: 79.95 years
Fertility Rate: 1.51 children born/woman
Religion:
Top Religion Percentages: Christian (89.94%), Muslim (6.27%), Nonreligious (3.54%), Jewish (0.13%), Atheist (0.08%)
Number of Christians: 31,028
Major Christian Groupings: Catholic (89%), Protestant/Independent (11%)

LUXEMBOURG

Geography:
Location: Western Europe, between France and Germany
Comparative Land Area: Slightly smaller than Rhode Island
Capital City: Luxembourg City
People:
Total Population: 486,006
Total Median Age: 39 years
Life Expectancy: 79.18 years
Fertility Rate: 1.78 children born/woman
Religion:
Top Religion Percentages: Christian (90.77%), Nonreligious (6.26%), Atheist (1.48%), Muslim (1.01%), Baha'i (0.31%)
Number of Christians: 441,148
Major Christian Groupings: Catholic (97%), Protestant/Independent (3%)

MALTA

Geography:
Location: Southern Europe, islands in the Mediterranean Sea, south of Sicily (Italy)
Comparative Land Area: About the size of Kansas City,
Capital City: Valletta
People:
Total Population: 403,532
Total Median Age: 39.2 years
Life Expectancy: 79.3 years
Fertility Rate: 1.51 children born/woman
Religion:
Top Religion Percentages: Christian (98.07%), Nonreligious (1.40%), Muslim (0.25%), Atheist (0.19%), Baha'i (0.07%)
Number of Christians: 395,744
Major Christian Groupings: Catholic (95%), Protestant/Independent (5%)

MONACO

Geography:
Location: Western Europe, bordering the Mediterranean Sea on the southern coast of France, near the border with Italy
Comparative Land Area: Less than 1 square mile
Capital City: Monaco
People:
Total Population: 32,796
Total Median Age: 45.5 years
Life Expectancy: 79.96 years
Fertility Rate: 1.75 children born/woman
Religion:
Top Religion Percentages: Christian (86.79%), Nonreligious (8.74%), Atheist (2.13%), Jewish (1.70%), Muslim (0.45%)
Number of Christians: 28,464
Major Christian Groupings: Catholic (97%), Protestant/Independent (3%)

NETHERLANDS

Geography:
Location: Western Europe, bordering the North Sea, between Belgium and Germany
Comparative Land Area: About the size of Switzerland
Capital City: Amsterdam

People:
Total Population: 16,645,313
Total Median Age: 40 years
Life Expectancy: 79.25 years
Fertility Rate: 1.66 children born/woman

Religion:
Top Religion Percentages: Christian (66.10%), Nonreligious (23.97%), Muslim (6.02%), Atheist (1.49%), Buddhist (1.18%)
Number of Christians: 11,002,684
Major Christian Groupings: Catholic (57%), Protestant/Independent (43%)

NORWAY

Geography:
Location: Northern Europe, bordering the North Sea and the North Atlantic Ocean, west of Sweden
Comparative Land Area: Slightly larger than New Mexico
Capital City: Oslo

People:
Total Population: 4,644,457
Total Median Age: 39 years
Life Expectancy: 79.81 years
Fertility Rate: 1.78 children born/woman

Religion:
Top Religion Percentages: Christian (92.09%), Nonreligious (3.50%), Muslim (2.81%), Buddhist (0.72%), Atheist (0.59%)
Number of Christians: 4,277,081
Major Christian Groupings: Protestant/Independent (98%), Catholic (2%)

PORTUGAL

Geography:
Location: Southwestern Europe, bordering the North Atlantic Ocean, west of Spain
Comparative Land Area: Slightly smaller than Indiana
Capital City: Lisbon

People:
Total Population: 10,676,910
Total Median Age: 39.1 years
Life Expectancy: 78.04 years
Fertility Rate: 1.49 children born/woman

Religion:
Top Religion Percentages: Christians (90.20%), Nonreligious (7.50%), Atheist (1.21%), Buddhist (0.56%), Muslim (0.24%),
Number of Christians: 9.630,573
Major Christian Groupings: Catholic (95%), Protestant/Independent (5%)

SAN MARINO

Geography:
Location: Southern Europe, an enclave in central Italy
Comparative Land Area: About the size of Manhattan Island in New York City, USA
Capital City: San Marino

People:
Total Population: 29,973
Total Median Age: 41.2 years
Life Expectancy: 81.88 years
Fertility Rate: 1.35 children born/woman

Religion:
Top Religion Percentages: Christian (91.88%), Nonreligious (5.27%), Atheist (1.82%), Baha'i (0.91%)
Number of Christians: 27,539
Major Christian Groupings: Catholic (96%), Protestant/Independent (4%)

SLOVENIA

Geography:
Location: Central Europe, eastern Alps bordering the Adriatic Sea, between Austria and Croatia
Comparative Land Area: Slightly smaller than New Jersey
Capital City: Ljubljana

People:
Total Population: 2,007,711
Total Median Age: 41.4 years
Life Expectancy: 76.73 years
Fertility Rate: 1.27 children born/woman

Religion:
Top Religion Percentages: Christian (90.16%), Nonreligious (5.25%), Atheist (2.75%), Muslim (1.82%), Baha'i (0.02%)
Number of Christians: 1,810,152
Major Christian Groupings: Catholic (95%), Orthodox (3%), Protestant/Independent (2%)

SPAIN

Geography:
Location: Southwestern Europe, bordering the Bay of Biscay, Mediterranean Sea, North Atlantic Ocean, and Pyrenees Mountains, southwest of France
Comparative Land Area: Slightly larger than Sweden
Capital City: Madrid

People:
Total Population: 40,345,716
Total Median Age: 40.7 years
Life Expectancy: 79.92 years
Fertility Rate: 1.3 children born/woman

Religion:
Top Religion Percentages: Christian (90.73%), Nonreligious (6.68%), Muslim (1.35%), Atheist (1.07%), Buddhist (0.10%)
Number of Christians: 36,605,668
Major Christian Groupings: Catholic (98%), Protestant/Independent (2%)

SVALBARD

Geography:
Location: Northern Europe, islands between the Arctic Ocean, Barents Sea, Greenland Sea, and Norwegian Sea, north of Norway
Comparative Land Area: Slightly smaller than West Virginia
Capital City: Longyearbyen

People:
Total Population: 2,165
Total Median Age: NA
Life Expectancy: NA
Fertility Rate: NA

Religion:
Top Religion Percentages: Christian (60.10%), Nonreligious (38.65%), Buddhist (1.24%)
Number of Christians: 1,301
Major Christian Groupings: Protestant/Independent (54%), Orthodox (46%)

SWEDEN

Geography:
Location: Northern Europe, bordering the Baltic Sea, Gulf of Bothnia, Kattagat, and Skagerrak, between Finland and Norway
Comparative Land Area: Slightly larger than California
Capital City: Stockholm

People:
Total Population: 9,045,389
Total Median Age: 41.3 years
Life Expectancy: 80.74 years
Fertility Rate: 1.67 children born/woman

Religion:
Top Religion Percentages: Christian (66.41%), Nonreligious (18.12%), Atheist (11.65%), Muslim (2.63%), Buddhist (0.42%)
Number of Christians: 6,007,043
Major Christian Groupings: Protestant/Independent (96%), Catholic (2%), Orthodox (2%)

SWITZERLAND	UNITED KINGDOM

Geography:
  Location: Central Europe, east of France, north of Italy
  Comparative Land Area: About the size of The Netherlands
  Capital City: Bern
People:
  Total Population: 7,581,520
  Total Median Age: 40.7 years
  Life Expectancy: 80.74 years
  Fertility Rate: 1.44 children born/woman
Religion:
  Top Religion Percentages: Christian (83.11%), Nonreligious (10.66%), Muslim (3.91%), Atheist (1.35%), Buddhist (0.32%)
  Number of Christians: 6,301,001
  Major Christian Groupings: Catholic (54%), Protestant/Independent (46%)
	Geography:
	  Location: Western Europe, islands including the northern one-sixth of the island of Ireland between the North Atlantic Ocean and the North Sea, northwest of France
	  Comparative Land Area: Slightly smaller than Oregon
	  Capital City: London
	People:
	  Total Population: 60,943,912
	  Total Median Age: 39.9 years
	  Life Expectancy: 78.85 years
	  Fertility Rate: 1.66 children born/woman
	Religion:
	  Top Religion Percentages: Christian (80.90%), Nonreligious (12.27%), Muslim (2.56%), Atheist (1.41%), Hindu (1.00%), Jewish (0.46%)
	  Number of Christians: 49,303,624
	  Major Christian Groupings: Protestant/Independent (88%), Catholic (12%)

NOTES

CHAPTER ONE: AT MANY TIMES AND IN MANY WAYS

1. Stephen Hawking, *A Brief History of Time* (New York: Bantam Books, 1996), p. 35.
2. Saint Augustine, *Confessions*, trans. Henry Chadwick (Oxford: Oxford University Press, 1991), p. 230.
3. Thomas Cahill, *The Gifts of the Jews* (New York: Doubleday, 1998), pp. 130–131.
4. Williston Walker, *A History of the Christian Church* (New York: Charles Scribner's Sons, 1918).
5. Kenneth Scott Latourette, *A History of Christianity* (New York: HarperSanFrancisco, 1953).
6. Kenneth Scott Latourette, *A History of the Expansion of Christianity* (New York: Harper and Row, 1937–1945).
7. Diarmaid MacCulloch, *Christianity: The First Three Thousand Years* (New York: Viking, 2010).
8. Mark Noll, *Turning Points: Decisive Moments in the History of Christianity* (Grand Rapids, MI: Baker Academic, 1997).
9. It is important to note that there are many other gospels. Christians normally believe that Christ's life was preserved most accurately in the four accepted gospels, but there are many other gospels. Scholars of religion disagree over whether the other gospels should be accepted as somewhat reliable or not. The Gospel of Thomas, for instance, is a very early gospel, and shares some features with the four accepted gospels.
10. Nazareth is today a town in Israel that is home to about 20,000 Arab Christians and 45,000 Arab Muslims.
11. Pliny is quoted in Dale Irvin and Scott Sunquist, History of the World Christian Movement, Vol. I: Earliest Christianity to 1453 (Maryknoll, NY: Orbis, 2001), p. 70.
12. Irvin and Sunquist, vol. 1, p. 83.
13. Irvin and Sunquist, vol. 1, p. 172.
14. Philip Jenkins, *The Lost History of Christianity* (New York: HarperOne, 2008), p. 54.
15. Jenkins, *The Lost History of Christianity*, p. 77.
16. "Philip the Evangelist" should not be confused with Philip the apostle (one of the twelve). Philip the Evangelist is mentioned in Acts 6, Acts 8, and Acts 21. He was one of the seven deacons appointed to work in the Jerusalem church. He became known as an evangelist and according to Acts 21 had four unmarried daughters who received the gift of prophecy.
17. Queen Makeda's encounter with Solomon is recorded in the biblical book of 1 Kings chapter 10. Most scholars believe Sheba is roughly the modern-day nation of Ethiopia.
18. The other emperor was Valerius Licinius (reigned from 308 to 324). Constantine ordered him executed in 325.
19. Christoph Baumer, *The Church of the East: An Illustrated History of Assyrian Christianity* (New York: I.B. Tauris, 2006), pp. 108–109.
20. Irvin and Sunquist, vol. 1, p. 356.
21. Irvin and Sunquist, vol. 1, p. 335.

22. Stephen Neill, *The Christian Society* (London: Nisbet and Co., 1952), p. 127.

23. Jenkins, *The Lost History of Christianity*, p. 98.

24. Johnson and Johnson, *Universal Religions in World History*, p. 110.

25. Jenkins, Lost History, pp. 130–32.

26. Leon Arpee, *A History of Armenian Christianity* (New York: The Armenian Association of America, 1946), p. 206.

27. Rodney Stark, *The Victory of Reason: How Christianity Led to Freedom, Capitalism, and Western Success* (New York: Random House, 2005), p. 233.

28. H.G. Haile, "Luther and Literacy," *PMLA 91*, no. 5 (Oct. 1976): 817.

29. Alister McGrath, *Christianity's Dangerous Idea* (New York: HarperOne, 2007).

30. Martin Marty, *The Christian World* (New York: Modern Library, 2007), p. 68.

31. Irvin and Sunquist, vol. 1, p. 473.

32. Irvin and Sunquist, vol. 1, p. 475.

33. See www.catholic-hierarchy.org/country/sc1.html.

34. Data compiled from David Barrett's *World Christian Encyclopedia* cited above. See summary of Barrett's conclusions in Wilbert Shenk, *Enlarging the Story: Perspectives on Writing World Christian History* (Maryknoll, NY: Orbis, 2002), p. xiii.

35. Martin Marty, *The Christian World*, p. 119.

36. See http://2001-2009.state.gov/g/drl/rls/irf/2008/108443.htm.

37. See Timothy Ware, *The Orthodox Church* (London: Penguin, 1997), chapter 8, "The Twentieth Century, II: Orthodoxy and the Militant Atheists," especially the chart on p. 162.

38. A.N. Wilson, *God's Funeral* (London: John Murray, 1999), pp. 281, 353–354.

39. Alister McGrath, *The Twilight of Atheism* (London: Doubleday, 2004).

40. See, for example, the *Cambridge History of Christianity: Volume 9: World Christianities* c. 1914–2000 (Cambridge: University Press, 2006), which briefly mentions the Armenian genocide in one sentence. Martyrdom does not occur in the index in the important work *Twentieth-Century Global Christianity* (Minneapolis: Fortress Press, 2008), ed. by Mary Farrell Bednarowski. Martin Marty does not include martyrdom in the index of his *sweeping The Christian World: A Global History* (2007).

41. Philip Jenkins, *Lost History of Christianity*, pp. 161–162.

42. Philip Jenkins, *Lost History of Christianity*, p. 163.

43. Jenkins, *Lost History of Christianity*, p. 171.

44. See Anthony Shadid, "Church Attack Seen as Strike at Iraq's Core," *New York Times*, November 1, 2010. Located at:
http://www.nytimes.com/2010/11/02/world/middleeast/02iraq.html

45. Baumer, *The Church of the East*, p. 273.

46. Stephen Neill, *A History of Christian Missions* (Harmondsworth, UK: Penguin, 1964), p. 538.

47. Stephen Neill, *Colonialism and Christian Missions* (London: Lutterworth, 1966), p. 421.

48. Stephen Neill, *A History of Christian Missions*, p. 538.

49. See Shenk, *Enlarging the Story*, p. xiv.

50. Augustine, *Confessions*, p. 221.

CHAPTER TWO: IN MY FATHER'S HOUSE ARE MANY ROOMS

1. Mary Farrell Bednarowski, *Twentieth Century Global Christianity* (Minneapolis: Fortress Press, 2008), p. 33.

2. Timothy Ware, *The Orthodox Church* (London: Penguin, 1997), p. 6.

3. Philip Jenkins, *Lost History of Christianity*, pp. 244–245.

4. Eastern Orthodox Christians still formally refer to the Archbishop of Constantinople as the Ecumenical Patriarch of Constantinople, in spite of the fact that the name of the city was officially changed to Istanbul in 1930.

5. Ware, *The Orthodox Church*, p. 7.

6. The Pentarchy was initially a Tetrarchy consisting of Jerusalem, Alexandria, Antioch, and Rome. When Constantine moved the seat of his empire to Constantinople, however, the bishopric of the imperial city gained immediate status. Canon XXVIII of Chalcedon refers to the Pentarchy, with "equal privileges" being granted to Rome and Constantinople. The Roman popes, however, have historically been reluctant to grant Constantinople equal status to Rome.

7. John H. Leith, *Creeds of the Churches* (Louisville: John Knox Press, 1982), p. 36.

8. Timothy Ware, *The Orthodox Church*, p. 43.

9. John Leith, *Creeds of the Churches*, p. 33.

10. Timothy Ware, *The Orthodox Church*, p. 46.

11. Joanne O'Brien and Martin Palmer, *The Atlas of Religion* (Los Angeles: University of California Press, 2007), pp. 36 and 109.

12. Catholic statistics come from International Bulletin of Missionary Research 33.1 (January 2009), p. 38.

13. The statistics in this paragraph are based on Philip Jenkins, *The Next Christendom*, pp. 66–67 and 227, O'Brien and Palmer, *The Atlas of Religion*, p. 37, and catholic-hierarchy.org.

14. O'Brien and Palmer, *The Atlas of Religion*, p. 108.

15. Special thanks to Shannon Shea of my Religion 301 class in "Christianity and Culture: World Christianity" at Pepperdine University. Our discussions took place in person and by email in January and February of 2009.

16. See www.catholic.org. In February 2009 there was a multiple article series written by Fr. Dwight Longenecker.

17. Dwight Longenecker, "What I Love About the Catholic Church 4," located at http://www.catholic.org/national/national_story.php?id=32127.

18. See for example "Benedict on Aquinas: Faith Implies Reason" by Fr. James V. Schall, S.J. Located at:
http://www.ignatiusinsight.com/features2007/schall_b16aquinas_feb07.asp.

19. Hans Küng, *The Catholic Church: A Short History* (New York: The Modern Library, 2003), pp. 162–168.

20. Küng, *The Catholic Church: A Short History*, p. 181.

21. Hans Küng was at the Second Vatican Council and contributed as a theological consultant. He has written extensively on the council. This overview, both positive and negative, is greatly informed by Küng's account and assessment of Vatican II in *The Catholic Church: A Short History*, pp. 181–196.

22. Küng, *The Catholic Church: A Short History*, p. 188.

23. Küng, *The Catholic Church: A Short History*, p. 188.

24. See the Pope's Lenten 2009 message at:
http://www.catholic.org/clife/lent/story.php?id=32255.

25. See "Why the Pope Is Boosting Latin Mass" at
http://www.time.com/time/world/article/0,8599,1641008,00.html.

26. Benedict's recent revival of the indulgences to reduce one's amount of time in Purgatory was reported widely in 2009. See for example "Why Catholic Indulgences Are Making a Comeback" at http://www.time.com/time/nation/article/0,8599,1881152,00.html. Also "For Catholics, a Door to Absolution Is Reopened" at http://www.nytimes.com/2009/02/10/nyregion/10indulgence.html.

27. See Martin Marty, *Martin Luther* (New York: Penguin, 2004), pp. 12-13.

28. Roland Bainton, *The Age of the Reformation* (Malabar, FL: Krieger Publishing Company, 1956), p. 24.

29. Alister McGrath, *Christianity's Dangerous Idea* (New York: HarperOne, 2007).

30. Alister McGrath, *Christianity's Dangerous Idea*, p. 251.

31. Margaret Miles, *The Word Made Flesh: A History of Christian Thought* (Oxford: Blackwell, 2005), p. 263.

32. Margaret Miles, *The Word Made Flesh: A History of Christian Thought*, p. 263.

33. Alister McGrath, *Christianity's Dangerous Idea*, p. 3.

34. Alister McGrath, *Christianity's Dangerous Idea*, p. 3.

35. Philip Jenkins, *The Next Christendom*, rev. ed. (2007), p. 45.

36. American universities consistently perform well in international rankings. One of the most recognized university ranking systems comes from the Chinese-based Center for World-Class Universities located at Shanghai Jiao Tong University. Its annual publication "Academic Ranking of World Universities" is insightful. In the 2011 rankings, the USA is home to over half of the top 100 universities in the world. Seventeen of the top twenty universities are in the United States. The 2011 publication is online at: http://www.shanghairanking.com/ARWU2011.html.

Chapter Three: And the Lord Added to Their Number Daily

1. Some of the unique doctrines include the special role of Joseph Smith, baptism for the dead, exaltation (humans may become gods/goddesses in the afterlife), and the Word of Wisdom health code. Mormons have an open canon that includes the Bible (King James Version), Book of Mormon, Pearl of Great Price, and Doctrine and Covenants. Mormons also believe in the inspiration of their denominational president.

2. Rodney Stark, *The Rise of Christianity: A Sociologist Reconsiders History* (Princeton, NJ: Princeton University Press, 1996), p. 11.

3. Rodney Stark, *The Rise of Mormonism* (New York: Columbia University Press, 2005), pp. 139, 145.

4. Stark, *The Rise of Mormonism*, pp. 139-140.

5. Stark is a decorated sociologist of religion. He is past president of the Society for the Scientific Study of Religion and of the Association for the Sociology of Religion. His illustrious track record includes more than 30 books and the title of Distinguished Professor of the Social Sciences at Baylor University.

6. Massimo Introvigne, "A Christmas Conversation with Rodney Stark," December 25, 2007. Introvigne is associated with CESNUR (Centro Studi sulle Nuove Religioni/Center for Studies on New Religions). See http://www.cesnur.org/2007/mi_stark.htm.

7. Max Müller (1823-1900) is the scholar usually credited with coining the term religionswissenschaft.

8. See Matthew 16:18-20.

9. Matthew 19:23-24.

10. 1 Timothy 6:10.

11. For the Franklin quotes, see
http://www.ushistory.org/franklin/quotable/singlehtml.htm. See also Ben's 13 Virtues
at http://www.pbs.org/benfranklin/pop_virtues_list.html.

12. See Max Weber, *The Religion of China: Confucianism and Taoism* (New York: Scribner,
1930). This book was originally published in German in 1904–1905.

13. For an analysis of this book see Otto B. Van Der Sprenkel, "Max Weber on China," in
History and Theory 3:3 (1964).

14. See Max Weber, *The Religion of India: The Sociology of Hinduism and Buddhism* (New York:
The Free Press, 1958). This book was originally published in German.

15. See Max Weber, *Ancient Judaism* (New York: Free Press, 1967). Originally published in
German between 1911 and 1920.

16. Werner Stark, *The Sociology of Religion: A Study of Christendom, Volume 5* (London:
Routledge and Kegan Paul, 1972), p. 2.

17. The percentages of world religious adherents are widely available and there is slight
variation in reputable sources as there is no one authoritative database. Currently, three
of the most comprehensive sources for worldwide religious statistics are the Central
Intelligence Agency (CIA) of the United States government, the World Christian
Encyclopedia, a resource originally intended for Christian academics in the 1980s that
has evolved into a major source for world religion due to its statistical rigor, and the
website Adherents.com. The CIA World Factbook lists Christianity as 33.32%, Islam as
21.01%, Hinduism as 13.26%, Buddhism as 5.84%. Every other religion is less than half
a percent. The World Christian Encyclopedia (WCE) was last printed in the year 2001
but continues to update its statistics through an academic website associated with Brill
Publishing   called   "The   World   Christian   Database."   See:
http://www.worldchristiandatabase.org/wcd/.   The 2001 edition of the WCE lists
Christianity as 33.0%, Islam as 19.6%, Hinduism as 13.4%, and Buddhism as 5.9%.
The WCE also groups the various Chinese religions under one heading "Chinese folk-
religionists" and has that category listed as 6.4%. Adherents.com has two advantages: it
draws from 43,000 different surveys into its overall numbers, and it rounds off the
numbers in order to avoid tenths of percentages. Adherents.com lists Christianity as
33%, Islam as 21%, Hinduism as 14%, and Buddhism as 6%. It is important to note
that the well-known and respected Pew Forum has begun a major research project to
map the religious world, country by country. Pew Forum injected new life into
discussions of religious statistics when they figured Islam constitutes 23% of the world's
population. This statistic for Islam is rather high and is attracting scholarly attention. See
www.pewforum.org.

18. Harm De Blij, *The Power of Place: Geography, Destiny, and Globalization's Rough Landscape*
(Oxford: Oxford University Press, 2008), p. 57.

19. John Hick wrote, "Consider a very obvious fact, so obvious that it is often not noticed,
and hardly ever taken into account by theologians. This is that in the vast majority of
cases, probably 98 or 99%, the religion to which anyone adheres depends upon where
they are born." See John Hick, "Believable Christianity," a lecture delivered on October
5, 2006. It is located on Hick's Web site: http://www.johnhick.org.uk/article16.html.

20. See: http://religions.pewforum.org/reports.

21. An excellent article on the history of the term "missions" (as evangelization) is Paul
Kollman, "At the Origins of Mission and Missiology: A Study in the Dynamics of
Religious Language," *Journal of the American Academy of Religion* 79.2 (June 2011), pp.
425–458. Kollman credits the term "mission," in the sense it is used today, to Ignatius of
Loyola in the sixteenth century.

22. For quarterly estimates of world Christian population, see David B. Barrett, *World
Christian Encyclopedia*, 2nd ed. (Oxford: Oxford University Press, 2001), p. 7. For

academic evaluations of the WCE and World Christian Database (WCD), see MacroData Guide: An international Social Science Resource: http://www.nsd.uib.no/macrodataguide/set.html?id=47&sub=1. One evaluation by Michael McClymond says the WCE is "generally even-handed," "fairly balanced," and "usually neutral." Perhaps the best evaluation of the WCD is by Becky Hsu, Amy Reynolds, Conrad Hackett, and James Gibbon (It was reviewed by Finke, Stark, Johnson, Norris, McCleary, and presented at the Society for Scientific Study of Religion, October 2006, Portland. It was published in the *Journal for the Scientific Study* of Religion in December 2008, vol. 47, Issue 4, pp. 678–693.). Hsu et al write: "On the whole we find that the WCD is reliable." See: http://www.princeton.edu/~bhsu/Hsu2008.pdf.

23. Andrew Walls, *The Cross-Cultural Process in Christian History* (Maryknoll, NY: Orbis, 2002), pp. 76, 78. Walls's italics.

24. Rodney Stark estimates the Christian population to have been around 34 million in the year 350. See Rodney Stark, *The Rise of Christianity* (Princeton, NJ: Princeton University Press, 1997), p. 6.

25. See Rodney Stark, *The Rise of Christianity*, p. 8.

26. Wilbert Shenk, *Enlarging the Story* (Maryknoll, NY: 2002), pp. xi–xiii.

27. Rodney Stark, *The Rise of Christianity*, p. 7.

28. Another expression for this concept that is gaining recognition is "the majority world."

29. Wilbert R. Shenk, ed., *Enlarging the Story*, p. xii. We must point out that Christianity was actually more of an Eastern faith until well into the second millennium A.D. In other words, Christianity was more affiliated with the Eastern side of the Roman Empire and Central Asia until 1100 or so.

30. Mary Farrell Bednarowski, ed., *Twentieth-Century Global Christianity* (Minneapolis: Fortress Press, 2008), pp. 32–33.

31. Paul Freston, "The Changing Face of Christian Proselytizing: New Actors from the Global South Transforming Old Debates," in *Proselytization Revisited: Rights Talk, Free Markets and Culture Wars*, ed. Rosalind Hackett (London: Equinox, 2008).

32. Harvey Cox, *Fire from Heaven: The Rise of Pentecostal Spirituality and the Reshaping of Religion in the Twenty-First Century* (New York: Addison-Wesley, 1995).

33. See Dyron Daughrity, *The Changing World of Christianity: The Global History of a Borderless Religion* (New York: Peter Lang, 2010).

34. CIA World Factbook. France hovers just under the two-children-per-woman mark, but the others are far from that benchmark.

35. Philip Jenkins, *God's Continent* (Oxford: University Press, 2007), p. 6.

36. Stephen Neill, *A History of Christian Mission*, p. 559.

37. See http://pewresearch.org/pubs/827/china-religion-olympics. Pew Forum refers to statistics from the World Christian Database and the Global China Center in addition to its own independent research. The WCD estimates 70 million unaffiliated Christians, while the Global China Center estimates 50 million Christians. According to Pew Forum, the Chinese government recognizes 21 million registered Christians. However, it is widely believed that membership in the unaffiliated churches is larger than membership in the state-sanctioned, nationally recognized churches.

38. Andrew Jacobs, "Illicit Church, Evicted, Tries to Buck Beijing," *NYTimes.com*, April 17, 2011, located at: http://www.nytimes.com/2011/04/18/world/asia/18beijing.html?scp=1&sq=christianity%20china&st=cse.

39. See: http://www.backtojerusalem.com/.

40. See Franklin Foer, "Baptism by Celluloid," *New York Times*, February 8, 2004, http://www.nytimes.com/2004/02/08/movies/baptism-by-

celluloid.html?pagewanted=all (accessed August 27, 2009). See also Giles Wilson, "The Most Watched Film in History," *BBC News Online Magazine*, July 21, 2003, located at: http://news.bbc.co.uk/1/hi/magazine/3076809.stm (accessed August 27, 2009).

41. See: http://www.jesusfilm.org/.

42. Mary Farrell Bednarowski, "Multiplicity and Ambiguity," in *Twentieth-Century Global Christianity*, p. 33.

43. Mary Farrell Bednarowski, "Multiplicity and Ambiguity," in *Twentieth-Century Global Christianity*, p. 33.

44. Ian Fisher, "Pope Warns Against Secularization in Germany," *New York Times*, Sept.10, 2006, located online at: http://www.nytimes.com/2006/09/10/world/europe/11pope.web.html?pagewanted=1 &_r=1.

45. Philip Jenkins, *The Next Christendom, Revised and Expanded Edition* (Oxford: Oxford University Press, 2007), p. 3.

46. Peter Berger, Brigitte Berger, and Hansfried Kellner, *The Homeless Mind: Modernization and Consciousness* (New York: Random House, 1973), pp. 163–167. Accessed in Noel Davies and Martin Conway, World Christianity in the 20th Century: SCM Reader (London: SCM Press, 2008), p. 203.

47. Peter Berger, Brigitte Berger, and Hansfried Kellner, *The Homeless Mind: Modernization and Consciousness*, pp. 163–167. Accessed in Noel Davies and Martin Conway, World Christianity in the 20th Century: SCM Reader (London: SCM Press, 2008), p. 204.

48. On the decline of church attendance throughout the 19th and 20th centuries, see Grace Davie, *Believing Without Belonging* (Oxford: Wiley Blackwell, 1994), and Hugh McLeod, *Secularization in Western Europe, 1848–1914* (New York: St. Martin's Press, 2000).

49. Grace Davie, "Europe: The Exception That Proves the Rule?" in Peter Berger, ed., *The Desecularization of the World: Resurgent Religion and World Politics* (Grand Rapids, MI: Eerdmans, 1999), p. 69.

50. Grace Davie, "Europe: The Exception That Proves the Rule?" p. 83.

51. Jason Palmer, "Religion May Become Extinct In Nine Nations, Study Says," *BBC Online*, 22 March 2011, located at: http://www.bbc.co.uk/news/science-environment-12811197.

52. Graeme Smith, *A Short History of Secularism* (London: I.B. Tauris, 2008), pp. 2–3.

53. See Jonathan Benthall, *Returning to Religion: Why a Secular Age is Haunted by Faith* (London: I.B. Tauris, 2008).

54. Grace Davie, *Believing Without Belonging* (Oxford: Wiley Blackwell, 1994). See also Abby Day, *Believing in Belonging:Belief and Social Identity in the Modern World* (New York: Oxford University Press, 2011)

55. See Dietrich Bonhoeffer, *Letters and Papers from Prison*, New Greatly Enlarged Ed. (New York: Macmillan, 1972), pp. 280–281, 285–286, 380–381.

56. Bonhoeffer, *Letters and Papers from Prison*, p. 286.

57. Bonhoeffer, *Letters and Papers from Prison*, p. 381.

58. See, for example, a PBS interview on "Chrislam," located at: http://www.pbs.org/wnet/religionandethics/episodes/february-13-2009/chrislam/2236/.

59. Job 1:20–21.

60. See "UK Among Most Secular Nations," *BBC News*, 26 February 2004, located at: http://news.bbc.co.uk/2/hi/programmes/wtwtgod/3518375.stm. See also Martin Beckford, "We Will Not Be Silenced, Pope Tells Secular Britain," in *The Telegraph*, 17 September 2010, located at: http://www.telegraph.co.uk/news/religion/the-pope/8010336/We-will-not-be-silenced-Pope-tells-secular-Britain.html.

61. See "Britain's Most Influential Black Church Leaders," located at: http://www.blackukonline.com/index.php?Itemid=39&id=228&option=com_content &task=view .

CHAPTER FOUR: GO AND MAKE DISCIPLES OF ALL NATIONS

1. I was in Ethiopia during the summer of 2010.
2. See UNESCO's Aksum site: http://whc.unesco.org/en/list/15.
3. See UNESCO's helpful descriptions of the rock-hewn churches of Lalibela: http://whc.unesco.org/en/list/18.
4. Francisco Alvarez, *The Prester John of the Indies* trans. by C.F. Beckingham and G.W.B. Huntingford (Cambridge: Hakluyt Society, 1961), p. 226. For further description of the churches, see appendix, pp. 526–542.
5. See Matthew 6:19-34.
6. Mark 16:15.
7. Dyron Daughrity, *The Changing World of Christianity: The Global History of a Borderless Religion* (New York: Peter Lang, 2010).
8. Acts 2:39.
9. Gay L. Byron, *Symbolic Blackness and Ethnic Difference in Early Christian Literature* (London: Routledge, 2002), p. 31.
10. Revelation 7:9.
11. Acts 2:5.
12. Acts 2:9-11.
13. Acts 2:12.
14. Jack Rogers, *Jesus, the Bible, and Homosexuality* (Louisville, KY: Westminster John Knox, 2006), p. 135.
15. Donna Lee Bowen and Evelyn A. Early, eds., *Everyday Life in the Middle East*, second edition (Bloomington, IN: Indiana University Press, 2002), p. 1.
16. See Hans Küng's speech, "The World's Religions: Common Ethical Values," at Santa Clara University, March 31, 2005. Located at: http://www.scu.edu/ethics/practicing/focusareas/global_ethics/laughlin-lectures/kung-world-religions.html.
17. Luke 13:33-35.
18. Carl Haub, "Tracking Trends in Low Fertility Countries: An Uptick in Europe?" in *Population Reference Bureau*, located at: http://www.prb.org/Articles/2008/tfrtrendsept08.aspx.
19. Paul Mojzes, "Orthodoxy under Communism," in Mary Farrell Bednarowski, ed., *Twentieth-Century Global Christianity* (Minneapolis: Fortress Press, 2008), p. 141.
20. Paul Mojzes, "Orthodoxy under Communism," p. 152.
21. See "Sharia law In UK Is 'Unavoidable'" at *BBC News*. Located at: http://news.bbc.co.uk/2/hi/7232661.stm.
22. Jared Diamond, *Guns, Germs, and Steel* (New York: W. W. Norton, 1999), p. 46.
23. Adrian Hastings, "Latin America," in Adrian Hastings, ed., *A World History of Christianity* (Grand Rapids, MI: Eerdmans, 1999), p. 331.
24. Matthew 19:24.
25. See U.S. census results for 1860 at: http://www.civil-war.net/pages/1860_census.html.
26. See Luke 4:18-19.
27. These statistics come from Terence Ranger, ed., *Evangelical Christianity and Democracy in Africa* (Oxford: Oxford University Press, 2008), p. x, but they are rooted in David Barrett and Todd Johnson's *World Christian Database*.

28. Mary Farrell Bednarowski, ed., *Twentieth Century Global Christianity* (Minneapolis: Fortress Press, 2008), pp. 32–33.

29. Terence Ranger, ed., *Evangelical Christianity and Democracy in Africa*, p. x.

30. "Africa is known to be by far the most linguistically diverse continent. The number of African languages is usually put at around 2000." See "Africa" on the UNESCO "Communication and Information/Culture" portal, located at: http://portal.unesco.org/ci/en/ev.php-URL_ID=8048&URL_DO=DO_TOPIC&URL_SECTION=201.html.

31. See the CIA World Factbook Publications: "Country Comparison: GDP (Purchasing Power Parity)," located at: https://www.cia.gov/library/publications/the-world-factbook/rankorder/2001rank.html?countryName=South%20Africa&countryCode=SF&regionCode=af#SF.

32. Mercy Oduyoye in Nicholas Otieno with Hugh McCullum, *Journey of Hope: Towards a New Ecumenical Africa* (Geneva: WCC, 2005), p. xix.

33. In Nicholas Otieno with Hugh McCullum, pp. xix–xxii. Oduyoye's "A Letter to My Ancestors" (pp. xv–xxii) is essentially a conversation with the ancestors in which she vows to help change Africa's trajectory through renewed spiritual commitment.

34. See, for example, the Oxfam publication "From Closed Books to Open Doors—West Africa's Literacy Challenge," April 2009, located at: http://oxfam.qc.ca/en/policy/2009-04-21_closed-books.

35. Oduyoye's "A Letter to My Ancestors" p. xix.

36. Lamin Sanneh, quoted in Terence Ranger, ed., *Evangelical Christianity and Democracy in Africa*, pp. 11–12.

37. This statement has been attributed to many African sources. See Nicholas Otieno with Hugh McCullum, *Journey of Hope*, p. 7.

38. Thomas C. Oden, *How Africa Shaped the Christian Mind* (Downers Grove, IL: Intervarsity Press, 2007), pp. 43–44.

39. See Dale Irvin and Scott Sunquist, *History of the World Christian Movement*, vol. 1 (Maryknoll, NY: Orbis, 2001), pp. 217–218.

40. Philip Jenkins, *The Lost History of Christianity* (New York: Harperone, 2008), pp. 146–147.

41. See Graham Duncan and Ogbu Kalu, "Bakuzufu: Revival Movements and Indigenous Appropriation in African Christianity," in Ogbu Kalu, ed., *African Christianity: An African Story* (Trenton, NJ: Africa World Press, 2007), pp. 250–253.

42. Ogbu Kalu, ed., *African Christianity: An African Story*, p. 36.

43. See Isabel Mukonyora, "The Dramatization of Life and Death by Johane Masowe," *Zambezia* 25.2 (1998), p. 205. See also G.C. Oosthuizen, "Isaiah Shembe and the Zulu World View," *History of Religions* 8.1 (August 1968), pp. 1–30.

44. For a transcript of Mandela's 1992 lecture, see: http://www.sahistory.org.za/pages/people/special%20projects/mandela/speeches/1990s/1992/1992_zcc_conference.htm.

45. John Mbiti, quoted in Noel Davies and Martin Conway, *World Christianity in the 20th Century* (London: SCM Press, 2008), p. 118.

46. Andrew Rice, "Mission From Africa," *New York Times*, April 8, 2009, located at: http://www.nytimes.com/2009/04/12/magazine/12churches-t.html.

47. See the church's website: http://www.godembassy.org/en/embassy.php.

48. Raeburn Lange, *Island Ministers: Indigenous Leadership in Nineteenth-Century Pacific Islands Christianity* (University of Canterbury, New Zealand: Macmillan Brown Centre for Pacific Studies, 2005), p. 8.

49. Rainer Buschmann, *Oceans in World History* (Boston: McGraw Hill, 2007), p. 93.

50. The research report is available online: http://pewforum.org/Christian/Global-Christianity-exec.aspx.

51. See "Executive Summary," of the Pew study, located at: http://pewforum.org/Christian/Global-Christianity-exec.aspx.

52. Sanneh has published many important works in the fields of church history and world Christianity. See for example *Translating the Message: The Missionary Impact on Culture* (Maryknoll, NY: Orbis, 1989) and *Disciples of All Nations: Pillars of World Christianity* (Oxford: Oxford University Press, 2007).

53. Philippians 2:10–11.

CHAPTER FIVE: WHO DO PEOPLE SAY I AM?

1. For pictures of Alexander Campbell's Bethany (West Virginia) office, see: http://www.therestorationmovement.com/lightfromabove.htm. For information on the mansion, see: http://www.bethanywv.edu/about-bethany/historic/campbell-mansion/.

2. Dyron Daughtry, *Bishop Stephen Neill: From Edinburgh to South India* (New York: Peter Lang, 2008).

3. See Acts 14:14.

4. See Acts 9:27.

5. See Acts 14:11–13.

6. See Matthew 10:39 and Philippians 1:21.

7. For Blandina's story, see Eusebius, *Church History*, Volume Two, Book Five, located at: http://www.newadvent.org/fathers/250105.htm.

8. See Ker Than, "Legendary Saints Were Real, Buried Alive, Study Hints," in *National Geographic News* (April 15, 2011), located at: http://news.nationalgeographic.com/news/2011/04/110415-saints-murdered-chrysanthus-daria-science-rome-roman-christians/.

9. See Ephesians 5:25–29.

10. See Galatians 3:26–29.

11. Christopher Beeley, *Gregory of Nazianzus on the Trinity and the Knowledge of God* (Oxford: Oxford University Press, 2008), p. 120.

12. See Timothy Frye, ed., *The Rule of Saint Benedict* (New York: Vintage Books, 1998).

13. Philip Jenkins, *The Lost History of Christianity* (New York: HarperOne, 2008), p. 6.

14. Philip Jenkins, *Lost History*, p. 185.

15. Will Durant, *The Age of Faith* (New York: Simon and Schuster, 1950), p. 537.

16. See "Pope Benedict IX," in *The Catholic Encyclopedia*. Originally published in New York by the Robert Appleton Company in 1913 under the editorship of Charles Herbermann, Edward Pace, Conde Pallan, Rt. Rev. Thomas Shahan, and John Wynne, S.J. The encyclopedia is now in the public domain, located at: http://www.newadvent.org/cathen/.

17. See information on the Poor Clares at the order's blog: http://poorclare.org/blog/.

18. See the English translation of the Syriac texts which recount the journeys of Bar Sauma and Bar Markos: *The Monks of Kublai Khan Emperor of China*, translated by Sir E. A. Wallis Budge, London: The Religious Tract Society, 1928, located online at: http://www.aina.org/books/mokk/mokk.htm#c28. For the year of their departure, see Jacques Gernet, A History of Chinese Civilization (Cambridge: Cambridge University Press, 1996), p. 376.

19. See James A. Montgomery, *The History of Yaballaha III and of His Vicar Bar Sauma, Mongol Ambassador to the Frankish Courts at the End of the Thirteenth Century* (New York: Columbia Press, 1927). Montgomery's fascinating book is online at:

http://link.library.utoronto.ca/booksonline/digobject.cfm?Idno=00001571. See also http://www.nestorian.org/history_of_rabban_bar_sawma_1.html.

20. After 1259 the Mongol Empire split into four major khanates, or empires: the Golden Horde in the northwest, the Chagatai Khanate in the west, the Ilkhanate in the southwest, and the Yuan Dynasty based in Beijing.

21. The first printed Greek New Testament was the Complutensian Polyglot, in 1514. However, it was not published until the early 1520s.

22. There is a dearth of scholarship on Katharina von Bora, but there is much hagiography, making it difficult to separate fact from legend. The Lutheran Church's "Concordia Historical Institute" has a helpful exhibit on Katharina. The Institute belongs to the Department of Archives and History of the Lutheran Church—Missouri Synod. See: http://www.lutheranhistory.org/katie/.

23. A good source for Luther and Katharina's marriage is Diana Severance, *Feminine Threads: Women in the Tapestry of Christian History* (Geanies House, Fearn, Ross-shire, Scotland: Christian Focus Publications, 2011).

24. Barnas Sears, *The Life of Luther: With Special Reference to its Earlier Periods and the Opening Scenes of the Reformation* (Philadelphia: American Sunday School Union, 1849), pp. 375–376.

25. See especially the writings of Giovanni Cavazzi da Montecuccolo (1621–1678). His *Historical Description of Three Kingdoms: Congo, Matamba, and Angola* is probably the most important source for this era of Kongolese history.

26. See Norbert Brockman, "Kimpa Vita," at the *Dictionary of African Christian Biography*, located at: http://www.dacb.org/stories/congo/kimpa_vita.html.

27. See Forrest Knapp, "The World Council of Christian Education," in *International Review of Mission* 37:4 (October 1948), pp. 437–441.

28. Gary Holloway and Douglas Foster, *Renewing God's People: A Concise History of Churches of Christ* (Abilene, Texas: ACU Press, 2006), p. 33.

29. This is part of Stone's Last Will and Testament of the Springfield Presbytery, written in 1804. See: http://www.mun.ca/rels/restmov/texts/esmith/hgl1808/LWT.HTM.

30. See Francis Chan, *Forgotten God: Reversing Our Tragic Neglect of the Holy Spirit* (Colorado Springs, CO: David C. Cook, 2009).

31. See The Last Will and Testament of the Springfield Presbytery, cited above.

32. See a timeline for Wurmbrand at: http://torturedforchrist.com/.

33. See the website for Voice of the Martyrs: http://www.persecution.com/.

34. Acts 1:8.

35. See Timothy Tennent's blog: http://asburyseedbed.com/feed/the-west-as-the-fastest-growing-mission-field-in-the-world-.

36. See John 20:28.

BIBLIOGRAPHY

"Aksum." UNESCO World Heritage Centre. Accessed May 9, 2012. http://whc.unesco.org/en/list/15.

Alvarez, Francisco. *The Prester John of the Indies*. Translated by C.F. Beckingham and G.W.B. Huntingford. Cambridge: Hakluyt Society, 1961.

Arpee, Leon. *A History of Armenian Christianity*. New York: The Armenian Association of America, 1946.

Bainton, Roland. *The Age of the Reformation*. Malabar, FL: Krieger Publishing Company, 1956.

Barrett, David, Todd Johnson, and George Kurian, eds. *World Christian Encyclopedia: A Comparative Survey of Churches and Religions in the Modern World*. Second edition. Oxford: Oxford University Press, 2001.

Baumer, Christoph. *The Church of the East: An Illustrated History of Assyrian Christianity*. New York: I.B. Tauris, 2006.

Beckford, Martin. "We Will Not Be Silenced, Pope Tells Secular Britain." *The Telegraph*, September 17, 2010.

Bednarowski, Mary Farrell, ed. *Twentieth-Century Global Christianity*. Minneapolis: Fortress Press, 2008.

Beeley, Christopher. *Gregory of Nazianzus on the Trinity and the Knowledge of God*. Oxford: Oxford University Press, 2008.

Benthall, Jonathan. *Returning to Religion: Why a Secular Age Is Haunted by Faith*. London: I.B. Tauris, 2008.

Berger, Peter, Brigitte Berger, and Hansfried Kellner. *The Homeless Mind: Modernization and Consciousness*. New York: Random House, 1973.

Bonhoeffer, Dietrich. *Letters and Papers from Prison*, New Greatly Enlarged ed. Translated by Eberhard Bethge. New York: Macmillan, 1972.

Bonk, Jonathan. "The Roman Catholic Church's Southward Shift." *International Bulletin of Missionary Research 33*, no. 1 (2009): 38.

Bowen, Donna Lee, and Evelyn A. Early, eds. *Everyday Life in the Middle East*, second ed. Bloomington, IN: Indiana University Press, 2002.

Budge, Sir E.A. Wallis, ed. and translator. *The Monks of Kublai Khan Emperor of China*. London: The Religious Tract Society, 1928.

Buschmann, Rainer. *Oceans in World History*. Boston: McGraw Hill, 2007.

Byron, Gay L. *Symbolic Blackness and Ethnic Difference in Early Christian Literature*. London: Routledge, 2002.

Cahill, Thomas. *The Gifts of the Jews*. New York: Doubleday, 1998.

Center for World-Class Universities, Shanghai Jiao Tong University. "Academic Ranking of World Universities." http://www.shanghairanking.com/ARWU2011.html.

Chadwick, Henry, trans. *Confessions of Saint Augustine*. Oxford: Oxford University Press, 1991.

Chan, Francis. *Forgotten God: Reversing Our Tragic Neglect of the Holy Spirit*. Colorado Springs, CO: David C. Cook, 2009.

Cox, Harvey. *Fire from Heaven: The Rise of Pentecostal Spirituality and the Reshaping of Religion in the Twenty-first Century*. New York: Addison-Wesley, 1995.

Daughrity, Dyron. *Bishop Stephen Neill: From Edinburgh to South India*. New York: Peter Lang, 2008.

—— *The Changing World of Christianity: The Global History of a Borderless Religion*. New York: Peter Lang, 2010.

Davie, Grace. *Believing without Belonging*. Oxford: Wiley Blackwell, 1994.

—— "Europe: The Exception That Proves the Rule?" In *The Desecularization of the World: Resurgent Religion and World Politics*, edited by Peter Berger. Grand Rapids, MI: Eerdmans, 1999.

Davies, Noel, and Martin Conway. *World Christianity in the 20th Century: SCM Reader*. London: SCM Press, 2008.

De Blij, Harm. *The Power of Place: Geography, Destiny, and Globalization's Rough Landscape*. Oxford: Oxford University Press, 2008.

Diamond, Jared. *Guns, Germs, and Steel*. New York: W.W. Norton, 1999.

Dictionary of African Christian Biography, s.v. "Kimpa Vita," by Norbert Brockman, accessed May 9, 2012, http://www.dacb.org/stories/congo/kimpa_vita.html.

Durant, Will. *The Age of Faith*. New York: Simon and Schuster, 1950.

Eusebius. *The Church History*, 4th ed. Translated by Paul L. Maier. Grand Rapids, MI: Kregel Academic, 1999.

Fisher, Ian. "Pope Warns against Secularization in Germany." *New York Times*, September 10, 2006.

Foer, Franklin. "Baptism by Celluloid." *New York Times*, February 8, 2004.

Freston, Paul. "The Changing Face of Christian Proselytizing: New Actors from the Global South Transforming Old Debates." In *Proselytization Revisited: Rights Talk, Free Markets and Culture Wars*, edited by Rosalind Hackett, chapter 5. London: Equinox, 2008.

"From Closed Books to Open Doors—West Africa's Literacy Challenge." Oxfam International. August 13, 2009. http://www.oxfam.org/en/policy/west-africa-closed-books-open-doors.

Frye, Timothy, ed. *The Rule of Saint Benedict*. New York: Vintage Books, 1998.

Gernet, Jacques. *A History of Chinese Civilization*. Cambridge: Cambridge University Press, 1996.

Haile, H.G. "Luther and Literacy." *PMLA 91*, no. 5 (1976): 816-828.

Hastings, Adrian, ed. *A World History of Christianity*. Grand Rapids, MI: Eerdmans, 1999.

Haub, Carl. "Tracking Trends in Low Fertility Countries: An Uptick in Europe?" *Population Reference Bureau*. September 2008. http://www.prb.org/Articles/2008/tfrtrendsept08.aspx.

Hawking, Stephen. *A Brief History of Time*. New York: Bantam Books, 1996.

Hick, John. "Believable Christianity." *John Hick: The Official Website*. http://www.johnhick.org.uk/article16.html.

Holloway, Gary, and Douglas Foster. *Renewing God's People: A Concise History of Churches of Christ*. Abilene, TX: ACU Press, 2006.

Hsu, Becky, Amy Reynolds, Conrad Hackett, and James Gibbon. "Estimating the Religious Composition of All Nations: An Empirical Assessment of the World Christian Database." *Journal for the Scientific Study of Religion 47*, no. 4 (2008): 678-693.

Introvigne, Massimo. "A Christmas Conversation with Rodney Stark." *Centro Studi sulle Nuove Religioni/Center for Studies on New Religions*, accessed May 9, 2012, http://www.cesnur.org/2007/mi_stark.htm.

Irvin, Dale, and Scott Sunquist. *History of the World Christian Movement, vol. 1: Earliest Christianity to 1453*. Maryknoll, NY: Orbis, 2001.

Israeli, Jeff. "Why the Pope Is Boosting Mass." *Time*, July 7, 2007.

Jacobs, Andrew. "Illicit Church, Evicted, Tries to Buck Beijing." *New York Times*, April 17, 2011.

Jenkins, Philip. *God's Continent*. Oxford: Oxford University Press, 2007.

—— *The Lost History of Christianity*. New York: HarperOne, 2008.

—— *The Next Christendom*. Revised and updated edition. New York: Oxford University Press, 2007.

Johnson, Donald, and Jean Johnson. *Universal Religions in World History*. New York: McGraw-Hill, 2007.

Kalu, Ogbu, ed. *African Christianity: An African Story*. Trenton, NJ: Africa World Press, 2007.

Knapp, Forrest. "The World Council of Christian Education." *International Review of Mission 37*, no. 4 (1948): 437–441.

Kollman, Paul. "At the Origins of Mission and Missiology: A Study in the Dynamics of Religious Language." *Journal of the American Academy of Religion 79*, no. 2 (2011): 425–458.

Küng, Hans. *The Catholic Church: A Short History*. New York: The Modern Library, 2003.

—— "The World's Religions: Common Ethical Values." Paper presented at Santa Clara University, Santa Clara, California, March 31, 2005.

Lange, Raeburn. *Island Ministers: Indigenous Leadership in Nineteenth Century Pacific Islands Christianity*. University of Canterbury, New Zealand: Macmillan Brown Centre for Pacific Studies, 2005.

Latourette, Kenneth Scott. *A History of the Expansion of Christianity*, 7 vols. New York: Harper and Row, 1937–1945.

—— *A History of Christianity*. New York: HarperSanFrancisco, 1953.

Leith, John H. *Creeds of the Churches*. Louisville, KY: John Knox Press, 1982.

MacCulloch, Diarmaid. *Christianity: The First Three Thousand Years*. New York: Viking, 2010.

Mandela, Nelson. Untitled speech at the Zion Christian Church Easter Conference, Moria, South Africa, April 20, 1992. Accessed May 9, 2012. http://www.sahistory.org.za/article/speech-nelson-mandela-zionist-christian-church-easter-conference.

Marty, Martin. *The Christian World*. New York: Modern Library, 2007.

—— *Martin Luther*. New York: Penguin, 2004.

McGrath, Alister. *Christianity's Dangerous Idea*. New York: HarperOne, 2007.

—— *The Twilight of Atheism*. London: Doubleday, 2004.

McLeod, Hugh, ed. *Cambridge History of Christianity, Vol. 9: World Christianities c. 1914–2000*. Cambridge: Cambridge University Press, 2006.

—— *Secularization in Western Europe, 1848–1914*. New York: St. Martin's Press, 2000.

Miles, Margaret. *The Word Made Flesh*. Oxford: Blackwell, 2005.

Mojzes, Paul. "Orthodoxy under Communism." In *Twentieth-Century Global Christianity*, edited by Mary Farrell Bednarowski, 131–156. Minneapolis, Fortress Press, 2008.

Montgomery, James A. *The History of Yaballaha III and of His Vicar Bar Sauma, Mongol Ambassador to the Frankish Courts at the end of the Thirteenth Century*. New York: Columbia University Press, 1927.

Mukonyora, Isabel. "The Dramatization of Life and Death by Johane Masowe." *Zambezia 25*, no. 2 (1998): 192–207.

Neill, Stephen. *A History of Christian Missions.* Harmondsworth, UK: Penguin, 1964.

—— *Colonialism and Christian Missions.* London: Lutterworth, 1966.

—— *The Christian Society.* London: Nisbet and Co., 1952.

Noll, Mark. *Turning Points: Decisive Moments in the History of Christianity.* Grand Rapids, MI: Baker Academic, 1997.

O'Brien, Joanne, and Martin Palmer. *The Atlas of Religion.* Los Angeles: University of California Press, 2007.

Oden, C. Thomas. *How Africa Shaped the Christian Mind.* Downers Grove, IL: Intervarsity Press, 2007.

Oduyoye, Mercy. "A Letter to My Ancestors." In *Journey of Hope: Towards a New Ecumenical Africa,* edited by Nicholas Otieno and Hugh McCullum. Geneva: World Council of Churches, 2006.

Oosthuizen, G.C. "Isaiah Shembe and the Zulu World View." *History of Religions* 8, no. 1 (1968): 1-30.

Palmer, Jason. "Religion May Become Extinct in Nine Nations, study says." *BBC Online,* March 22, 2011. http://www.bbc.co.uk/news/science-environment-12811197.

Pew Forum on Religion and Public Life: Global Christianity, A Report on the Size and Distribution of the World's Christian Population. December 19, 2011.
http://www.pewforum.org/Christian/Global-Christianity-worlds-christian-population.aspx.

Rice, Andrew. "Mission from Africa." *New York Times,* April 8, 2009.

Rochman, Bonnie. "Why Catholic Indulgences Are Making a Comeback." *Time,* February 22, 2009.

"Rock-Hewn Churches, Lalibela." UNESCO World Heritage Centre. Accessed May 9, 2012. http://whc.unesco.org/en/list/18.

Rogers, Jack. *Jesus, the Bible, and Homosexuality.* Louisville, KY: Westminster John Knox, 2006.

Sanneh, Lamin. *Disciples of All Nations: Pillars of World Christianity.* Oxford: Oxford University Press, 2007.

—— *Translating the Message: The Missionary Impact on Culture.* Maryknoll, NY: Orbis, 1989.

Sears, Barnas. *The Life of Luther: With Special Reference to Its Earlier Periods and the Opening Scenes of the Reformation.* Philadelphia: American Sunday School Union, 1849.

Severence, Diana. *Feminine Threads: Women in the Tapestry of Christian History.* Geanies House, Fearn, Ross-shire, Scotland: Christian Focus Publications, 2011.

Shadid, Anthony. "Church Attack Seen as Strike at Iraq's Core." *New York Times,* November 1, 2010.

"Shariah Law in UK is 'Unavoidable'." BBC News Online. February 7, 2008.
http://news.bbc.co.uk/2/hi/7232661.stm.

Shenk, Wilbert. *Enlarging the Story: Perspectives on Writing World Christian History.* Maryknoll, NY: Orbis, 2002.

Smith, Graeme. *A Short History of Secularism.* London: I.B. Tauris, 2008.

Stark, Rodney. *The Rise of Christianity.* Princeton, NJ: Princeton University Press, 1996.

—— *The Rise of Mormonism.* New York: Columbia University Press, 2005.

—— *The Victory of Reason: How Christianity Led to Freedom, Capitalism, and Western Success.* New York: Random House, 2005.

Stark, Werner. *The Sociology of Religion: A Study of Christendom,* vol. 5. London: Routledge and Kegan Paul, 1972.

Than, Ker. "Legendary Saints Were Real, Buried Alive, Study Hints." *National Geographic News.* April 15, 2011. http://news.nationalgeographic.com/news/2011/04/110415-saints-murdered-chrysanthus-daria-science-rome-roman-christians/.

"The Hierarchy of the Catholic Church: Current and Historical Information about Its Bishops and Dioceses," accessed May 9, 2012. http://www.catholic-hierarchy.org/country/sc1.html.

The World Factbook 2009. Washington, DC: Central Intelligence Agency, 2009. https://www.cia.gov/library/publications/the-world-factbook/index.html.

"UK Among Most Secular Nations." BBC News Online. February 26, 2004. http://news.bbc.co.uk/2/hi/programmes/wtwtgod/3518375.stm.

U.S. Department of State. "2008 Report on International Religious Freedom." 2008. http://2001-2009.state.gov/g/drl/rls/irf/2008/index.htm.

Van Der Sprenkel, Otto B. "Max Weber on China." *History and Theory 3,* no. 3 (1964).

Vitello, Paul. "For Catholics, a Door to Absolution Is Reopened." *New York Times,* February 9, 2009.

Walker, Williston. *A History of the Christian Church.* New York: Charles Scribner's Sons, 1918.

Walls, Andrew. *The Cross-Cultural Process in Christian History.* Maryknoll, NY: Orbis, 2002.

Ware, Timothy. *The Orthodox Church.* London: Penguin, 1997.

Weber, Max. *Ancient Judaism.* New York: The Free Press, 1967.

—— *The Religion of China: Confucianism and Taoism.* New York: Scribner, 1930.

—— *The Religion of India: The Sociology of Hinduism and Buddhism.* New York: The Free Press, 1958.

Wilson, A.N. *God's Funeral.* London: John Murray, 1999.

Wilson, Giles. "The Most Watched Film in History." *BBC News Online Magazine,* July 21, 2003. http://news.bbc.co.uk/2/hi/uk_news/magazine/3076809.stm.

INDEX